Enlightenment is Levels 600-900 @ 600+ ego is not Present.

The ego IS A Separate Reality from God

MEDITATION AND KABBALAH

DAVID HAWKINS Level of Consciousness
200-1000 (TRUTH)
0-199 (False)

Kabbalah calibrates in its original form @ Level 600 (Enlightenment)
THE Zohar Level 900 (Enlightenment)

Hawkins Kinesiology = Muscles go Strong when TRUTH is Present. Muscles go Weak when TRUTH is Absent

P9-DBV-144

MEDITATION AND KABBALAH

Containing Relevant Texts from
***The Greater Hekhalot*, Textbook of the Merkava School**
The works of Abraham Abulafia
Joseph Gikatalia's *Gates of Light*
The Gates of Holiness
***Gate of the Holy Spirit*, Textbook of the Lurianic School**
Hasidic Classics

BY

ARYEH KAPLAN

WEISERBOOKS
San Francisco, CA / Newburyport, MA

This book contains Divine Names.
Do not take it into the bathroom or any other unclean place.

First published in 1982 by
Red Wheel/Weiser, LLC
With offices at
500 Third Street, Suite 230
San Francisco, CA 94107
www.redwheelweiser.com

First paperback edition, 1985

Copyright © 1982 Aryeh Kaplan
All rights reserved. No part of this publication may be reproduced or transmitted in any form or by any means, electronic or mechanical, including photocopying, recording, or by any information storage and retrieval system, without permission in writing from Red Wheel/Weiser. Reviewers may quote brief passages.

Library of Congress Catalog Card Number: 81-70150

ISBN-10: 0-87728-616-7
ISBN-13: 978-0-87728-616-5

Cover design by Bima Stagg

Printed in the United States of America
MG
20 19 18 17 16 15

The paper used in this publication meets the minimum requirements of the American National Standard for Information Sciences—Permanence of Paper for Printed Library Materials Z39.48-1984.

Contents

בדחילו ורחימו

With trepidation and love...

ברשות רבותי

By authority from my masters...

ACKNOWLEDGMENTS

Dr. Perle Epstein.

Library of Jewish Theological Seminary of America, New York, New York, particularly to Ms. Susan Young and Mr. Micha Falk Oppenheim.

Hebrew University Libraries, Jerusalem.

Bodleian Library, Oxford, England.

Biblioteque Nationale, Paris, France.

British Museum, London, England.

Biblioteca Apostolica Vatican, Vatican City.

Columbia University Library, Manuscript Division, New York, New York.

Lenin State Library, Guenzburg Collection, Moscow.

Introduction

It is with great trepidation that one begins to write a work such as this, involving some of the most hidden mysteries of the Kabbalah. Many would question the wisdom and propriety of placing such information in a printed book, especially in an English translation. But so much misinformation has already been published that it is virtually imperative that an authentic, authoritative account be published. It is for this reason, as well as other reasons which I am bound by an oath to conceal, that the great living masters of Kabbalah have voiced their approval that such a book be published.

The science of Kabbalah is divided into three basic areas: the theoretical, the meditative, and the practical.

The theoretical deals with the form of the mysteries, teaching the structure of the angelic domains as well as of the Sefirot, or Divine Emanations. With great success, it deals with problems posed by the many schools of philosophy, and it provides a conceptual framework into which all theological ideas can be fitted. More important for the discussion at hand, it also provides a framework through which the mechanism of both the meditative and practical Kabbalah can be understood.

Some three thousand Kabbalah texts exist in print, and, for the most part, the vast majority deal with the theoretical Kabbalah. Falling within this category are the best known Kabbalah works, such as the Zohar and the *Bahir*, which are almost totally theoretical in their scope. The same is true of the writings of Rabbi Isaac Luria, the Ari, considered by many to have been the greatest of all Kabbalists. With the passage of time, this school probed deeper and deeper into the philosophical ramifications of the primary Kabbalistic concepts, producing an extremely profound, self-consistent and satisfying philosophical system.

The practical Kabbalah, on the other hand, was a kind of white magic, dealing with the use of techniques that could evoke supernatural powers. It involved the use of divine names and incantations, amulets and talismans, as well as chiromancy, physiognomy and astrology. Many theoretical Kabbalists, led by the Ari, frowned on the use of such techniques, labeling them as dangerous and spiritually demeaning. As a result, only a very small number of texts have survived at all, mostly in manuscript form, and only a handful of the most innocuous of these have been published.

It is significant to note that a number of techniques alluded to in these fragments also appear to have been preserved among the non-Jewish school of magic in Europe. The relationship between the practical Kabbalah and these magical schools would constitute an interesting area of study.

The meditative Kabbalah stands between these two extremes. Some of the earliest meditative methods border on the practical Kabbalah, and their use is discouraged by the latter masters, especially those of the Ari's school. Within this category are the few surviving texts from the Talmudic period. The same is true of the teachings of the Thirteenth Century master, Rabbi Abraham Abulafia, whose meditative works have never been printed and survive only in manuscript.

Most telling is a statement at the end of *Shaarey Kedushah* (Gates of Holiness), which is essentially a meditative manual. The most important and explicit part of this text is the fourth section, which actually provides instructions in meditation. When this book was first printed in 1715, the publisher omitted this last, most important section, with the following note:

> The printer declares that this fourth section is not to be copied or printed since it consists entirely of divine names, permutations and concealed mysteries, and it is not proper to bring them on the altar of the printing press.

Actually, upon examining this section, we find that "divine names and permutations" play a relatively small role, and could easily have been omitted. But besides this, the section in question also presents explicit instructions for the various techniques of Kabbalah meditation, and even this was considered too secret a doctrine to be published for the masses.

The Ari himself also made use of a system of meditation involving *Yechudim* (unifications), and this was included in the main body of his writings, particularly in the *Shaar Ruach HaKodesh* (Gate of the Holy Spirit). But even here, it is significant to note that, although the Ari lived in the Sixteenth Century, this text was not printed until 1863. For over three hundred years, it was available only in manuscript.

With the spread of the Hasidic movement in the Eighteenth Century, a number of meditative techniques became more popular, especially those centered around the formal prayer service. This reached its zenith in the teachings of Rabbi Nachman of Breslov (1772–1810), who discusses meditation in considerable length. He developed a system that could be used by the masses, and it was primarily for this reason that Rabbi Nachman's teachings met with much harsh opposition.

One of the problems in discussing meditation, either in Hebrew or in English, is the fact that there exists only a very limited vocabulary with which to express the various "technical" terms. For the sake of clarity, a number of such terms, such as "mantra" and "mandala" have been borrowed from the various meditative systems of the East. This is not meant in any way to imply that there is any connection or relationship between these systems and the Kabbalah. Terms such as these are used only because there are no Western equivalents. Since they are familiar to most contemporary readers, they have the advantage of making the text more readily understood.

Many people express surprise that the Jewish tradition contains a formal meditative system, that, at least in its outward manifestations, does resemble some of the Eastern systems. This resemblance was first noted in the Zohar, which recognized the merit of the Eastern systems, but warned against their use.

The fact that different systems resemble each other is only a reflection on the veracity of the technique, which is primarily one of spiritual liberation. The fact that other religions make use of it is of no more consequence than the fact that they also engage in prayer and worship. This does not make Jewish worship and prayer any less meaningful or unique, and the same is true of meditation. It is basically a technique for releasing oneself from the bonds of one's physical nature. Where one goes from there depends very much on the system used.

CHAPTER ONE

Meditation

1. THE SCHOOLS

It is universally accepted by the Kabbalists that the first ones to engage in these meditative methods were the patriarchs and prophets, who used them to attain enlightenment and prophecy. Although there are many allusions to this in the Bible, the scripture is virtually silent when it comes to providing explicit descriptions of their methods. Still, if one looks at the appropriate texts, one can gain considerable insight into the methods that were in use in the time of the prophets.[1]

The earliest direct statement regarding method comes from the First Century, from the early Talmudic period. Here we find some of the greatest Talmudists engaged in the mystical arts, making use of a number of meditative techniques to attain spiritual elevation and ascend to the transcendental realm. Many of these techniques consisted of the repetition of divine names, as well as intense concentration on the transcendental spheres. What little we know of their methods is preserved in a few fragments, as well in a remarkable complete text, *Hekhalot Rabatai* (The Greater Chambers), of which the main parts are presented for the first time in translation in this book.

It was during this period that some of the main classics of Kabbalah were written. These include the *Sefer Yetzirah* (Book of Formation), the Bahir and the Zohar. These involved even higher levels than those described in the *Hekhalot*, and for the most part, only the barest hints are provided as to how these levels were reached.

With the close of the Talmudic period, these methods became restricted to a few very small closed secret societies. Both the Bahir and the Zohar remained completely unknown outside of these societies, and were not revealed until the late Twelfth and Thirteenth Centuries respectively. The publication of the Bahir in particular gave impetus to the study of the mysteries, and a number of individuals began to openly teach the secret methods.

Most remarkable among these was Rabbi Abraham Abulafia (1240–1295). Having received the tradition from earlier sources, he was the first to actually put them in writing. For this, he weas condemned in many circles, although most Kabbalists consider his methods to be authentic and based on a reliable tradition. Several of his contemporaries, most notably, Rabbi Isaac of Acco and Rabbi Joseph Gikatalia, also speak of meditative methods.

Most of their work, however, was eclipsed by the publication of the Zohar in the middle 1290's. This great classic gripped the imagination of almost all Kabbalists of the time, and the teachings of other schools was virtually forgotten. It is therefore no accident that many books written before this were never published, and among those which have not been lost, a good number exist only in manuscript.

Since the Zohar has little to say about meditative methods, many important Kabbalists began to ignore the subject completely. They were too involved in trying to unravel the mysteries of this ancient book that had been concealed for many centuries. There were a few exceptions, however, and these Kabbalists made use of the methods of Abulafia, Gikatalia and Isaac of Acco. For over two hundred years, however, we find virtually nobody exploring the Zohar itself to ascertain the meditative methods used by its authors.

The main attempts in this direction occurred in the Safed School, which flourished during the Sixteenth Century. It reached its zenith in the teachings of Rabbi Isaac Luria (1534–1572), commonly known as the Ari, who showed how the various letter combinations found in the Zohar were actually meant to be used as meditative devices. Although the Ari wrote almost nothing himself, his teachings were arduously copied by his disciplies, and fill almost two dozen large volumes. To a large extent, all this was an introduction to the methodology involved in his system of meditation.

Just as the Zohar had overshadowed everything when it was published, so did the writings of the Ari overwhelm the other schools three centuries later. His teachings were seen as the ultimate expression of the Kabbalah, and for the next two hundred years, the greatest part of Kabbalah literature devoted itself to their interpretation. Although the Ari's meditative methods were used by a few individuals, and possibly by one or two minor schools, for the most part the Kabbalists devoted themselves to theory rather than practice.

The next great renascence came with the rise of the Hasidic movement, founded by Rabbi Israel, the Baal Shem Tov (1698–1760).

When their works are studied, it becomes obvious that the Baal Shem and his closest disciples were ardent students of the earlier meditative texts of the Kabbalah, and in the Hasidic classics, these texts are often paraphrased. During the second half of the Eighteenth Century, and perhaps the first decade or two of the Nineteenth, many people engaged in the classical meditative techniques of Kabbalah, often describing the high spiritual states that they attained.

The opposition to this, especially where it involved teaching these methods to the masses, was very strong. An entire group, known as the *Mitnagdim* (opposers), arose to combat the Hasidim, vigorously denouncing their methods. As a result, the Hasidim themselves began to de-emphasise their meditative practices, and eventually these were virtually forgotten.

2. METHODS

Meditation is primarily a means of attaining spiritual liberation. Its various methods are designated to loosen the bond of the physical, allowing the individual to ascend to the transcendental, spiritual realm. One who accomplishes this successfully is said to have attained *Ruach HaKodesh*, The "Holy Spirit," which is the general Hebraic term for enlightenment.

The best-known contemporary method of meditation is that which involves a mantra, a word or phrase that is repeated over and over for a designated period of time. One concentrates on the mantra to the exclusion of all else, thus clearing the mind of all extraneous thoughts and divorcing it from the normal stream of consciousness. In this method, the mantra may be repeated verbally, or the repetition may be completely mental. This type of meditation is found in the Kabbalah, especially among the earlier schools. In the *Hekhalot*, for example, one begins his spiritual ascent by repeating a number of Divine Names 112 times.

Mantra meditation is an example of structured, externally directed meditation. It is externally directed, insofar as one concentrates on a word or phrase, rather than on the spontaneous thoughts to the mind. Since it involves a specific practice, repeated for a fixed length of time, it is considered a structured meditation.

Another example of structured externally-directed meditation is contemplation, where one gazes at an object, placing all of one's concentration on it. In occult practices, the best-known type of contemplation involves gazing into a crystal ball.[2] Other types of contemplation involve mandalas, pictures or letter designs, where one gazes upon them, emptying the mind of all other thought. In Kabbalah meditation, the simplest contemplative device is the Tetragrammaton itself, and this is discussed even in non-Kabbalistic works.[3] More mplex forms are also used, and this method seems to have reached its zenith under the influence of Rabbi Shalom Sharabi (1702—1777).

Very closely related to this is the method of *Yechudim* (Unifications), which plays an important role in the system of the Ari. Here one does not contemplate a physical picture, but rather a mental image, asually consisting of various combinations of divine names. Since the structures and combinations of these names are predetermined, and do not arise spontaneously in the mind, this is also considered to be an externally-directed meditation.

The second basic method of meditation is that which is internally-directed. This consists of meditating on thoughts, feelings or mental images that arise spontaneously in the mind. Usually, this is best accomplished by focusing on a general area, around which these thoughts will be evoked. Since there is no formal or predetermined method of evoking such thoughts, this is most commonly an unstructured meditation.

Internally-directed meditation can be practiced purely in thought, or, as in some systems, one's thoughts can also be verbalized. One of the best methods of verbalizing such thoughts while keeping them concentrated on a single focus is to express them as spontaneous prayer. It is this method that forms the basis for the meditative system of Rabbi Nachman of Breslov.

The third basic type of meditation is that which is non-directed. Such meditation strives for a stillness of the mind and a withdrawal from all perception, both internal and external. It plays an important role in the advancd states of many other methods, but at the same time, it can also be used as a method in its own right. Very little is expressly written about this method, but it appears to play a role in the teachings of such Hasidic masters as Rabbi Dov Baer, the Maggid of Mezrich (1704—1772) and Rabbi Levi Yitzchak of Berdichov (1740—1809).

There is evidence that this method was used, at least for the most advanced, in the very terminology of the Kabbalah. Indeed, in a number of cases, it is only when looked upon in this sense that some terminology is comprehensible. Thus, for example, the Kabbalists call the highest level of transcendence *Ayin,* literally "Nothingness." Actually, this alludes to the ultimate level reached by non-directed meditation, where all perception and imagery cease to exist.

Besides being divided into these three basic methods, meditation can be classified according to the means used. The three basic means are the intellect, the emotions, and the body.

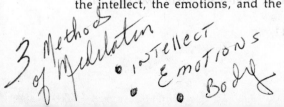

The path of the intellect is very prevalent among the theoretical Kabbalists, and was also used outside of the Kabbalistic schools. The most common method was simply to contemplate on various aspects of the Torah, probing the inner meaning of its commandments. It also included delving deeply with the intellect into the structure of the supernal universes, and, as it were, becoming a denizen of these worlds. For many, this method lead to a very high state of ecstasy, and this method forms the basis of the Habad system of Hasidism.[4]

Another form of intellectual meditation involves the study of devotional works, carefully contemplating each concept in an effort to attain self-improvement. It was primarily this method that formed the basis of the Mussar Movement, which arose in the Nineteenth Century as a response to Hasidism. Such contemplation, or *Hitbonenut,* plays an especially important role in the devotional work *Mesilat Yesharim* (Path of the Just), by the great Kabbalist Rabbi Moshe Chaim Luzzatto (1707—1747). In this remarkable book, the author outlines all the steps leading up to, but not including, *Ruach HaKodesh* the ultimate enlightment. The method of attaining these desired traits is that of *Hitbonenut*—contemplation on the teachings germain to that step and rectifying one's life in the light of these teachings. Incidentally, although it is not widely known, the ten levels discussed in this text clearly parallel the ten mystical *Sefirot* of the Kabbalists.

The path of the emotions also plays an important role in the systems of the Kabbalists. One place where it is particularly important is in *Kavanah*-meditation, the system that makes use of the formal daily prayers as a sort of mantra, especially in the Hasidic schools. Here one is taught to place all of his feelings and emotions into the words of his worship, thus attaining a divestment of the physical *(hitpashtut hagashmiut).* This path is also found in meditations involving music, which played an important role in the meditations of the ancient prophets of the Bible.

A path combining the intellect and emotions is the path of love, described in detail by the leading philosopher, Rabbi Moses Maimonides (1135—1204). He writes that when a person deeply contemplates on God, thinking of His mighty deeds and wondrous creations, he becomes profoundly aware of His wisdom, and is brought to a passionate love for God.[5] He speaks of a level of love called *Cheshek* (passion), where the emotion is so intense that every thought is exclusively engaged with its object. This love for God can be so intense that the soul can literally be drawn out of the body by it, and this is what occurs when a saint dies by the "Kiss of God." This is considered to be one of the highest possible levels of enlightenment, usually attained only at very advanced age.[6]

The third path is that of the body. It includes both the body motions and breathing exercizes that play a key role in the system of Rabbi Abraham Abulafia. The swaying and bowing that accompanies formal prayer also involves the path of the body, enhancing the meditative uuality of the worship.

One of the most important techniques of body meditation involves dancing. This is especially true among the Hasidic schools, where even after other meditative methods were abandoned, dance was still used as a means of attaining ecstasy and enlightenment. This, however, was not a Hasidic innovation, since even in most ancient times dance was an important method for attaining enlightenment.

The Talmud teaches that on the festival of Succot (Tabernacles), during the "Festival of Drawing," in Jerusalem, "saints and men of deed would dance before the assemblage, holding torches and singing hymns of praise." [7] This festival was a particularly propitious time for attaining enlightenment, as the Jerusalem Talmud states, "Why was it called a 'Festival of Drawing'? Because it was a time when people drew in *Ruach HaKodesh*." [8] So closely was dance associated with enlightenment, that the Future World, which is viewed as the ultimate place of enlightenment, is described as "A dance conducted by the Blessed Holy One, where each individual points a finger at Him." [9]

3. VOCABULARY

One reason why so little is known about the various systems of Kabbalah meditation is that all of this literature is in Hebrew, and it has never been accurately translated. Since most of these methods are no longer practiced, the vocabulary associated with them has also been forgotten. So great is this confusion that even the very Hebrew word for meditation is not generally known. This has even led to the use of the wrong term in an article on the subject in a major Judaic encyclopedia. Once a basic vocabulary is established, however, one can gain an appreciation of how often meditation is discussed in classical texts, particularly in the Kabbalistic classics.[10]

There is one word that is consistently used as a term for meditation by the commentators, philosophers and Kabbalists. The word which most often denotes meditation is *Hitbodedut* (הִתְבּוֹדְדוּת). The verb, "to meditate," is represented by the word *Hitboded* (הִתְבּוֹדֵד).

The word *Hitboded* is derived from the root *Badad* (בדד), meaning "to be secluded." Literally, then, *Hitbodedut* actually means self-isolation, and in some cases, actually refers to nothing more than physical seclusion and isolation.[11] In many other places, however, it is used to denote a state of consciousness involving the isolation of the self, that is, the isolation of he individual's most basic essence.

Thus, when discussed in a Kabbalistic context, the word *Hitbodedut* means much more than mere physical isolation. It refers to a state of internal isolation, where the individual mentally secludes his essence from his thoughts. One of the greatest Kabbalists, Rabbi Chaim Vital (1543—1620), often speaks of such mental seclusion, saying that "one must seclude himself *(hitboded)* in his thoughts to the ultimate degree." [12] In doing this, one separates his soul from his body to such a degree that he no longer feels any relationship to his physical self. The soul is thus isolated, and as Rabbi Chaim Vital concludes, "the more one separates himself from the physical, the greater will be his enlightenment."

This state of mental seclusion is very important to the prophetic experience. The clearest description of this state is presented by Rabbi Levi ben Gershon (1288—1344), a major Jewish philosopher, often known as Gersonides, or simply by the acrostic, "the Ralbag." He writes that the attainment of prophetic revelation "requires the isolation *(hitbodedut)* of the consciousness from the imagination, or both of these from the other perceptive mental faculties." [13]

Rabbi Isaac of Acco also uses the same definition. Speaking of individuals seeking prophecy, he writes, "They fulfil the conditions of meditation *(Hitbodedut)* which has the effect of nullifying the senses and divorcing the thought porcesses of the soul from all perception, clothing it in the spiritual essence of the transcendental." [14]

One of the clearest expressions of this has been developed by Rabbi Abraham Maimonides (1186—1237), son of the famed Moses Maimonides. He writes that there are two different types of self-isolation *(hitbodedut)*, external and internal. External *hitbodedut* is nothing more than physical isolation, and this is usually desirable when one wishes to meditate. Internal *hitbodedut*, on the other hand, consists of isolating the soul from the perceptive faculty. When the mind is completely hushed in this manner, one becomes able to perceive the spiritual realm.[15]

The word *Hitbodedut* therefore primarily is used to denote the isolation of the soul or ego from all external and internal stimuli. Any method or practice that is used to accomplish this is also called *Hitbodedut*. Since these are the practices that are usually referred to as "meditation," this is how the word *Hitbodedut* should be translated.

Another closely related term, *Hitbonenut* (הִתְבּוֹנְנוּת), is also often translated as "meditation." (Indeed, this is the term used in the above-mentioned encyclopedia article.) From context, however, we see that a more precise definition of *Hitbonenut* is "contemplation," that is, intense concentration on an object or image. Of course, contemplation is a meditative technique, but it is significant to note that the term is hardly ever used in the classical Kabbalah texts in describing the attainment of the higher states of consciousness.

CHAPTER TWO

Talmudic Mystics

Recurring Dream

Thru Practice of Meditation I will find my Vehicle (Merkava) = my way Back Home

↓

LOST = No Being able to find my way Back Home (Spiritual Home)

↓

Dream of Losing my Vehicle (CAR) = LOSING (HAVING LOST) CONNECTION TO G-d

1. THE TALMUDISTS

With the destruction of Solomon's Temple, the age ofthe prophets came to a close, and a dark age descended over their heirs. The Biblical canon was sealed, and after this, almost no important literature was produced until the time of he Talmud. Although there are some historical records of this period, the most important being found in the Apocrypha, virtually no mystical literature exists.

Some of the mystical teachings of the prophets had survived, but they were only taught in the narrowest circles, and were most probably confined to small secret societies. Thus, Rabbi Yochanan ben Zakkai, a leader in the First Century, taught,"The workings of the *Merkava* should not be taught even individually, except to one who is wise, understanding with his own knowledge." [1] These mysteries were not publicly taught, even within the secret societies but were given over individually, to one worthy disciple at a time.

The term "Workings of the *Merkava*," as used in the Talmud, refers to the mystery of Ezekiel's vision. Although the term is not found in the vision itself, it does occur in the verse, "Gold for the pattern of the Chariot *(Merkava)*, the Cherubs" (1 Chronicles 2:18). The word *Merkava* is used to describe the Cherubs on the Ark, but Ezekiel himself identifies the Cherubs as the angels seen in his vision.[1]

The word *Merkava* (מֶרְכָּבָה) comes from the root *Rakhav* (רכב), meaning "to ride," and hence means a "chariot" or "riding vehicle." In general, the concept of riding involves travelling and leaving one's natural place. When the Bible says that God "rides," it means that He leaves His natural state where He is absolutely unknowable and inconceivable, and allows Himself to be visualized by the prophets. One who "sees" God in this manner is said to experience a *Merkava* vision.

The term *Maaseh Merkava* or "Workings of the *Merkava*" refers to the setting up of a *Merkava*, that is, attaining a state where a

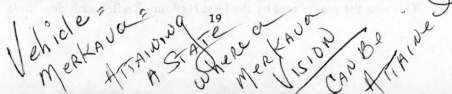

Merkava vision can be attained. From the context in which this term is used in the Kabbalah texts, it is obvious that *Maaseh Merkava* refers to the meditative techniques involved in attaining this mystical experience. The Ari explicitly describes an individual involved in the "Workings of the *Merkava*" as being engaged in meditation *(hitbodedut)*.[3] The *Hekhalot* speaks of the individual making a "Chariot of Light," with which he then ascends to the supernal chambers.[4]

These mysteries were entrusted to the religious leaders of each generation. Rav Zeira, a sage of the Fifth Century, thus taught, "Even a summary of these mysteries should be given over only to the chief justice of the court." [5] The chief justices had more than mere judicial authority. Each major community had its own ecclesiastical court, and these chief justices were normatively the religious leaders of their communities. In order to prevent the mysteries from degenerating into heresy, they were safeguarded by the religious leadership, and taught individually only to those considered worthy.

Among the early mystical schools, there is a group that the Talmud cryptically refers to as the "First Hasidim." Among the things that the Talmud says about them is that they were zealous in bringing sacrifice, and scrupulously buried refuse containing sharp objects so as not to cause harm to others.[6] According to Rabbi Chaim Vital, these First Hasidim were among the important heirs to the prophetic tradition.[7]

The Mishnah states that "the First Hasidim would linger an hour and then pray." To this, the Talmud adds that they would also wait an hour after their prayers, and that the prayer itself would also take an hour.[8] Since there were three daily prayer services, they would spend a total of nine hours each day involved in such devotion.

There is no mention in the Talmud as to what these Hasidim did during the hours before and after prayer, but the Kabbalists explain it in terms of classical meditative techniques.[9] In order to place oneself in the frame of mind necessary for successful deep meditation, one must sit calmly beforehand, quietly building up spiritual energy. Similarly, after intense meditation, one must also sit quietly, absorbing the effects of ths experience. This would then clearly indicate that the prayer itself was used as a type of meditation among these First Hasidim.

This is actually easy to understand. In the time of Ezra, shortly after the close of prophecy, the Great Assembly had composed the Eighteen Blessings, a prayer that was to be recited three times daily. This was the prayer said by the First Hasidim. Recited each day, three times, this prayer itself became almost like a mantra. While the words could be said almost automatically, the mind became totally absorbed by the words, inducing a very deep meditative state. The intensity of their concentration is evident, since the Eighteen Blessings can normally be recited in two or three minutes, and the First Hasidim spent an entire hour on them.

Most types of *Merkava* meditation involved the use of Divine Names. As far back as the time of Hillel, a leader in the First Century b.c.e., we find warnings against using such Names for one's own purposes. Hillel thus taught, "He who makes use of the Crown will pass away." [10] A very early source interprets this to refer to one who makes use of God's names for his own purposes.[11]

One of the earliest names associated with the *Merkava* school is that of Rabbi Yochanan ben Zakkai. While he is said to have been completely versed in all aspects of the tradition, both mystical and otherwise, he was still considered among the least disciples of Hillel. The greatest of Hillel's disciples, Rabbi Jonathan ben Uziel, was the mystic *par excellence,* but very little is know of his life. Rabbi Yochanan ben Zakkai, on the other hand, is a well-known figure in the Talmud, and a vast majority of its legalistic material is derived from the school that Rabbi Yochanan founded in Yavneh after the destruction of the Second Temple in the year 70.

Rabbi Jonathan ben Uziel is mentioned only a few times in the Talmud, but is credited with having authored the Targum, the authorized Aramaic translation, to the books of the Prophets. It is in this context that we see that he had a direct tradition regarding the mystical teachings of the prophets embodied in their books, and was thus one of the greatest students of the esoteric tradition in his generation.

Rabbi Yochanan ben Zakkai was the most important religious leader after the destruction of the Second Temple. Among his major disciples were the Great Rabbi Eliezer, Rabbi Joshua, and Rabbi Eleazar ben Arakh, who were counted as the greatest sages and religious leaders of their time. Rabbi Yochanan ben Zakkai taught them the mysteries of the *Merkava,* but did not take these teachings lightly, going to great lengths to teach his disciples proper respect for them.

The Talmud tells us that the main one to whom Rabbi Yochanan ben Zakkai taught the mysteries was Rabbi Joshua, who in turn taught it to Rabbi Akiba.[12] Besides being the greatest religious leader of his generation, and one of its supreme logicians,Rabbi Akiba was also one of the leading mystics of his time. The Talmud tells how, alone of the four greatest sages of his generation, he was able to penetrate the deepest mysteries and remain unscathed.

There are some mystical books attributed to Rabbi Akiba and his school, the most prominent being *Otiot deRabbi Akiba* (The Letters of Rabbi Akiba), which discusses the mystery of the letters of the alphabet. Some also attribute to Rabbi Akiba the present recension of *Sefer Yetzira* (The Book of Formation), one of the most important and mystical classics of the Kabbalah.

As an adept in the science of meditation, we would expect to find Rabbi Akiba familiar with the various manifestations of the higher states of consciousness. An important experience in high meditative states is synesthesia, where sound is seen and colors are heard. On the verse, "And all the people saw the voices" (Exodus 20:15), Rabbi Akiba states that they saw the sounds and heard visions, a clear example of synesthesia.[13] Since Rabbi Akiba was able to speak of this state, it is also highly probable that he experienced it.

SOURCES

Hillel had eighty disciples. . . . The greatest was Rabbi Jonathan ben Uziel, while the least was Rabbi Yochanan ben Zakkai.

It is said of Rabbi Yochanan ben Zakkai that he was not ignorant of anything. [He knew] Mishnah, Talmud, law, exposition, grammatical analysis of the Torah, analysis of the Scribes, logical inference, similar wordings, astronomical calculations, *gematriot*, incantations for angels, incantations for demons, incantations to palm trees, proverbs of washwomen, proverbs of foxes, a "Great Thing," and a "Small Thing."

A "Great Thing" is the Workings of the *Merkava*, while a "Small Thing" is the discourses of Abaya and Rava. . . .

Since this was true of the least of them, it was certainly true of the greatest. It is said that when Rabbi Jonathan ben Uziel was sitting and studying Torah, any bird that flew by was immediately consumed.

Talmud.[14]

The translation *(Targum)* on the Prophets was authored by Jonathan ben Uziel, based on a tradition from [the prophets,] Haggai, Zechariah and Malachi.

When he wrote it, an earthquake shook an area four hundred parsangs square in the Land of Israel. A heavenly voice *(bat kol)* declared, "Who is it who reveales My mysteries to man?"

Jonathan ben Uziel stood on his feet and said, "It is revealed and known before You that I have not done this for my own glory, nor for the glory of my father's house. I have done it for Your glory so that controversy not increase in Israel."

Talmud[15]

It happened that Rabbi Yochanan ben Zakkai was on a journey, riding on a donkey. His disciple, Rabbi Eleazar ben Arakh, who was driving the donkey, said, "Master, teach me a lesson in the Workings of the *Merkava.*"

Rabbi Yochanan ben Zakkai said, "Did I not teach you that the Workings of the *Merkava* may not even be taught individually, except to one who is wise, understanding from his own knowledge?"

The other replied, "Then let me repeat something that you have already taught me."

Rabbi Yochanan ben Zakkai immediately got down from the donkey, wrapped himself in his Tallit, and sat on a stone under an olive tree.

The disciple asked, "Rabbi, why did you get down?"

The master replied, "Is it then proper that you should expound on the Workings of the *Merkava,* when the Divine Presence joins us and angels are all around, while I am sitting on a donkey?"

Rabbi Eleazar ben Arakh then began to expound on the Workings of the *Merkava.* Fire came down and surrounded all the trees of the field. . . .

When this was told to Rabbi Joshua, he was on a journey together with Rabbi Yosi the Priest. They decided that they too would expound on the workings of the *Merkava* [out in the fields]. Rabbi Joshua began the discourse.

This was during the dry summer season, but the sky clouded over, and a rainbow appeared in the sky. Angels gathered to listen to them, like people thronging to the entertainment at a wedding.

Rabbi Yosi the Priest later told Rabbi Yochanan ben Zakkai about this experience. He replied, "Happy are you, and happy are those who bore you. Happy are my eyes that have seen this."

Talmud[16]

Four entered the Orchard *(Pardes)*. They were Ben Azzai, Ben Zoma, the Other, and Rabbi Akiba. Rabbi Akiba warned them, "When you enter near the stones of pure marble, do not say 'water water,' since it is written, 'He who speaks falsehood will not be established before My eyes'' (Psalms 101:7).

Ben Azzai gazed and died. Ragarding him it is written, "Precious in God's eyes is the death of His saints" (Psalms 116:15).

Ben Zoma gazed and was stricken. Regarding him it is written, "You have found honey, eat moderately lest you bloat yourself and vomit it" (Proverbs 25:16).

The Other (Elisha ben Abuya) gazed and cut his plantings (became a heretic).

Rabbi Akiba entered in peace and left in peace. . . .

The angels also wished to cast down Rabbi Akiba but the Blessed Holy One said, "Leave this elder alone, for he is worthy of making use of My glory."

Talmud[17]

Entered the Orchard: They ascended to heaven by means of a [Divine] Name.

Pure Marble: As transparent as clear water.

Do not say 'water water': is here and how can we procede?'

Ben Zoma gazed: toward the Divine Presence *(Shekhinah)*.

And was stricken: He lost his mind.

Precious in God's eyes is the death of His saints: This death is harsh in His eyes, since [Ben Azzai] died unmarried. Still, it is impossible that he should not have died, since it is written, "No man can see Me and live" (Exodus 33:20).

Rabbi Shlomo Yitzchaki-Yarchi
(Rashi: 1040—1105), Commentary ad loc.

They did not physically ascend, but it appeared to them as if they had ascended on high.

Tosafot (Twelfth Century),
Commentary ad loc.

[The Sages] use the term "Orchard" (*Pardes,* Paradise) to denote the Garden of Eden, the place set aside for the righteous. It is the place in Aravot (the highest heaven) where the souls of the righteous are stored.[18]

In the *Hekhalot* it is explained that sages who were worthy of such undertakings would pray and purify themselves of all uncleanliness. They would fast, immerse [in the *Mikvah*] and purify themselves. Then they would make use of various Names and gaze into the Chambers [on high]. There they would see how the watches of angels stand. They would see how one Chamber follows another, and what is in each Chamber.

Rabbi Akiba warned them, "When you gaze into the profound depths (*avanta,* אַבְנְתָּא) of your heart, approaching the stones of pure marble, do not say, 'water water.' " There is actually no water there at all, but only a form is seen. If one says there is water there, he is blaspheming.

This is explained in *Hekhalot Rabatai.*[19] The Watcher of the Chamber of the Marble Door casts forth thousands upon thousands of waves of water, but actually not even a single drop is there. Rabbi Akiba says, "It appears as if the waves are of water, but there is actually not even a single drop. All that one sees is the glow in the air from the stones of pure marble, which are included in the Chamber. Their radiance resembles water. But if one says, 'What is the purpose of this water,' he is a blasphemer."

They did not actually ascend into heaven, but gazed and saw it in the profound depths of the heart. They saw it like one gazing through a dull mirror.[20]

Ben Azzai gazed. This means that he continued uttering Divine Names so as to be able to see in a clear mirror, and as a result he died.

Ben Zomah gazed and was stricken, that is, he lost his mind.

The Other cut his plantings. Since the place is called an Orchard, the sages say that he "cut his plantings." This means that he blasphemed. He saw [the angel] Metatron, who was given authority to sit for one hour to inscribe the merit of Israel. He said, "I have learned that it is not permitted to sit in that place on high. Perhaps there are two Authorities."

Rabbi Chananel ben Chushiel (990–1055),
Commentary ad loc.

The sages taught that four entered the Orchard. In the Greater and Lesser *Hekhalot,* it is explained that they engaged in certain practices, uttered prayers in purity, and "made use of the Crown." [21] They were then able to gaze at the Chambers. . . .

This does not mean that they actually ascended on high, but that they gazed and saw it in the chambers of their heart, viewing it just like something seen clearly with the eyes. They hear, see and speak with an eye that views with *Ruach HaKodesh.* This is the explanation of Rav Hai Gaon.

Rabbi Nathan ben Yechiel (1035–1106), Lexicographer.[22]

Many sages maintain that one who possesses all the necessary qualifications has methods through which he can gaze at the *Merkava* and peek into the chambers on high. One must first fast for a certain number of days. He then places his head between his knees, and whispers into the ground many songs and praises known from tradition.

From his innermost being and its chambers he will then perceive the Seven Chambers. In his vision, it will be as if he is entering one chamber after another, gazing at what is in each one.

There are two tractates in which this is taught. These are called the Greater *Hekhalot* and the Lesser *Hekhalot,* as is well known.

It is with regard to such an experience that the Talmud teaches, "Four entered the Orchard."The chambers are likened to an orchard and are given this name. The four who entered the *Merkava* and passed through the Chambers are likened to people entering an orchard. . . .

It is taught that Ben Azzai gazed and died. This is because it was his time to leave the world.

It is also taught that Ben Zoma gazed and was stricken. This means that he became insane because of the confounding visions that his mind could not tolerate. He was like the "stricken ones," regarding which the 91st Psalm was written.[23]

When the Talmud states that the Other "cut his plantings," it is again using the allegory of the orchard. Since one of the four did irreparable damage, he is likened to one who enters an orchard and cuts down its trees. The Other assumed that there are two Authorities, very much like the Magii, who believe in Ormuzd and Ahriman, as well as independent domains of good and evil, like light and darkness.[24] This is the intent of the Talmud.

Rabbi Akiba was the most perfect of them all. He gazed properly, not exceeding his limitations, and his mind was able to encompass these mighty confounding visions. God gave him power so that as long as he gazed he kept proper thoughts in his mind and maintained a proper mental state.

This was known to all the early sages and none denied it. They maintained that God would accomplish wonders and fearsome things through the saints, just as He did through the prophets. . . . . They do not deny the Talmudical accounts of miracles, such as those involving Rabbi Chanina ben Dosa and the like.[25]

When Mar Rav Samuel Gaon [who headed the academy between 730 and 748 c.e.] and others like him flourished, they began to read the books of the philosophers. They claimed that such visions were only seen by the Prophets, and that only the Prophets could invoke miracles. They denied all the accounts which told of miracles occurring to the saints. They say that this is not Law. The same is true of the account of Rabbi Akiba's gazing into the Chambers, and the account of Rabbi Nehuniah ben Hakana and Rabbi Ishmael. Regarding all these, they say it is not the Law.

But our opinion remains that God does wonders and miracles to His saints, and also allows them to see the Chambers.

Hai Gaon (938–1038).[26]

2. THE ZOHAR

Among the disciples of Rabbi Akiba, the most prominent mystic was Rabbi Shimon bar Yochai, best known as the author of the Zohar. Although Rabbi Shimon obviously received a good part of the mystical tradition from Rabbi Akiba, he was not considered his prime disciple in this area. This honor was reserved for a colleague of Rabbi Shimon, Rabbi Chananya ben Chanikai.[27]

With Rabbi Shimon, however, a new school was developed. The account of Rabbi Shimon's thirteen-year stay in a cave with his son, hiding from the Roman officials, is well known. Rabbi Shimon had denounced the Romans and had been sentenced to death, barely escaping to this cave. During his stay there, Rabbi Shimon engaged in esoteric meditations and prayers, until he was worthy of a mystical revelation of the prophet Elijah. Elijah taught him the deepest of mysteries, which were later to make up the main body of the Zohar.

Rabbi Shimon left the cave around the year 138, shortly after the death of Hadrian, and established a new school of mysticism. This school continued after his death, and some seventy years later, his disciples wrote down his main teachings, forming the main body of the Zohar. These later writings were distinguished from the "first Mishnah," which was written by Rabbi Shimon himself.[28]

Rabbi Shimon's school survived for many years, during which minor additions were made to the Zoharic literature. For over a thousand years, this body of literature consisted of volumes of notes, restricted to a very small secret society. With the final disbandment of this society, the manuscripts were hidden in a vault, and were not uncovered until the Thirteenth Century. They finally came to the hands of Rabbi Moshe de Leon, one of the most prominent Kabbalists of that time, and he finally edited and published them in the 1290's. Enough was known of the Zoharic literature by the Kabbalists of that generation to recognize it as being authentic, and it was accepted by them with virtually no controversy.

There has always been some question as to the authenticity of the Zohar, especially among secular historians and opponents of the Kabbalah. Some even claim that Rabbi Moshe de Leon was its actual author. The main basis of this allegation is an account by another prominent Kabbalist of the time, Rabbi Isaac of Acco. He writes that he went to visit Rabbi Moshe to see the original manuscripts of the Zohar, but by the time he arrived, he found that Rabbi Moshe had passed away. He was informed that the manuscripts had never existed, and that Rabbi Moshe himself was the actual author of the Zohar. It is upon this account that most of the speculation regarding medieval authorship of the Zohar is based.

There are, however, strong questions regarding the veracity of the story told to Rabbi Isaac. It is well known that the ignorant often destroyed manuscripts, or on occasion, sold them so that the parchment could be reused. It is quite possible that the wife did this, and then embarrassed at not having them, claimed that they never existed. What is most important, however, is the fact that Rabbi Isaac of Acco investigated the matter, determined to ascertain the truth. Although the exact results of his investigation are not known, it is obvious that he eventually accepted the authenticity of the Zohar. This will be discussed at greater length in the section on Rabbi Isaac of Acco.

On its face, the Zohar contains virtually nothing regarding the methods of mystical meditation. It does contain many allusions of names and letter permutations, but does not provide a key as to how they should be used. It remained for the Ari to open the door of the Zohar, and demonstrate how its methods are to be used.

Excerpts from
THE ZOHAR

[After the death of Rabbi Shimon bar Yochai,] Rabbi Chiyah prostrated himself on the earth and kissed the ground. He cried out and said, "Dust, dust, how stiffnecked you are! How brazen you are! The most desirable things decay in you. You consume and pulverize all the world's pillars of light. How dastardly you are! The holy light who illuminated the world, the great master who oversaw the community, in whose merit the world stood, is now decaying in you."

"O Rabbi Shimon, shining lamp, light of the world, you are decaying in the dust. But you are still alive, directing the community."

He was astounded for an instant. Then he said, "Dust, dust, be not proud! The pillars of the world will not be given over to you. For Rabbi Shimon is not decaying in you."

When Rabbi Chiyah rose, he was crying. He left, and Rabbi Yosi went along with him. He fasted for forty days so that he should be able to see Rabbi Shimon, but he was told, "You are not worthy to see him." He wept and then fasted for another forty days.

He was then shown a vision. He saw Rabbi Shimon and his son Eliezer studying a concept that he had discussed with Rabbi Yosi. Many thousands were listening to his words.

At that moment, he saw many great lofty Wings. Rabbi Shimon and his son Eliezer mounted them, they ascended to the Academy of the Heavens. While they were there, the Wings waited for them.

He then saw [Rabbi Shimon and his son Eliezer] returning. They shone with a renewed glory, brighter than the sun.

Rabbi Shimon opened and said, "Let Rabbi Chiyah enter. Let him see to what extent the Blessed Holy One will renew the faces of the righteous in the World to Come. Happy is he who comes here without shame. Happy is he who can stand in this world like a mighty pillar."

[Rabbi Chiyah then] saw [himself] enter. Rabbi Eliezer was standing, and all the others who were sitting there [stood up before Rabbi Chiyah] He was very ashamed, but he entered, going to the side and sitting at the feet of Rabbi Shimon.

A Voice was heard, proclaiming, "Lower your eyes. Do not raise your head. Do not gaze." He lowered his eyes, but saw a light shining at a great distance.

The Voice came back as before, and said, "O you on high, who are hidden and concealed, open your eyes. O you who fly through all the worlds, gaze and see. O you who sleep with sealed eyes down below, wake up.

"Who among you has transformed darkness into light or bitterness into sweetness before he came here? Who among you waited each day for the light that shines when the King visits the Doe? For it is at this time that the Glory is increased, and He is called King over all the kings of the world. One who does not look forward to this each day in the world below has no portion here."

At that instant, [Rabbi Chiyah] saw a number of the group surrounding all the standing pillars, and he saw them being elevated to the Heavenly Academy. Some were ascending while others were descending. And above them all, was the Master of Wings.[29]

He made an oath and heard from behind the barrier that each day the King remembers the Doe who lies in the dust and visits her.[30] At that time, He kicks out at 390 firmaments, and they all are confounded and tremble before Him. He sheds tears because of this, and those tears, boiling like fire, fall into the great sea. The tears remain and endure there, and as a result of their power, the Master of the Sea is able to sanctify the Name of the Holy King. He accepts upon himself to swallow up all the waters of creation, and gather them into himself. Then, all peoples will come together to the Holy People, and the waters will be dried up so that they will be able to pass over on dry land.

While this was happening, he heard a voice proclaiming, "Make way, make way, for the King, the Messiah, is coming to the academy of Rabbi Shimon."

(All the righteous are heads of the academies on high, and all the earthly academies have their counterparts there. All the fellows of each academy ascend from their own school to the Heavenly Academy. The Messiah comes into all these academies, sealing Torah from the lips of the sages.)

At that moment, the Messiah came to [the academy of Rabbi Shimon]. He was wearing the highest crowns, given to him by the heads of the academies.

All the fellows stood up and Rabbi Shimon also rose, with his light ascending to the heights of the Firmament. [The Messiah] said to him, "O Rabbi, happy are you. Your Torah teachings ascend with 370 lights, and each light separates into 613 meanings.[31] These rise and are immersed in a river of pure balsamum. The Blessed Holy One seals Torah from your academy, as well as from the academy of Hezekiah king of Judah, and from the academy of Ahiyah the Shilonite.[32]

"I did not come to seal Torah from your academy, but only because the Master of Wings came here. I know that he does not enter any academy other than yours."

Rabbi Shimon then told him of the oath uttered by the Master of Wings. The Messiah lifted his voice and trembled. The firmaments, the great sea, and the Leviathan all trembled, and it seemed as if the world would be overturned.

At that moment [the Messiah] saw Rabbi Chiyah sitting at the feet of Rabbi Shimon. He said, "Who allowed a person wearing the clothing of the physical world to come here?"

Rabbi Shimon replied, "He is Rabbi Chiyah, the shining light of the Torah."

[The Messiah] said, "Let him and his sons die so that they can enter your academy."

Rabbi Shimon responded, "Let him be given more time [on earth]. He was then given additional time. He left that place, trembling, with tears streaming from his eyes. Rabbi Chiyah trembled, wept and said, "Happy is the portion of the righteous in that world. And happy is the portion of the son of Yochai, who is worthy of all that."

Zohar 1:4a

Rabbi Abba said:

One day I came to a city of the people of the East, and they told me some wisdom that they had inherited from ancient times. They also had books explaining this wisdom, and they brought me one such book.

In this book it was written that when a person meditates in this world, a spirit *(ruach)* is transmitted to him from on high. The type of spirit depends on the desire to which he attaches himself. If his mind attaches itself to something lofty and holy, then that is what he transmits down to himself. But if his mind attaches itself to the Other Side, and he meditates on this, then that will be what he transmits down to himself.

They said, "It all depends on word, deed, and the individual's desire to attach himself. Through these, he transmits downward to himself that side to which he becomes attached."

In that book I found all the [idolatrous] rites and practices involved in the worship of the stars and constellations. It included the things needed for such rites, as well as instructions how one must meditate in order to transmit their [influence] to himself.

In the same manner, one who wishes to attach himself on high through *Ruach HaKodesh* must do so with deed, word, and desire of the heart, meditating in that area. This is what it depends on when on wishes to bind himself to something and transmit its influence to himself. . . .

I said to them, "My children, the things in that book are very close to the teachings of the Torah. But you must keep yourselves from these books in order that your hearts not be drawn to their [idolatrous] practices and all the [other] facets mentioned there, and lest you be drawn away from serving the Blessed Holy One."

All these books can confuse a person. This is because the people of the East were great sages, who inherited this wisdom from Abraham. He had given it to the sons of his concubines, as it is written, "To the sons of the concubines that Abraham had taken, Abraham gave gifts"

(Genesis 25:6).[33] [This was originally true wisdom] but later it was drawn into many [idolatrous] sides.

Zohar 1:99b.

Happy is he who elevates his faith in God, taking te Divine Presence, which consists of Ten Sayings, and placing it in a single thought, a single desire, without any admixture whatsoever. Each and every *Sefirah* (Divine Emanation) is planted in it, and it is the Garden in which all the *Sefirot* are one. . . .[34]

When a person wishes to unify the Blessed Holy One and His Divine Presence (the male and female aspects of the Divine), he must banish all other thoughts. [Such thoughts] are the *Klipot* (קְלִיפּוֹת, Husks), regarding which it is written, "There are many thoughts in the heart of man" (Proverbs 19:21). One must then bring the Divine Presence into his mind, as the verse continues, 'But the counsel of God will abide."

When a man comes together with his wife, he must remove all clothing, to be together with her as one, as it is written, "They shall be one flesh" (Genesis 2:21). In a similar manner, one must remove all other [thoughts, which serve as the soul's] garments, when he makes the Unification twice each day, declaring, "Hear O Israel, God is our Lord, God is One" (Deuteronomy 6:4).[35]

Tikuney Zohar 66 (98a).

This is the mystery of Unification (*Yichud*, יִחוּד). The individual who is worthy of the World to Come must unify the name of the Blessed Holy One. He must unify the upper and lower levels and limbs, uniting them all and bringing them all to the necessary place, where the knot can be bound.[36]

This is the mystery of, "Hear O Israel, God is our Lord, God is One."

The mystery of "Hear" (*Sh'ma*, שְׁמַע) is the Name (*Shem*, שֵׁם) which becomes seventy (Eyin, ע) names.

This is the unifying category, Israel. It is called the Elder Israel (*Yisrael Sabba*), since there is also a lesser [Israel]. Regarding [the latter] it is written, "Israel is a child and I will love him" (Hosea 11:1). But [the one alluded to in "Hear O Israel] is the Elder Israel.

[This Elder Israel is] a single mystery and a single unifying category. "Hear O Israel" thus includes the [supernal archetype] Female and her Husband.

After the two are included in each other, in a single unifying category [which is the Elder Israel] one must unify their limbs. One must combine the two Tabernacles, making them into one in every limb.

This unification is accomplished when one meditates and ascends, attaching himself to the Infinite Being (*Ain Sof*, אֵין סוֹף). It is here that all things, both on high and below, are bound together in a single desire.

This is the mystery of "Will Be" (*YiHYeH*, יִהְיֶה), in the verse "God will be (*Yihyeh*) One" (Zechariah 14:9). It means that [He "will be One"] in the mystery of *YiHYeH*.

The Yod (י) must be attached to the Heh (ה) to make YH (יה). This is the Inner Chamber [since these are the first two letters of the Tetragrammaton, YHVH (יהוה)]. This is the place that conceals the highest point, which is the Yod (י).

This is the mystery of "God is our Lord." The two Divine Names represent the letters Yod (י) and Heh (ה).

One must then include all limbs in the place from which they emanate, this being the Inner Chamber. One brings them back to their place in their essence, foundation and root, elevating them to the place that is the Root of the Covenant.

Then one must concentrate on the second pair of letters [in YiHYeH (יִהְיֶה)]. He must bind [the second] Yod (י) to [the second] Heh (ה).

Yod is the mystery of the Holy Covenant. Heh is the Chamber, the place in which the Holy Covenant, which is the Yod, is concealed. And even though we have stated [elsewhere] that this is the Vav (ו) [in the Tetragrammaton, YHVH, (יהוה),] here it is a Yod. The mystery is that the two are united as one.

"[God is] One." This indicates that one must take everything from there and above and unify them as one.

One must elevate the mind so as to bind them all in one knot, and then, one must elevate the mind with awe and love until it reaches the Infinite Being (*Ain Sof*). At the same time, however, one must not allow the mind to leave all the other levels and limbs. But the mind should ascend with all of them, binding them so that all of them are a single knot in the Infinite Being (*Ain Sof*).

This is the Unification (*Yichud*) of the Elder Rav Hamnuna. He learned it from his father, and his father learned it from his master, who had a tradition from the lips of the Prophet Elijah.

Zohar 2:216a.

3. THE HEKHALOT SCHOOL

Another important mystical school was headed by Rabbi Nehuniah ben Hakaneh, a mysterious personality about whose life virtually nothing is known. A contemporary of Rabbi Yochanan ben Zakkai, he flourished in the First Century, living to extreme old age. In one Talmudical account, we find him in the presence of Rabbi Yochanan ben Zakkai when the latter was asking his disciples to interpret a certain Biblical passage. When Rabbi Nehunia gave his opinion, Rabbi Yochanan declared that it was better than his own.[37] The true stature of Rabbi Nehuniah becomes evident in the *Hekhalot*, where we find the greatest sages of that generation sitting at his feet as disciples. It is quite evident that he was the greatest esoteric master of his time.

It is from Rabbi Nehuniah that we have the Bahir, one of the oldest of all Kabbalistic texts. It is in this book that we find the earliest discussion of the *Sefirot*, as well as the doctrine of reincarnation. Although no details are given as to how they are to be used, a number of esoteric Names are discussed, as well as the general concept of "descending to the *Merkava*."

The Bahir states that it is impossible to become involved in the *Merkava* without falling into error, but that one should pursue it nonetheless, since it leads to the "way of life." [38] The reason why the mystics call it "descending to the *Merkava*" is because one's vantage point is the highest level of thought, from which one must actually descend to visualize the mysteries of the *Merkava*.[39]

The most important disciple of Rabbi Nehuniah was Rabbi Ishmael ben Elisha, who served as High Priest in the last days of the Second Temple. The Talmud relates how Rabbi Ishmael learned from Rabbi Nehuniah how to derive lessons from every word in the Torah, no matter how insignificant.[40] But most important, Rabbi Ishmael was the prime disciple in areas of mystical meditation, and it is from him that most sources have survived.

In one place, the Talmud provides us with an example of Rabbi Ishmael's mystical experience, where he sees "Akhteriel Yah the Lord of Hosts sitting on a high and exalted throne." The association of an angel, Akhteriel (אַכְתְּרִיאֵל), with God's name is somewhat difficult to understand. This is a very important point, however, since similar expressions occur many times in the early mystical writings, particulary in the *Hekhalot*.

In the commentaries, there appears to be some confusion as to whether Akhteriel is the name of an angel, or an appelation of the Glory itself. This can be understood, however, in terms of the teaching that prophecy and vision must always come through an *Ispaklaria* (אִסְפַּקְלַרְיָא) which is translated to mean a mirror or a lens. Although the initiate actually perceives God's Glory, it is not seen directly, but must be reflected through the *Ispaklaria*. The *Ispaklaria* can be an angel or some other transcendental being, and in this case, it was the angel Akhteriel.[41]

The same is true whenever an angel's name precedes that of God in mystical literature. This merely means that the angel is serving as the lens or mirror for the vision, or as God's spokesman. In many places in the Bible we find that an angel speaks in God's name, and this is the inner meaning of what God said regarding an angel, "My Name is in him" (Exodus 23:11).[42] This angel is usually identified as Metatron (מֶטַטְרוֹן), and regarding this angel, the Talmud says, "his name is like that of his Master."[43]

Elsewhere, the Talmud relates that Rabbi Ishmael said, "Suriel, Prince of the Face, spoke to me."[44] The name of the angel Suriel or Suriah occurs many times in the *Hekhalot*, and this angel is seen to be a spokesman for the "Face." From all these sources, it is obvious that Rabbi Ishmael was accustomed to such visions.

From these earlier generations, the esoteric tradition was given over to Rabbi Judah the Prince (120—189), who is best known as the redactor of the Mishnah, the earliest part of the Talmud.[45] From him it was given over to Rabbi Yochanan, redactor of the Jerusalem Talmud, and then to his disciple, Rabbi Assi. The tradition finally reached Rav Joseph and Rav Zeira, both of whom were versed in the mysteries of the *Merkava*. The mysteries were therefore in the hand of the Talmudic sages, and were in use until the middle of the Fifth Century.[46]

Rabbi Chaim Vital points out that many practices involving the use of Divine Names cannot be successful unless the initiate has been purified with the ashes of the Red Heifer. This is an important teaching of the Ari, mentioned a number of times in his writings. The Red Heifer was a special sacrifice, discussed in detail in Numbers 19, and it is the only means through which defilement resulting from contact with a dead body can be removed.

The main need for the Red Heifer arose because one was not permitted to enter the Temple grounds while in a defiled state. If a person had ever come in contact with the dead, he would have to be purified with the ashes of the Red Heifer before he could enter the sanctuary. Similarly, those engaged in the esoteric practices could not recite the Divine Names unless they were first purified in this manner.

The Red Heifer was a type of sacrifice, however, and sacrifice could only be offered when the Temple stood. When the Temple was destroyed in the year 70, only a small quantity of the ashes remained, and as long as these were still available, such purification was possible. The last of these ashes were used up in the Fifth Century, and after that, the method of Divine Names outlined in the *Hekhalot* could no longer be used.

This is verified by an account in the *Hekhalot* itself, where Rabbi Ishmael and Rabbi Akiba wished to bring Rabbi Nehuniah out of his mystical state. They did so by touching him with a cloth that had come in contact with a menstruous woman, and immediately upon touching this cloth, he was dismissed from before the Throne of Glory. Similarly, an individual who has not cleansed himself of all spiritual and ritual defilement, including the purification of the Red Heifer, cannot enter into these mysteries. The *Hekhalot* clearly spells out the dangers waiting for those who are not properly prepared and attempt to enter the *Merkava.*

SOURCES

Rabbi Ishmael said: I once entered the innermost chamber [of the Holy of Holies] to burn incense [on Yom Kippur] I saw Akhteriel Yah the Lord of Hosts (אַכְתְּרִיאֵל יָהּ יהוה צְבָאוֹת) sitting on a high and exalted throne. He said to me, "Ishmael, My son, bless Me."

I replied, "May it be Your will that You withhold Your anger, and let Your mercy be revealed over Your attributes. May You deal with Your children with the attribute of Mercy, and enter with them beyond the call of the Law."

He then nodded His head.

Talmud.[47]

Rabbi Ishmael said: I was thirteen years old when I went to study with Rabbi Nehuniah ben Hakanah. I asked him, "Who is the Prince of the Torah," and he replied, "His name is Yofiel (יופיאל)."

I was already fasting, but I decided to increase my mortification. I separated myself from all enjoyment for an additional forty days, beyond my previous fasts. At the end of the forty days, I pronounced the Great Name and brought down [the angel Yofiel]. He descended in a flaming fire, and his face was like a flash of lightning. When I saw him, I trembled and was confounded. My limbs seemed to dismember themselves, and I fell over backward.

He said to me, "Son of man, how dare you agitate the great Assembly on high?"

I fortified myself and replied, "It is known and revealed before the One who spoke and brought the world into being that I did not bring you down to earth for my own honor, but only to do the will of your Master."

He immediately said to me, "Son of man, you putrid drop, you worm, you maggot! Even if your soul has begun [to purify itself], you are still attached to a defiled body. If you wish that I reveal myself to you, fast for forty days, and immerse yourself twenty-four times each day. Do not taste anything that causes an odor, nor eat any kind of beans or vegetables. Sit in a dark room and do not look at any woman.

After I had done this, he taught me a Divine Name, with which I would ascend and descend.

Midrash.[48]

Rabbi Akiba related that he asked Rabbi Eliezer the Great, "How does one bind the Angel of the Face (*Sar HaPanim*) by an oath so that he should come down to earth and reveal the mysteries of things above and below?"

He replied to me, "My son, I once brought him down, and he wanted to destroy the world. He is a mighty prince, greater than any in the Family on high. He constantly stands and serves the King of the universe in cleanliness, abstinence and purity, in terror and fear for the glory of his Master, since the Divine Presence is with him in every place."

I said to him, "I will oblige him with an oath. Through the knowledge that he will reveal to me, I will oblige him and learn from him."

He replied, "If one wishes to oblige himself, he should sit fasting for the entire day when he brings him down. Before that day, he should purify himself for seven days [with the ashes of the Red Heifer]. He should immerse himself in a stream of water, and not speak any idle words.

"At the end of these days of fasting and purification, he should sit in water up to his neck. Before binding [the angel] with an oath, he should say, 'I bind you by an oath, princes of pride and terror, who are appointed to strike down one who is not pure and clean and who dares to reach out to make use of the servants on high. I do this through the glorious and fearsome Name. . . .' "

Razo Shel Sandelfon.[49]

[There are four universes, *Atzilut* (Nearness), the universe of the Sefirot, *Beriyah* (Creation), the universe of the Throne, *Yetzirah* (Formation), the universe of angels, and *Asiyah* (Making), the universe of forms.]

The prophets were able to see into *Atzilut,* although it was completely clothed in the lights of *Beriyah* when they saw it. Ezekiel lived after the destruction [of Solomon's Temple], and he therefore only received prophecy from *Atzilut* after it was clothed in *Beriyah,* with *Beriyah* itself clothed entirely in *Yetzirah.*

After this, the lights of *Atzilut* and *Beriyah* were no longer revealed at all. This is the meaning of the teaching that after Hagai, Zechariah and Malachi, prophecy ended completely, and only *Ruach HaKodesh* (Holy Spirit) remained.[50]

[This *Ruach HaKodesh*] consists of a transmission of the lights of *Yetzirah* itself, as well as lower levels. Attaining this level is called "Ascending to the Orchard (*Pardes*)." [51] This refers to *Yetzirah,* which is called "the Universe of [the angel] Metatron."

There are given techniques through which one can open the gates of the physical world so as to enter *Asiyah* and *Yetzirah.* These consist of Unifications (*Yechudim*) and prayers pertaining to the Universe of *Yetzirah* and its Ten Sefirot. It is these techniques that are taught in the Chapters of *Hekhalot,* and these practices were used by Rabbi Nehuniah, Rabbi Akiba, Rabbi Ishmael, and the members of the Great Assembly.

These techniques were then forgotten. Besides this, the ashes of the Red Heifer were lost in the period of the later Talmudic sages

(*Amaraim*), during the generation of Abaya and Rava [who lived in the Fifth Century], as mentioned in the Talmud.[52] After this, they no longer made use of these techniques to ascend to the Orchard.

From then on, people only made use of techniques involving the universe of *Asiyah*. Since this is the lowest of the universes, its angels have only a little good, and are mostly evil. Besides this, this is a level where good and evil are closely intertwined [and it is very difficult to separate them]. This does not bring any enlightenment, since it is impossible to perceive good alone, and one's perception is therefore a combination of good and evil, truth and falsehood.

This is the significance of the Practical Kabbalah. It is forbidden to make use of it, since evil necessarily attaches itself to the good. One may actually intend to cleanse his soul, but as a result of the evil, he actually defiles it.

Even if one does gain some perception, it is truth intermingled with falsehood. This is especially true today, since the ashes of the Red Heifer no longer exist. [Since one cannot purify himself,] the uncleanliness of the Husks (*Klipot*) attaches itself to the individual who attempts to gain enlightenment through the Practical Kabbalah.

Therefore, "he who watches his soul should keep far from them." [53] For besides polluting his soul, he will also be punished in purgatory (*Gehinom*). We also have a tradition that such an individual will be punished in this world. Either he or his children will become sick, will be impoverished, or will become apostates. Learn a lesson from Joseph Della Reina and Rabbi Shlomo Molcho, who made use of the Practical Kabbalah and were destroyed from the world.

All this is because of the above-mentioned reason. This involves a realm where there is no good devoid of evil. Besides this, it involves coercing angels with oaths against their will. These angels retaliate by enticing this individual, drawing him into evil ways until his soul is destroyed.

Beyond this, the methods involving these oaths were concealed by earlier generations, and we are not well-versed in the proper techniques. One must therefore keep himself far from these things.

Rabbi Chaim Vital (1543–1620).[54]

4. THE HEKHALOT TEXT

The *Greater Hekhalot* is one of the most ancient of all mystical texts, dating back to the First Century. It is also one of the few ancient tracts that explicitly describe the methods through which one enters the mystical state. The key appears to be a type of mantra meditation where a series of Divine Names is repeated 112 times. Through the repetition of this formula, one enters the threshold of the mystical Chambers, and one must then proceed from one Chamber to the next.

The ascent through the Chambers seems to be a sort of spiritual projection. One creates for himself a spiritual "body," and with the hands of this "body," he holds the Seals that must be shown to the angels guarding each gate in order to gain admittance. Since the initiate is ascending mentally rather than physically, these Seals must also be mental images of the Names in question.

The most probable meaning is that one must concentrate on these names, and possibly depict them in his mind. If this is the case, then this method would be very closely related to the method of Unifications (*Yichudim*) taught by the Ari. In the selection just quoted, Rabbi Chaim Vital states that the initiate would make use of Unifications in his ascent.

When one reaches the step before the seventh and final chamber, he is placed in a chariot (*Karon*, קָרוֹן). It should be recalled that the general word for this type of mystical experience is *Merkava*, which also means a chariot. The *Merkava* is a spiritual vehicle that one creates for himself, with which he ascends into the mystical state.

Also of great interest is the interpretation given to the *Nogah* (נֹגַהּ, glow) and *Chashmal* (חַשְׁמַל) seen in Ezekiel's vision. These are mentioned in the verse, "I saw, and behold a stormy wind coming from the north, a great cloud and flashing fire, a Glow *(nogah)* round about, and from its midst, a vision of the Speaking Silence (*Chashmal*), in the midst of the fire" (Ezekiel 1:4). These two concepts are important elements in the ascent into the transcendental realm.

In the *Hekhalot,* we find that the person descending into the *Merkava* is the first carried away by a stormy wind (*sa'arah,* סְעָרָה). This is the same stormy wind that lifted up Elijah, described in the verse, "There appeared a chariot of fire, and horses of fire, which separated the two, and Elijah went into heaven in a stormy wind (*sa'arah)" (2 Kings 2:11).* This is also obviously the "stormy wind" described by Ezekiel at the beginning of his vision. He is then brought upward in a chariot of *Nogah,* This being the glow seen by Ezekiel. The *Nogah* that Ezekiel saw was therefore the vehicle that brings the initiate into the heavenly realm.

Finally, when he is about to enter the highest levels of the *Merkava* the initiate is tested by the *Chashmal* to see if he is worthy. This fits very well into the Kabbalistic teaching that the *Chashmal* is the spiritual element that forms a barrier between good and evil, preventing evil from treading on the domain of the Holy.[55] In the *Hekhalot* it is also the final barrier, excluding all who have not purified themselves sufficiently.

Crucial to the entire process is a precise knowledge of the names of the angels, as well as the various formulas and seals needed to ascend from one chamber to the next. Here, unfortunately, we are faced with a serious difficulty, since these exhibit considerable variation in different manuscripts and printed texts of the *Hekhalot,* and it is impossible to determine which versions are correct. The only way to do this would be through a logical derivation of these formulas, and this is presently beyond our means. What is presented here is a synthesis of the best readings found in the various editions.[56]

THE GREATER HEKHALOT

Chapter 1

Rabbi Ishmael said: What is the meaning of the hymns that one must chant when he desires to gaze into a vision of the *Merkava,* to descend in peace and to ascend in peace?

When one is on a higher level, he can enter, and is brought in and led to the heavenly Chambers, where he is allowed to stand before the Throne of Glory. He then knows what will happen in the future, who will be raised and who will be lowered, who will be made strong and who will be cut off, who will be made poor and who will be made rich, who will die and who will live, who will have his inheritance taken from him, and who will have it given to him, who will be invested with the Torah, and who will be given wisdom.

When one is on a [still] higher level, he can see all the secret deeds of man. He knows and recognizes the adulterer, the murderer, and the one who is only suspected of these things. All this he knows and recognizes.

When one is on a [still] higher level, he knows all kinds of sorcery.

When one is on a [still] higher level, whoever raises his hand to strike him is clothed in leprosy. . . .

When one is on a [still] higher level, whoever speaks against him maliciously is taken and cast down. He is dealt severe blows, and suffers from infected wounds.

When one is on a [still] higher level, he is separated from all men, and distinguished from all humanity by his traits. He is honored by those on earth and by those on high. Whoever sins against him, sins greatly, and evil falls upon him from heaven. Whoever casts a hand against him, suffers retribution by the hand of the heavenly tribunal.

Chapter 2

When one is on a [still] higher level, all humanity stands before him like silver before a refiner who can distinguish when silver is pure and which is adulterated. Similarly, this individual can look at a family and see how many converts it contains, how many with mutilated genitalia and how many conceived from a menstruous woman, how many slaves, and how many uncircumcised.

When one is on a [still] higher level, whoever is disrespectful in his presence has his eyesight diminished.

When one is on a [still] higher level, whoever insults him is torn out, root and branch, and is not left with any heir.

When one is on a [still] higher level, whoever speaks badly of him is beset with destruction and bewilderment, and none have mercy.

When one is on a [still] higher level, when he gives permission, they sound the Shofar and excommunicate [whoever he wills]. Three times a day do they pronounce the ban of excommunication.

Permission was granted to the proper, the meek, the humble, the wise, the upright, the pious, the chosen, the ascetics (*perushim*), the righteous, and the perfected ones to descend and ascend in the *Merkava*. They say, "[The wrongdoer] shall be excommunicated to

TATzSh (טעצש), The Lord, God of Israel—to Him, to His Throne, to the Crown of His head, to the Tribunal on high, to the tribunal below, to all the host on high, to all His [angelic] servants who stand before Him, and to those who engage in the *Merkava.*" They all abandon him.

Rabbi Ishmael said: This has been taught about gazing in the *Merkava.* A person so engaged may not stand, except in three cases: before a king, before the High Priest, and before the Great Tribunal (*Sanhedrin*), when the President is with them. But if the President is not among them, he may not stand, even before the Great Tribunal. If he stands, his blood is on his head, since he diminishes his days, and reduces his years.

Rabbi Ishmael said: What is the meaning of the songs that a person sings in order to descend into the *Merkava*? He starts with praise and begins with song. . . . .

. . . .

Chapter 16

Rabbi Ishmael said: I stood up and gathered the entire Great Tribunal (*Sanhedrin*) and the Lesser Tribunal, bringing them to the great third hall of the House of God. I sat on a couch of pure marble, given to me by my father Elisha. . . .

Those who came included Rabban Shimon ben Gamaliel, Rabbi Eliezer the Great, Rabbi Eleazar ben Dama, Rabbi Eliezer ben Shamua, Rabbi Yochanan ben Dahavai, Rabbi Chananya ben Chanikai, Rabbi Jonathan ben Uziel, Rabbi Akiba, and Rabbi Yehuda ben Bava. We all came and sat before [Rabbi Nehunia ben Hakana]. The throngs of our companions stood on their feet, for they saw rivers of fire and brilliant flames separating them from us.

Rabbi Nehunia ben Hakana sat and explained everything involving the *Merkava.* He described its descent and ascent; how one who descends must descend, and how one who ascends must ascend:

When a person wishes to descend to the *Merkava,* he must call upon Surayah, the Prince of the Face. He must then bind him by an oath 112 times, in the name of TUTRUSYAY (טוטרוסיאי), the Lord, who is called:

TUTRSYAY TzURTK TUTRBYAL	טוטרסיאי צורטק טוטרביאל
TOFGR ASHRUYLYAY ZVUDIAL	טופגר אשרויליאי זבודיאל
and ZHRRYAL TNDAL SHUKD	וזהרריאל טנדאל שוקד
YOZYA DHYVURYN and ADIRYRON	יוזיא דהיבורין ואדירירון
the Lord, God of Israel.	

One should not add to these 112 times, nor should he subtract from them. For if one adds or subtracts, his blood is on his head. But his mouth should utter the names, and with his fingers, he should count up to 112. He then immediately descends and has authority over the *Merkava*.[57]

Chapter 17

Rabbi Ishmael said, this is the teaching of Rabbi Nehunia ben HaKana:

TUTRSYAY (טוטרסיאי), the Lord, God of Israel sits in seven chambers, one within the other. At the door of each chamber are eight gatekeepers, four to the right of the lintel, and four to the left.

These are the names of the watchers at the door of the First Chamber: Dahaviel, Kashriel, Gahuriel, Buthiel, Tofhiel, Dahariel, Mathkiel, and Shaviel (and some substitute Shiviel).

These are the names of the watchers at the door of the Second Chamber: Tagriel, Mathpiel, Sarchiel, Arpiel, Shahárariel, Satriel, Ragaiel, and Sahiviel.

These are the names of the watchers at the door of the Third Chamber: Shaburiel, Ratzutziel, Shalmiel, Sabliel, Zachzachiel, Hadariel, and Bazriel.

These are the names of the watchers at the door of the Fourth Chamber: Pachadiel, Geburathiel, Cazviel, Shekhinyael, Shathakiel, Araviel, Capiel, and Anpiel.

These are the names of the watchers at the door of the Fifth Chamber: Techiel, Uziel, Gatiel, Gatchiel, Saafriel, Garfiel, Gariel, Dariel, and Paltriel.

These are the names of the watchers at the door of the Sixth Chamber: Dumiel, Katzpiel, Gahgahiel, Arsbarsabiel, Agromiel, Partziel, Machakiel, and Tofriel.

And at the door of the Seventh Chamber erectly stand all the mighty ones, terrifying, powerful, fearsome. . . . Sharp swords are in their hands, flashing lightning shoots from their eyes, streams of fire come from their nostrils, and burning coals from their mouths. They are garbed with helmet and armor, with spears and lances hanging at their sides.

Chapter 18

Their horses are horses of darkness, horses of deathly shadow, horses of gloom, horses of fire, horses of blood, horses of hail, horses of iron, horses of cloud. . . .

This is a description of the guardians at the door of the Seventh Chamber, and the horses at the door of each chamber.

All the masters who would descend into the *Merkava* would also ascend again and not be harmed, even though they saw everything in this Chamber. They would descend in peace and return, and would stand and bear witness to the fearsome, confounding visions of things not found in the palace of any mortal king. Then they would bless, praise, sing out . . . and give glory to TUTROSYAY, the Lord, God of Israel, who rejoices in those who descend to the *Merkava*. . . .

Chapter 19

Rabbi Ishmael said: When you come and stand at the door of the First Chamber, take two seals in your hand, one of TUTROSYAY, the Lord, and one of Surayah, Prince of the Face.[58] That of TUTROSYAY show to those standing to the right, and that of Surayah, show to those standing to the left.

Dehaviel, the angel who is the chief guardian of the door of the First Chamber, and overseer of the First Chamber, who stands at the right of the lintel, and Tofhiel, the angel who stands at the left of the lintel with him, will immediately grasp you. They will give you over to Tagriel, the angel who is chief guardian of the door of the Second Chamber, who stands to the right of the lintel, and to Mathpiel, the angel who stands with him to the left of the lintel.

Show them two seals, one of ADRYHRON (אדריהרון), the Lord, and one of Ohazyya, the Prince of the Face. That of ADRYHRON show to those who stand at the right, and of Ohazyya, Prince of the Face, show to those who stand at the left.

Immediately they will grasp you, one to the right and one to the left. Perfecting and illuminating you, they will bring you and give you over to Shaburiel, the angel who is the chief guardian of the Third Chamber, who stands to the right of the lintel, and to Ratzutziel, the angel who stands with him to the left.

Show them two seals, one of TzURTK (צורתק)the Lord, and one of Dahavyoron, the Prince of the Face. That of TzURTK, the Lord, show to those who stand to the right, and that of Dahavyoron, Prince of the Face, show to those who stand to the left.

Immediately they will grasp you, one to your right, and one to your left, and two angels will precede you and two will follow you.

Perfecting and illuminating you, they will bring you to Pachdiel, the chief guardian of the door of the Fourth Chamber, standing at the right of the lintel, and to Geburathiel, the angel who stands to the left of the lintel with him.

Show them two seals, one of ZVUDIEL (זבודיאל), the Lord, and one of Margiviel, Prince of the Face. That of ZVUDIEL, show to those who stand to the right, and that of Margiviel, Prince of the Face, show to those who stand to the left.

Immediately, they will grasp you, one to the right and one to the left. Perfecting and illuminating you, they will bring you and give you over to Techiel, the angel who is head of the Fifth Chamber, who stands to the right of the lintel, and to Uziel, the angel who stands to the left of the lintel with him.

Show them two seals, one of TUTRBYAL (טוטרביאל), the Lord, and one of Zachapniryai, Prince of the Face. That of TUTRBYAL show to those standing at the right, and that of Zachapniryai, Prince of the Face, show to those standing to the left. Immediately [six] angels will grasp you, three from in front, and three from behind.

The guardians of the Sixth Chamber will attack those who descend into the *Merkava* but do not descend into the *Merkava*, [attempting this] without authority. They throng around such individuals, striking at them and burning them, and then they send others in their place who do the same. They have no compunction, nor do they ever stop to think and ask, "Why are we burning them? What enjoyment do we have when we attack those individuals who descend to the *Merkava* but do not descend, without authority?" This is still the trait of the guardians at the door of the Sixth Chamber.

Chapter 20

Rabbi Ishmael said: The entire company said to me, "Son of the haughty, you rule with the light of the Torah, just like Rabbi Nehunia ben Hakana. See if you can bring him back from his gazing perception. Let him sit with us and tell us the meaning of those who 'descend to the *Merkava* but do not descend.' Why are they attacked by the guardians of the Sixth Chamber? Why do they not touch those who [actually] descend into the *Merkava* at all? What is the difference between the two?"

Rabbi Ishmael said: I immediately took a cloth of feathery down and gave it to Rabbi Akiba. Rabbi Akiba gave it to our servant, telling him to take this cloth and touch it to a woman who had immersed in the

Mikvah, but had not done so correctly. This was to be a case that if brought to the sages, one would say that she was forbidden, but the majority would say that she was permitted. [The servant was instructed to] tell the woman, "Touch this cloth with the tip of your middle finger. Do not press on it, but touch it lightly, as if you were removing a cinder from your eye, where you barely brush it."

They did this, and placed the cloth before Rabbi Ishmael. He caught it up on a perfumed twig of myrtle, which had been soaked in pure balsamum. He then placed it on the knees of Rabbi Nehunia ben Hakana, and the latter was immediately dismissed from before the Throne of Glory. . . .

We then asked him, "Who are the ones who descend into the *Merkava,* but do not descend into the *Merkava*?"

He replied to us: These are the individuals taken along by those who descend into the *Merkava*. [Their guides] stand them above their heads, and sit them in front of them, and say to them, "Gaze, look and listen, and write all that I say, and all that we hear from before the Throne of Glory." These people are not worthy of this, and are therefore attacked by the guardians of the Sixth Chamber. You should therefore be careful that you choose for yourselves proper individuals, and they should be members of the society who have been screened.

When you come and stand before the door of the Sixth Chamber, show three seals to the guardians of the door.

Show two seals to Katzpiel, the angel whose sword is unsheathed in his hand. Lightning flashes from him, exploding and blinding all who are not worthy of gazing at the King and the Throne. Nothing can hold him back. His outstretched sword screams out, "Destruction and Annihilation!" He stands at the right of the lintel.

Then show one to Dumiel.

Is Dumiel then his name? Is his name not the mighty Gahidriham?

Rabbi Ishmael said: This is what Rabbi Nehunia ben HaKana taught. Each day a heavenly voice (*Bat Kol*, בַּת קוֹל) emanates from *Aravot* (the Seventh Heaven), and proclaims in the name of the Supernal Tribunal, "TEUM (טעום) and BaR MNTzH ZPUCY GShSh GEShTh (בר מנצה זפוכי גשש געשת), the Lord, God of Israel, calls him Dumiel by name. What I see I silence (*dum*, דום). The same is true of Dumiel (דוּמִאֵל)."

His authority is over the right lintel, and it is the same as the angel Kaptziel. But there is no enmity, hatred, jealousy, or competition between them, since both of them serve only for His Glory.

Chapter 21

The two seals of ZHRRYAL (זהרריאל) and those who do His works, show to Kaptziel. The [seal of] Broniah show to the angel Dumiel, an upright and humble angel.

Kaptziel immediately then draws his bow and fires it. This brings a stormy wind (*Sa'arah*), and places you in a chariot of Brightness (*Nogah*). They trumpet before you with eighty million horns, thirty million shofars, and forty million bugles. The angel Dumiel then grasps a prize and goes before you.

And what is this prize?

Rabbi Ishmael said: This is what Rabbi Nehunia ben Hakana my master taught. The prize that the angel Dumiel holds before the chariot of the individual who is worthy of descending to the *Merkava* is not one of silver or gold. But the prize is that this individual is left alone. He is not interrogated, not in the First Chamber, not in the Second Chamber, not in the Third Chamber, not in the Fourth Chamber, not in the Fifth Chamber, and not in the Sixth Chamber. He can show them all the seal [of Dumiel], and they allow him to enter.

At the right of the door of the Sixth Chamber is the angel Dumiel, keeper of the gate, to the right of the door. He sits on a couch of pure platinum,[59] glowing like the radiance of the heavens, like the covenant of the universe. ARSTAN (ארסטאן), MYRA ARSTAN (מירא ארסטאן), and CNPYNN TzMNSh ERNH. (כנפינן צמנש ערנה) the Lord, God of Israel,[60] and the angel Dumiel receive this individual with a pleasant countenance, sitting him on a couch of pure platinum. They then sit by him to his right.

He used to say: I bear witness regarding two things and warn you. One dare not descend to the *Merkava* unless he has two qualifications. First, he must have read and reviewed the Torah, Prophets and Writings (that is, the entire Bible), and have mastered the Mishnah, the Law, the Agadah, as well as the deeper meaning of Law regarding what is permitted and what is forbidden. Secondly, he must be an individual who keeps the entire Torah, and heeds all of its prohibitions, decrees, judgments and laws, taught to Moses on Sinai.

Chapter 22

If the individual has these two qualifications, then the angel Dumiel entrusts him to Gabriel the scribe. He writes a note with red ink and hangs it on the chariot (*karon*) of that individual. The note describes the individual's Torah scholarship and his deeds, and states that he wishes to come before the Throne of Glory.

When the guardians of the door of the Seventh Chamber see Dumiel, Gabriel and Kaptziel coming before the chariot of the individual worthy of descending to the *Merkava*, they cover their faces, and since they were previously standing, they sit down. They also unloosen their drawn bows and return their swords to their sheaths. Even so one must still show them the great Seal and fearsome crown of AER SOBR MTzUGYYH (אער סובר מצוגייה) and BEShPTSh (בעשפטש),[61] the Lord, God of Israel.

They then bring him before the Throne of Glory. They take out all kinds of musical instruments and play before him until they elevate him and sit him next to the Cherubim, next to the Ophanim, and [finally], next to the Holy Chayot. He then sees wonders and power, majesty and greatness, holiness, purity, terror, humility, and uprightness.

Rabbi Ishmael said: All the fellows likened this to a person who has a ladder in his house. He goes up and down on it and no one can prevent him. Blessed are You, O Lord, Wise of Mysteries and Master of Secrets. Amen Amen.

Rabbi Ishmael said: Rabban Shimon ben Gamaliel was enraged at me. He said to me, "In an instant we all could have been struck down by PTRYAY (פטריאי), the Lord, God of Israel. Why? Because we have been guilty of error. Do you then think that Jonathan ben Uziel is a minor figure in Israel [that he sat at the feet of Rabbi Nehuniah ben Hakana]? What would have happened if we would have approached the door of the seventh chamber?"

Rabbi Ishmael said: I immediately went to Rabbi Nehuniah ben Hakana and angrily said, "The President [of the Great Tribunal, Rabbi Shimon ben Gamaliel,] is angry with me. What pleasure have I in life?"

He replied, "Son of the haughty, if this is so, what honor have I from you? I have placed in your mouths the Torah, the Prophets, the Writings, Mishnah, Midrash, Laws, Agadah, and the legal decisions regarding what is permitted and what is forbidden. If not for the mysteries of the Torah that I have concealed from you, would you ever come and show yourself before me? I know why you have come. It is only to [learn] about the guardians of the Seventh Chamber.

"Go tell the President: You have authority to utter the names of all the guardians at the doors of the Chambers and to influence them. But the sound of the names of the guardians at the door of the Seventh

Chamber dumbfounds a person. How can one influence them, since each one of them are named after the King of the Universe. These I have not revealed.

"Now that you wish me to reveal them, let all of you come and stand on your feet. When the names leave my mouth, prostrate yourselves and fall on your faces."

Immediately, all the [spiritual] giants of the society, together with the aristocrats of the Academy, came, and they stood on their feet before Rabbi Nehuniah ben Hakana. The scribes wrote, and they fell on their faces.

Chapter 23

When one is ascending, these are the names of the guardians of the Seventh Chamber [that he encounters:[62]

Zehpanuryay YVY, an honored and beloved angel.

Abirzehyay YVY, an honored, beloved and fearsome angel.

Atarigiash YVY, an honored, beloved, fearsome and astounding angel.

Nagarniel YVY, an honored, beloved, fearsome, astounding and precious angel.

Anpiel YVY, an honored, beloved, fearsome, astounding, precious and exulted angel.

Naazuriel YVY, an honored, beloved, fearsome, astounding, precious, exulted and mighty angel.

Sastiel YVY, an honored, beloved, fearsome, astounding, precious, exulted, mighty and majestic angel.

Anpiel YVY, an angel whose name is uttered before the Throne of Glory three times each day.

[The name of Anpiel has been] praised [in this manner] from the day that the world was created until now. And why? Because the Ring containing the seal of heaven and earth is given over into his hand.

When all [the host] on high see him, they bow, fall on their faces, and prostrate themselves before him. This is not true, however, of those on the highest level.

You may wonder if these are the same ones who bow down before the Prince of the Face. But those who stand before the Throne of Glory do not bow down to the Prince of the Face, but they do bow down before the angel Anpiel. This is with the authority and permission of

ANTOROS (אנטורוס), the Great Master, and YAPYMYL ShNTh MRTzE (יאפימיל שנת מרצע),[63] the Lord, God of Israel.

These are the names of the guardians of the Seventh Chamber [that one encounters] when one descends. These are not the same ones [encountered] when one ascends:[64]

Nurpiel YVY, an honored, beloved, fearsome angel, who is called Abirhyay YVY.

Dalukiel YVY, an honored, beloved, fearsome angel, who is called Levkapiel YVY.

Yakriel YVY, an honored, beloved and fearsome angel, who is called Atrigiel YVY.

Yasisiel YVY, an honored, beloved and fearsome angel, who is called Banaaniel YVY.

Nurpiniel YVY, an honored, beloved and fearsome angel, who is called Shakadyahiel YVY.

Naaruriel YVY, an honored, beloved and fearsome angel, who is called Zuhaliel YVY.

Anpiel YVY, an honored, beloved, fearsome, astounding, precious, exalted, mighty, majestic, powerful, upright, and stupendous angel, who is called Tufriel YVY.

Why is he called Anpiel (עֲנָפִיאֵל)? It is because of the foliage (*Anaph*, עֲנָף) of crowns upon crowns that is on his head. These cover and surround all the rooms in the Chamber in the [highest] heaven, [which is called] Aravot. In this respect, he is like the One who formed all creation.

Regarding the One who formed creation, it is written, "The heavens cover His glory" (Habakkuk 3:3). This is also true of the angel Anpiel, a servant who is called by his Master's name.[65]

And why is he beloved more than all the guardians of the six doors of the Chambers? This is because he opens the door of the Seventh Chamber.

Chapter 24

Each of the holy Chayot that stand opposite the door of the Seventh Chamber has 256 faces. These great [angels] therefore each have 512 eyes.[66]

There are four Chayot opposite the door of the Seventh Chamber. Each of these [four] Chayot has the face of a man, [the face of a lion, the face of an ox, and the face of an eagle]. Each [of these four] faces in turn has sixteen faces.

When an individual wishes to descend to the *Merkava* the angel Anpiel opens the door of the Chamber. The individual then stands on the threshold of the door of the Seventh Chamber. The holy Chayot then lift up their 512 eyes to gaze at him, and each eye of the Chayot is like a huge bushel.[67] The gaze of their eyes is like a lightening flash. All this is besides the eyes of the mighty Cherubs and the Ophanim of the Divine Presence, which are like scintillating flames and the fire of glowing coals.

The individual then trembles, shakes and shudders, is stricken and faint, and he falls backwards. He is then supported by the angel Anpiel and the 63 other guardians of the seven doors of the Chambers. All of them support him and say, "Fear not, O son of the beloved seed. Enter and see the King in His glory. You will not be destroyed. You will not be burned.

[He must then chant a praise to the Mighty King.][68]

They strengthen this individual. Then, immediately, a horn is sounded above him, from the firmament that is over their head.[69] The holy Chayot cover their faces, and the Cherubim and Ophanim turn their faces around. The individual then stands alone before the Throne of God's Glory.

Chapter 25

When the individual stands before the Throne of His Glory, it begins to sing. For each day the Throne of Glory sings . . . to HHRRYAL (ההרריאל) the Lord, God of Israel, the exalted King, crowned with a tapestry of song. . . .

Chapter 26

"I saw the likeness of the Speaking Silence (*Chashmal*)" (Ezekiel 1:27). This tests the individual and determines whether or not he is worthy of descending to the *Merkava*.

If the individual is worthy to descend to the *Merkava*, they bid him to enter. If he does not enter, they again bid him to enter. He then enters immediately. They then praise him and say, "He is among those who have descended to the *Merkava*."

But if the individual is not worthy to descend to the *Merkava*, they warn him not to enter. If he still enters, they immediately cast thousands of steel axes at him.

The guardians at the door of the Sixth Chamber act as if they are casting millions of waves of water at this individual. Actually, however, there is not even a single drop. If the individual says, "What is the purpose of this water," they pursue him and say, "You miserable creature! You are probably a descendent of those who kissed the Golden Calf! You are not worthy of seeing the King and His Throne." He does not have a chance to move before they cast millions of steel axes at him.

[But if one enters successfully, he must sing praise.][70]

CHAPTER THREE

Rabbi Abraham Abulafia

1. THE MAN

One of the most important early figures in Kabbalah meditation is Rabbi Abraham Abulafia. Not only was he party to many important traditions, but he also wrote voluminously regarding them. Indeed, very little would be known about many of these traditions if not for his writings.

Unfortunately, however, very few of his writings have ever been published. Most exist only in manuscript form, either in major libraries or in the hands of Kabbalists who refuse to publicize the fact. Finding and correctly identifying Abulafia's manuscripts has been a difficult task, since many of these were catalogued incorrectly or not catalogued at all. In a number of cases, important manuscripts were tracked down by word of mouth and discovered in the libraries of individuals who had no idea as to their content. Although much important work has been done by library scientists, manuscriptologists and other scholars, the study of Abulafia's writings requires much basic research into the largely unexplored world of ancient manuscripts.

An important problem in working with manuscripts is the fact that many were written in ancient scripts that are almost illegible to the modern reader. Others were privately made, written hurriedly by individuals with poor handwriting. When added to the fact that their basic script may now be obsolete, the reading of these manuscripts becomes next to impossible. Much study has to be done to decipher the alphabets of many manuscripts, and in some cases, relevant portions had to be transcribed letter by letter before they could be read.

One reason why Abulafia's works were not published was undoubtedly related to the general retincence surrounding the publication of materials dealing with meditation and the mystical arts. But another reason was the controversy that surrounded Abulafia as a person. In many places in his writings, Abulafia indicates that he is a prophet, and in others, he hints that he has a special mission. There are also many veiled allusions that could be interpreted to reflect messianic delusions on his part. For the most part, however, these are ambiguous, and it is probable that when he speaks of himself as the "anointed one," he means that he is enlightened, and not that he is the promised messiah. In a number of places, he speaks of the prophet experience as one resembling being anointed with oil.[1] In no place did Abulafia ever attempt to actually implement a messianic role for himself, so this interpretation appears highly probable.

All of his alleged claims, however, did not escape the notice of the religious leaders of his generation. His strongest opposition came from the Rashba (Rabbi Shlomo ben Adret, 1235—1310). Five years older than Abulafia, the Rashba had been appointed rabbi in Barcelona in 1280, and he enjoyed a reputation as the leading sage of his time. Even today, his Talmudic commentaries are counted among the most important, and his responsa are considered basic to Jewish Law.

It is evident that while Abulafia was in Sicily, the Rashba mounted a scathing attack against him. This involved his own letters as well as messages that he influenced the leaders of other congregations to send to Sicily, denouncing Abulafia. In the early 1290's, the Rashba wrote a responsum to the community of Saragosta, Abulafia's birthplace, regarding a self-proclaimed prophet in Avila, possibly a disciple of Abulafia. In it, he alludes to his earlier attacks on Abulafia, denouncing him in no uncertain terms.

This attack by the leading figure of the generation was enough to virtually guarantee that the religious establishment would shun and ignore Abulafia's works. In some ways, however, the intensity of the attack is understandable, considering the status of the Kabbalah at the time. The Zohar had not yet been published, and although the Bahir had been published in 1175, it was far from being universally accepted. A very strong school opposed the Kabbalah, denouncing its teachings as approaching heresy. This is best exemplified by a statement by the Rashbash (Rabbi Shlomo ben Shimon Duran, 1400—1467), a century later, who wrote, "The Christians believe in the Three, while the Kabbalists believe in the Ten."[2]

As a strong defender of the Kabbalah, the Rashba might have seen Abulafia's statements as being very dangerous to its healthy growth. Abulafia was very much hurt by the Rashba's attacks, and it was as a reply to them that he wrote his famous epistle, *VeZot LiYehudah* (And This is to Judah).

The Rashba's responsum was taken up by another major Kabbalist, Rabbi Judah Chayit, who lived around the time of the

Spanish Inquisition. The entire attack against Abulafia was then expanded upon by the Yashar of Candia (Rabbi Yoseph Shlomo Delmedigo, 1591—1655), one of the most important defenders of the Kabbalah.[3]

In view of all this, one would expect that Abulafia and his writings would be relegated to the dustbin of history, and not have any influence whatsoever on the Kabbalah tradition. This, however, turns out to be far from true, and his works are quoted, albeit guardedly, by many of the most important Kabbalists. Thus, the Ramak (Rabbi Moshe Cordevero, 1522—1570), dean of the Safed school, considers Abulafia to be an authority on the pronunciation of Divine Names, and quotes a lengthy section from his *Or HaSekhel* (Light of the Intellect).[4] In the unpublished fourth section of his *Shaarey Kedushah* (Gates of Holiness), Rabbi Chaim Vital cites Abulafia's methods as being techniques for meditation. He speaks of his *Chayay Olam HaBah* (Life of the Future World) as if it were a well-known book in Kabbalistic circles, and quotes at length from his *Sefer HaCheshek* (Book of Passion). Another major figure, the Radbaz (Rabbi David abu Zimra, 1470—1572), mentions Abulafia's works in a positive context.[5]

The final word regarding the acceptability of any Hebraic text is usually given to the Chida (Rabbi Chaim Yosef David Azulai, 1724—1806). Quoting a number of attacks against Abulafia, the Chida then cites the fact that his works have been accepted by the greatest Kabbalists, and have been found to be beneficial.

In view of this opinion, the general trend among knowledgeable Kabbalists has been to accept the teachings of Abulafia, even though his methods are considered to be very advanced and dangerous. His manuscripts have been copied and circulated among many Kabbalists, and they form an important part of the curriculum in some secret schools. While the personality of Abulafia may be questioned, it is generally recognized that he was in possession of authentic traditions, and that he recorded them faithfully and accurately.

SOURCES

There are many frauds whom I have heard and seen. One is the disgusting creature, "may the name of the wicked rot," whose name is Abraham [Abulafia]. He proclaimed himself as a prophet and messiah in Sicily, and enticed many people with his lies. Through the mercy of God, I was able to slam the door in his face, both with my own letters and with those of many congregations. If not for this, he would have actually been able to begin.

He invented many false ideas, totally foolishness which resembles high wisdom, and with this, he could have done much damage. Making use of a certain consistence, he places his mind on an idea for many days, and comes up with elaborate numerical exercizes (*gematriot*) involving both scripture and the words of our sages.

The Rashba.[6]

I have also seen books written by a scholar by the name of Rabbi Abraham Abulafia. In his foolishness and pride . . . he calls himself a prophet. But it is taught that since the Temple has been destroyed, "prophecy has been given over to the insane." [7] . . . His books are filled with his own inventions, imaginations and falsehood.

He may have written *Or HaSekhel* (Light of the Intellect) but he actually walks in darkness. He wrote the *Moreh HaMoreh* (Guide to the Guide) as a Kabbalistic commentary on [Maimonides'] *Guide to the Perplexed*. How idiotic it is to invent a Kabbalistic commentary to the *Guide*! Maimonides would never even dream of such an interpretation!

He also wrote a *Book of the Name* (this is *Chayay Olam HaBah:* "Life of the Future World") as a commentary on the Name of Seventy-Two. He writes the entire book as a series of circles so as to confuse those who look at it.[8] As if this would make up for its lack of true content! He filled this book with word manipulations, made up by his own deficient mind.

Rabbi Judah Chayit.[9]

Chayah Olam HaBah (Life of the Future World) is a book written by Rabbi Abraham Abulafia, in circles, concerning the Name of Seventy-Two. I have seen a manuscript of it, written on parchment.

The Rashba, in Chapter 544 [of his responsa] and Rabbi Yashar [of Candia] in his *Metzaref LeChokhmah* (Purifier of Wisdom), denounce him like one of worthless and worse.

Still, I must tell the truth, I saw a great rabbi, one of the major masters of the mysteries, of great reputation. According to his words, there is no question that he made use of this book and benefited greatly from it.

The Chidah.[10]

2. GROWTH OF A PROPHET

Abulafia included considerable autobiographical material in his writings, and much is therefore known about his life, even though there are some important blank spots. From all this material, we obtain a picture of a sincere, inspired individual, who also possessed many human failings.

He was born in the year 1240. This does not appear very significant until we realize that on the Hebrew calendar, which counts from the birth of Adam, this was the year 5000, literally the beginning of a new millennium. Abulafia was very much aware of this distinction, and in a number of places, cites it as proof that he was destined for a special mission.

In his autobiography, Abulafia speaks about many of his disciples. The most important of these was Rabbi Joseph Gikatalia, who later was to become one of the greatest Kabbalists of that period. Eight years younger than Abulafia, it can be ascertained that he came under the influence of Abulafia in the year 1273, when he was twenty-five years old.[11] Gikatalia's *Shaarey Orah* (Gates of Light) became one of the most important Kabbalistic classics, and in many places, it reflects the teachings of Abulafia.

Another disciple mentioned in the autobiography is a certain Shem Tov of Burgos. We shall meet him again as one of the possible authors of *Shaarey Tzedek* (Gates of Righteousness), an important exposition of Abulafia's techniques.

It has often been stated that Abulafia was opposed to the Talmud and deficient in its knowledge, but this is an inaccurate conclusion. As a teenager, Abulafia learned Scripture, Mishnah and Talmud from his father, attaining what was then considered an adequate knowledge of these subjects. When the Rashba accused him of being an ignoramus, he replied that he had completed the entire Talmud, and had learned how to render decisions in religious law from two prominent masters. He also states that he had mastered *Chullin,* the Talmudic tract that deals with the fine points of the dietary laws, and that which forms the core of traditional rabbinical training.[13]

In a number of places, we clearly find that Abulafia held the masters of Talmud in high esteem. Once, he openly states that if not pressed by his disciples, he would rather study the Talmud than write books on the mysteries.[14]

Abulafia's earliest study consisted largely of the works of the great Jewish philosophers, and he writes that he originally considered philosophy to be the greatest of all disciplines.[14] Maimonides' famed *Guide to the Perplexed* remained one of his favorite books, and he was later to write three different commentaries on it.

Abulafia mentions that he was introduced to the *Guide* by a certain Rabbi Hillel in Capua. This is most certainly Rabbi Hillel of Verona (1220—1295), who lived in Capua between 1260 and 1271. Rabbi Hillel had been a disciple of the famed Rabbi Jonah Gerondi (1194—1263). Rabbi Jonah had been a vehement opponent of Maimonides' *Guide,* but toward the end of his life, he made a public confession regretting this opposition. Rabbi Hillel followed his master, and also became a staunch advocate of Maimonides' teachings. When Shlomo Petit, a leading Kabbalist from Acco, attempted to reintroduce a ban against the *Guide,* Rabbi Hillel became one of its most important defenders. Besides this, Rabbi Hillel is best known for his book *Tagmuley HaNefesh* (Reward of the Soul), written in 1290 in the city of Forli.[15] It was from Rabbi Hillel that Abulafia gained a strong positive impression of Maimonides' teachings, in direct opposition to many important Kabbalists of that period.

Besides this, Abulafia was thoroughly familiar with the mystical works from the Talmudical period, such as the Bahir, which he calls the greatest of all Kabbalah texts.[16] In at least one place, he uses a term prominent in the Zohar, indicating that he might also have had some access to that body of literature, even though it had not yet been published.[17]

It is of great significance that Abulafia also refers to the *Hekhalot,* which we have discussed in the previous chapter. Although he was familiar with this text, in no place does he mention the actual use of its methods, but instead, advocates a different system entirely. This would appear to indicate that, like the Ari, he realized that the techniques described in the *Hekhalot* require a system of purification that was no longer in existence.

Another reason may be the fact that Abulafia considered himself a follower of the way of the *Sefer Yetzirah* (Book of Formation), a system that he considered unique and different than other Kabbalistic teachings. In one place, he discussed the Kabbalistic school utilizing the Ten Sefirot, and clearly states that the way of the *Sefer Yetzirah* is different and higher, involving the Twenty-Two Letters of the Hebrew alphabet rather than the ten numbers.[18]

There is no question that the *Sefer Yetzirah* played a most important role in Abulafia's career. In his autobiographical sketch, he writes that he considered his initiation into the mysteries of the *Sefer Yetzirah* as the major turning point in his life. Elsewhere, he writes that he had studied the *Sefer Yetzirah* with twelve of its major commentaries, both philosophical and Kabbalistic.[19]

His master in the *Sefer Yetzirah* was Rabbi Baruch Torgami, who also apparently influenced Rabbi Isaac of Acco. Rabbi Baruch wrote a book *Maftechot HaKabbalah* (Keys of Kabbalah), a commentary on the *Sefer Yetzirah* involving numerical manipulations (*gematria*) in a style very much like that of Abulafia.[20] Besides this, it appears that Abulafia learned a good deal of the mystical tradition from Rabbi Baruch. The surname Torgami would indicate that Rabbi Baruch came from Turkey (*Togarmah*). This would imply that the mystical tradition may have been preserved there in an unbroken tradition. This is quite likely, since at the time, Turkey had a Jewish community that had flourished there since the time of Alexander the Great.

There has been much confusion regarding the temptations that Abulafia mentions in his autobiographical sketch. A key is provided by his statement that "for fifteen years, the Satan was at my right hand to mislead me." In a number of places, Abulafia indicates that Satan (שָׂטָן) has a numerical value of 359, the same as that of *Zera Lavan* (זֶרַע לָבָן), meaning "white seed." [21] This "white seed" clearly refers to semen, as Abulafia clearly states elsewhere.[22] It would therefore appear that the "Satan" indicates sexual temptation, most probably involving masturbation. This is supported by his poem at the beginning of *Chayay Olam Habah*, where he speaks of his body "defiled with seed," worthy of death, and apparently guilty of murder.[23] This is an allusion to Er and Onan, who died for spilling their seed in vain, and to the Talmudic statement that one who emits semen in vain is likened to a murderer.[24]

This is particularly significant, since it is well established in Kabbalistic teachings that masturbation is one of the worst of sins, as clearly stated in the Zohar.[25] The main task of the mystic is to use the intellect and imagination to reach the highest spiritual levels, and this process is totally disrupted when one uses his imagination to conjure up sexual fantasies while masturbating. A later mystic, Rabbi Nachman of Breslov (1772—1810), considered it one of his greatest accomplishments that he was able to discover a General Rectification (*Tikun HaKelali*) to undo the spiritual damage caused by masturbation.[26]

Although Abulafia clearly recognized the primacy of the Hebrew language in his mystical system, he also recognized the value of other languages and cultures. In a number of places, he makes use of foreign terms to prove a point, and even incorporates them into his numerical calculations.[27] Once, he makes use of the Arabic or Indian number system to prove a point.[28] He also had discussions with Christian mystics, and praises them for their insight. In one place he states, "There is no question that there are individuals among the Christians who know this mystery. They discussed the mysteries with me and revealed that this is unquestionably their opinion, whereupon I judged them to be among the pious of the gentiles. One need not worry about the fools of any nation, since the Torah was only given to those with intelligence." [29]

Abulafia's relationship with the Christians was not confined to debates, nor was he particularly impressed with their theology. In a number of places, he speaks of such Christian ideas as the Trinity and Incarnation as being false.[30] But, in what is probably the most dramatic episode in Abulafia's life, he went on a mission to attempt to convert the Pope to Judaism.

This Pope was Nicholas III, who, according to historical records, died in Saronno, Italy on August 22, 1280 (25 Elul, 5040). This was just a few days before *Rosh HaShanah,* the Hebrew New Year. This Pope was best known for having established the Vatican as a permanent seat of the papacy, and for sending missionaries to Persia and China. Abulafia came to see him shortly before *Rosh HaShanah,* and it was only the Pope's sudden death that saved him from being burned at the stake.

Abulafia himself wrote an autobiographical account of this conversion attempt in his *Sefer HaEdot* (Book of Testimonies).[31] In this account, he calls himself Raziel, an anonym that he frequently used, this being the name of the angel who taught the mysteries to Adam. Raziel (רָזִיאֵל) has a numerical value of 248, this being the same as that of

Abulafia's first name, Abraham (אַבְרָהָם). As Abulafia himself indicates, this relationship is more than a simple *gematria,* but it is a *mishkal* (balance), since both the numerical value and the number of letters in both names are equal.[32]

It appears that Abulafia returned to Barcelona shortly after this, since we find him leaving there in 1281. This is particularly significant, since the Rashba, the main opponent of Abulafia, had assumed the post of Rabbi in Barcelona in 1280. It may well have been the denunciation on the part of the Rashba that Abulafia refers to when he states that he "was captured by gentiles because of denunciation on the part of the Jews."

From Barcelona, Abulafia moved his base of operations to Palmyra, Sicily, and here he wrote his *Metzaref LaSekhel* (Refinement of the Intellect) in 1282. It was also here that he gained Rabbi Achitov the physician as a disciple. It was to this Rabbi Achitov that the Rashba sent a scathing denunciation of Abulafia's methods.[33]

A short time after this, Abulafia moved to Messina, also in Sicily. He calls this city *Mi-Sinai,* meaning "from Sinai," possibly indicating that it was a place of revelation. His opposition, however, grew even stronger, and by 1288, he had been forced to move to the tiny island of Comino near Malta. After this, very little is known of his personal life, although a few of his existant works seem to have been written during this period.

An excellent autobiographical account of this last period, couched in apocalyptic language, is found in Abulafia's *Sefer HaOt* (Book of the Sign). Here Abulafia uses another anonym, Zechariyahu (זְכַרְיָהוּ), which also has the same numerical value as Abraham.

SOURCES

In everything that I have written until now, my main intent was to come to what I will now reveal.

I, [Abraham Abulafia], the individual mentioned in the introduction, was born in Saragossa, in Argon, which is in the kingdom of Spain. Before I was weaned, while I was still an infant suckling milk from the breasts of my mother, I moved to [Navarra], some sixteen parsangs from the city where I was born, together with my brothers and sisters. I thus grew up on the Ebro River, which passes through both of these cities.

I began to read the Scriptures with their commentaries, and also learned Hebrew grammar, completing all twenty-four books [of the Bible] under the tutelage of my father, of blessed memory. It was from him that I also learned the Mishnah and Talmud, and most of my learning was under this instruction.

I was eighteen years old when he died.

I remained in the land of my birth for two years after my father passed away. At the age of twenty, God's spirit moved me, and I left, heading straight for the Land of Israel by sea and by land. My intent was the rearh the land of the Sambation,[34] but I did not get further than Acco. Because of the conflict between Ishmael (the Arabs) and Esau (the Christians), I was forced to flee. I left [the Holy Land] and returned [to Europe] by way of Greece.

It was while passing through [Greece] that I got married. God then aroused me, and, taking along my wife, I set out for the "waters of desire" where I could study the Torah. This I found in Capua, a journey of five days from Rome.

It was here that I found a distinguished sage, philosopher, and master physician by the name of Rabbi Hillel. We became friends, and it was from him that I learned philosophy, which I found very pleasant. Exploring this discipline with all my might, I kept at it day and night. I was not satisfied until I had gone through the entire *Guide to the Perplexed* many times.

In Capua I also had four disciples whom I taught occasionally. They were senseless young men, however, and when they went out to evil ways, I abandoned them. There were also another ten disciples, but these too did not benefit, and they lost both ways, the first and the second.

In Agropoli there were four disciples. But these also did not benefit from my teachings. They had very strange ideas, especially concerning the depths of wisdom and mysteries of the Torah. I did not find any who were worthy that I should even give them the barest hints of the Truth.

In Rome, there were two old men, Rabbi Tzadakia and Rabbi Yeshiah who entered into my covenant. With these I had some success, but they were very old and they died.

In Barcelona I had two disciples. One, by the name of Rabbi Kalonymos, of blessed memory, an older man who was quite distinguished. The other was a brilliant unmarried man, a distinguished sage, and one of the leaders of the community, by the name of Rabbi Yauda, also called Solomon.[35]

In Burgos, I taught two men, a master and his disciple. The name of the master is Rabbi Moshe Sifno.[36] The disciple is Rabbi Shem Tov, a pleasant young man, but his youth prevented him from mastering the subject. Both he and his master only learned a few external points of the Kabbalah from me.

In Medina Celi there were two disciples. One was Samuel the Prophet, to whom I taught some Kabbalah. The other was Rabbi Joseph Gikatalia, may God continue to guide him. He had great intelligence, and will undoubtedly have great success if God is with him.

I am now in Messina, which is "from Sinai" (*Mi-Sinai*). Here I found six men, and I also brought a seventh along with me. These learned from me for a very short time, each one taking what he could, some much and some little. They all eventually left me, except for one. He was their leader, and he brought all the others to learn from me.

The name of this disciple is Rabbi Saadia ben Yitzchak Sanalmapi of blessed memory. He was followed by Rabbi Abraham ben Shalom, and then by the latter's son, Yaakov, and then by his friend Yitzchak. These were followed by other acquaintances, until I had three disciples on one level, and four on a lower level.[37] The seventh disciple was Natronai the Frenchman, of blessed memory, but for various reasons, he immediately left us. He was the one who prevented the others from attaining what they could. It was here that some desired things occurred, and there were some normal events, some accidents, and some things that had to take place.

When I was thirty-one years old, in Barcelona, God awakened me from my sleep, and I learned the *Sefer Yetzirah* with its commentaries. God's hand was upon me, and I wrote books of wisdom and also some wondrous prophetic books. My soul awakened within me, and a spirit of God touched my mouth. A spirit of holiness fluttered through me, and I saw many fearsome sights and wonders, through signs and miracles.

But at the same time, spirits of jealousy gathered around me, and I was confronted with fantasy and error. My mind was totally confused, since I could not find anyone else like me, who would teach me the correct path. I was therefore like a blind man, groping around at noon. For fifteen years, the Satan was at my right hand to mislead me.

All this time, I was driven mad from what my eyes saw.[38] But I was able to keep the Torah, and seal in the second curse for fifteen years, until God granted me wisdom and counsel. God was thus with me from the year One (5001 = 1241) until the year 45 (5045 = 1285), protecting me from all misfortune.

At the beginning of the year "Elijah" (*Elyah*, אֵלִיָּה = 46; that is, 5046, or the end of 1285 c.e.) God had mercy on me and brought me to the Holy Palace. It is at this time that I completed this book (*Otzar Eden HaGanuz*), which was written here in Messina. It was written for . . . the above-mentioned Saadia, the first of the seven mentioned earlier. Seeing the affection with which he attached himself to me, [I wrote this for him] so that he should remember what he learned from me, since forgetfulness is rampant. When he has it, I know that it will also help his above-mentioned companions, since it is most probable that they will also learn from it.

I realize that if not for various "accidents" [39] and fantasies, they would have never left me. The fantasies that caused them to leave me and keep away from me are precisely the ones that I myself once had. God helped me to stand my ground, and withstanding the test enlightened my heart, since because of them I guarded my mouth and tongue. I kept my lips from speaking and my heart from thinking, and I returned to the proper place.

I continued to keep the covenant recognizing and perceiving what was hidden from me at the time. And I praise the name of the Lord, my God and God of my fathers, who did not withdraw His love and truth during all these times. . . .

Otzar Eden HaGanuz.[40]

Conversion of the Pope

This is the *Book of Testimonies (Sefer HeEdot)*, the fourth commentary written by Raziel (an anonym of Abulafia), the third book of the volume. The first was the *Book of the Upright (Sefer HaYashar)*, written in the city of Mount Patrai in Greece in the year 5039 (1279). The author was then 39 years old, and this was the ninth year of his prophecy. Until that year he did not write any prophetic books, even though he wrote many other books of wisdom, some dealing with the deepest mysteries of the Kabbalah.

In that ninth year, God aroused him to go to Rome, as He commanded him in Barcelona in those years.[41] On the way, he passed through Tarni, where he was imprisoned by the gentiles because he had been denounced by the Jews. A miracle occurred and he escaped.

He then settled in Capua for a short time. In the tenth year, after he had left Barcelona, he wrote a scond book, which is called the *Book of Life (Sefer HaChaim)*.

In the fifth month after Nissan, the eleventh month after Tishrei, that is, the month of Ab (July), in the tenth year, he came to Rome. He had planned to appear before the Pope on the day before the [Hebrew] New Year. The Pope was then in Saronno, a day's journey from Rome, and he instructed the gatekeepers that if Raziel should come to speak to him in the name of Judaism, he should be detained, and should not be granted an audience. They were given instructions to take him out of the city and burn him at the stake. The wood was already prepared near the inner gate of the city.

Raziel was informed of this, but he paid no heed to those who told him. He meditated (*hitboded*) and saw wonders, and at that time he wrote them down in his *Book of Testimonies*. It would be a testimony between him and God that He had saved him from his enemies.

On the day that he was to see the Pope, he was given two mouths. When he entered the outer gate of the city, a messenger greeted him and informed him that on the previous night, the one who had sought to kill him had suddenly died, as if from a plague. One was killed that night, and [the other] was saved.

In Rome he was then imprisoned by the "Little Brothers" (Franciscans) and he remained in their academy for twenty-eight days . . . He finally went free on the first of Cheshvan (October 18, 1240). I write this to tell the praise of God, and His miracles and wonders with Raziel and His true servants.

Metzaref LaSekhel.[42]

Zecharyahu

And God said to Zecharyahu (an anonym for Abulafia) the proclaimer, raise your voice, your tongue, with a pen, and with three fingers, write the words of this book. And God was with him to help him, and Zecharyahu wrote all that God commanded him.

He went quickly, declaring and announcing the living words of God to the Jews, circumcised in flesh, but uncircumcised in heart. But the poor to whom he was sent, and for whom he was revealed, did not pay attention to his coming. They began to speak about him and his God, saying things that should not be spoken.

And God commanded him to speak in His name to the gentiles, uncircumcised in heart and uncircumcised in flesh. He did this, and they believed in the announcement from God. But they did not return to God, for they believed in their sword and bow, and God had hardened their unclean uncircumcised hearts. God's anger was then kindled against them, and He had mercy on His people Israel.

And He then chose a time and season for the day of the proclamation. . . .

And it was on that day, God went with joy and gladness, with seven lamps and five bright lights, seeking on all the tops of the mountains. Between the lions and bears, He found a lost sheep, without shepherd, but no lion had torn it, and no bear had eaten it.

And God found the top of a high mountain, and its name is Mount Naples. The shepherd of is sheep sat on it for twenty years, until the passing of the time of anger and the instant of rage, during which the shepherd slept. At that time, the God of Israel will awaken the heart of the shepherd, and he will be aroused from his sleep, and he will awaken the hearts that sleep in the dust. The dead will then come to life, and the sheep will come home, never again to be scattered. . . .

In the year 5045 (1285), in the third lunar month, that is the month of Kislev, this being the ninth solar month (September), in the tenth cycle, in the fifth year of the cycle, on the first of the month, on the sixth day (Friday) . . . God awakened the spirit of Zecharyahu to review and double his prophetic books and to complete half of this book. On that day Zecharyahu the shepherd began to write wonders. . . .

And God sent a physician to his people to heal the pain of their wound by teaching their sages His Name. And the sages of wisdom were sick and wounded, with "every sickness and wound that is not written in this book of the Torah" [43]

And God said to Zecharyahu the healthy one, "Go, and I will send you to the people who are stricken in heart, to heal their sickness. Take with you the remedy of 'My Name' and 'My Remembrance'." [44]

And God gave a gift of grace and a portion of love in the hands of Zecharyahu, and he went about in the lands of the nations where Israel is scattered. He began to speak, and as he spoke, he ended. For he called out in the name of the Lord, the everlasting God, from the beginning to the end, walking a straight line, not straying to the right or to the left.

But only a few of the sages of Israel wished to hear the wisdom of God and the excellence of His ways from his mouth. God appeared to the healthy among them, and asked them to heal the sick in spirit by the word of Zecharyahu.

And those who would deny the highest wisdom stood up, sick and stricken with deadly wounds. They spoke high words against God and His anointed, and against all the healthy ones who had gone along with them, who recognized the depth of their sickness and pursued a cure. The hearts of those who followed melted, and their spirit became weak, and they stopped following those who knew the Name and are counted with it.

Because of such things, God became angry at those who provoked Him and denied His Name. He sent one to rebuke them, and his words were a shame and an insult to their name. So they chased him from city to city, from place to place, until he came to the land of Mastina (Malta), to the island of Comino. There he sat for many days against his will.

And it was in those days that God said to Zecharyahu, "Write for you this book, which will go against the sages of Israel in this generation, who boast about that which I do not desire. They say, why should we consider God's Name, how will it help us when we utter it, and how will it benefit us if we calculate it?"

Sefer HaOt.[45]

3. WRITINGS

It is not because of his personal life that Abulafia is so fascinating, but because of the remarkable treasure of mystical lore that he has included in his writings. While this tradition was known to other masters of that period, none wrote down more than the barest hints regarding the explicit practices of the Kabbalah. Abulafia himself writes, "no other Kabbalist before me wrote explicit books on this subject." [46] Elsewhere he states that the earlier authors who did write about this subject made a point of concealing its practices. They did not make it obvious that this was the main point of their books, but only mentioned it in passing. "But I have made it the main point and root of all that I have ever written." [47]

It apparently was not pride that led Abulafia to do this, but rather, a feeling of divine calling. In one place he states that he was commanded by Elijah and Enoch in a vision to reveal these secrets.[48] According to his calculations, prophecy was destined to return around the year 1285, and his books were intended to teach the methods of attaining this level for those who were worthy of it.[49] He writes that he was not motivated by ulterior motives, because he considered himself greater than the earlier Kabbalists, or because he felt that no one else would ever reveal it if not for him. Instead, he wrotes, he did so for two reasons, one theological and one human. The theological reason is related to the final redemption, for which these mysteries are necessary, while the human reason is due to the lack of Kabbalah masters in his generation.[50]

Abulafia was very much aware that criticism would be directed at him because of his revelations. He had already been persecuted by the Rashba, and was shunned by other Kabbalists for revealing their mysteries. He writes that the mysteries involving the letters were revealed to the prophets, and they, in turn, revealed them to all Israel.

Since it was almost forgotten, it is important to write it down. He concludes, "Even though I know that people will denounce both me and my books, I will not desist from writing." [51]

All this was not mere words. In a letter to Abraham Comti of Messina, Abulafia indicates that he had already written 26 books on the mysteries,and 22 prophetic books.[52] Even these numbers are significant, since 26 is the numerical value of the Tetragrammaton (*YHVH*, יהוה), while 22 is the number of letters in the Hebrew alphabet.

Abulafia's "prophetic" books were those written while he was in a quasi-prophetic meditative state. In at least one place, he clearly states that such a book was written after he had meditated.[53] The only surviving example of these prophetic books is his *Book of the Sign (Sefer HaOt)*, which is also one of the very few of his books that was ever published. It is written in a style that attempts to mimic that of the Biblical prophets, and tells about his mystical experiences. Most of his other books are guides to meditation or expositions of the Kabbalah, often involving long strings of numerically related words or phrases.

With a few very minor exceptions, none of Abulafia's works were ever printed. Even those that were, were not published until relatively recently, and then by secular scholars or historians. Still, his writings did enjoy a fair degree of circulation in the mystical community, and a considerable number of manuscripts survive, both in libraries and in private collections.

The following is a list of Abulafia's known works:

1. *Key to the Bind (Mafteach HaRayon)*. Vatican, M291.
2. *Divorce of Names (Get HaShemot),* where the author divorces himself from the use of all of God's names other than the Tetragrammaton. Oxford, Ms. 1658.
3. *Life of the Soul (Chayay Nefesh),* the first of his three commentaries of Maimonides' *Guide to the Perplexed.* Written in 1279. Munich, Ms. 408, Jewish Theological Seminary, Ms. 96.
4. *Mysteries of the Torah (Sithrey Torah),* the second commentary on the Guide. Written in 1280. Munich, Ms. 32.
5. *Book of Redemption (Sefer HaGeulah),* a third commentary on the *Guide.* Leipzig, Ms 39. Existent in Latin translation by Flavius Mitradates.
6. *Life of the Future World (Chayay Olam HaBah).* Abulafia's most important book teaching meditation as a means of attaining enlightenment. Written 1280. In many manuscripts, notably, Jewish Theological Seminary, Mss. 2158, 2165, 8126; Jerusalem, Ms. 8° 540.

7. *Book of the Upright (Sefer HaYashar).* Written in Urbino in 1279. No copy available. See #15.
8. *The Book of Life (Sefer HaChaim).* Written in Capua in 1280. No copy available.
9. *The Book of Testimonies (Sefer HaEdot).* Written in Rome in 1281. No copy available.
10. *The Book of the Covenant (Sefer HaBrit).* No copy available.
11. *The Book of the Interpreter (Sefer HaMelitz).* No copy available.
12. *The Book of Human Man (Sefer Ish Adam).* No copy available.
13. *The Book of the Haftorah (Sefer Haftorah).* Written in Capua in 1280. No copy available.
14. *Seal of the Haftorah (Chotem Haftorah).* No copy available.
15. *Refinement of the Intellect (Matzaref LaSekhel),* a "commentary" on books #7–14, all of which appear to be "prophetic" books written between 1279 and 1282. Written in Sicily in 1282. Munich, Ms. 285.
16. *Treasury of the Hidden Eden (Otzar Eden HaGanuz),* a commentary on the *Sefer Yetzirah* containing important autobiographical material. Written in Sicily in 1285. Oxford, Ms. 606.
17. *Light of the Intellect (Or HaSekhel),* an important exposition of Abulafia's system and meditative techniques. Written in Sicily in 1285 for his two disciples in Messina, Abraham Comti and Nathan Charar. Vatican, Ms. 233, Munich, Ms. 92, Jerusalem, Ms. 8° 3009.
18. *Keeper of a Commandment (Shomer Mitzvah),* a commentary on the Priestly Blessing. Written in 1287 for a disciple from the Holy Land who had come to Sicily. Paris, Ms. 853.
19. *Sealed Garden (Gan Naul),* commentary on *Sefer Yetzirah.* Written in Sicily in 1289. Munich, Ms. 58. Printed in part as a section in *Sefer HaPeliyah* (Koretz, 1784), pp. 50c–56c.
20. *Book of the Sign (Sefer HaOt),* a prophetic work. Written in 1288, after Abulafia had fled to Comino near Malta. Published by Jellinek, Leipzig, 1853.
21. *Key of Wisdoms (Mafteach HaChokhmot),* commentary on Genesis. Written in 1289. Jewish Theological Seminary, Mss. 1897, 1686.
22. *Key of Names (Mafteach HaShemot),* commentary on Exodus. Jewish Theological Seminary, Ms. 1897.
23. *Key of Offerings (Mafteach HaKorbanot),* commentary on Leviticus. Mentioned in introduction of *Mafteach HaChokhmot,* p. 90b. No known manuscript.
24. *Key of Sefirot (Mafteach HaSefirot),* commentary on Numbers. Milan (Ambriosana), Ms. 53.
25. *Key of Admonishment (Mafteach HaTokhachah)* , commentary on Deuteronomy. Oxford, Ms.

26. *Words of Beauty (Imrey Shefer)*, an introduction to Abulafia's system. Written 1291. Munich, Ms. 285.
27. *The Lamp of God (Ner Elohim)*. Munich, Ms. 10.
28. *And This is to Judah (VeZot LiYehudah)*, a reply to the Rashba's accusations. Written in Sicily as a letter to Judah of Barcelona, known as Solomon. Published by Jellinek in *Philosophie und Kabbalah,* Leipzig, 1854.
29. *Seven Paths of the Torah (Sheva Netivot HaTorah)*, regarding the methods of Torah study. Published by Jellinek in *Philosophie und Kabbalah*, Leipzig, 1854.
30. *A Refinery for Silver and a Furnace for Gold (Metzaref LaKesef VeKur LaZahav)*, discussion of the Name of 42 letters. Sasoon, Ms. 56.
31. *The Book of Passion (Sefer HaCheshek)*, an important work on Abulafia's meditative system, paralleling *Chayay Olam HaBah*. Jewish Theological Seminary, Ms. 1801.
32. *The Book of Blendings (Sefer HaTzeruf)*. An important work regarding the manipulation of letters and words. Attribution to Abulafia not definite. Jewish Theological Seminary, Ms. 1887, Paris, Ms. 774.

Besides these, a number of other books are known, either in small fragments, or in unnamed manuscripts. Others are thought to have been written by Abulafia, but identification is not positive.

4. TEACHINGS

In the literature, there is considerable discussion regarding the term *Kabbalah*(קַבָּלָה). Most authorities state that it comes from the root *Kabal* (קבל), meaning "to receive." Abulafia takes this a step further, maintaining that a mystic is called a Kabbalist because he has *received* (*Kibel*, קִבֵּל) the tradition from either the prophets or those who received fom them.[54] Like most other Kabbalists, he saw his tradition as being that of the prophets, and assumed that his methods were the same as those that the prophets used to attain their high mystical experience.

The use of Divine Names plays a very important role in Abulafia's system. This is one tradition that he clearly saw as being derived from the patriarchs and prophets. Thus, when the Torah states that Abraham "called in the Name of God" (Genesis 12:8), most commentaries interpret this to mean that he prayed, or that he proclaimed God's greatness. Together with a number of other Kabbalists, however, Abulafia takes this literally, stating that Abraham actually pronounced God's Name, and through this practice was able to attain the highest mystical levels.[55]

The *Sefer Yetzirah*, which is attributed to Abraham, seems to support this interpretation. It states:[56]

> When Abraham gazed, he looked, saw, probed, and understood. He graved *(chakak)*, hewed *(chatzav)* and combined *(tzaraf)*. He was successful and the Master of all, blessed be He, revealed himself to him.

The three key words here are graved (*chakak*, חקק), hewed (*chatzav*, חצב), and combined (*tzaraf*, צרף). According to a number of Kabbalists, these processes involve the manipulation of letters, and it is from this that Abulafia derived his main system. Over a hundred years before Abulafia, a major commentator, Rabbi Yehudah ben Barzilai of

Barcelona, had explained that the word "graved" (*chakak*) denotes writing. He also stated that "hewed" (*chatzav*) denoted the formation of the letters, while "combined" (*tzaraf*) indicated that Abraham permuted them.[57]

In one of his books, Abulafia virtually paraphrases this interpretation, and it was apparently well known among the Kabbalists. Thus, the method used by Abraham, as outlined in the *Sefer Yetzirah*, was primarily one of writing and permuting the letters of the alphabet. This activity served as a meditative method, through which he reached high prophetic states. This is also the core of Abulafia's system. He calls it the "Kabbalah of letters," distinguishing it from the "Kabbalah of Sefirot."[58]

Another important Talmudic teaching, often quoted by Abulafia, is the statement that "Betzalel knew how to permute (*tzaraf*) the letters with which the heaven and earth were created."[59] Betzalel was the one who was given the task of erecting the Tabernacle in the desert after the Exodus. Through this mystical ability to manipulate the letters of creation, he was able to build it in such a manner that it would act as a channel for the spiritual energies of creation.

Very closely related to this is the fact that all of creation took place by means of sayings. At each stage in the creation of the universe, the Bible introduces the account by stating, "And God said." Creation therefore took place through words. These words, however, consisted of letters, and therefore the letters of the Hebrew alphabet are the most basic building blocks of creation.[60] Therefore, if an individual knows how to correctly manipulate the letters of the alphabet, he is able to make use of the same spiritual forces that originally brought the universe into being.

Abulafia finds a hint for this in the verse, "God's way is perfect (*tamim*), God's word is permuted (*tzerufah*)" (Psalms 18:31).[61] Although the word *tzerufah* (צְרוּפָה) in this verse is usually interpreted to mean "refined" or "purified," Abulafia used it in the sense of the *Sefer Yetzirah*, where means "blended" or "permuted." This is also indicated by the word *tamim* (תָּמִים), which indicates a spiritual experience and a state of enlightenment.[62] Elsewhere, Abulafia states that the permutation of the letters itself serves as a test and a "refining" for the initiate. Through the manner in which an individual permutes the letters, one can know the nature of his innermost self.[63]

Here we see an entirely new method of meditation. Instead of chanting a word over and over, as in mantra meditation, one writes a word, permuting and cycling the letters in every possible manner. As the initiate progresses to higher and higher states, he no longer needs to actually write the letters, but can permute them verbally or mentally. All this is an initiation to the higher levels, which actually involve the Divine Names.[64] An entire handbook dealing with the various methods of manipulating letters in this manner is attributed to Abulafia, and similar books were written by other members of his school.[65]

A similar word with two meanings is *rakhav* (רכב), which means "to ride," but also has a connotation of "grafting" and "attaching." This is especially significant since *rakhav* is the root of the word *Merkava* (מֶרְכָּבָה), which denotes the highest mystical experiences. As Abulafia points out, this also has the connotation of grafting and combining, and therefore, the "Mystery of the *Merkava*" involved the combination of letters, words and Divine Names.

Abulafia thus discusses the phrase, "One who looks at the gazing (*tzefiyat*) of the *Merkava*."[66] He states that the meaning of this was known to the sages by a tradition from the prophets, and consisted of "grafting (*harkava*, הַרְכָּבָה) of one letter to another, one word to another, one Divine Name to another."

Each such *Merkava*-combination combines the power of the Divine Names, the Sefirot, and the letters. When these influence an individual, they direct him in forming every possible permutation. Because their essence is sealed in these permutations, every key of wisdom is given over to the individual who "gazes, sees, and understands."

When an individual looks into these permutations in a proper manner, he can see all of creation. He is like a person looking into a glass mirror, who sees both his own face, and the faces of all who pass by.[67] Abulafia writes that, "when the power of the influx begins to manifest and reveal itself to the one gazing into the 'mirror,' the letters and Sefirot begin to appear before him, like lightning flashes. This is like the vision of the *Chayot*, regarding which it is written, 'The *Chayot* ran and returned, like a vision of lightning' (Ezekiel 1:14)."[68]

This is also the meaning of what the *Sefer Yetzirah* says, "Ten Sefirot of Nothingness, their vision (*tzafiyah*, צְפִיָּה) is like a flash of lightning."[69] The word "vision" (*tzafiyah*) here, is a term that has a special connotation of prophecy and the mystical vision.

Although Abulafia considered the "Method of Sefirot" to be different than the "Method of Letters" that he taught, he does occasionally speak in guarded tones about ascending through the "ladder of the Sefirot."[70] Still, he was very careful not to stress this method. He realized that if one meditated on the Sefirot, it would be very easy to see them as independent entities, thus introducing an element of plurality into the absolute unity of the Godly realm.[71] This, in turn, can lead to the actual worship of the Sefirot, and according to at least one Kabbalistic source, this was the first step that eventually led to pagan polytheism.[72]

Another type of meditation that Abulafia hints at is contemplation. He particularly speaks about this with respect to the blue thread in the *Tzitzit,* the ritual tassel worn on the Prayer Shawl *(Tallit).* Speaking of the *Tzitzit,* the Torah says, "You shall gaze at it, and remember all of God's commandments" (Numbers 15:39). The Talmud expounds on this, saying, "the blue thread resembles the sea, the sea resembles the firmament, and the firmament resembles the Throne of Glory."[73] What the Talmud is actually doing is alluding to the fact that this thread is to be used as an object of meditative contemplation, outlining the steps of spiritual ascent.

This thread was colored with a blue dye taken from the *chilazon,* a mollusc related to the murex. Abulafia notes that the word *chilazon* (חִלָזוֹן) has the same letters as *la-chazon* (לְחָזוֹן), meaning, "for a vision."[74] Through this dye, one could attain a vision approaching that of prophecy.

Still, Abulafia's main method involved the permutation of letters, and, on a higher level, pronouncing the letters of the Divine Names. Such pronunciation was to be accompanied by specific head motions, as well as particular breathing exercises.

The true mystical experience is beyond description, and cannot be explained to one who has not experienced it himself. Just as a person who has been blind from birth cannot comprehend the concept of color, so one who has been spiritually blind cannot grasp the brilliant spectrum of the spiritual world. Abulafia thus writes, "One who reaches the highest level cannot reveal it to anyone. All he can do is give over the keys, so that the enlightened individual can open the gates which are sealed to exclude the unworthy."[75]

Both the opportunities and dangers facing one who enters the mysteries are graphically described by Abulafia. He writes that divine wisdom has both a right side and a left side. This mystery is the highest level, since it teaches the individual how to attain true enlightenment. But still, even if one makes use of all the necessary techniques, he cannot attain the higher levels unless he is properly prepared for this.

Abulafia writes that, "many great men and sages have stumbled and fell, were trapped and snared, because they exceeded the bounds of their knowledge." [76]

Abulafia then continues, speaking of the highest level, which is the Crown. The word for Crown is *Keter* (כֶּתֶר), and Abulafia notes that when these letters reversed, they spell *karet* (כָּרֵת), which means "cut off." [77] Thus, when an individual attempts to reach the highest level of the Crown, if he is not worthy, he can end up being "cut off" spiritually. Abulafia therefore warns in the strongest terms that one who attempts to enter these mysteries must be adequately prepared, and that one not enter unless he is thoroughly familiar with all the necessary introductions.

An especially strong warning is given against spiritual dilettantism. If a person enters the mysteries as a whim, without preparation, he can be destroyed, both spiritually and psychologically. In pronouncing this warning, Abulafia writes to the uninitiated, "You mind will be confused, your thoughts confounded, and you will not find any way to escape the reveries of your mind. The power of your imagination will overwhelm you, making you imagine many utterly useless fantiasies. Your imaginative faculty will grow stronger, weakening your intellect, until your reveries cast you into a great sea. You will not have the wisdom ever to escape from it, and will therefore drown." [78] He warns that before one attempts to attain the "small still voice," he must first grasp the mysteries of the Kabbalah with his intellect.

The ultimate mysteries are alluded to by the Garden of Eden.[79] The Torah relates that after Adam sinned and was expelled, this garden was protected by "the flame of a rotating sword" (Genesis 3:24). Abulafia explains that the manner in which this sword rotates depends on the readiness of the individual attempting to enter. If he is worthy, it becomes the mirror through which he perceives, while if he is not worthy, he is burned out and "cut off" by the fire of this sword. The one who oversees the sword, preventing the unworthy from entering is the angel Metatron. The turning sword itself is the cycle of the intellect.[80]

Abulafia writes that the letters, used by the initiate, are engraved on the cycle of the intellect, and it is through this cycle that one perceives the transcendental. The source of his vision is the Holy Palace, which is the precise center of that cycle.[81]

The sphere of the intellect has the power to travel through the spiritual realm, which is the realm of Pure Intellect. As one begins to enter this realm, he can climb the revolving sphere of the intellect as if it were a ladder. When he actually ascends, his thought processes are turned over and his entire perception is altered, so that he retains nothing of his normal mental state.

Entering such a state of consciousness can be extremely dangerous. Abulafia writes that, "one must completely alter his nature and personality, transporting himself from a state of feeling to one of intellect, from the path of the imagination to one of burning fire. Otherwise, he will ultimately find his visions altered, his thought processes demolished, and his reveries confounded. The sphere is what refines and tests, and regarding it the Scripture states, 'A refinery (*metzaref*, מְצָרֵף) is for silver, a furnace is for gold, but God tries the heart' (Proverbs 17:3)."[82]

Abulafia goes on to state that "God gave us the Torah, teaching us the way of permutations, and the steps of the ladder involving the mystery of letters. Without such information, it is impossible to reach the level of knowing God." He explains that the higher one ascends, the more barriers must be sundered.[83] Speaking at length of these barriers, he discusses the Biblical passages which appear to indicate that God is hidden by gloom and cloud. Since God is infinite, it is impossible for anything to encompass Him, but this "gloom and cloud" is actually in the human intellect, which cannot actually perceive God.[84]

While one must break through the barriers, one must also be careful not to enter too close. One who goes beyond the proper boundary can be swallowed up by the light and die of rapture, very much like Ben Azzai. According to Abulafia and other Kabbalists, this was the death known as the "kiss of God," which, according to the Talmud was reserved for the greatest saints.[85] One method of avoiding this is to bind one's own soul with an oath that it not leave the body.[86] But even more important, one must constantly avert his gaze, going "back and forth." This is the meaning of what the *Sefer Yetzirah* teaches:[87]

> Ten Sefirot of Nothingness: Close your mouth that it not speak of them, and your heart that it not think. And if your heart runs, return to its place, It is thus written, "The Chayot ran and returned" (Ezekiel 1:14). Regarding this, a covenant has been made.

Abulafia maintained that when an individual is on the highest meditative levels, he can actually alter the laws of nature through sheer spiritual force.[88] Still, he was generally very much opposed to using these powers for such a purpose, seeing their main goal as being spiritual enlightenment, and not mere magic tricks. In a number of places he graphically describes the magical techniques of the practical Kabbalah, denouncing them in no uncertain terms.[89]

The best time for the deepest levels of meditation is in old age, when the intellect is well developed and the pull of the body is weak. Although young people may try to enter the mysteries, Abulafia taught that they will not reach the higher levels until they are advanced in age.[90] This reflects the Talmudic teaching that such mysteries should not be taught to an individual unless he is "halfway through his years." [91]

Highly controversial was Abulafia's claim to have attained true prophecy, even though he did not live in the Holy Land. According to the Midrash, prophecy can only be attained in the Holy Land, and not anyplace else, except under sharply restricted conditions.[92] Abulafia refused to accept this literally, and said that the Holy Land discussed in this teaching referred to a specific spiritual level. If an individual reached this level, he could attain prophecy, no matter what his geographical location.[93]

5. THE HIDDEN EDEN

Many types of meditation involve the repetition or chanting of certain words and phrases. In Abulafia's system, however, writing also plays a very important role. Rather than recite various letter combinations, the initiate was to write them down. An especially effective technique was to take a word and permute its letters in every possible way. From this, the initiate would procede to manipulate the word in other ways, making use of various ciphers and numerical values of the letters.

This is alluded to in the *Sefer Yetzirah,* which speaks of the number of ways in which various words can be permuted. Thus, a word containing three letters has six permutations, one containing four has 24, one containing five has 120, and a word with six letters has 720 permutations.[94] There is a special technique, known as cycling (*galgal,* גלגל) through which one permutes the letters of a word in a prescribed manner.[95] Writing in this manner is a type of meditation, where one makes use of both the path of the body and that of the intellect.

Another important reason for the effectiveness of this method is the fact that the letters are the very essence of creation, and therefore, when one writes and permutes them, he can channel these forces into his spiritual being. Abulafia notes that *d'yo* (דְיו), the Hebrew word for ink, has the same letters as *Yod* (יוד), the initial letter (י) of the Tetragrammaton (*YHVH,* יהוה), and the substance of the spiritual realm.[96] The ink with which one writes is therefore the substance of his spiritual experience, from which all else follows.

Abulafia wrote much about the permutation and combination of letters, devoting his entire *Sefer HaTzeruf* (Book of Blendings) to the subject. There, however, he writes very little regarding the actual method in which one makes use of such permutations. There is, however, one place where Abulafia goes into this at length, and this is in his *Otzar Eden HaGanuz* (Treasury of the Hidden Eden).[97]

An Excerpt From

Otzar Eden HaGanuz

I have explained what you need to do this, and you lack nothing. Take the pen, parchment and ink, and write the letters, permuting them in such a manner as to denote good. "Depart from evil, do good, seek peace and pursue it." (Psalms 34:15)[98]

. . .

These things cannot be know unless one knows the Name . . . It is written, "Every word of God is permuted *(tzeruf)*, He is a shield to those who take refuge in Him" (Proverbs 30:5) . . . This teaches that true knowledge depends on God's sayings, which must be permuted, and tested through such permutation. It is the permutation of letters that tests these things, as it is written, "A permuter (*metzaref*) for silver, a furnace for gold, but God tests the heart" (Proverbs 17:3).[99]

The way of Permutations (*Tzeruf*, צֵרוּף) is the closest way to truly know God, more so than any other way. The individual who wishes to enter the Way of permutations should immediately test and permute (purify) his heart with the great fire, which is the fire of darkness.[100]

If one has the power to endure the way of rebuke with great passion, and if his mind can control its fantasies, then he can ride [his mind] like a horse. He can control it as he desires, spurring it on to go forward, or reigning it to stop where he pleases. At all times, his imagination remains subject to his will, not straying from its authority, even by a hairbreadth.

A person with this power is truly a mighty warrior . . . He is like Uriel, who constantly gazes at the Light of God, delighting in God's mysteries. . . .

Now I will tell you the mystery of the true discipline, through which you can alter the laws of nature. . . . This is the path along which you must travel to attain the mystery of true discipline:

Take in your hand a scribe's pen. Write speedily, letting your tongue utter the words with a pleasant melody, very slowly. Understand the words that leave your lips. The words can consist of anything that you desire, in any language that you desire, for you must return all languages to their original substance. I have alluded to this elsewhere, . . . but this is its correct place. . . .

You already know that Isaiah said, "Declare the letters backward, and then we will know that you are gods, that you can do good and evil, and we will meditate (וְנִשְׁתָּעָה, from *sha'ah*, שעה) and see together" (Isaiah

41:23). He also said [in God's name], "Ask Me of letters, and command Me over My sons and the work of My hands" (Isaiah 45:11). Again, he said [in God's name], "Tell them of the letters that will come" (Isaiah 44:7).[101] These three verses are trusted witnesses to the power of the letters.

Take the pen in your hand, like a spear in the hand of a warrior. When you think of something, uttering it in your heart with specific letters, also express it with your mouth. Listen carefully, and "watch what emanates from your lips" (Deuteronomy 23:24). Let your ears hear what your lips speak, and with your heart, understand the meaning of all these expressions.

Write each expression down immediately. Manipulate the letters, and seek out other words having the same numerical value, even if they do not follow my path. And know that this will be your key to open the fifty gates of wisdom. . . .

You must be alone when you do this. Meditate (*hitboded*) in a state of rapture so as to receive the divine influx, which will bring your mind from potential to action.

Permute the letters, back and forth, and in this manner, you will reach the first level. As a result of the activity and your concentration on the letters, your mind will become bound to them. The hairs on your head will stand on end and tremble.

Your life blood is in your heart, and regarding this it is written, "the blood is the soul" (Deuteronomy 12:23). It is likewise written, "the blood in the soul will atone" (Leviticus 17:11). This blood within you will begin to vibrate because of the living permutations that loosen it. Your entire body will then begin to tremble, and all your limbs will be seized with shuddering. You will experience the terror of God, and will be enveloped with fear of Him.

You will then feel as if an additional spirit is within you, arousing you and strengthening you, passing through your entire body and giving you pleasure. It will seem as you have been annointed with perfumed oil, from head to foot.[102]

You will rejoice and have great pleasure. You will experience ecstasy and trembling — ecstasy for the soul, and trembling for the body. This is like a rider who races a horse, the rider rejoices and is ecstatic, while the horse trembles under him.

There will be no question that, through this wondrous method, you will have reached one of the Fifty Gates of Understanding.[103] This is the lowest gate. But once you have entered this gate, you are protected from the gatekeeper whose name is AZ (אָז). Regarding this gatekeeper it is written, "[God acquired me (Wisdom) at the beginning of His way,] the first of His works from AZ" (Proverbs 8:22).[104] This is the mystery of "the beginning of His way."

The Divine Presence will then rest on you, and the Fifty Gates of Understanding will be opened in your heart. From then on, you will realize Who is with you, Who is over your head, and Who is in your heart. You will then recognize the true way.

Treasury of the Hidden Eden.

6. LIGHT OF THE INTELLECT

Once one has mastered the technique of letter permutation, the next step in Abulafia's system involves the pronunciation of the various names of God. The simplest of these involves the four letters of the Tetragrammaton, YHVH (יהוה). These letters are combined with the letter Alef (א), together with the five primary vowels.

This method is presented in detail in Abulafia's *Or HaShekhal* (Light of the Intellect), and it is one of the very few cases where his meditative techniques have found their way into a standard published Kabbalah classic. This entire selection is presented by the Ramak (Rabbi Moshe Cordevero, 1522—1570), in his *Pardes Rimonim* (Orchard of Pomegranates), one of the most important of all Kabbalah classics.[105]

In this selection, however, the Ramak does not attribute this method to Abulafia, but rather to an obscure *Sefer HaNikud* (Book of Dots). While there are a number of books with this name, none of them are known to speak of this method. Several of these books have been lost and are only known because they are mentioned in other texts, the most important being attributed to Rabbi Aaron of Baghdad, a Kabbalist of the Ninth Century.[106] It is entirely possible that both Abulafia and the Ramak are actually quoting from a much older text known as *Sefer HaNikud*, and this is supported by the manner in which it appears in Abulafia's manuscripts. It is equally possible, however, that only this small portion was copied, and that it was generally called *Sefer HaNikud*. In any case, it is well established that the Ramak was familiar with Abulafia' system.[107]

Techniques very similar to those presented here are also discussed by other Kabbalists, even by opponents of Abulafia, such as Rabbi Judah Chayit.[108] It is also most interesting to note that a very similar method is prescribed for the creation of a Golem.[109]

Briefly, the system of *Or HaSekhel* involves the combination of the four letters of God's name, Yod (י) Heh (ה) Vav (ו) Heh (ה), with the letter Alef (א), and then cycling it through the five basic vowels. These vowels are:

Cholam (˙), having the sound of o.
Kametz (ָ), having the sound of a.
Tzeré (ֵ), having the sound of e.
Chirek (ִ), having the sound of i.
Shurek (וּ), having the sound of u.

Together with each pronunciation, one must move his head in a motion resembling the actual form of each vowel. At the same time, one must breath in a specific manner, with a certain number of breaths permitted between letters, and more between lines.

An Excerpt From
The Light of the Intellect

It is known that the [consonant] letters do not have any sound by themselves. God therefore gave the mouth the power to express the letters, pronouncing them as they are found in a book. For this purpose, he provided vowel points for the letters, indicating the sound with which they must be expressed when they are translated from a book to the mouth. These vowels are what allow the letters to be sounded, and they can also be written as letters in a book.

The vibrations of these sounds must also be associated with space. No vibration can occur except in a definite time and place.

The elements of space are the dimensions and distances. The elements of time are the cycles, through which it is measured. This includes such divisions as years, months and days.

One must therefore know how to draw out the sound of each letter as it is related to these dimensions.

This is the mystery of how to pronounce the Glorious Name:

Make yourself right. Meditate (*hitboded*) in a special place, where your voice cannot be heard by others. Cleanse your heart and soul of all other thoughts in the world. Imagine that at this time, you soul is separating itself from your body, and that you are leaving the physical world behind, so that you enter the Future World, which is the source of all life distributed to the living.

[The Future World] is the intellect, which is the source of all Wisdom, Understanding and Knowledge, emanating from the King of Kings, the Blessed Holy One. All creatures fear Him with a great awe. This is the fear of one who actually perceives, and it is double the fear of one who merely has experienced love or awe.

Your mind must then come to join His Mind, which gives you the power to think. Your mind must divest itself of all other thoughts other than His Thought. This becomes like a partner, joining you to Him through His glorious, awesome Name.

You must therefore know precisely how to pronounce the Name. Its form [is given in the tables].

This is the technique. When you begin to pronounce the Alef (א) with any vowel, it is expressing the mystery of Unity (*Yichud*). You must therefore draw it out in one breath and no more. Do not interrupt this breath in any manner whatsoever until you have completed the pronunciation of the Alef.

Draw out this breath as long as you extend a single breath. At the same time, chant the Alef, or whatever other letter you are pronouncing, while depicting the form of the vowel point.

The first vowel is the *Cholem* (o, ˙), above the letter.

When you begin to pronounce it, direct your face toward the east, not looking up or down. You should be sitting, wearing clean, pure white robes over all your clothing, or else, wearing your prayer shawl (*Tallit*) over your head and crowned with your Tefillin. You must face the east, since it is from that direction that light emanates to the world.

With each of the twenty-five letter pairs, you must move your head properly.

When you pronounce the *Cholem* (o), begin facing directly east. Purify your thoughts, and as you exhale, raise your head, little by little, until when you finish, your head is facing upward. After you finish, prostrate yourself on the ground.

Do not interrupt between the breath associated with the Alef and the breath associated with the other letter in the pair. You may, however, take a single breath, and it may be long or short.

Between each pair of letters, you may take two breaths without making a sound, but not more than two. If you wish to take less than two breaths, you may do so.

After you finish each row, you may take five breaths, but no more. If you wish to take less, you may do so.

Pronunciation with the Yod (י)

AoYo AoYa AoYe AoYi AoYu	אֹיֹ אֹיָ אֹיֵ אֹיִ אֹיֻ
AaYo AaYa AaYe AaYi AaYu	אָיֹ אָיָ אָיֵ אָיִ אָיֻ
AeYo AeYa AeYe AeYi AeYu	אֵיֹ אֵיָ אֵיֵ אֵיִ אֵיֻ
AiYo AiYa AiYe AiYi AiYu	אִיֹ אִיָ אִיֵ אִיִ אִיֻ
AuYo AuHa AuYe AuYi AuYu	אֻיֹ אֻיָ אֻיֵ אֻיִ אֻיֻ
YoAo YoAa YoAe YoAi YoAu	יֹאֹ יֹאָ יֹאֵ יֹאִ יֹאֻ
YaAo YaAa YaAe YaAi YaAu	יָאֹ יָאָ יָאֵ יָאִ יָאֻ
YeAo YeAa YeAe YeAi YeAu	יֵאֹ יֵאָ יֵאֵ יֵאִ יֵאֻ
YiAo YiAa YiAe YiAi YiAu	יִאֹ יִאָ יִאֵ יִאִ יִאֻ
YuAo YuAa YuAe YuAi YuAu	יֻאֹ יֻאָ יֻאֵ יֻאִ יֻאֻ

Pronunciation with the Heh (ה)

AoHo AoHa AoHe AoHi AoHu	אֹהֹ אֹהָ אֹהֵ אֹהִ אֹהֻ
AaHo AaHa AaHe AaHi AaHu	אָהֹ אָהָ אָהֵ אָהִ אָהֻ
AeHo AeHa AeHe AeHi AeHu	אֵהֹ אֵהָ אֵהֵ אֵהִ אֵהֻ
AiHo AiHa AiHe AiHi AiHu	אִהֹ אִהָ אִהֵ אִהִ אִהֻ
AuHo AuHa AuHe AuHi AuHu	אֻהֹ אֻהָ אֻהֵ אֻהִ אֻהֻ
HoAo HoAa HoAe HoAi HoAu	הֹאֹ הֹאָ הֹאֵ הֹאִ הֹאֻ
HaAo HaAa HaAe HaAi HaAu	הָאֹ הָאָ הָאֵ הָאִ הָאֻ
HeAo HeAa HeAe HeAi HeAu	הֵאֹ הֵאָ הֵאֵ הֵאִ הֵאֻ
HiAo HiAa HiAe HiAi HiAu	הִאֹ הִאָ הִאֵ הִאִ הִאֻ
HuAo HuAa HuAe HuAi HuAu	הֻאֹ הֻאָ הֻאֵ הֻאִ הֻאֻ

If you change anything or make any mistake in the order in any row, go back to the beginning of the row. Continue until you pronounce it correctly.

Just like you face upward when pronouncing the *Cholem*, face downward when you pronounce the *Chirek* (i, ִ). In this manner, you draw down the supernal power and bind it to yourself.

When you pronounce the *Shurek* (u, ֻ or וּ), do not move your head upward or downward. Instead, move it straight forward (neither lowering or raising it).

When you pronounce the *Tzeré* (i, ֵ), move your head from left to right.

When you pronounce the *Kametz* (a, ָ), move it from right to left.

Pronunciation with the Vav (ו)

AoVo AoVa AoVe AoVi AoVu	אֹוֹ אֹוָ אֹוֵ אֹוִ אֹוֻ
AaVo AaVa AaVe AaVi AaVu	אָוֹ אָוָ אָוֵ אָוִ אָוֻ
AeVo AeVa AeVe AeVi AeVu	אֵוֹ אֵוָ אֵוֵ אֵוִ אֵוֻ
AiVo AiVa AiVe AiVi AiVu	אִוֹ אִוָ אִוֵ אִוִ אִוֻ
AuVo AuVa AuVe AuVi AuVu	אֻוֹ אֻוָ אֻוֵ אֻוִ אֻוֻ
VoAo VoAa VoAe VoAi VoAu	וֹאֹ וֹאָ וֹאֵ וֹאִ וֹאֻ
VaAo VaAa VaAe VaAi VaAu	וָאֹ וָאָ וָאֵ וָאִ וָאֻ
VeAo VeAa VeAe VeAi VeAu	וֵאֹ וֵאָ וֵאֵ וֵאִ וֵאֻ
ViAo ViAa ViAe ViAi ViAu	וִאֹ וִאָ וִאֵ וִאִ וִאֻ
VuAo VuAa VuAe VuAi VuAu	וֻאֹ וֻאָ וֻאֵ וֻאִ וֻאֻ

Pronunciation with the Final Heh (ה)

AoHo AoHa AoHe AoHi AoHu	אֹהֹ אֹהָ אֹהֵ אֹהִ אֹהֻ
AaHo AaHa AaHe AaHi AaHu	אָהֹ אָהָ אָהֵ אָהִ אָהֻ
AeHo AeHa AeHe AeHi AeHu	אֵהֹ אֵהָ אֵהֵ אֵהִ אֵהֻ
AiHo AiHa AiHe AiHi AiHu	אִהֹ אִהָ אִהֵ אִהִ אִהֻ
AuHo AuHa AuHe AuHi AuHu	אֻהֹ אֻהָ אֻהֵ אֻהִ אֻהֻ
HoAo HoAa HoAe HoAi HoAu	הֹאֹ הֹאָ הֹאֵ הֹאִ הֹאֻ
HaAo HaAa HaAe HaAi HaAu	הָאֹ הָאָ הָאֵ הָאִ הָאֻ
HeAo HeAa HeAe HeAi HeAu	הֵאֹ הֵאָ הֵאֵ הֵאִ הֵאֻ
HiAo HiAa HiAe HiAi HiAu	הִאֹ הִאָ הִאֵ הִאִ הִאֻ
HuAo HuAa HuAe HuAi HuAu	הֻאֹ הֻאָ הֻאֵ הֻאִ הֻאֻ

In any case, if you see any image before you, prostrate yourself before it immediately.[110]

If you hear a voice, loud or soft, and wish to understand what it is saying, immediately respond and say, "Speak my Lord, for Your servant is listening" (1 Samuel 3:9). Do not speak at all, but incline your ear to hear what is being said to you.

If you feel great terror and cannot bear it, prostrate yourself immediately, even in the middle of pronouncing a letter.

If you do not see or hear anything, do not use this technique again all that week.

It is good to pronounce this once each week, in a form that "runs and returns." For regarding this, a covenant has been made.[111]

What can I add? What I have written is clear, and if you are wise, you will understand the entire technique.

If you feel that your mind is unstable, that your knowledge of Kabbalah is insufficient, or that your thoughts are bound to the vanities of the time, do not dare to pronounce the Name, lest you sin all the more.

Between the tablet of the Yod and that of the Heh, you can take twenty-five breaths, but not more. But you must not make any interruption at this time, not with speech and not with thought.

The same is true between the Heh and the Vav, and between the Vav and the final Heh. But if you wish to take less than twenty-five breaths, you may do so.

Light of the Intellect.[112]

7. LIFE OF THE FUTURE WORLD

Of all Abulafia's books, the one that explains his methods most completely is his *Chayay Olam HaBah* (Life of the Future World). This was well known to the Kabbalists, and in the unpublished fourth section of his *Shaarey Kedushah* (Gates of Holiness), Rabbi Chaim Vital speaks of it as being the most important guide for attaining meditative enlightenment. To this day, *Chayay Olam HaBah* is known to Kabbalists, and it exists in many manuscripts, both in libraries and in private collections. While its methods are considered to be very highly advanced, there are still some closed Kabbalistic circles that actually make use of them.

The main method discussed in *Chayay Olam HaBah* is very similar to that found in *Or HaSekhel,* also involving the same head motions as well as controlled breathing. Instead of making use of the Tetragrammaton, however, this book utilizes the Name of Seventy-Two Combinations.

This Name was known from most ancient times, and is discussed in both the Bahir and the Zohar, but significantly, not in the *Hekhalot.*[113] By the Eleventh Century, it had been popularized in Rashi's commentaries, and is also mentioned in a late Midrash.[114] But while the Name itself was known earlier, the actual methods of its use had never been written down until Abulafia did so.

The Name of Seventy-Two is derived from three very interesting verses (Exodus 14:19—21), reproduced on the following page. Counting the letters of these three verses, one immediately discovers that each one contains exactly seventy-two letters. These verses then form the basis for the seventy-two triplets in the Name.

The process of constructing the Name is outlined in the Bahir, and is very straightforward. One takes the letters of the first verse in direct order, those of the second in reverse order, and those of the third verse in direct order.

Thus, one begins with the first letter of the first verse, which is a Vav (ו). Then one takes the last letter of the middle verse, which is a Heh (ה), and finally, the first letter of the third verse, which is a Vav (ה). Combining these, one obtains the first triplet, VHV (והו).

In order to construct the second triplet, one procedes in a similar manner. One takes the second letter, Yod (י), of the first verse, the

Derivation of the Name of Seventy-Two

The Three Verses: Exodus 14:19—21

ויסע מלאך האלהים ההלך לפני מחנה ישראל וילך מאחריהם ויסע עמוד
הענן מפניהם ויעמד מאחריהם:

And the angel of God, who went before the camp of Israel, moved, and went behind them, and the pillar of cloud moved from before them and went behind them.

ויבא בין מחנה מצרים ובין מחנה ישראל ויהי הענן והחשך ויאר את
הלילה ולא קרב זה אל זה כל הלילה:

And it came between the camp of Egypt and the camp of Israel, and cloud and darkness were there, yet it gave light in the night, and one did not come near the other all that night.

ויט משה את ידו על הים ויולך יהוה את הים ברוח קדים עזה כל הלילה
וישם את הים לחרבה ויבקעו המים:

And Moses stretched out his hand over the sea, and God caused the sea to go back with a strong east windall the night, and it made the sea into dry land, and the waters were parted.

THE NAME OF SEVENTY-TWO

והו	ילי	סיט	עלם	מהש	ללה	אכא	כהת
הזי	אלד	לאו	ההע	יזל	מבה	הרי	הקם
לאו	כלי	לוו	פהל	נלך	ייי	מלה	חהו
נתה	האא	ירת	שאה	ריי	אום	לכב	ושר
יחו	להח	כוק	מנד	אני	העס	רהע	ייז
ההה	מיכ	וול	ילה	סאל	ערי	עשל	מיה
והו	דני	החש	עמם	ננא	נית	מבה	פוי
נמם	ייל	הרח	מצר	ומב	יהה	ענו	מחי
דמב	מנק	איע	חבו	ראה	יבם	היי	מום

second letter from the end of the middle verse, Lamed (ל), and the second letter of the last verse, Yod (י). This results in the second triplet, YLY (ילי). One then continues in this manner until all seventy-two triples are completed.

This, however, only provides the consonants of the Name. The vowels used when pronouncing the Name are the "natural vowels" associated with each consonant.[115]

Abulafia explains that the "natural vowel" is the first vowel found in the letter's own name. Thus, for example, the first vowel in the name of the letter Bet (ב, written out as בֵּית) is "e," and therefore, "é or the *Tzeré* (..) is the natural vowels of the Bet. Similarly, the first vowel in Gimel (ג, written out as גִמֶל) is "i," and hence "i," or *Chirek* (.), is the natural vowel for Gimel. The same is true of all the other letters.

The Natural Vowels					Numerical Value
Alef	א	◌ָ	a	*Kametz*	1
Bet	ב	◌ֵ	e	*Tzeré*	2
Gimel	ג	◌ִ	i	*Chirek*	3
Dalet	ד	◌ָ	a	*Kametz*	4
Heh	ה	◌ֵ	e	*Tzeré*	5
Vav	ו	◌ָ	a	*Kametz*	6
Zayin	ז	◌ָ	a	*Kametz*	7
Chet	ח	◌ֵ	e	*Tzeré*	8
Tet	ט	◌ֵ	e	*Tzeré*	9
Yod	י	◌ֹ	o	*Cholem*	10
Kaf	כ	◌ָ	a	*Kametz*	20
Lamed	ל	◌ָ	a	*Kametz*	30
Mem	מ	◌ֵ	e	*Tzeré*	40
Nun	נ	◌ֻ	u	*Shurek*	50
Samekh	ס	◌ָ	a	*Kametz*	60
Ayin	ע	◌ָ	a	*Kametz*	70
Peh	פ	◌ֵ	e	*Tzeré*	80
Tzadi	צ	◌ָ	a	*Kametz*	90
Kof	ק	◌ֹ	o	*Cholem*	100
Resh	ר	◌ֵ	e	*Tzeré*	200
Shin	ש	◌ִ	i	*Chirek*	300
Tav	ת	◌ָ	a	*Kametz*	400

In general, *Chayay Olam HaBah* is a book that speaks most elequently for itself. The selection cited here should provide an adequate overview of the use of the Name of Seventy-Two.

An Excerpt From

Life of the Future World

"Prepare to meet your God, O Israel."[116] Prepare yourself, unify your heart, and purify your body. Choose a special place for yourself, where your voice will not be heard by anyone else. Meditate *(hitboded)* alone, with no one else present. Sit in one place in a room or attic. Do not reveal your secret to anyone.

If you engaged in this by day, do so in a darkened room. It is best, however, that you do it at night.

At this time, when you prepare yourself to speak to your Creator and you desire to witness His might, be careful to cleanse your thoughts of all worldly folly.

Wrap yourself in your Tallit. If the time is proper, also place your Tefillin on your head and arm. This will increase your awe and trembling before the Divine Presence which will visit you at this time.

Wear clean clothing. If possible, all your clothing should be white. This is of great help for one's concentration on fear and love [of God].

If it is at night, light many candles, so that your eyes are well illuminated.

Then take in your hand a tablet and some ink. These will serve as your witnesses that you are coming to serve God with joy and good heart.

Then begin to permute a number of letters. You may use only a few, or you may used many. Transpose and permute them quickly, until your heart is warmed as a result of these permutations, their motions, and what is derived from these permutations.

As a result of these permutations, your heart will become extremely warm. From the permutations, you will gain new knowledge that you never learned from human traditions nor derived from intellectual analysis. When you experience this, you are prepared to receive the influx *(shefa,* שֶׁפַע*)*.

The influx will then come, bestowed to you. It will arouse in you many words, one after the other.

Then prepare your inner thoughts to depict God and His highest angels. Depict them in your heart as if they were human beings, sitting or standing around you. You are in their midst, like a messenger whom the King and His servants wish to send on a mission. You are ready to hear the words of the message, whether it is from the King or from one of His servants, from His mouth, or from the mouth of any one of them.

After you have depicted all this, prepare your mind and heart so that your thoughts should understand the many things that come to you through the letters that your heart imagines. Understand each concept and its reasons, both as a whole and in its parts. Ponder them, like a person who has a parable or example revealed in a dream, or like one who delves into a very deep concept in a book of wisdom.

Take each concept that you hear, and interpret it with the best and closest interpretation that you can. Judge yourself according to what you understand from it. And what you are told can also relate to others.

All this will take place after you have cast the tablet from your hand and the pen from between your fingers, or after they have fallen of their own accord because of your many thoughts.

The divine influx will begin to prevail in you, and will weaken your external and internal organs. Your entire body will begin to tremble, until you think that you are about to die. This is because your soul is separating itself from your body as a result of the great joy that you experience when you perceive and recognize these things.

In your mind, you will then choose death rather than life. For death only involves the body, and as a result, the soul lives forever when it is resurrected.

You then know that you have reached a level where you are receiving the divine influx.

At that time, you may wish to honor the glorious Name and serve Him with the life of your body and soul. Conceal your face, and be afraid to gaze upon God. "Do not come closer. Remove your shoes from your feet, for the place upon which you stand is holy ground" (Exodus 3:5).

Instead, involve yourself with your body once again. Stand up, eat something, drink something, smell a pleasant fragrance, and let your spirit once again return to its sheath. Let your heart rejoice with its portion, and know that God loves you. He teaches you for your benefit, He teaches man knowledge.[117]

After you have done this successfully many times, you will become an expert in "choosing life." When you are strong and stable, you can make use of another, higher method.

When attempting this method, prepare yourself in the manner discussed earlier. Clear your mind completely.

Then, with complete concentration and with a proper, pleasant, sweet melody, pronounce the Name [of Seventy-Two].

Using the natural vowels of each letter, [begin by pronouncing these six triplets]:

VaHeVa YoLaYo SaYoTe וָהֵו יֹלָי סִיט
EaLaMe MeHeShi LaLaHe עָלָם מֵהֵשׁ לָלָה

These six triplets of the Holy Name pronounce with eighteen breaths.

If the divine influx does not force you to stop, continue pronouncing the Name in this manner until you reach the triplet MVM (מום), [the last of the seventy-two].

We have a tradition that the divine influx will come to a perfected individual after he completes [the number of letters in] the first verse, that is, after he pronounces twenty-four triplets.

This is alluded to in the word "my Beloved" — *Dodi* (דודי = 24). It is thus written, "The sound of my Beloved (*Dodi*) knocking" (Song of Songs 5:2).

You may then see the image of a child (*Naar*, נער = 320) or that of a Sheik (שך = 320). In Arabic, the word "Sheik" means an "elder." You see the image of an old man (*Zaken*, זקן), since the numerical value of *Naar* is the same as "Elder and Elder" (*Zaken VeZaken*, זקן וזקן = 320).

The mystical name of the one who appears to you is Metatron, whose name is also *Naar*.[118]

His name is also Enoch (*Chanokh*, חנוך). This is alluded to in the verse, "Train (*Chanokh*) a child (*Naar*) in his way, and when he is old (*Zaken*), he will not depart from it" (Proverbs 22:6).

Combine "raise" (*Chanokh*, חנוך = 84) and "his way" (*Darko*, דרכו = 230), and you will discovery his mystery.[119]

Thus, "our way is his strength" (*Dark-enu Koch-o*, דרכנו כחו = 314). Likewise, "our strength is his way" (*Koch-enu Dark-o*, כחנו דרכו = 314). [The numerical value of Metatron (מטטרון) is 315.]

When you see him, strengthen your heart and understand his ways. "Take heed of him and hearken to his voice — do not rebel against him, for he will not forgive your sin — for My Name is in him" (Exodus 23:21).[120]

Behold God's Name, *Shaddai* (שדי = 314). This is Metatron.[121] He is the "Prince of Names" (*Sar HaShemot*, שר השמות), who speaks with the "authority of the Name" (*Reshut HaShem*, רשות השם). [Both expressions contain the same letters.]

These twenty-four triplets contain seventy-two letters.

Therefore, when he speaks, respond and say, "Speak my Lord, for Your servant (*Avdekha*) is listening" (1 Samuel 3:9).[122] [Both of these numbers are alluded to in the word *Avdekha* (עבדך), which can be broken into] *Av* (עב = 72) and *dekha* (דך = 24).

The angel who teaches you the mystery of God (YHVH, יהוה) and His Name is Gabriel. He speaks out of the first verse (*pasuk*) of the Holy Name that is pronounced by your mouth, and he provides you with a vision (*mareh*) of prophecy. This is the mystery of the verse, "I make Myself known to him in a vision (*mareh*), I speak to him in a dream (*chalom*)" (Numbers 12:6).

A vision (*Mareh*, מראה = 246) is the mystery of the verse (*Pasuk*, פסוק = 246). This is Gabriel (גבריאל = 246).

A dream (*Chalom*, חלום = 84) is the mystery of "my Witness" (*Ed-iy*, עדי = 84). This is Enoch (*Chanoch*, חנוך = 84).

"And now, also, my Witness (*Ed-iy*) is in heaven, and He who testifies for me is on high" (Job 16:19), that this Kabbalah tradition is true.

If, heaven forbid, you do not receive anything when you pronounce the first verse, start again and begin the second verse.

Pronounce [the second set of triplets]:

NuThaHe HeAaAa YoReTha — נֻתָהֵ הֵאָאָ יֹרָתָ
ShiAaHe ReYoYo AaVaMe — שִׁאָהֵ רֵיֹיֹ אָוָמֵ

Concentrate as much as you can. As you pronounce each letter, exhale while you sound out the accompanying vowel together with its proper motion.

There are only five vowels, and their order is *o a e i u* (אֹ אָ אֵ אִ אֻ). The exhalation for all of them is the same. . . .

The Name contains 21 different letters. [These are all the letters of the Hebrew alphabet, except for the Gimel (ג), which is lacking.]

The letters having the first vowel [*Cholem* (o)] are Yod (יֹ) and Kof (קֹ).

The letters containing the second vowel [*Kametz* (a)] are Alef (אָ), Dalet (דָ), Vav (וָ), Zayin (זָ), Kaf (כָ), Lamed (לָ), Samekh (סָ), Ayin (עָ), Tzadi (צָ), and Tav (תָ). They are ten in all.

The letters containing the third vowel [*Tzeré* (e)] are Bet (בֵ), Heh (הֵ), Chet (חֵ), Tet (טֵ), Mem (מֵ), Peh (פֵ), and Resh (רֵ). There are seven in all.

The letter containing the fourth, special vowel [*Chirek* (i)] is Shin (שִׁ). This is the only such letter [in the Name].

There is one other letter that has the vowel [Shurek (u)] to itself, and this is the Nun (נֻ).

There is also another letter, Gimel (גִ), that shares the vowel [*Chirek* (i)] with the Shin. But although it is found in the alphabet and in books, it does not exist in the Name, because of a reason already discussed elsewhere.[123]

As you begin to pronounce each letter, begin to move your heart and your head. Since your heart is internal, move it mentally. But your head is external, and therefore, you must move it physically.

Move your head following the actual form of the vowel point associated with the letter that you are pronouncing.

This is the form of the head motions:

The vowel point written above the letter is called *Cholem (o,* אֹ). This is the only vowel point above the letter, since all the others are written beneath the letter.

When you pronounce [the *Cholem*] together with the letters Yod (י) or Kof (ק), begin facing directly straight ahead. Do not incline your head to the right or left, upward or downward. Keep your head straight and even, like the balance of a scale, just as it would be if you were speaking face to face to a person of the same height as yourself.

Then, as you draw out the sound of the letter while you pronounce it, begin to move your head so as to face upward, toward the sky. Close your eyes, open your mouth, and let the words shine. Clear your throat of all phlegm, so that it should not disturb your pronunciation. As you exhale, continue to raise your head at the same rate, so that you complete the exhalation and head motion simultaneously. If you complete the head motion before the exhalation, do not lower your head until you have exhaled completely.

Between each letter, you may rest and prepare yourself. At this time, you can take as many as three breaths, like those associated with the pronunciation. [Each triplet will therefore involve twelve breaths.]

The mystery of these "twelve breaths" (*YB Neshimot,* י"ב נשימות = 818) is the "Seventy-Two Names" (*EB Shemot,* ע"ב שמות = 818).

These are bound	הם משבעות = 818
Until they raise	אשר ישאו = 818
A change, a change in nature	שנוי שנוי הטבע = 818

Through Names when they build בשמות בבנוי = 818
In the calculation of attributes בחשבון מדות = 818
Which are [HH] beneath the Name. תחת ה ה = 818

However, the mystery of all
the letters האווית = 828
depends on
twenty-two breaths כ״ב נשימות = 828
which are
under the glory. תחת ההוד = 828
Furthermore,
their parts are tripled חלקים שליש = 828
and they parallel the
seventy-two Sefirot ע״ב ספירות = 828
which in man are
seventy-two thoughts. ע״ב מחשבות = 828

But the
twelve breaths, י״ב נשימות = 828
whose mystery is the
seventy-two Names, ע״ב שמות = 818
are the
seal of the Satan. חותם השטן = 818

["The Satan"(השטן), plus an additional unit for the word itself, adds up to 365, the days of the year.] For this mystery, we must pronounce the twelve months. [The reason for this is that the word for "month," *Chodesh* (חדש = 312), is equal to twelve Divine Names (יהוה = 26); 12 × 26 = 312.] This is for the sinners in Israel, whose bodies are judged in Gehinom for twelve months.[124]

And two "houses" (triplets) ושני בתים = 818
contain
twelve breaths. י״ב נשימות = 818.

Their mystery if Vav Vav (ו ו), that is, six and six,
as I alluded in the
seventy-two names ע״ב שמות = 818

that are pronounced.

These breaths give rise to a third triplet, and this gives a total of eighteen [meaning "life" (*Chai*, חי = 18).]

They will increase for you
years of life — שנות חיים = 824
which are
eighteen breaths — י״ח נשימות = 824
from the two Chayot — משני חיות = 824
in which there is
the lifeforce of breath. — חיות הנשמה = 824

You have
two nostrils — שני נחירים = 678
whose mystery is the heaven called
Aravot. — ערבות = 678
Understand this, for these are
the nostrils of the soul — נחירי הנשמה = 678
and their mystery is
two Cherubs — כרובים שנים = 678
which make
the Divine Presence descend — מבריכי השכינה = 678

The Divine Presence then dwells on earth, speaking to man, "from above the ark cover, from between the two Cherubs" (Exodus 25:22).

For the
primeval substance — חמר ראשון = 805
is on the ark cover — על הכפרת = 805
like the form of
the rainbow. — הקשת = 805

The two Cherubs allude to the Divine Presence (*HaShekihnah*, השכינה = 390). They are cause and effect, male and female (*Zachar U'Nekevah*, זכר ונקבה = 390). They were therefore forged (*miksheh*) as a single body with two forms.[125] They look at each other, and the Name was between them.

All of this was like a tree
on the ark cover, — על הכפרת = 805
and because of
the rainbow (*HaKeshet*) — הקשת = 805
it had to be
forged (*Miksheh*). — מקשה = 445
These are the overseers
over the Name — על השם = 445
which is

the name of the category	שם המין = 445
out of which comes	
every soul.	כל נשמה = 445
And now	
the sorcerer	המכשיף = 445
depends on these techniques, and therefore	
every soul	כל נשמה = 445
is a witch.	מכשיפה = 445

The Torah, however, says, "Do not let a witch live" (Exodus 22:17). This means that "every soul" shall not live. Regarding the vengeance against the wicked, God therefore commanded, "Do not let 'every soul' live" (Deuteronomy 20:16).[126]

However,	
the breath	הנשימה = 410
which is	
from the second one	מהשניה = 410
is a	
holy	קדש = 410
tabernacle	משכן = 410
in the heart.	
One ascends	
with the Unique Name	בשם מיוחד = 410
to the sky	לרקיע = 410
to depict with Unifications	לציר ביחודים = 410
the relationship	ההקש = 410
between everything that	
is difficult	הקשה = 410
in this	בזאת = 410
science of pronunciation.	החכמה מן ההזכרה = 410
It alone is	
life in the Name.	חיים בשם = 410
It is remembered and sealed	
in the Book of Life	בספר החיים = 410
to make the individual live	
with passion	בחשק = 410
which enlightens [the soul]	המשכילה = 410
constantly, when	
every thought,	כל מחשבה = 410
every soul	כל נשמה = 410
is concentrated on it.	

Therefore, one who pronounces the Name so as to always live with it, is serving God with love, and all the reward is his alone. In His wisdom, this is what God desired.

The vowel point which is called *Kametz (a,* ָ), looks like a line with a dot below it.

When you pronounce it with one of the ten associated letters, chant the letter, and move your head from left to right in a straight line, as if to trace the top of this vowel point. Then bring your head back so that you are facing directly forward, toward the east, since you are facing this direction when you pronounce the Name. This practice must be done while one faces the east, just as in the case of formal worship.

Conclude by bowing down slightly [so as to parallel the dot beneath the line of the *Kametz*]. Complete [the exhalation and head movement] simultaneously, as I instructed you by the first vowel.

The next vowel is the *Tzeré* (e, אֵ), which looks like two dots next to each other, one to the right, and one to the left.

As you pronounce it with one of its seven associated letters, begin the pronunciation and the motion simultaneously. Move your head from right to left, the reverse of what you did the the *Kametz* . . .

When you pronounce the Shin, you will make use of the *Chirek* (i, אִ) which has the form of a single dot below the letter.

As you pronounce it, move your head downward, as if you were bowing down to God, who is standing before you, and to whom you are speaking. This is the precise opposite of the head motion associated with the *Cholam*.

With these four vowels, you have crowned God as King [over the four directions].

When you pronounce a Nun, also make Him King. Begin by looking straight ahead, stretching your neck forward as much as you can. Do not raise or lower your head, but keep it facing straight forward.

This is the form of the *Shurek*. It consists of three dots, one under the other, like this (אֻ). It can also be a single dot in the center of a Vav, like this (אוּ). Both cases imply the same thing.

Through these five vowels, you have crowned God as King in all six directions of the universe. These are up and down with o (אֹ) and i (אִ), right and left with the a (אָ) and e (אֵ), and backward and forward with the u (אֻ).

[These vowels are often written together with their associated letters: AoO (אוֹ = 7), AaH (אָה = 6), AeY (אֵי = 11), AiY (אִי = 11), and AuU (אוּ = 7). They all add up to 42.]

All the vowels therefore point to the fact that they are "in God's Hand" (*BeYad YHVH*, ביד יהוה = 42). This is alluded to in the verse, "Let us fall *in God's Hand,* for His mercies are great, but let me not fall into the hand of man" (2 Samuel 24:14).

Their mystery is:

God	אלוה = 42
my only One	יחידי = 42
in them	בם = 42
my heart	לבי = 42
will be worthy.	יזכה = 42

And this mystery is

Enough! Enough! Enough! די די די = 42

And if, heaven forbid, when you pronounce these two verses, you still do not receive the divine influx, speech, or a visible vision of a man or some other prophetic vision, start again, and begin the third verse.

This is its form:

VaHeVa DaNuYo HeChe Shi וְהֶוָ דָנֻיֹ הֶחֶשִׁ
EaMeMe NuNuAa NuYoTha עָמֶמֶ נֻנֻאָ נֻיֹתָ

When you complete the entire Name, and receive from it whatever God wishes to grant you, praise God and thank Him.

If you are not successful in attaining what you have sought from God, you must realize that you must repent completely. Cry because of your lack of elevation, and because you pronounced the Name with ulterior motives, which is an extraordinary sin. You have not been fit to receive God's blessing. In the Torah, God promised that He would bless us with His Name, as it is written, "In every place where (*asher*) I will pronounce My Name, I will come to you and will bless you" (Exodus 20:21). [God is saying,] "I will pronounce My Name when you pronounce my Name."

[The word "where" (*Asher,* אשר)in this verse has the same letters as *Rosh* (ראש), the word for "head."] The mystery indicated here is that one must pronounce the Name with his head, as I have taught you.

The priest blesses the people with the Name, and he himself is also blessed. Every priest who does not bless, is himself not blessed.

With all this, "My son, despise not the rebuke of God, and do not spurn His correction" (Proverbs 3:11). Wait a while and then make another attempt to pronounce His fearsome Name, until you are worthy of something.

You may also attempt to use one of the Ten Names [of God used in the Bible. God says, "I will come to you and bless you,"] and the numerical value of "I will come" (*Aboa*, אבוא) is ten.

All of this may also be a test. God may be testing you to see whether you will deny Him or will still have faith. So be careful and guard your soul, lest you see any iniquity or unfairness in God. . . . "If it is empty, it is from you." [127]

This completes the entire Kabbalah tradition regarding the pronunciation of the Name. If you accustom yourself to do it, you will be successful and will attain enlightenment.

Life of the Future World.[128]

8. GATES OF RIGHTEOUSNESS

Although Abulafia presents an excellent overview of his methods, he does not fit them together into a single system, nor does he discuss the form of his experiences in any detail. This is left to an anonymous disciple, author of *Shaarey Tzion* (Gates of Righteousness), a book that was most probably written in the year 1295 in Hebron.[129] A clue to the identity of the author is provided in another manuscript, which indicates that the author's name was Shem Tov. As mentioned earlier, Abulafia had a disciple by the name of Shem Tov of Borgus, and it is highly probable that he is the author of this book.

There is very little question that the master mentioned in this book is none other than Abulafia himself. And for the most part, the material here appears to parallel that in other works by Abulafia.[130] Most important, however, is an autobiographical sketch, where the author speaks of his experience with Abulafia, describing his initial skepticism and ultimate enlightenment. We will not include this here, however, since it has already been published elsewhere in English.[131]

Numerous copies of this book were made, and it exerted an important influence on the later Kabbalists of the Holy Land. Almost an entire chapter was copied two hundred years later in the main work of Rabbi Judah Albotini, whom we shall discuss in the next section. Another important Kabbalah text, *Shoshan Sodot* (Rose of Mysteries), actually quotes it by name.

The author speaks of three ways through which one can divest himself of the physical: the common way, the philosophical way, and the Kabbalistic way. The common way involves a method called "erasure" (*mechikah*), where one attempts to erase all images from the mind.[132] The author notes that he was aware that the Moslem Sufis also made use of this technique, and that one method involved the repeated chanting of the name "Allah."[133] Although the Sufis are able to attain a degree of ecstasy in this manner, the author writes that they cannot know its significance, since they are not party to the Kabbalah tradition.

Discussing the philosophical way, the author speaks of a certain philosopher by the name of Ben Sina, who wrote many volumes while in a state of meditation (*hitbodedut*). When an idea was particularly difficult, he would concentrate on it and ponder it, often drinking a cup of strong wine, enabling him to sleep on it.[134] This is of particular interest, since a very similar procedure is also discussed by Rabbi Isaac of Acco, and this is one indication that the two shared a common tradition.[135]

It is in discussing the way of Kabbalah that the author mentions his master, who is identified as Abulafia. The master spent four months teaching him the methods of letter permutations, telling him to erase everything from his mind. Finally he told him, "The goal is not to stop at any finite form, even though it is of the highest order. Through the way of Divine Names, one can reach a level where the power is not under his control. The more incomprehensible the Names, the greater is their advantage."[136]

The master then showed him books composed of utterly incomprehensible Names and number combinations, saying, "This is the Path of Names." The author spent two months deeply meditating on these, and finally, one night, he awoke to see a light shining from his face. At first he did not believe what he was seeing, but no matter where he walked in the dark, this light followed him, even when he hid under a blanket. He was aware that this was something that could not be explained in any natural manner.

Upon informing the master of this experience, the author was told to spend half his time permuting letters, and half making use of the Divine Names. One night while permuting the letters of the Name of Seventy-Two, he began to see the letters expanding before his eyes, growing until they looked like great mountains.[137] His hair stood on end, and he began to speak automatically, saying words of wisdom.

On a later occasion, the author made use of a technique involving the Tetragrammaton. At first, he felt as if he would die, but after saying a sincere prayer, he suddenly felt as if he were being anointed with oil from head to toe.[138] He then felt a tremendous spiritual experience, which he speaks of as indescribable sweetness of rapture and ecstasy.

An excerpt from

The Rose of Mysteries[139]

"The power of the prophets to liken a form to its Creator" is a very great mystery. . . . I found an ancient teaching that explains this, and I will write it down here. . . . These are the author's words:

The following was told to me by the enlightened sage, Rabbi Nathan, of blessed memory:[140]

When an individual completely enters the mystery of prophecy, he suddenly sees his own image standing before him. He becomes totally unaware of his own essence, as if it were concealed from him. Then he sees his own image standing before him, speaking to him and telling him of the future. It is regarding this mystery that our sages say, "Great is the power of the prophets, since they liken a form to its Creator."[141]

Rabbi [Abraham] ibn Ezra (1089—1164) likewise taught, "He who hears is a man, and he who speaks is a man." [142]

Regarding this, another sage writes:

Through letter combinations and meditation (*hitbodedut*), I had a number of experiences. One involved a light, that followed me wherever I went, as I discussed in *Shaarey Tzedek* (Gates of Righteousness). However, I was never worthy of attaining a level where I could see my own image standing in front of me.

Still another sage writes:

I am aware how insignificant I am, and I realize that I am certainly not a prophet or a disciple of the prophets. I have neither attained *Ruach HaKodesh* (Holy Spirit), nor have I made use of a heavenly voice (*Bat Kol*). Of such things, I have not been worthy, for I have not divested myself of my "cloak" or "washed my feet." [143] But I call heaven and earth as my witnesses, that this account is true.

One day, I was sitting and writing mysteries in the manner of Truth. Suddenly, it was as if I had ceased to exist. I then saw my own image standing in front of me. As a result of this, I was forced to stop writing.

In his commentary on the *Guide to the Perplexed*, Rabbi Moshe of Narbonne (d. 1362) writes:[144]

When the sages teach that the prophets "liken a form to its Creator," they mean that they liken the form which is in the prophet's own soul . . . to its Creator, that is, to God. It is thus written, "Over the form of the Throne there was a form like an image of a Man" (Ezekiel

1:26). These forms and images exist in the soul of the prophet. . . .

This also happened to us when we were writing this book. Once, in the late afternoon, we were placing the vowel points on the Explicit Name. All at once, our eyes were confronted with visions, appearing like definite forms made of red fire. This occurred a number of times while we were writing this book.

9. THE LADDER OF ASCENT

The teachings of Abulafia are known to have come to the Holy Land through the author of *Shaarey Tzedek*, and it appears that they took firm root there. Over two hundred years later, we find one of the prominent sages of the Holy Land, a chief rabbi of Jerusalem, involved in these mysteries and authoring an important book on Abulafia's teachings. This is none other than Rabbi Judah Albotini (1453—1519), author of *Sulam HaAliyah* (Ladder of Ascent).

Albotini is known to Talmudic scholars as the author of a supercommentary on Maimonides' commentary on the Mishnah. This was published by Rabbi Shlomo Idni (1567—1626), author of another important commentary on the Mishnah.[145] Written in 1501, this supercommentary is included in the most important edition of the Mishnah. Not as well-known is Albotini's monumental commentary on Maimonides' code, which exists only in manuscript.[146]

Not too much is known of the personal life of Albotini, other than the fact that his father, Moshe Albotini, was a prominent scholar in Lisbon. It is highly probable that the family was exiled in 1496, during the general expulsion of Jews from Portugal. This is significant, since Rabbi Judah Chayit, a strong opponent of Abulafia's teachings, also left Portugal during this same expulsion. The fact that Chayit found it necessary to denounce Abulafia's writings indicates that they enjoyed a degree of popularity in his homeland.

Albotini migrated to the Holy Land, and by 1509, we find him as a member of the Jerusalem academy, where he signed an ordinance exempting scholars from the head tax. He succeeded Rabbi Jacob of Triel as head of the Jerusalem Academy, making him the official head of all the Rabbis of Jerusalem. It would appear that Abulafia's school of meditative Kabbalah was sufficiently accepted in Jerusalem at the time that a practitioner and teacher of these methods could be chosen as a chief Rabbi. A short time later, we find another teacher of these methods, Rabbi Joseph Tzayach, also holding a rabbinical post in Jerusalem.

A manuscript of *Sulam HaAliyah* was in the hands of the great Kabbalist, Rabbi Sasoon bekhor Moshe Presiado (d. 1903), and from what he writes, he actually intended to publish it.[147] Although he never succeeded in doing so, a number of key chapters have been published in scholarly journals. Several manuscripts of this book exist, both in libraries and in private collections.[148]

In this book, Albotini speaks about the Meditative Kabbalists (*MeKubalim HaMitbodedim*), as if they were a well-established group in his time.[149] Speaking about other books on the subject of letter manipulation (*tzeruf*) that had recently been written, he warns that they contain many errors.[150] He is thoroughly familiar with Abulafia's system, upon many of whose teachings he expands, presenting them in a clear and well-ordered manner. In two places, he mentions Abulafia's *Chayay Olam HaBah* (Life of the Future World) by name.[151]

The first few chapters of the book deal mostly with word and letter manipulation (*tzeruf*), drawing heavily on Abulafia's works. Because this involves the letters of the Hebrew alphabet, it is virtually impossible to do justice to this method in English. The individual interested in pursuing the subject further can find an excellent summary in the published works of the Ramak.[152]

Another idea that Albotini discusses in detail is that of "jumping" (*kefitzah*) and "skipping" (*dilug*). Although this is mentioned by Abulafia, and the method was undoubtedly used by him, he does not present a clear picture how one makes use of it.[153] Albotini not only clearly describes these techniques within Abulafia's system of *Tzeruf*, but he also provides a number of examples showing how they are used.

Briefly, "skipping" consists of a sort of free association, using any one of the standard methods of letter manipulation. This can consist of simple letter permutation, the use of ciphers, or finding other words with similar numerical values (*gematria*). Words can also be expanded in a number of ways, the simplest being to spell out different letters of the word. As long as one is making use of a single system, such as *gematria* for example, he is said to be "skipping." When he goes from one system of letter manipulation to another, then he is said to be "jumping." All of this was seen as an important meditative technique through which one could attain a high level of enlightenment.[154]

An important prerequisite for attaining the meditative experience is stoicism (*hishtavut*,הִשְׁתַּוּוּת), and this is discussed at great length by

Albotini.[155] This has been discussed by a number of later kabbalists, but Abulafia only speaks about it in passing, writing, "One who has attained true passion (*cheshek*), is not influenced by the blessings or curses of others. It is as if they were speaking in a language that he does not understand." [156] Albotini's teachings regarding stoicism, however, seems to come from Rabbi Isaac of Acco, who speaks of this idea at length. This is of particular significance, since it would indicate that Albotini was a student of Rabbi Isaac of Acco as well as of Abulafia.

Albotini also expands on Abulafia's discussion of Hewing (*chatzivah*) and Engraving (*chakikah*), mentioned in the *Sefer Yetzirah*. When a person reaches a high meditative level, "the mind is no longer concealed in the prison of the physical faculties, and it emerges . . . entering the spiritual domain." In this domain, the individual may see various visions or letter combinations, and the connotation of Hewing is that he "splits" and analyzes these visions while still in a meditative state. Engraving then implies that he "engraves" these revelations in his soul so that they are never forgotten.[157]

Although Albotini speaks of a number of standard meditative techniques, Albotini maintained that any proper teaching could serve as the subject of one's meditation. He thus writes, "Those who meditate (*hitboded*), concentrate on an idea or on a very deep lesson. They close their eyes, and virtually nullify all their faculties in order to allow their hidden intellect to emerge from potential to action. They then absorb the lesson, permanently engraving it in their soul." [158]

Through the use of Divine Names in meditation, one can channel extremely powerful spiritual forces. Albotini writes that Moses made use of this to save Israel, and that, "with the power of the Divine Names, which he pronounced in his prayers, he was able to turn back the anger and fury." [159] More remarkable, he states that the Ten Martyrs could have saved themselves by using these Names, and that the sages could have even prevented the destruction of Jerusalem at the hand of the Babylonians and Romans. But, seeing that this had been God's decree, they refrained from doing anything.

The Talmud speaks of three oaths that Israel made not to improperly hasten the coming of the Messiah. This is based on the verse, "I bind you by an oath, O daughters of Jerusalem, . . . that you not awaken, that you not arouse the love, until it is desired" (Song of Songs 3:5).[160] There has been much discussion of this oath, and some rabbis have even used it as a refutation of Zionism.

Albotini provides a very novel interpretation of this oath, saying that the great masters of Kabbalah meditation were bound by an oath not to use their methods to hasten the redemption. He thus writes, "Even though the coming of the Messiah is a great concept, necessary for the rectification of all Universes, the sages and saints who knew the mystery of God's name were bound by an oath not to arouse the redemption until they knew that God desired that it should occur." [161]

In general, Albotini warns against pronouncing any of the Divine Names, even those discussed by Abulafia. Anticipating the Ari, he understands that, while earlier generations may have been able to purify themselves sufficiently so that they could actually pronounce the Names, later generations are no longer able to do this. But still, he maintains that it is not actually necessary to pronounce the Names, and that much can be accomplished by merely knowing them and pondering their significance.

This is evidenced from the verse, "He was enraptured in Me, I will bring him forth, I will raise him up, because he knew My Name" (Psalms 91:14). Albotini notes that the verse does not say, "he pronounces My name," but rather, it says, "he knows My name." He concludes, "from this we see that the main thing is the knowledge of the Divine Names, of their existence, essence, and meaning." [162] A similar explanation is also provided to the verse, "Before they call I will answer them" (Isaiah 65:24). "Even though one concentrates on a given name and only thinks about it, without 'calling' and actually pronouncing it, he will be answered."

CHAPTER FOUR

Other Early Schools

1. THE GATE OF KAVANAH

Although much of the early explicit material regarding Kabbalah meditation stems from Abulafia's writings, there were also a number of other schools contemporary to him. The most important was the school in Provence, France, which was heir to the mystical teachings of the Bahir, and eventually published this book in the late 1100's.

Until the Twelfth Century, the Kabbalah had been a carefully concealed mystery, in the hands of a few very small and restricted secret societies. So hidden were these that some of the greatest rabbinical leaders were not even aware of their existence. The first ones to break this silence were the great Kabbalists of Provence.

The earliest known members of this school were Isaac and Jacob Nazir, both of Lunel. The title Nazir indicated that they had separated themselves from all worldly activities, devoting all their time to worship and the study of the Torah. The community supported a number of such individuals, creating an atmosphere where the contemplative life necessary for the teaching of the Kabbalah and its methods could flourish.

Another important member of this group was Rabbi David ben Isaac, head of the rabbinical court, whose son was the famed Raavad (Rabbi Abraham ben David of Posqueres, 1120—1198), renowned as the author of the standard gloss on Maimonides' Code. A master of the mystical arts, the Raavad received the tradition from his father, as well as from his father-in-law, the famed Rabbi Abraham ben Isaac of Narbonne, best known as the author of the *Eshkol*. In his legal commentaries, the Raavad actually writes that his school was subject to divine inspiration and the revelations of mysteries.[1]

The Raavad's son, known as Isaac the Blind, inherited leadership of the school from his father, and brought it to Provence. Even though he was blind, he was reputed to be able to look into a person's soul and see his thoughts. In his commentary on the Torah, Rabbi Bachya ben Asher (1276—1340) calls him the "father of Kabbalah." [2]

Rabbi Isaac the Blind had two disciples, Rabbi Ezra and Rabbi Azriel, both of Gerona. They assumed leadership of the school, and authored a number of very interesting books on the Kabbalah. It is from them that the Kabbalah tradition passed to the Ramban (Rabbi Moshe ben Nachman, Nachmanides, 1194—1270), one of the most important religious scholars and leaders of that period.

It is most probably from Rabbi Azriel of Gerona that we have one of the very few works describing the meditative methods used by the Provence school. This is the *Shaar HaKavanah LeMekubalim HaRishonim (The Gate of Kavanah* of the Early Kabbalists). This short essay exists in a large number of manuscripts, and is reproduced in its entirety in the unpublished Fourth Section of Rabbi Chaim Vital's *Shaarey Kedushah.*[3] Here, we find a system of meditation very different than that of Abulafia, even though it appears that he was aware of it.

This text speaks of *Kavanah* (כַּוָּנָה)in a very remarkable context. The word itself is very difficult to translate, having a number of important connotations. At various times, the word *Kavanah* has been defined as concentration, attention, devotion, and intention. It actually means all of these things and more, the sum being greater than its parts. In many places in this book, we have translated *Kavanah* as "concentration." Here, however, it appears to have the connotation of actual meditation, and a similar use of the word seems to be found in the writings of the Ari.

The *Gate of Kavanah* speaks of meditation based on light, where one elevates the mind from one light to a higher one. It is significant to note that two of these lights are called *Bahir* (brilliant) and *Zohar,* (radiant), alluding to the two most important Kabbalistic classics.[4] One ascends until he reaches the Infinite, which is called *Ain Sof* (אין סוף). Since one reaches this level by meditating on light, the highest level is often spoken of as the Infinite Light (*Or Ain Sof*) in Kabbalistic literature. There is considerable speculation as to the symbolism of light in the spiritual realm, but from this text, it appears to be related primarily to the meditative technique through which it is visualized.

Although a number of different types of light are mentioned in this brief essay, they are not clearly defined. The *Gate of Kavanot,* however, appears to have been well-known to Rabbi Moshe de Leon

Correspondence Between the Lights and the Sefirot

Light		Sefirah	
Tov	Good	*Chesed*	Love
Nogah	Glow	*Gevurah*	Strength
Kavod	Glory	*Tiferet*	Beauty
Bahir	Brilliance	*Netzach*	Victory
Zohar	Radiance	*Hod*	Splendor
Chaim	Life	*Yesod*	Foundtion

(See Part Four of *Shaarey Kedushah*, p. 19b.)

(1238—1305), best known as the publisher of the Zohar. In his *Shekel HaKodesh* (Holy Coin), written in 1292, he clearly explains the meaning of these types of light. It is significant to note that although the Zohar speaks of different colors with regard to fire, its system appears quite different from that of its publisher.[5]

The Gate of Kavanah[6]

When a person sets his mind on something, its essence returns to him.

Therefore, if you wish to pray, or if you wish to grasp the true nature of an idea, do the following:

Imagine that you yourself are light, and that all of your surroundings, on every side, are also light.

In the middle of this light is a Throne of light.

Above this Throne is a light called *Nogah* (Glow).[7]

Facing this is [another] Throne. Above the [second Throne] is a light called *Tov* (Good).[8]

You are standing between the two.

If you wish to take revenge, turn to the *Nogah*.

If you wish to seek mercy, turn to the *Tov*.

The words that you speak should be directed toward [this light].

Now turn yourself to the right of it, and there you will find [another] light. This is a light that is called *Bahir* (Brilliant).[9]

To its left you will [also] find a light. This is a light called *Zohar* (Radiant).[10]

Above these two, directly between them, is a light called *Kavod* (Glory).

Around it is a light called *Chaim* (Life).

Above it is the Crown.

This is the light that crowns the desires of the mind and illuminates the paths of the imagination, enhancing the radiance (*zohar*) of the vision. This light has no end, and it cannot be fathomed. From the glory (*Kavod*) of its perfection comes desire, blessing, peace, life (*chaim*), and all good (*tov*) to those who keep the way of its unification.

It is hidden from those who stray from the path of this light, and is transformed into its precise opposite. [It then results] in rebuke and punishment.

[The true path is] straight, depending on the concentration (*kavanah*) of the individual. He must know how to concentrate on its truth with attachment of thought and desire, derived from its unfathomable power.

According to the strength of his concentration, he will then transmit power through his desire, desire through his knowledge, imagination through his thoughts, strength through his effort, and fortitude through his contemplation.

When there is no other thought or desire intermingled with [his concentration] it can become so strong, that it can transmit an influence from the Infinite (*Ain Sof*).

The entire process is then consciously completed, according to the individual's desire. One must know how to trim away the surrounding fringes, the conscious desires [which draw him away] from the primary goal. These all come from the individual himself, and he can therefore elevate himself above them through the power of his concentration.

He can then probe very deeply, and break away from the crooked path.[11] Through the power of his meditation, the individual can then blaze a new path.

He elevates himself over them[12] with the power of his concentration, which comes from the glory *(kavod)* of the perfection of the Concealed Light. [This is a light that] cannot be seen, depicted, measured, estimated or probed, and it has neither boundary or end. It is infinite in every way.

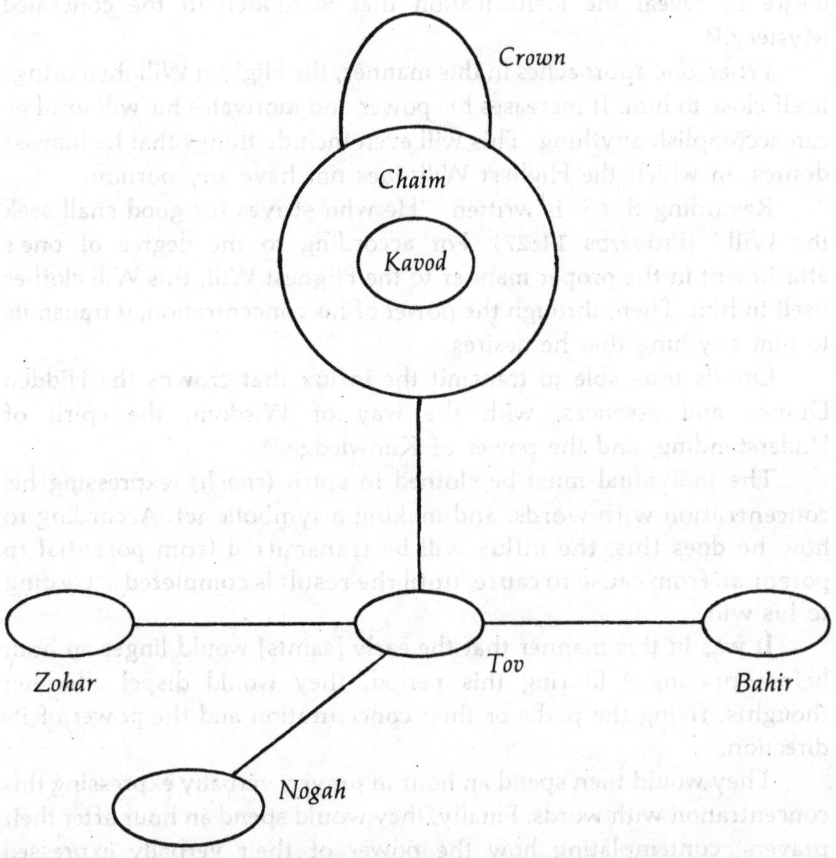

An individual thus ascends with the power of his concentration from one thing to the next, until he reaches the Infinite (*Ain Sof*).

He must then direct his concentration in a proper manner so as to perfect it, so that the Highest Will should be clothed in his will, and not only that his will should be clothed in the Highest Will.

The highest influx does not descend except when the individual does this correctly. He must bring himself to the Highest Will in such a manner that the Highest Will clothes itself in the will of his desire.

The Highest Will and the lower will are then unified. The individual identifies himself with his attachment to the Unity. The divine influx can then be transmitted in order to perfect him.

The lower will is not perfected when the individual approaches for his own needs. Rather, one must approach while clothed in the will and desire to reveal the identification that is hidden in the concealed Mystery.[13]

When one approaches in this manner, the Highest Will then brings itself close to him. It increases his power and motivates his will until he can accomplish anything. This will even include things that he himself desires, in which the Highest Will does not have any portion.

Regarding this it is written, "He who strives for good shall seek the Will" (Proverbs 11:27). For according to the degree of one's attachment in the proper manner to the Highest Will, this Will clothes itself in him. Then, through the power of his concentration, it transmits to him anything that he desires.

One is thus able to transmit the influx that crowns the Hidden Desires and essences, with the way of Wisdom, the spirit of Understanding, and the power of Knowledge.[14]

The individual must be clothed in spirit (*ruach*), expressing his concentration with words, and making a symbolic act. According to how he does this, the influx will be transmitted from potential to potential, from cause to cause, until the result is completed according to his will.

It was in this manner that the early [saints] would linger an hour before praying.[15] During this period, they would dispel all other thoughts, fixing the paths of their concentration and the power of its direction.

They would then spend an hour in prayer, verbally expressing this concentration with words. Finally, they would spend an hour after their prayers, contemplating how the power of their verbally expressed concentration would have a visible effect.

[The Talmud thus teaches that] "Since they were saints (*Hasidim*), their Torah learning preserved itself and their work blessed itself." [16]

This is one of the ways of prophecy. One who accustoms himself to it will be worthy of attaining the prophetic level.[17]

An Excerpt From the Works of
Rabbi Moshe de Leon

The four appearances of light are the radiant *(zohar)* lights which are hidden and concealed. These come into being from the mysterious reality of [God's] essence, which is also hidden and concealed.

This is like the glow (*nogah*) that surrounds the eye's vision in the concealed sphere of radiance (*zohar*). It is not openly seen.

This sphere [of radiance] stands between four [paths of] concentration *(kavanah)* involving this glow *(nogah)*. These involve the light that is Scintilating (*Muvhak*), Brilliant (*Bahir*), Radiant (*Zohar*), like the "radiance of the sky." [18]

There are four type of radiance (*zohar*). They are Bahir light, Zohar light, Muvhak light, and light that receives Zohar.

Physical light always receives from spiritual light.

Thus, there are four different types of fire, and these are the ones that God showed to Moses. These are red fire, yellow fire, white fire, and black fire.[19] God told Moses about these four types of fire, and showed them to him on Mount Sinai.

These four types of fire parallel the four luminations under discussion. In a mystical sense, these four lights are the four "lights of the hosts" [that God showed Moses].[20]

The light under discussion, however, is hidden and concealed. It rotates the true Zohar light when the light [seen by] the closed eye rotates.

This is a hidden light that is never revealed. It cannot be seen in any way, other than in a concealed manner.

It is regarding this hidden, concealed light that [Moses] said, "Show me Your Glory" (Exodus 33:18).

This is the Light that gives rise to the four luminations under discussion, which are Bahir light, Zohar light, Muvhak light, and light that receives Zohar. These are the lights that can be seen.

Bahir light is the Shining Glass (*Ispaklaria*), which has the power to reflect.[21]

Zohar light is a glass that absorbs light. It then cannot be recognized except when it is revealed near a shining light.

Muvhak light is a Shining Glass in which the color of all lights is recognizable. Through its colors, all other Glasses are illuminated.

Light that receives Zohar is a Glass that does not shine. It receives all the other lights like a reflector that receives the radiance (*zohar*) of the sun, and it can be recognized in it.

The same is true of the light that receives Zohar. This light absorbs all other colors, and they are then visible inside it. When other colors come near it and shine into it, it absorbs them and gathers them in. The mark of each one is then recognizable in it.

This light is more readily revealed, since it is not very bright. Zohar light, on the other hand, is so bright that the eye cannot grasp it in any way. It is like the light of the sun, which is so intense (*zahir*) that the eye has no power [to see] it. Light that is less bright, however, can be grasped and revealed, and the eye is able [to see] it.

Whoever looks at this color can recognize the other colors, which are hidden and concealed in it, and which stand over it.

Contemplate that the other, higher colors can be recognized inside it. Still, they never appear to be scintillating (*Muvhak*) and radiant (*Zohar*), since they must be seen through visible light.

The prophets and other enlightened individuals only saw through this [light that receives Zohar, which is the] Glass that does not shine.[22] What they actually saw, however, was the Zohar, the Shining Glass.

When you look into the steps, you will find that all is one.

Gaze at a candle. You will find the black light at the bottom,[23] and the Bahir light at the top. But it is all one mystery and one light, and there is no separation whatsoever.

The Holy Coin.[24]

2. GATES OF LIGHT

One of the most important teachings of the Kabbalah involves the Ten Sefirot (Divine Emanations). It is therefore surprising to find that they hardly seem to find any place in Kabbalah meditation. Although there are some allusions, they are usually tenuous at best. There are a number of hints that the great early Kabbalists meditated on the Sefirot, using them as a ladder to reach the highest levels, but very little is mentioned about the method that they used. In general the early literature is silent about the relationship between meditation and the Sefirot.

There is, however, one important exception. This is a remarkable book *Shaarey Orah* (Gates of Light), by Rabbi Joseph Gikatalia (1248—1323).

Considered as one of the greatest Kabbalists of all time, Gikatalia was born in Medina Celi in Castile. It was there that, as a young man, he came under the influence of Abulafia, who apparently taught him his entire system. Shortly after this, he wrote his first book, *Ginat Egoz* (The Nut Garden), a title suggested by the verse, "I went down into the nut garden" (Song of Songs 6:11). Besides this, the word *Ginat* (גִּנַּת) is an acronym of *Gematria Notrikion Temurah*, three important methods of letter manipulation used by Abulafia. It is significant to note that the word *Ginat* is used in the same manner by Rabbi Baruch Targomi, one of Abulafia's teachers.[25]

Gikatalia's most important work, however, was his *Shaarey Orah*, which has been published in over a dozen editions. This book consists of an exposition of the Ten Sefirot and the Ten Divine Names that are associated with them. Strongly influenced by the Bahir, *Shaarey Orah* can actually be considered to be a key to this ancient Kabbalah classic. The Ari calls *Shaarey Orah* the key to the mystical teachings.

The Sefirot and Associated Names of God

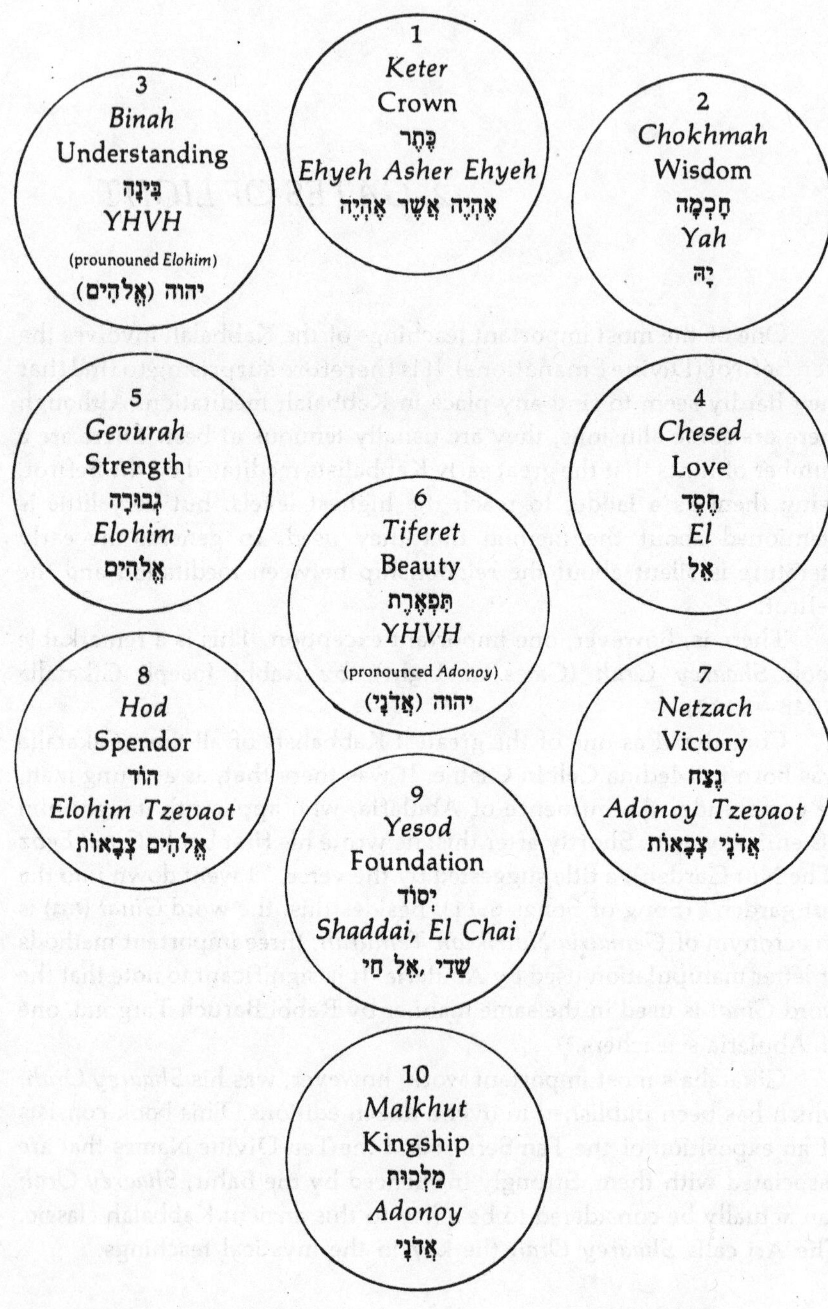
1
Keter
Crown
כֶּתֶר
Ehyeh Asher Ehyeh
אֶהְיֶה אֲשֶׁר אֶהְיֶה
3
Binah
Understanding
בִּינָה
YHVH
(prounouned *Elohim*)
יהוה (אֱלֹהִים)
2
Chokhmah
Wisdom
חָכְמָה
Yah
יָהּ
5
Gevurah
Strength
גְּבוּרָה
Elohim
אֱלֹהִים
4
Chesed
Love
חֶסֶד
El
אֵל
6
Tiferet
Beauty
תִּפְאֶרֶת
YHVH
(pronounced *Adonoy*)
יהוה (אֲדֹנָי)
8
Hod
Spendor
הוֹד
Elohim Tzevaot
אֱלֹהִים צְבָאוֹת
7
Netzach
Victory
נֶצַח
Adonoy Tzevaot
אֲדֹנָי צְבָאוֹת
9
Yesod
Foundation
יְסוֹד
Shaddai, El Chai
שַׁדַּי, אֵל חַי
10
Malkhut
Kingship
מַלְכוּת
Adonoy
אֲדֹנָי

At first, *Shaarey Orah* seems to be just another book on the theoretical Kabbalah, without any practical application. In a number of places, however, the author hints at the practical applications of this system. At the end of the book, he explicitly states, "I have given over to you ten keys, and with them you can enter gates that are otherwise closed."

Upon close examination, then, the book can be taken as a guide for those who wish to ascend spiritually through meditation on the ladder of the Sefirot. Indeed, in the unpublished Fourth Part of his *Shaarey Kedushah,* Rabbi Chaim Vital presents two selections from this book in precisely this light.[26] Abulafia might also have been alluding to this method when he speaks of using the Ten Names in meditation.[27]

When examined in this light, *Shaarey Orah* can be seen in its entirety as a guide to meditation on the Sefirot. The words and Divine Names associated with the Sefirot can be viewed as guides, helping one to meditate on particular Sefirot. They provide mental or verbal images upon which one can meditate, although the precise method of doing so is not explicitly defined. A chart of the Sefirot, as presented in *Shaarey Orah,* along with the Divine Names associated with them is provided here.

It is interesting to note that this book also exerted a profound influence on the "Christian Kabbalists." In 1516, forty-five years before the first Hebrew edition was printed, a Latin translation was published. This had been translated by Paul Ricci, and it came to the attention of the Christian mystic, Johann Reuchlin (1455—1522). When a group of Dominicans tried to convince Pope Leo X to confiscate and burn all Jewish books, Reuchlin made use of the Latin version of *Shaarey Orah* to convince the Pope of the value of Judaic teachings. As one of the few Kabbalistic works published in translation, *Shaarey Orah* exerted a powerful influence on many occult groups in Europe.

There are a number of places where *Shaarey Orah* speaks specifically about meditative techniques, and these will be presented here.

Excerpts From

The Gates of Light

You have asked me, my brother, beloved of my soul, to enlighten you regarding the path involving God's names so that through them you will gain what you wish and reach what you desire. Since I see that your intent is upright and good, I will go beyond your request and show you where the Light can be found, explaining what God desires and what He does not desire. When you grasp this knowledge, then you will be among those close to God — "You will call, and God will answer" (Jeremiah 58:9).

The earlier sages had many Holy Names, which they had received as a tradition from the Prophets. These included the Name of Seventy-Two, the Name of Forty-Two, the Name of Twelve, and many other Holy Names. Through these names, they were able to bring about miracles and wonders, but they never used them for their own needs. Such was reserved for a time of evil decree, or to sanctify God's holy Name....

The boundary of truth and the tradition ofthe covenant is this. If one wishes to attain what he desires through the use of God's Names, he must first study the Torah with all this might, so that he can grasp the meaning of every one of God's Names mentioned in the Torah. These names are Ehyeh (אֶהְיֶה), Yah (יָהּ), YHVH (יהוה), Adonoy (אֲדֹנָי), El (אֵל), Elo'ah (אֱלוֹהַּ), Elohim (אֱלֹהִים), Shadai (שַׁדַּי), and Tzevaot (צְבָאוֹת). One must know and understand that each of these names is like a key for all of his needs, no matter what they are.

When a person contemplates these Names, he will find that the entire Torah and all the commandments depend on them. If one knows the meaning of all these Names, he will understand the greatness of He who spoke and brought the universe into being. He will fear God, yearning and pining to bind himself to Him through his knowledge of these Names. He will then be close to God, and his prayers will be answered.

Regarding this, it is written, "I will raise him up because he knows My Name" (Psalms 91:14). The verse does not say, "I will answer him," but "I will raise him up." Furthermore, it does not say, "because he pronounced My Name," but "because he knows My Name." This is because the main thing is knowledge.[28]

[When a person has such a knowledge,] then he can call and God will answer him. This means that when he needs something and concentrates on the Name associated with his need, he will be answered.[29]

. . .

The first Name is closest to all created things. It is through this Name that one enters the presence of God the King. Other than through this Name, there is no other way whatsoever that one can see the face of the Blessed King.

This Name is Adonoy (אֲדֹנָי). [It is the name associated with Malkhut-Kingship, the lowest Sefirah.]

The Unique Name, YHVH (יהוה), denotes the essence of our Blessed Creator, and everything depends on it. However, the first gate, and the opening through which one enters to reach God, is the Name Adonoy.

This is the lowest level of the Divine. From the level of Adonoy and above, we find the mystery of Unity. . . . Below this is the world of separation. . . .

The Name Adonoy is like a storehouse and a treasury. It holds all influx and every emanation that is transmitted through all spiritual channels from YHVH.

There are three names, one above the other. Adonoy is on the bottom, YHVH is in the middle, and Ehyeh is on top. It is from the Name Ehyeh that all kinds of sustenance emanate, coming from the Source, which is the Infinite (*Ain Sof*). It then proceeds through a series of steps until it reaches the blessed name, YHVH. From the Name YHVH all spiritual channels flow and the flux is transmitted to the name Adonoy. The Name Adonoy is therefore the storehouse containing all of the King's devices, and it is the essence that distributes these to all creation. It nourishes and sustains all things, through the power of YHVH that is in it.

It is by the order [of Adonoy] that all who approach to attach themselves to YHVH may enter and leave. There is absolutely no way that one can attach himself to YHVH except through Adonoy.

[Adonoy] is therefore the treasury of the Unique Name [YHVH] It is the Palace in which YHVH dwells.[30] It is for this reason that whenever the name YHVH appears in the Torah, it is read as Adonoy. This is because one who seeks YHVH only finds it in the name Adonoy.

There are a total of 54 ways in which the four letters of YHVH can be permuted. [Since each of these permutations contains four letters] all of them yield a total of 216 letters. These 54 names are the mystery of the transmission of power to all that exists, in all creation. They are like a soul to the 216 letters of the Name of Seventy-Two Triplets.[31]

. . .

One who attaches himself to [Adonoy] is worthy of eternal life.

Permutations of the Tetragrammaton

Form		*Number of Permutations*
YHVH	יהוה	12
YYVH	ייוה	12
YVVH	יווה	12
YYVV	ייוו	6
YYHH	ייהה	6
VVHH	ווהה	6
		54

This is alluded to in the verse, "And you, who are attached to YHVH your God, you are all alive today" (Deuteronomy 4:4).

Our sages question this, and ask, "Is it then possible to attach oneself to the Divine Presence?" [32] Although their question is valid, this is only true in a homeletic sense. In a mystical sense, one can indeed attach himself.

God therefore said, "You shall fear YHVH your God, Him shall you serve, and to Him you shall attach yourself" (Deuteronomy 10:20). . . .

Know and believe that there is a method involving the mystical purification of the limbs, through which it is possible for a human being to attach himself to the Divine Presence, even though it is a "consuming fire." [33] Actually, it is a fire that provides delight and ecstasy to those who attach themselves to it with a pure soul.

It is therefore called the Lamp of God. It is what lights the Lamp of the Soul. The soul is then attached to it, and this is its desire.[34]

. . .

One who wishes to perceive Eternal Life should attach himself to the attribute of El Chai (Living God), [which is associated with the Sefirah of Yesod-Foundation].

This means that through his prayers, one should bring El Chai into Adonoy. It was regarding this that King David had passion and desire when he said, "My soul thirsts for God, for El Chai" (Psalms 42:3).

When the attribute (Yesod), which is called El Chai, is bound to Adonoy (Malkhut), then one can draw down all his needs. He can overcome his enemies, and no one can stand up to him. . . .

We must bind the Sefirot together, attaching all levels through the attribute of Adonoy (Malkhut-Kingship). We therefore say, "He chooses song of praise, King (Malkhut), Life (Yesod) of the world." [35] If one wishes to seek a good life, he should bind himself to the attribute of El Chai.

When a person is attached to Adonoy in purity, then he is also attached to El Chai. It is thus written, "And you, who are attached to YHVH your God, you are all alive (Chai) today" (Deuteronomy 4:4).[36]

. . .

If one wishes to attain these three things, [life, food or children], he cannot attain them as a matter of right in this world. They cannot be attained through merit, which [involves] the Tribunal on high.

How then can he attain these things?

One must elevate his concentration (*kavanah*) higher and higher. He must probe deeper than the Future World (Binah-Understanding), until he reaches the level of Keter-Crown, which is Ehyeh, which is [associated with] the Infinite (*Ain Sof*).

One thus reaches the level of the Thirteen Attributes of Mercy. One of these Thirteen Attributes is called Destiny (*mazal*, מַזָּל). The sages therefore teach, "Life, children and food do not depend on merit, but on Destiny." [37]

There is one thing that you must know and understand. Even though we say that one who wishes to attain what he desires from God should concentrate on a particular Divine Name, this does not mean that he should concentrate on that name and go no farther.

But the true intent is this: One must concentrate on the Name associated with the thing that he needs. He must then elevate his concentration on that Name until the top of the Ten Sefirot. He then reaches the Highest Source, which is called the Source of Desire. When one reaches the Source of Desire, then his request and the desire of his heart are fulfilled.

This is the meaning of the verse, "You open Your hand (*yadekha*), and satisfy all life desire"(Psalms 145:16). Do not read *Yadekha* (יָדֶךָ)– "Your hand" – but Yod-ekha (יוֹדֶךָ)–"Your Yod." [38] This means that God opens the mystery of the Yod (י) in the name YHVH (יהוה), which is the Source of Desire. He then fulfills the desire of all who ask.

One who wishes to attain from God what he desires must contemplate the Ten Sefirot. He must transmit Will and Desire from the highest to lowest, until he brings it to the Final Desire, which is the name Adonoy. The Sefirot are then blessed through him, and he is blessed through the Sefirot.

This is the mystery of the verse, "He who blesses himself on earth (Malkhut), blesses himself by the God of Amen" (Isaiah 65:16). The word Amen (אָמֵן) alludes to the mystery through which blessing is transmitted from the names Ehyeh and YHVH to the name Adonoy.

From this you learn that when one prays, he must concentrate in the manner that I have described. He must unify the Sefirot, and bring them close to each other...

When a person prays, he must concentrate and ascend from Sefirah to Sefirah, from desire to desire. He must continue in this manner until in his heart he reaches the Source of the Highest Will, which is called the Infinite (*Ain Sof*).

King David therefore said, "A song of steps, from the depths I call You O God (YHVH)" (Psalms 130:1). He is saying that he is calling God from His depths, that is, from the highest source, which is called the Infinite (*Ain Sof*). This is the depth which is the apex of the Yod of YHVH. He therefore said, "From the depths I call You YHVH."

And how does one concentrate?

One does so through a series of *steps* in an upward direction. He enters through the final Heh (ה) of the Name [which is associated with Malkhut-Kingship]. He then ascends from attribute to attribute, from Sefirah to Sefirah, until his mind elevates itself to the apex of the Yod, which is Keter-Crown. This is called the Infinite (*Ain Sof*), and it is the mystery of "the depths." [King David therefore called this] "A song of *steps*." . . .

These "depths" denote everything that is hidden, concealed, and difficult to grasp. It is therefore written, "That which was is far off, deep, deep, who can find it" (Ecclesiastes 7:24). The great mystery that includes all this is the verse, "Very deep are Your thoughts" (Psalms 92:6). You already know that the mystery of thought is the Yod of the Name YHVH. . . .

Now that we have taught you this, we can return to the main idea. When one concentrates, he must focus all his thoughts, until with absolute concentration, he reaches the Source of Will. This is the apex of the Yod, and it is the Depth of Thought. Regarding this it is written, "from the depths I call You, O God."[39]

. . .

The Tetragrammaton, YHVH, is like the trunk of a tree, while the other divine Names are like its branches.[40]

. . .

The Name YHVH is occasionally connected to Adonoy.

Sometimes YHVH comes first, and is followed by Adonoy. An example of this is the verse, "YHVH Adonoy is my strength, he makes my feet like hinds" (Habakkuk 3:19). Another example is, "God is to us a God of deliverance, and to YHVH Adonoy are the issues of death" (Psalms 68:21). Still another is, "My eyes are to You, YHVH Adonoy, in You I have taken refuge" (Psalms 141:8).

When the two names are pronounced together, YHVH is not read as Adnoy, but as Elohim. This alludes to the attribute of Binah-Understanding, which is being united with the attribute of Malkhut-Kingship, which is called Adonoy. Through Binah, it is unified with YHVH.

When one pronounces YHVH Adonoy (Elohim Adonoy) in this order, the influx descends through all the Sefirot, from the highest to the lowest, until the influx of blessing and essence reaches the name Adonoy. When this occurs, all the world is enhanced with a perfect blessing.

At other times, Adonoy is pronounced first, followed by YHVH. An example of this is, "Abraham said: Adonoy YHVH, what will You give me" (Genesis 15:2). Another example is, "Adonoy YHVH, You have begun to show Your servant Your greatness" (Deuteronomy 3:24). Still another is, "Adonoy YHVH, destroy not Your people" (Deuteronomy 9:26).

When the Name is pronounced Adonoy YHVH (Adonoy Elohim), it denotes the mystery of the ascent of the Sefirot and their unification with one another, until a person's concentration reaches the Source of Will.

This is like an individual who wishes to grasp a place in the supernal Light and attach himself to it. The name Adonoy (Malkhut-Kingship) yearns to elevate itself and grasp on to Binah-Understanding. YHVH is then vocalized as Elohim.

When the name is written YHVH Adonoy, it denotes the mystery of the divine influx of Binah-Understanding, which descends through the channels and reaches the name Adonoy. When this happens, all the universe is blessed.[41]

. . .

The great, glorious, fearsome name, YHVH, is a name that included all the other divine names that are mentioned in the Torah. There is no divine name that is not included in the name YHVH.

Realizing this, you must be aware how careful you must be when you pronounce this name. When you pronounce the name YHVH, you take on your lips all the holy names. It is then as if your mouth and tongue are carrying all the holy names, upon which depend the universe and everything in it.

When you realize this, you will understand the mystery of the [Third] Commandment, "You shall not take the name of YHVH your God in vain" (Exodus 20:7). For how can a lowly, insignificant creature take on his tongue the great name YHVH which upholds all creation, both on high and below. Even more so, [how can one use it for his own needs], as an ax with which to cut? . . .

You must realize that when one pronounces the name YHVH, sounding out its letters with the motions of his tongue, he agitates all the universes, both on high and below. All the angels rise up and ask each other, "Why is the universe trembling?" And they answer, "Because some wicked person is pronouncing the Explicit Name, sounding it out with his lips. As a result of these vibrations, every name and appelation that depends on it, reverberate, and heaven and earth tremble."

Then they say, "And who is this wicked person who makes the universe tremble, pronouncing the Great Name without reason? He is this wicked person, who did these sins on this day, and those misdeeds another day." As a result, all of this individual's sins are recalled.

When you shake the trunk of a tree, you cause all of its branches and leaves to tremble. Likewise, when a person pronounces the name YHVH, all the host on high and below tremble, since they all depend on it.

The only place where this was not true was in the Holy Temple. When the High Priest would pronounce this Name in the Temple, all the host of heaven would rejoice and would receive the divine influx. For in doing this, the High Priest would rectify all the supernal channels, and blessing would be brought to everything in the universe.[42]

. . .

Many saints were afraid to touch the attribute of Adonoy when it was alone. They would therefore transmit love and good to it from the highest Keter-Crown and from the other Names associated with mercy. King David did this, when he said, "But You Adonoy (Malkhut-Kingship) are El (Chesed-Love), full of compassion and mercy, slow to anger, with great love and truth. Turn to me and have mercy on me" (Psalms 86:15).

If you understand this, you will enter many chambers. You will know how the prophets and saints would direct the channels of love and mercy to the name Adonoy, so that they would not enter into it when it was dry and empty.

It was in this manner that the Talmudic sages knew how to rectify the channels and direct all the Names associated with mercy, until everything would be transmitted into the name Adonoy. Since they knew how to concentrate through all the channels to the name Adonoy, they could do anything they wished in the world.[43]

. . .

The blessed name, YHVH, which is the mystery of the Middle Pillar, is called *Atah* (Thou). This is the mystery of all of God's banners and appelations. He clothes Himself in them all, and prides Himself in them, this being the mystery of the word *Atah*.

This mystery teaches that everything in the universe, and every *Merkava*, was created through permutations of the letters of the alphabet. This is the Kabbalah tradition found in the *Sefer Yetzirah*, which speaks of the permutation and cycling of the letters.

Through the permutations of the 22 alphabets, heaven and earth, and all their host, on high and below, were created. Know this and ponder it carefully. . . .

Letter permutations are therefore a door to the most profound depths. Through them, he can discern the depth of Wisdom, and the wonder of the creation of everything that was formed, each thing according to its kind. He can also discern the structure of every *Merkava*, and the mystery of every male and female.

The permutations and cyclings of the 22 letters are all concealed in the mystery of the word *Atah* (אַתָּה). [The first two letters of this word are Alef (א) and Tav (ת),] the first and last letters of the alphabet, and the beginning and end of every *Merkava*.

This is the meaning of what the *Sefer Yetzirah* says, "Ten Sefirot of Nothingness, their end is embedded in their beginning, and their beginning in their end, like a flame bound to a coal."[44]

All this is the mystery of the 22 letters, and the five channels of Binah-Understanding. Through these all forms of the *Merkava* are depicted, as well as all things, both on high and below.

This is the mystery of the Torah. It is written with the 22 letters, and consists of Five Books. [Five is the numerical value of Heh (ה), the last letter of *Atah*.] All of these together, [the Alef (א), the Tav (ת), and the Heh (ה)], spell out *Atah* (אַתָּה).[45]

• •

Contemplate on the keys that I have given you here. With them, you can open many gates, sealed with many locks, since everyone is not worthy to enter through them.[46]

• • •

The Sefirah [of Chokhmah-Wisdom] is called Somethingness in the Torah. The reason for this is that the first Sefirah, Keter-Crown, is hidden from the eyes of all. Since no one can contemplate it, it is called Nothingness. . . .

If a person seeks [Keter-Crown] he will find Nothingness. No one can contemplate the depth of its depth and excellence. It is for this reason that it is not connotated by any letter in the alphabet, but only by the apex of the Yod.

The beginning of thought, and the first revelation of the array, is the second Sefirah, which is called Chokhmah-Wisdom.[47]

• • •

Gazing at the *Merkava* is called a descent, and the sages therefore speak of "descending to the *Merkava.*"

One who gazes in the *Merkava* must first ascend to the highest level, which is the place of the Light. It is here that he receives the influx of insight. Only then can he descend and look into the *Merkava.*[48]

• • •

The Sefirah [of Chokhmah-Wisdom] is called Fear. The reason for this is that when a person's thoughts reach this high and deep place, he has reason to fear, lest his thoughts become confounded, running and meditating beyond the proper measure.

Regarding this the *Sefer Yetzirah* says, "Ten Sefirot of Nothingness, close your mouth that it not speak, and your heart that it not think. And if your heart runs, return to your place." One must return to his place, since he is entering a place of fear and terror when one thinks of its depth and essence. . . .

Therefore, wherever you find the word Fear, contemplate that it is referring to the Sefirah [of Chokhmah-Wisdom]. It is a place of fear, since it has no measure or boundary, and therefore the mind does not have the power to grasp it. This alluded to in the verse, "He says to man, behold the fear of God is Wisdom, and to depart from evil is Understanding" (Job 28:28).

3. RABBI ISAAC OF ACCO

A contemporary of both Abulafia and Gikatalia, Rabbi Isaac of Acco was the third great Kabbalist of that period to speak of meditation. Tlthough he does not provide any clear examples of his methodology, he does speak of many important meditative principles, and his writings have had an important influence on the meditative Kabbalists. Even more than Abulafia and Gikatalia, he was renowned as a master of letter permutations, and Rabbi Chaim Vital taught that when Rabbi Isaac of Acco would practice the art of *Tzeruf*, he would be visited by angels.[49]

Rabbi Isaac (1250—1340) was born in the Holy Land, and grew up in Acco, which had an important Jewish community. The city had come under the Kabbalistic influence of the Ramban (Rabbi Moshe ben Nachman), who had arrived in the Holy Land in 1267. Considered one of the brightest students in Acco, Rabbi Isaac studied in the Academy of Rabbi Shlomo Petit, and there is some evidence that he also studied with the Ramban himself. It is interesting to note, that while Abulafia studied the *Guide to the Perplexed* under Rabbi Hillel of Verona, one of its staunchest defenders, Rabbi Isaac of Acco was a disciple of Rabbi Hillel's major opponent in the dispute raging over Maimonides' philosophical system.

Living in Acco, Rabbi Isaac was surrounded by this controversy. His master, Rabbi Shlomo Petit, had seized on the fact that Maimonides both quoted and praised Aristotle. Since Aristotle's works are often diametrically opposed to the teachings of Judaism, Petit condemned Maimonides' works as being heretical. He traveled to Europe, to gain support, seeking to place a ban on the learning or teaching of the *Guide*. Maimonides was not without his supporters, however, and the controversy virtually tore the community of Acco into two opposing factions. Ultimately, Maimonides' supporters won out, and in the summer of 1289 a ban was pronounced against Petit, proscribing any

The Seven Mystical Seals

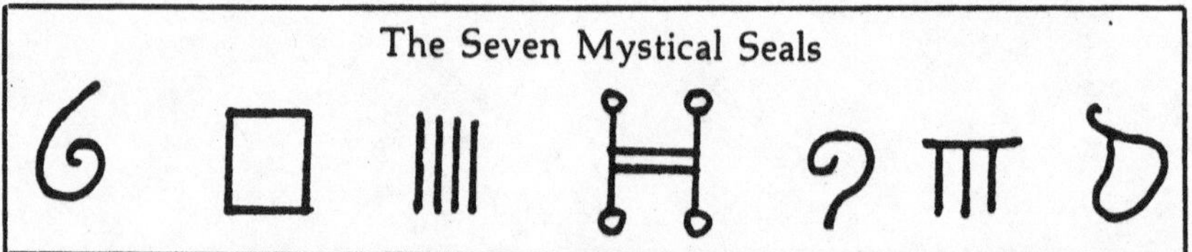

further attacks on the *Guide*. Testimonials in favor of Maimonides' classic were sent to Barcelona, most probably to the Rashba.

The city of Acco had long been an important scene of conflict between the Crusaders and the Saracens. It had finally been wrested from the Moslems in 1191 by King Richard the Lion Hearted, and had subsequently enjoyed a century of peace, during which the Jewish community prospered. However, on May 18, 1291 (18 Sivan, 5051), after a month of seige, it was retaken by the Saracen Almalek Alshraf, and a good portion of both the Jewish and Christian community was put to the sword. The remainder of the populace was imprisoned, and included among them was Rabbi Isaac of Acco.

It appears that Rabbi Isaac remained in the Holy Land for a few years after this. From there he went to Italy, where we find him in 1305. He then travelled through Toledo, and it was at this time that he met with Rabbi Moshe de Leon, publisher of the Zohar.

Although Isaac of Acco does not mention Abulafia by name, he is highly critical of Gikatalia's *Ginat Egoz* (Nut Garden), which was written under Abulafia's influence. Rabbi Isaac complains of Gikatalia's extensive use of Divine Names, and writes, "If I had not heard that he is Godfearing, I would say that when he does this, he is not among those who do not fear God." [50] Later, however, when Gikatalia lived in Segovia, and probably after he had written *Shaarey Orah* (Gates of Light), Rabbi Isaac counts him among the greatest Kabbalists of his generation.[51]

Since both Abulafia and Isaac of Acco were contemporaries who spoke of meditative techniques, it would be interesting to seek a connection between the two. One possiblity is that they both had the same teacher, Rabbi Baruch Targomi. I have a fragment where Rabbi Isaac of Acco discusses the Seven Mystical Seals, which he attributes to Nohaniel Gaon (?), and which are elsewhere attributed to the Ramban.[52] Rabbi Isaac states that he heard an explanation as to the meaning of these seals from a certain Rabbi Baruch.[53] In his commentary on the Torah, Rabbi Isaac likewise speaks of Rabbi Baruch in a number of places.[54] It seems evident that this is the same Rabbi Baruch Targomi who was Abulafia's teacher.

There are a number of places where Rabbi Isaac's teachings seem to parallel those of Abulafia. Both taught that prophecy can exist in any place, and that the Midrashic doctrine that prophecy can only be attained in the Holy Land, is actually speaking of a spiritual level.[55] The initial letters of the Hebrew words for "Beginning, Middle, End," *Rosh, Tokh, Sof* (ראש תוך סוף), spell out the word *Seter* (סֶתֶר) meaning "mystery," and this, too, is discussed by both in the same manner.[56] The Name of Seventy-Two Triplets contains a total of 216 letters, which is the numerical value of "Fear" (*Yirah*, יִרְאָה) and "Lion" (*Aryeh*, אַרְיֵה). This, too, appears in the works of both Abulafia and Isaac of Acco.[57]

All of this could be coincidence, either discovered independently or the product of independent traditions. There is one gematria, however, which both of them use, and since it involves a foreign word, it is difficult to imagine it coming from two independent traditions. The Talmud states that the angel Metatron (מֶטַטְרוֹן) is called *Naar* (נַעַר), meaning a "youth" or "child," since both words have a numerical value of 320. Both Abulafia and Isaac of Acco point out that this is also the numerical value of Sheik (שֵׁיךְ), which in Arabic means an elder. Metatron the "youth," is therefore actually an elder.[58] It would be difficult to say that two individuals would independently arrive at the same gematria, and it therefore seems highly probable that Isaac of Acco either took it from Abulafia's writings or that they both received it from the same source.

It is very possible that Rabbi Isaac learned of Abulafia's teachings from the author of *Shaarey Tzedek* (Gates of Righteousness), who lived in the Holy Land. Both were in the Holy Land at the same time, and there are important similarities between *Shaarey Tzedek* and Isaac of Acco's *Otzar Chaim* (Treasury of Life). Thus, for example, both books, speaking of man's inability to perceive the Divine, cite the example of a bat, who can see in the dark, but is blinded by daylight.[59]

Another idea that is almost too similar to be coincidence involves the philosophers who would use wine to help them resolve difficult problems, as discussed in *Shaarey Tzedek*.[60] Rabbi Isaac almost paraphrases this, writing, "I heard that when one of the most spiritual of the philosophical sages was confronted with a difficult problem, he would drink a cup of strong wine, and fall asleep with his thoughts on that subject. While in a state of semi-sleep, full understanding would come to him, and then he would awaken and write it down." [61] Since *Otzar Chaim* was written at least ten years after *Shaarey Tzedek*, it is highly probable that Isaac of Acco saw this in the earlier text.

One of Rabbi Isaac of Acco's important teachings involves *Hishtavut* (הִשְׁתַּוּוּת), a term derived from the root *Shava* (שוה), meaning "equal." The term denotes making all things equal for oneself, and can be translated as equanimity, or more accurately, as stoicism. It involves total indifference to all outside influences good or bad. This is seen by Rabbi Isaac as a prerequisite for any true level of meditation, an idea that is mentioned by Abulafia, and discussed at length by Albotini.[62]

The idea of *Hishtavut* is also found in earlier, non-Kabbalistic sources, the earliest beng *Chovot HaLevavot* (Duties of the Heart), by Rabbi Bachya ibn Pakuda (1050—1120).[63] Actually, however, this concept is also found in the Talmud, where it is called "overcoming one's [natural] tendencies." Thus, the Talmud relates that the great mystic, Rabbi Nehunia ben HaKana, the central figure of the *Hekhalot,* said that this was one of the main traits responsible for his attainments.[64] The Talmud also teaches that the mysteries involving the Name of Forty-Two can only be given over to one who has attained this level of stoicism.[65] In another place, the Talmud speaks of prayer being answered immediately in a mystical manner, and again states that the reason was because the individual leading the prayers had been able to "overcome his tendencies." [66]

The Talmud clearly states that those who attain this level of stoicism are able to radiate spiritually. It teaches, "Regarding those who are insulted but do not insult, who hear themselves scorned, but do not respond, who serve [God] with love and rejoice in suffering, it is written, 'Those who love [God] shall be like the sun, when it shines forth with [all] its strength' (Judges 5:31)." [67]

This teaching had a profound effect on later Kabbalists. It is discussed at length in *Sulam HaAliyah* (Ladder of Ascent), and Isaac of Acco's primary teaching regarding this is quoted in its entirety in the unpublished Fourth Part of Rabbi Chaim Vital's *Shaarey Kedushah.*[68] A similar idea was taught to Rabbi Joseph Caro by his angelic teacher.

It is significant to see that this very same idea is also found in early Hasidic teachings. The Baal Shem Tov, founder of the Hasidic movement, speaks at length regarding *Hishtavut*-stoicism and states that this is the intent of the verse usually translated as, "I have set (*shivi-ti*) God before me at all times" (Psalms 16:8). According to the Baal Shem, the word *Shivi-ti* (שִׁוִּיתִי), instead of being translated, "I have set," should be translated, "I have been stoic." The verse then reads, "I have been stoic, God is before me at all times."

At first this interpretation may seem far-fetched to Bible scholars, but actually, it makes a number of other very difficult verses much more understandable. Thus, instead of, "I have placed (*shivi-ti*) and have quieted my soul" (Psalms 131:1), we can now read this verse, "I have become stoic and have quieted my soul." Another verse where this interpretation fits well is, "I have chosen a path of faith, through Your judgments I have become stoic" (Psalms 119:30). The same is true of the verse in Isaiah, "I made myself stoic (*shivi-ti*) like a lion until morning" (Isaiah 38:13). In all these verses, it would be very difficult to translate *Shivi-ti* as "I have placed."

In a number of places, Rabbi Isaac speaks of *Mitbodedim* (מִתְבּוֹדְדִים) or "meditators" as if there were regular organized groups of these individuals.[69] The very fact that so many Kabbalistic schools contemporary to him speak of various meditative techniques also seems to support this. In a number of places, he also speaks of the science of letter combination (*tzeruf*) citing this as an important means for attaining enlightenment.[70]

Rabbi Isaac of Acco wrote a number of books, none of which were ever published, except for fragments in scholarly journals. His best known work is *Meirat Eynayim* (Light of the Eyes), a commentary on the Torah explaining the teachings of the Ramban. Another important Kabbalistic work is his *Otzar Chaim* (Treasury of Life), which consists mostly of mysteries revealed to him while in a meditative state.[71] He also wrote commentaries on *Sefer Yetzirah,* and *Pirkey Rabbi Eliezer,* an ancient Midrash. Parts of these have been published in journals.[72] Highly significant is his autobiographical *Divrey Yamim* (Chronicles), which he mentions in his *Otzar Chaim,* but no manuscript of this exists.[73] Also mentioned there is another work, *Chaim DeOraita* (Life of the Torah), which is not noted by historians, but may be the mystical unknown book of his that is occasionally quoted by the Kabbalists.[74]

TEACHINGS

I, the insignificant Isaac, son of Solomon, of Acco, proclaim this both to individuals and the masses, who wish to know the mystery of binding one's soul on high.

One can attach his thoughts to God, and when one does so consistently, there is no question that he will be worthy of the World to Come, and God's Name will be with him constantly, both in this world and in the next.

The Tetragrammaton in Ashurit Script

You should constantly keep the letters of the Unique Name in your mind as if they were in front of you, written in a book with Torah (*Ashurit*) script. Each letter should appear infinitely large.

When you depict the letters of the Unique Name (יהוה) in this manner, your mind's eye should gaze on them, and at the same time, your heart should be directed toward the Infinite Being (*Ain Sof*). Your gazing and thought should be as one.

This is the mystery of true attachment, regarding which the Torah says, "To Him you shall attach yourself" (Deuteronomy 10:20).

[If you are able to do this,] no evil will befall you, you will not be subject to errors caused by logic or emotion, and you will not be the victim of accidents. As long as you are attached to God, you are above all accidents, and are in control of events.

You must respect God, and be careful not to attach your thoughts to Him when you are not in a clean place. Do not do so in filthy alleys, when your hands are not clean, or when you are in the presence of idols.

I heard the following from a pious sage who had served Rabbi Isaac [the Blind], son of the Raavad (Rabbi Abraham ben David of Posqueres, 1120—1198):

[Rabbi Isaac] had been born blind, and had never seen with his physical eyes. Whenever he would go any place, he would tell his attendant, "When we pass by a place of idolalatry, quicken your pace as much as you can." [75]

It appears to me that this was done for the glory of God. His thoughts were always bound to God, and because of the unclean spirit that dwells in the idols, he could not think such thoughts [while in proximity to them]. This was a place of ultimate uncleanness, while his thoughts were on the Root of ultimate holiness. He would therefore hurry away from there, so that he could return to his normal state of mind.

You may ask why one should bind his thoughts to the Tetragrammaton more than any other name. The reason is that this Name is the cause of causes and the source of all sources. Included in it are all things, from Keter-Crown (the highest Sefirah) to the lowliest gnat. Blessed be the Name of the glory of His kingdom forever and ever.

It is regarding this name that the Psalmist said, "I have placed YHVH before me at all times" (Psalms 16:8). This alludes to what we have said, that his eyes and heart were always directed toward God, and it is as if the Name (YHVH) was written before him.[76] . . .

When an individual is worthy of the mystery of Attachment (*Devekut*), he can also be worthy of the mystery of Stoicism (*Hishtavut*). After he is worthy of Stoicism, he can also be worthy of Meditation (*Hitbodedut*). And after he is worthy of Meditation, he can be worthy of *Ruach HaKodesh* (Holy Spirit, enlightenment). From there, he can reach the level of Prophecy, where he can actually predict the future.

In explaining the mystery of Stoicism, Rabbi Abner related the following account:[77]

A sage once came to one of the Meditators (*Mitbodedim*) and asked that he be accepted into their society.

The other replied, "My son, blessed are you to God. You intentions are good. But tell me, have you attained stoicism or not?"

The sage said, "Master, explain your words."

The Meditator said, "If one man is praising you and another is insulting you, are the two equal in your eyes or not?"

He replied, "No my master. I have pleasure from those who praise me, and pain from those who degrade me. But I do not take revenge or bear a grudge."

The other said, "Go in peace my son. You have not attained stoicism. You have not reached a level where your soul does not feel the praise of one who honors you, nor the degradation of one who insults you. You are not prepared for your thoughts to bound on high, that you should come and meditate (*hitboded*). Go and increase the humbleness of your heart, and learn to treat everything equally until you have become stoic. Only then will you be able to meditate.

Light of the Eyes.[78]

One who is worthy to reach the level of meditation (*hitbodedut*) has peace in this life. To reach this level, one must bind himself to three traits, and keep himself from their opposite. He will then have peace in this world, and certainly in the next.

These are the three traits: One must rejoice in his portion, he must love meditation, and he must flee from position and honor. This involves the subjugation of the heart.[79]

Rabbi Isaac of Acco writes in the name of Rabbi Moshe, a disciple of Rabbi Joseph Gikatalia:

If a person's heart impels him to rectify his traits, perfecting his personality and deeds, he should pursue humility to the ultimate degree. He should "be insulted but not insult, hear himself scorned but not respond."[80] The Divine Presence will then immediately rest on him and he will not have to learn from any mortal being, for the spirit of God will teach him.[81]

Elsewhere, [Rabbi Isaac of Acco] writes:

We found this in the books of the Kabbalists who were worthy of the way of truth:

One of the great rectifications for one who wishes to know God is that he should be among those who are "insulted but does not insult." This should even be true with regard to people of whom he is not afraid and before whom he has no shame, such as his wife and children. Even if members of his household insult him, he should not answer, except to correct their ways. . . . But inwardly, he should feel no anger, but his heart should always be joyful, attached [to God] no matter what happens.[82]

PARALLELS

It is related that one of the Hasidim asked one of his companions, "Have you attained stoicism (*hishtavut*)?" When the other asked the meaning of his question, he explained, "Have you [reached a level where] praise and insult are equal in your eyes?" The other replied negatively, and he said, "If this is true, then you have not reached the [necessary level]. Continue to strive in this direction, and you may be able to reach this level. It is the highest level of piety and its desired end.

Rabbi Bachya ibn Pekudah (1050–1120).[83]

[My angelic master taught me this:] Do not worry about anything in the world, other than that which will influence your worship of God. With regard to all worldly things, everything should be the same as its opposite.

This is the mystery of the words of the sage, who asked an initiate who wished to involve himself in Unifications *(Yichudim),* "Have you attained stoicism?"

If a person does not see that all good in the physical world is exactly the same as its evil, it is impossible for him to Unify all things.

Rabbi Joseph Caro (1488–1575).[84]

"I have been stoic, God is before me at all times." (Psalms 16:8). This denotes a level of stoicism with regard to all that befalls a person. Whether people insult him or praise him, it should all be equal. The same is true of eating, whether he eats sweetmeats or gall, it should all be equal to him. In this manner, one can dispel the Evil Urge (*Yetzer HaRa*) completely.

Rabbi Israel Baal Shem Tov (1698–1760).[85]

It is told that one of the Hasidim was once asked, "What was the happiest occasion in your life?" He told the following story:

I was once travelling on a ship along with merchants carrying costly goods. I wished to meditate (*hitboded*) on my Creator, and I went down into the bowels of the ship, lying there in the lowest place. The young son of one of the merchants stood himself over me, insulting me and spitting in my face. He then uncovered himself and urinated on me. I was astounded at his brazenness.

But as God lives, my soul was not downcast as a result of this. After he left, I was exceedingly happy, realizing that my soul had reached a level of true humility. I realize that through this trait, one can "walk among the Ones who stand."[86] This trait dominated me so much that I felt absolutely nothing whatsoever.

Rabbi Eliahu di Vidas (16th Century).[87]

4. PUBLICATION OF THE ZOHAR

In the 1270's, a number of manuscripts began to circulate among the Kabbalists, creating a tremendous stir. Rumors began to fly that an ancient text had been discovered, stemming from the famed Second Century mystic, Rabbi Shimon bar Yochai. This remarkable manuscript was being published by an important Kabbalist of that time, Rabbi Moshe de Leon (1238—1305). By 1281, a number of mystical texts were already quoting passages from this text, which soon became known as the Zohar.[88]

Even though the manuscripts included some two dozen texts, they were considered to be a single body of literature. Stories began to be told how these manuscripts had been hidden in a vault for a thousand years and had been dug up by an Arabian king and sent to Toledo.[89] Others said that the Ramban (Rabbi Moshe ben Nachman, 1194—1270) had sent them by ship to his son, but the ship had been diverted and they ended up in the hands of Rabbi Moshe de Leon. There were also some whispers that Rabbi Moshe himself had written these books, using mystical powers derived from the "Name of Writing."

The Zohar itself provides a clue, stating that it should be revealed in preparation for the final redemption, twelve hundred years after the destruction of the second Temple.[90] Since the Temple was destroyed in the year 69, this would mean that the Zohar was meant to be revealed in 1269. The secret society, who were guardians of these mysteries, entrusted this task to Rabbi Moshe de Leon, who was possibly a member of this group.

Seeing parts of the text and hearing conflicting rumors surrounding it, Rabbi Isaac of Acco decided to investigate the matter. He met with Rabbi Moshe de Leon, and the latter swore that the manuscript was an authentic text from Rabbi Shimon bar Yochai. It is difficult to imagine that a saint such as Rabbi Moshe would violate the Third Commandment and swear falsely regarding this, no matter what his motive. Excited, Rabbi Isaac asked him to see the original manuscript, a request to which Rabbi Moshe readily agreed. Again, it would hardly seem likely that one would be so ready to display a manuscript that did not exist, or even one that had been forged.

Before Rabbi Isaac was able to view the manuscript, however, Rabbi Moshe had died. Upon inquiring as to the manuscripts, he was informed by David of Pancorbo that Rabbi Moshe's widow had claimed that the manuscript had never existed, and that the entire text had been made up. Stunned, Rabbi Isaac decided to explore the matter further.

In his search, he is informed by a prominent Kabbalist, Rabbi Joseph HaLevi, that he had once tested Rabbi Moshe regarding the Zohar. Claiming to have lost a manuscript, he had Rabbi Moshe write him a new one, and found to be precisely identical to the first. This was a clear indication that the writer had a manuscript from which he had made copies. Encouraged, Rabbi Isaac of Acco is determined to investigate until he comes to a final conclusion.

The entire account is in Rabbi Isaac's *Divrey HaYamim* (Chronicles), and no manuscripts of this text have survived. The pertinent selection, however, was published by Rabbi Abraham Zacuto (1448—1515) in his *Sefer HaYuchasin* (Book of Geneologies), but it was deleted from all editions of this book other than the first edition, which was published by the author in 1510 in Constantinople.[91] Unfortunately, the published account ends abruptly, probably because the author did not have the succeeding pages, and therefore, we are not told of Rabbi Isaac of Acco's conclusion.

Besides this, however, a number of other points are also left hanging. For example, if Rabbi Moshe did indeed write a copy for himself, what happened to it? Why did no one recall ever having seen it?

It seems obvious that none of Rabbi Moshe's contemporaries considered him to have been capable of authoring the Zohar. Whoever claimed that he himself had written it said that he did so through the "Name of Writing," which would enable a person to write in a manner far beyond his natural capabilities. Furthermore, anyone familiar with Rabbi Moshe's writings, which are extensive, immediately sees that his entire system is very different from that of the Zohar.[92]

David of Pancorbo's story can be explained in many ways. First of all, it was told third hand, from Rabbi Moshe's wife to that of a certain

Joseph, then to Joseph himself, and finally to David, who in turn related it to Rabbi Isaac. This leaves much room for error. And how reliable was the widow? Parchment was quite expensive in those days, and as a result of her intense poverty, she might have sold the manuscripts as a scrap parchment, to be erased and reused, as was common in that period. When later asked about the manuscripts, she may have been ashamed to have disposed of a valuable volume in such a manner, and simply made up a story denying that the manuscripts had ever existed, a perfectly natural response.

Another possibility is that either David or Joseph were ashamed to admit that they had tried to swindle these priceless documents from Rabbi Moshe's widow. They might have actually obtained them, but would not want an outsider to know that they had done so without informing the widow of their true value. Under Jewish law, this would have been a most reprehensible act, and she could even have sued to recover the manuscripts. One's suspicions are further raised, since David speaks very unkindly of Rabbi Moshe, while among his contemporaries in general, he seems to have enjoyed a reputation as a sage and saint.

But what was Rabbi Isaac of Acco's own conclusion? This is the most important question. It is critical to any discussion of the Zohar, and has not been sufficiently explored. Looking at his own words, we find that he writes in his *Otzar Chaim:* "Rabbi Shimon bar Yochai clearly realized that the supernal spiritual Forces are very jealous of those who engage in the Workings of Creation, which is natural wisdom, and in the Workings of the *Merkava,* which is divine wisdom. Together with his son Rabbi Eliezer and the ten sages who were with them in the cave (!) he therefore wrote the Zohar in Aramaic rather than in Hebrew [since these forces do not understand Aramaic].[93]

Quoting the Zohar in another place, Rabbi Isaac likewise writes, "These are the words of Rabbi Shimon bar Yochai, and it is forbidden to depart from them. They are the living words of God . . . sweeter than honey. For authority was given to him from on high, such as had never been given to any other sage. Compared to the other sages, he is like Moses compared to the other prophets."[94]

In a number of other places, he likewise cites the Zohar as the work of Rabbi Shimon.[95] The fact that he quotes the Zohar would in itself not be proof that he accepted it as an authentic ancient text. But he would hardly attribute it to Rabbi Shimon bar Yochai so openly if he did not consider it authentic.

A most important point is that the *Otzar Chaim* was written after Rabbi Isaac had investigated the origin of the Zohar. We recall that the entire account of this investigation is quoted from his *Divrey HaYamim.* This was clearly written before his Otzar Chaim, since in a number of places in the later book, he actually mentions his *Divrey HaYamim.*[96]

We therefore come to a highly significant conclusion. The one person best in the position to investigate the authenticity of the Zohar, after a thorough investigation, openly states that it was written by Rabbi Shimon bar Yochai. This fact has escaped the notice of historians, and may be highly instrumental in dispelling their doubts as to the authenticity of the Zohar.

An excerpt from **Sefer HaYuchasin**

In the month of Adar, Rabbi Isaac writes that Acco was destroyed in the year 5050 (1291), and the saints of Israel were killed in the most brutal manner. Rabbi Isaac survived, and by 5065 (1305), had been in Navarra in the province of Asti, Italy. In the year 5065 (1305), he came to Toledo.

The following account is found in his *Divrey HaYamim.* He also wrote a Kabbalah text in the year of the Angel (*HaMalach,* המלאך = 96), [that is, in the year 5096 (1336)].[97] It was in his time that Acco was destroyed, and many were taken into capitvity, including the Ramban's grandson, and the grandson of Rabbi David, son of Rabbi Abraham, son of Maimonides.

He later went to Spain to investigate how the Zohar was found in his time. This had been written by Rabbi Shimon and his son Eliezer in the cave. Happy are those who are worthy of its truth, for in its light they see light.[98]

He vouched for its authenticity, although some similar manuscripts had been forged. He said that he knew from tradition that everything written in Aramaic was actually from Rabbi Shimon. That which is in Hebrew, however, was a later addition, since the original book was written completely in Aramaic.[99]

These are his words:

When I saw the Zohar, I realized that its words are wondrous, drawn from a high place, from the Fount that gives without receiving, blessed be the Name of the glory of His Kingdom forever and ever. I pursued it, and asked scholars who have large sections of the text about it. These were wondrous words, known by Kabbalah-tradition that had been transmitted orally, but they were never permitted to be written down in a book, where they are clearly available to all who can read.

I inquired as to their source, but the answers that I received did not all agree. Some said one thing, but others had a completely different story.

Some said that the faithful Ramban had sent it from the Holy Land to his son in Catalonia, but that the wind had brought the ship to the land of Aragonia. Others said that it had come to Alicante. Eventually, it came to the hands of the sage, Rabbi Moshe de Leon, who is also called Rabbi Moshe of Guadalhajara.

Others claimed that Rabbi Shimon bar Yochai never actually wrote the book, but that Rabbi Moshe knew the Name of Writing, and through its power, had written these wondrous things. In order to fetch a high price and obtain much money for the manuscripts, he had "hung his words on great trees." [100] He therefore said that he had transcribed it from a book written by Rabbi Shimon bar Yochai, his son Rabbi Eliezer, and their school.

When I came to Spain, I arrived in the city of Valladolid, where the king had his capitol. It was there that I met Rabbi Moshe, and we became friendly and discussed [the Zohar]. He made a solomn oath and swore to me, "May God strike me down, and may He continue to do so if [the Zohar] is not an ancient book written by Rabbi Shimon bar Yochai. At this very moment, the manuscript is in my house, in Avila, were I live. Come and visit me there, and I will show it to you."

Soon after this, we separated, and Rabbi Moshe left for Arevalo, on the way home to Avila. He became sick in Arevalo, and died there.

When I heard this news, I was deathly upset, but I decided to visit Avila. When I arrived there, I found an elderly sage whose name is Rabbi David of Pancorbo. I found grace in his eyes, and bound him by an oath, saying, "Resolve for me the mystery of the Zohar. Some say one thing and others say the opposite. Rabbi Moshe himself vowed [that the Zohar was authentic], but died before he could verify it to me. I do not know who is reliable and whose word to believe."

He replied, "The truth is this: I have determined without question that this book called the Zohar never existed, and never came to the hand of Rabbi Moshe. But he was a master of the Name of Writing, and through the power of that name, wrote everything in that book. Listen and I will tell you how I determined this.

"Rabbi Moshe was a great spendthrift, tossing away money very generously. Today his house could have been filled with silver and gold, given to him by the rich who understand the great mysteries that he gave them, written through the Name of Writing. But tomorrow it would be completely empty.

"His wife and daughter are presently virtually naked, hungry and thirsty, and totally destitute.

"When I heard that he had died in Arevelo, I went to the wealthiest man in the city, whose name is Joseph de Avila, and I said to him, 'The time has finally arrived when you can obtain the priceless [original] manuscript of the Zohar. Just listen to my advice.'

"I advised Joseph to instruct his wife, 'Send a generous gift to Rabbi Moshe's widow with you maid.' She did this, and on the next day, he told her to go to the house of Rabbi Moshe's widow and say, 'I would like my son to marry your daughter. If you agree, for the rest of your life, you will never lack food or clothing. I want nothing from you other than the manuscript of the Zohar, from which your husband transcribed the copies that he distributed.'

"[Joseph] told his wife, 'Speak to the mother and daughter separately and tell them this. Listen carefully to their answer, and see whether or not the two say the same thing.'

"Rabbi Moshe's widow swore to Joseph's wife, and said, 'May God strike me down [if I lie to you], but my husband never owned such a book. Everything that he wrote was made up, from his own mind.'

"She related that she would often see him writing without any other book in front of him, and she would ask him, 'Why do you tell people that you are transcribing this from a book? You do not have a book, but are making it all up out of your head. Wouldn't it be better if you say that you are the author if this book, and that it is the product of your intellect? Would you not have more honor?'

"He would answer, 'If I would reveal my secret, that I am making this up from my own mind, they would not pay any attention to what I write. They would not give me a penny for my writings, since they would consider them nothing more than the product of my imagination. But now, when they hear that it is taken from the Zohar, written by Rabbi Shimon bar Yochai, with *Ruach HaKodesh*, and that I am only transcribing it, they pay a high price for it. You can see this yourself.'

"After this, Joseph's wife spoke to Rabbi Moshe's daughter, saying the same things that she had said to her mother. She proposed that the daughter marry her son, and that the mother would be provided with food and clothing. She answered exactly the same as her mother, adding nothing and subtracting nothing.

"Do you need any clearer evidence than this?"

After hearing this, I was confused and dismayed. At the time, I was certain that there had never been any original manuscript. All that existed was that he had composed using the Name of Writing and had distributed to people.

I then left Avila and travelled to Talavera. There I found an extraordinary sage, with a generous heart and a good eye, by the name of Rabbi Joseph HaLevi, son of the great Kabbalist, Rabbi Todros.[101] I asked him about the Zohar.

He replied, "You must know and believe that the manuscript of the Zohar which Rabbi Moses had was written by Rabbi Shimon bar Yochai. It was this manuscript that he transcribed, giving copies to those whom he deemed worthy. I myself tested Rabbi Moshe to see if he was actually copying from an ancient text, or he was merely inventing it through the power of the Name of Writing.

"This was the test: He had written for me many large volumes of the Zohar. Many days after he had written them, I hid one of the folios and told him that I had lost it, pressing him to write me another copy. He said, 'If you show me the end of the folio before it and the beginning of the next folio, I will be able to provide you with an exact copy.'

"I did this, and after several days, he brought me a copy of the missing folio. I compared it with the original copy, and there was absolutely no difference between them. Nothing had been added or left out, and there was no change in wording. Both wording and content was exactly the same, just as if it had been copied from my original.

"Can there be a better test than this?"

I then left Talavera and came to Toledo, where I continued to investigate the book, inquiring among the sages and their disciples. There I also found that the subject was controversial, where opposite opinions were being expressed.

I told them about Rabbi Joseph's test, but they replied that it was by no means conclusive. It was quite possible that [Rabbi Moshe] had used the Name of Writing to make a copy for himself, and then transcribe from his own copy. He would therefore have a primary text, and it would be just as if he were copying it from an ancient manuscript.

But then I discovered something new there. The disciples told me that they had seen an old man, whose name was Jacob, who had been a foremost disciple of Rabbi Moshe, and who had been loved by him like a son. [I spoke to him, and] he called heaven and earth as his witnesses that the Zohar that Rabbi Shimon bar Yochai wrote (The text ends abruptly at this point).

5. OCCULT SCHOOLS

The line between meditation and magic is often a tenuous one, and in many areas of Kabbalah the distinction is difficult to discern. How, for example, do we describe a process where a magical incantation is repeated over and over, and for all practical purposes, is used as a mantra? Do we ascribe the effect to the supernatural powers of the Name or incantation, or to the meditative state that it induces? This question has never been fully resolved in the Kabbalah, and hence, the magical and meditative schools often appear to overlap.

The controversy regarding this type of magical Kabbalah was quite strong in the 1200's. Maimonides (1135—1204) was aware of these magical practices, and he denounces them in no uncertain terms, deeming them fit only for the ignorant and unlearned.[102] Abulafia follows this philosophical ideal, describing these cryptic rites in detail and denouncing their practitioners as charlatans of the lowest kind.[103] Isaac of Acco, on the other hand, not only appears to have approved of such practices, but he actually seemed to have used them.[104]

This controversy seemed to have lasted well into the Sixteenth Century. The Ari tried to abolish these practices completely, and in general, strongly denounced the use of the Practical Kabbalah (*Kabbalah Maasiut*), as it was called. On the other hand, his chief disciple, Rabbi Chaim Vital, was not only familiar with these practices, but also appeared to have made use of them.[105] Another important Kabbalist of that period, Rabbi Joseph Tzayach, describes a number of magical rites, but warns the reader to keep his motives absolutely pure when using them.[106] There is no question that these rites were widely known and used during that period.

One of the foremost practitioners of the Practical Kabbalah was Rabbi Joseph Della Reina (1418—1472), who lived in the Holy Land.

Many magical formulas are preserved in his name, and it is obvious that he was considered to be one of the greatest masters of these occult arts.[107] Tradition teaches that he made use of his powers in an attempt to bring the final redemption, but was unsuccessful and spiritually injured in the process. According to some accounts, he became an apostate, according to others he went mad, while others say that he committed suicide. In many texts, his example is cited as a warning against practicing these methods.[108]

Many techniques of the magical schools of Kabbalah involved incantations and amulets, and these were often used for trivial and even questionable purposes. Some are for practical things, such as protection while travelling, quieting a stormy sea, or aiding a woman having a difficult childbirth. Others are for "opening the heart" and similar enlightenment. We also find formulas for protection against one's enemies, or even some for doing away with them.

Some of these methods, however, were used for objectives as trivial as catching fish.[109] Others were for questionable goals, such as for luck in gambling.[110] We find formulas for love, some which even involve physical contact with the desired woman.[111] Some practices include the use of "grasses," which were possibly psychedelic drugs.[112] In general, it is not difficult to understand why these practices were widely condemned or at least discouraged by Kabbalists involved in serious meditation and philosophical analysis.

Still, the traditions of the Magical or Practical Kabbalah were very ancient, and although often perverted, still contained methods through which one could attain high meditative states. Such texts as *Charba DeMoshe* (The Sword of Moses), *Sefer HaCasdim* (Book of the Chaldees), *Sefer HaRazim* (Book of Secrets), and *Sefer HaMalbush* (Book of the Garment), had been around for many centuries, possibly even from the Talmudic period.[113]

There are many texts involving the Practical Kabbalah from the Sixteenth Century and earlier, but most of these consist of little more than fragments. In many cases, a "book" is nothing more than a number of single, unrelated, incomplete pages, bound together in a single volume. For the most part, our knowledge of the practical Kabbalah comes from these fragments. A few small booklets involving these methods have been published, the most notable being *Toledot Adam* (Generations of Adam) attributed to Rabbi Eliahu Baal Shem Tov (1537-1653).[114]

One of the most complete collections of such practices is found in a remarkable manuscript, *Shoshan Yesod Olam* (The Rose, Foundation of the Universe), compiled around 1550 by a certain Rabbi Joseph Tirshom.[115] This book contains over two thousand magical formulas from the Practical Kabbalah. From a number of remarks by the redactor, it appears that the text was compiled from many ancient manuscripts that he had in his hand.[116] Although many of these practices are purely magical, many others combine elements of both magic and meditation, and can therefore be included in the latter category.

One interesting practice frequently encountered in this genre of literature involves induced dreams. This is usually referred to as a "Dream Request" *(Shaalat Chalom)*, where one poses a question and attempts to induce an answer to appear in a dream. The practice itself is very ancient, alluded to even in the Talmud, and examples are found from as early as the Tenth Century.[117] While the methods for inducing dreams are often purely magical, there are some that have important meditative overtones. This is particularly significant because of the general relationship between prophecy, enlightenment and dreams.

6. MAGIC SQUARES

One of the most mysterious Kabbalists of the Sixteenth Century was Rabbi Joseph Tzayach (1505—1573), who was also one of the leading rabbinical figures of that period. Aside from his many mystical works, a large body of Responsa exist from him in manuscript, and he is known to have corresponded with the leading religious leaders of that time.[118] The great codist, Rabbi Joseph Caro quotes a number of his responsa in his *Avkat Rokhel.*[119]

Rabbi Joseph Tzayach was apparently born in Jerusalem, and from there he was chosen to serve as rabbi in Damascus. There were two Jewish communities in Damascus, one being an immigrant community from Spain, consisting of some five hundred families, and the other being the native communities, known as the Mostarabians, who had been there from ancient times. It was the Mostarabian community that chose Tzayach as its leader, but it also seems that he learned many ancient mysteries from them.

Tzayach commuted frequently between Damascus and Jerusalem, and we find him in the Holy City on numerous occasions between 1538 and 1555. It was in Jerusalem that he wrote his main Kabbalistic work, *Evven HaShoham* (The Onyx Stone) in 1538. A year later, he wrote a second book, *Tzeror HaChaim* (The Binding of Life), a mystical commentary on the Talmud.[120] His *Sheirit Yosef* (Remnant of Joseph) an expansion of *Evven HaShoham*, was written in 1549, also in Jerusalem.[121] Besides these, he also mentions another book, *Tzafanat Paneach*, which is no longer extant.[122]

At least three of his books are dedicated to Abraham Castro, who apparently supported Tzayach, while he was in Jerusalem. This Abraham Castro was a leader of the Jewish community in Egypt, and was famed as a philanthropist, distributing more than three thousand gold florens each year. The Turkish Sultan, Selim I (1467—1520), had conquered Egypt in the battle of Aleppo in 1517. Soon after this, he appointed Abraham Castro, a Jew of Spanish descent, as Master of the Mint, responsible for issuing the new Turkish coinage in Egypt.

Besides his high government position, Castro was also an important leader in the Jewish community. It was he who secured the appointment of the Radbaz (Rabbi David abu Zimra, 1480—1574), one of the most prominent religious authorities of that period, as chief rabbi of Cairo. From his dedications, it is apparent that he was also a patron of Rabbi Tzayach. As we shall see, the fact that Tzayach corresponded with the Radbaz is also highly significant.[123]

Rabbi Joseph Tzayach apparently was influenced by Abulafia's school, and many ideas that he discusses seem to be taken verbatum from Abulafia's writings. Thus, for example, Abulafia warns that one striving for the highest level, which is called the Crown, or *Keter* (כֶּתֶר), must be careful, lest he be "cut off" (*Karet,* כָּרֵת). He notes that both words contain the same letters, and the exact same idea is also mentioned a number of times in Tzayach's works.[124]

Even more obvious is an interpretation of the Hebrew word for "letters," which is *Otiot* (אוֹתִיוֹת). The word can be divided into two, spelling out *Tav Alef* (תָּו א'), "a line of Alef," and *Tav Yod* (תָּו י'), "a line of Yod (= 10)." This is said to be indicative of a strong relationship between the letters of the alphabet and the ten digits, which are ten units. A virtually identical discussion of this is found both in Abulafia's *Or HaSekhel* and in Tzayach's *Tzeror HaChaim.*[125]

One book that Tzayach mentions numerous times is the Bahir.[126] It also appears that he was familiar with *Shoshan Yesod Olam* or one of its precursers. In one place, he speaks of a book called *Yesod Olam,* which quotes a certain Aramas, a disciple of Chalatino the Magician.[127] While there is apparently no reference to this magician in *Shoshan Yesod Olam,* it may be on one of the many missing pages in the manuscript. It is also possible that *Shoshan Yesod Olam* was an expansion or supplement of an earlier book called *Yesod Olam,* and this would help explain its name.

Particularly noteworthy is the fact that Tzayach does not mention the Zohar. Indeed, in his discussions of chiromancy, he does not follow the Zohar's system, but uses an alternative method, still used by western occultists.[128] When one takes into account that in his *Sulam HaAliyah,* Rabbi Judah Albotini also fails to mention the Zohar, this becomes highly significant. The Zohar was the main text of the theoretical Kabbalists, but it appears that the meditative Kabbalists followed a completely different tradition that did not include the Zohar. One reason for this may have been the fact that, at least outwardly, the Zohar makes virtually no reference to meditation.

Tzayach's most important work is his *Evven HaShoham*, literally "the Onyx Stone." As he mentions in his introduction, the onyx paralleled the tribe of Joseph in Aaron's breastplate, and the title therefore alludes to the name of the author.[129] He also notes that the word *Shoham* (שֹׁהַם) has the same letters as *HaShem* (הַשֵּׁם), meaning "the Name," since this is the main point of the book.

This text, as well as *Sheirit Yosef*, was explicitly written as a meditative text, as the author clearly states in his introduction. The books contain what appears to be an extremely complex meditative system, but the author purposely conceals the key to its use. Many ideas mentioned in this book appear to be unique in Kabbalah, and it may well represent a tradition that has otherwise been lost.[130] There is much numerical manipulation (*gematria*) in the book, as well as a numerology that is more sophisticated than anything else that I have seen in any Kabbalistic text.

Also found here is considerable insight into common human behavior. An interesting example is his discussion of how the five fingers parallel the five senses, and the manner in which the two are unconsciously associated. The pinky is associated with hearing, and one therefore cleans one's ear with the pinky. The ring finger parallels the sense of sight, and one often uses it to wipe the eye, while the middle finger is used for touch. The forefinger is related to smell, and is used to clean the nose. Finally, the thumb is associated with the sense of taste, and it is for this reason that small children often suck their thumbs.[131]

This would seem like nothing more than a humorous insight, but the author then associates these five concepts with the five divisions of the Hebrew alphabet mentioned in the Sefer Yetzirah.[132] He then goes on to associate them with the five methods of manipulating letters through *Tzeruf*. He concludes by saying, "I have already discussed this, but it is not permissible to put in in writing."

Even more interesting, and to my knowledge unique, is his association of the Ten Sefirot with the lines of the fingers, as indicated in the figure on the opposite page. These account for the upper nine Sefirot, and the triplet array parallels that of conventional Kabbalah. The lowest Sefirah, which is Malkhut-Kingship, is represented by what is called the Heart Line in conventional chiromancy, or perhaps by the

Girdle of Venus. Tzayach concludes, "The line on the palm that begins under the middle finger and extends to the pinky indicates the Coronet (*Malkhut*). This goes 'to the east of Ashur' (Genesis 2:14), encompassing the Ten Holy [Sefirot]. Surrounding them are the Ten Unclean Ones. All of this is alluded to in the lines of the palm, and is understood by those who know these mysteries." [133]

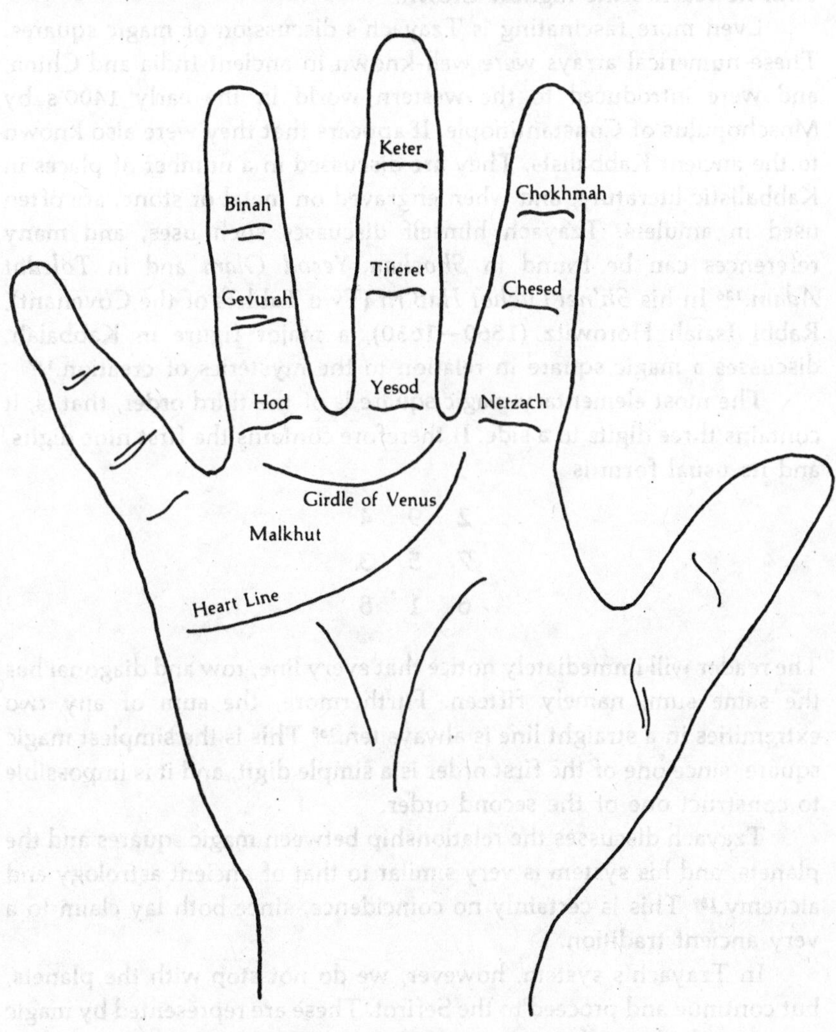

Tzayach's System of Chiromancy

Tzayach is very reticent when it comes to discussing how this system can be used, and in his introduction openly states that he is obscuring such things.[134] One gets a very strong impression, however, that he advocates contemplating these lines in a meditative sense. One can gaze at his palm until these lines begin to glow, and they actually begin to resemble the Sefirot. The initiate sits, gazing at his own hand, and using the finger lines as steps, he can climb the ladder of the Sefirot until he reaches the highest Crown.[135]

Even more fascinating is Tzayach's discussion of magic squares. These numerical arrays were well-known in ancient India and China, and were introduced to the western world in the early 1400's by Moschopulus of Constantinople. It appears that they were also known to the ancient Kabbalists. They are discussed in a number of places in Kabbalistic literature, and when engraved on metal or stone, are often used in amulets. Tzayach himself discusses such uses, and many references can be found in *Shoshan Yesod Olam* and in *Toledot Adam*.[136] In his *Sh'nei Luchot HaB'rit* (Two Tablets of the Covenant), Rabbi Isaiah Horowitz (1560—1630), a major figure in Kabbalah, discusses a magic square in relation to the mysteries of creation.[137]

The most elementary magic square is of the third order, that is, it contains three digits to a side. It therefore contains the first nine digits, and its usual form is

2	9	4
7	5	3
6	1	8

The reader will immediately notice that every line, row and diagonal has the same sum, namely fifteen. Furthermore, the sum of any two extremities in a straight line is always ten.[138] This is the simplest magic square, since one of the first order is a simple digit, and it is impossible to construct one of the second order.

Tzayach discusses the relationship between magic squares and the planets, and his system is very similar to that of ancient astrology and alchemy.[139] This is certainly no coincidence, since both lay claim to a very ancient tradition.

In Tzayach's system, however, we do not stop with the planets, but continue and proceed to the Sefirot. These are represented by magic squares of the order ten to twenty.[140] These magic squares are apparently used for a very special meditation, where each horizontal

Magic Squares

Order n	*Correspondence*	*Sum of Side* $S = (n^3 + n)/2$
3	Saturn	15
4	Jupiter	34
5	Mars	65
6	Sun	111
7	Venus	175
8	Mercury	260
9	Moon	369
10	Keter-Crown	505
11	Chokhmah-Wisdom	671
12	Binah-Understanding	860
13	Chesed-Love	1105
14	Gevurah-Strength	1379
15		1695
16	Tiferet-Beauty	2056
17	Netzach-Victory	2465
18	Hod-Splendor	2925
19	Yesod-Foundation	3439
20	Malkhut-Kingship	4010

row is a "house," while each number in this row is a "room." Thus, in the magic square of the tenth order, which represents Keter-Crown, the first "room" of the first "house" is 1, the second room is 2, the third is 98, and the fourth is 97.

In the meditative system, each number represents a "thousand myriad" (10,000,000) parsangs, and a "thousand myriad" colored lights. As one mentally travels from room to room and from house to house, going through the magic square of Keter-Crown, one must apparently attempt to depict these lights. These exercises thus allow one to elevate himself through the Sefirot in a very graphic manner.

The magic square for Keter-Crown is presented in three places in his works.[141] He warns against trying to change or improve the squares, as some tried to do. He writes that he "received this from my master, of blessed memory. One should not add to the squares that we have

Magic Square of Order Ten
Corresponding to Keter-Crown

1	2	98	97	96	5	94	93	9	10
90	12	13	87	86	85	84	18	19	11
80	79	23	24	76	75	27	28	22	71
70	69	68	34	36	35	37	33	62	61
41	59	58	57	45	46	44	53	52	50
51	49	48	47	55	56	54	43	42	60
31	32	38	64	65	66	67	63	39	40
30	29	73	74	25	26	77	78	72	21
20	82	83	14	16	15	17	88	89	81
91	92	3	7	6	95	4	8	99	100

drawn, since they allude to the highest and most concealed concepts, as we have explained. One who attempts to improve them, actually diminishes them, for he does not consider the glory of God. . . . Each house and each room has a specific function, but this I did not learn from my master." [142]

In a number of places, Tzayach stops just short of explicitly explaining exactly how these squares are to be used. In one place he states, "If you look carefully at the order of numbers in the houses and rooms, you will understand a wondrous concept regarding the mystery of the order of Atzilut. But I do not have the authority to explain the mystery of these luminaries, or to write down with my pen why there are more in some rooms and less in others." [143]

Elsewhere, he repeats that he does not have the authority to reveal the reasons for the numbers associated with each room. He concludes, "This is among the deepest mysteries of the highest *Merkava.* It cannot be deliniated by books or scrolls. The mysterious reason for this is that they are cycled by the Infinite Being (*Ain Sof*), where no eye can penetrate. May He and His name be blessed. But from what I have written, the intelligent will understand." [144]

There is considerable discussion as to whether one should meditate alone, or together with an instructor. The Baal Shem Tov explicitly taught that one should always meditate with a companion, since this can otherwise be very dangerous.[145] Tzayach anticipates this, and writes, "It is necessary for the initiate's master to stand over him the first time, until he becomes accustomed [to enter these states. His master] can help bring him back to his normal state of consciousness. . . . [One must do this] until he is properly initiated into these new states [of consciousness], lest he gaze and lose his mind [like Ben Zoma]".[146]

Finally, Tzayach was probably the last Kabbalist to advocate the use of the prophetic position, where one places his head between his knees. This position was used by Elijah on Mount Carmel, and occasionally, by the sages of the Talmud. It is also mentioned by Hai Gaon (939—1038), head of the Babylonian academy at Pumbedita.[147] Some five hundred years later, Tzayach discusses the same position. Speaking of individuals who meditate (*hitboded*), he says, "They bend themselves like reeds, placing their heads between their knees until all their faculties are nullified. As a result of this lack of sensation, they see the Supernal Light, with true vision and not with allegory."[148]

This position is also associated with meditation on the houses and rooms in the magic squares. He writes, "If you wish to enter into their mystery, concentrate on all that we have said. Contemplate (*hitbonen*) the rooms that we have discussed, together with their lights, colors, and letter combinations. Meditate (*hitboded*) on this for a while, either briefly or at length. Begin by placing your head between your knees."[149]

He then includes a remarkable prayer that should be said while in the prophetic position:

> *Ehyeh Asher Ehyeh,* Crown me *(Keter).*
> *Yah,* grant me Wisdom *(Chokhmah).*
> *Elohim Chaim,* grant me Understanding *(Binah).*
> *El,* with the right hand of His Love, make me great *(Chesed).*
> *Elohim,* from the Terror of His Judgment, protect me *(Gevurah).*
> YHVH, with His mercy, grant me Beauty *(Tiferet).*
> *Adonoy Tzevaot,* watch me Forever *(Netzach).*
> *Elohim Tzevaot,* grant me beatitude from His Splendor *(Hod).*

El Chai, make his covenant my Foundation *(Yesod).*
Adonoy, open my lips and my mouth will speak of Your praise *(Malkhut).*

The reader will immediately notice that this chant includes the Ten Sefirot, as well as the Divine Names associated with them. This is the only place where we find an actual meditative practice involving the prophetic position. The chant involving the Sefirot is also unique.

The fact that Tzayach mentions such an early method strongly suggests that he was heir to a very ancient tradition, possibly one coming from Hai Gaon. Tzayach lived in Damascus, a city that had a continuous Jewish community dating back to Biblical times. It is very possible that these very ancient traditions had been preserved within this community.

CHAPTER FIVE

Safed

1. THE RAMAK

One of the greatest of all theoretical Kabbalists, and one of the main systematisers of its philosophy, was Rabbi Moshe Cordevero (1522—1570) of Safed. So respected was he that he was the first Kabbalist honored by being called by his initials, and even today, initiates call him "the Ramak." Until his time, only the greatest Talmudic masters had been given this distinction, having the word "the" added before their initials to indicate that they were a solid part of the tradition. Thus for example, Rabbi Moshe ben Maimon (Maimonides) became known as "the Rambam," Rabbi Moshe ben Nachman (Nachmanides) became "the Ramban," and Rabbi Sh'lomo ben Adret became "the Rashba."

The Ramak was born in Safed, a city that was to become famed as a center of the Kabbalah. At a very tender age, he gained a reputation as a most extraordinary genius. Besides his knowledge in Kabbalah, he was a Talmudic scholar and philosopher of the highest rank, and was widely respected in these fields. But his main interest was the systematisation of the Kabbalah, setting it into a philosophical structure, a task that had already been started by Rabbi Judah Chayit (1462—1529) and Rabbi Meir Gabbai (1480—1547).

The Zohar had been accepted as the foundation of Kabbalah, but for the most part, its system appeared as complex and unstructured as that of the Bible and Talmud. It took a genius of the stature of Maimonides to unravel and systematise the philosophical system of the Bible and Talmud, clearly outlining the organizing principles underlying its structure. What the Rambam had done for the more conventional tradition, the Ramak was to do for the Kabbalah.

Like Maimonides, the Ramak defended his system against its detractors, and in most cases his words were directed against those philosophers who refused to accept the authority of the Kabbalah. In one place, he states that the philosophers can only surmise what exists in the metaphysical realm, while the Kabbalist can actually see it.[1] But besides being the pre-eminent philosopher of the Kabbalistic world, the Ramak was also thoroughly familiar with its mystical elements. He was an expert in the various systems of meditative and practical Kabbalah, and although he rarely speaks about these areas, there is enough in his writings to indicate an intimate familiarity. Thus, in one place he quote a long section from Abulafia's *Or HaSekhel.*[2] Elsewhere, he actually mentions the book and its author by name, saying that this is the most important system involving the pronunciation of the Divine Name.[3]

No mere theorist, the Ramak was also actively engaged in Kabbalah meditation, through a method known as *Gerushin* or "Divorce." We know very little of this method, even though an entire booklet, called *Sefer Gerushin* (Book of Divorce) was written regarding the insight that the Ramak gained through this method.[4] Most probably it consisted of meditating on a given scripture, or perhaps repeating it over and over like a mantra until one could relate to it on a high meditative state. One would then gain deep insight into it, without having to analyze it logically.

The word "Divorce" in this context, most probably meant divorce from the physical, even though it also obviously had the connotation of separation and seclusion from inhabited places. In this respect, it is very much like the word *Hitbodedut*, which refers to both physical and mental seclusion.

The Ramak founded a Kabbalah academy in Safed, and until the rise of the Ari, was considered the dean of the Safed school. Among his disciples were many of the luminaries of Safed, including Rabbi Eliahu di Vidas, author of *Reshit Chokhmah* (Beginning of Wisdom), and Rabbi Chaim Vital, who later became the Ari's Boswell. It is reported that the prophet Elijah revealed himself to the Ramak, and when he died, the Ari said that he saw a pillar of fire following his bier.

It was largely under the leadership of the Ramak that Safed became the greatest center of Kabbalah that the world has ever known — a city whose very name is synonymous with the Kabbalah. But there were also other factors that contributed to this, and it seems as if all the forces of Providence had conspired to create this great city of saints and scholars. Three events in the late 1400's were to have a most important influence.

The first was the discovery of printing. Guttenberg had printed his Bible around 1450, and by 1475 the first Hebrew book had been printed. By the 1490's, over a hundred Hebrew titles had been published, putting the tools of scholarship into the hands of almost everyone. Whereas scholars had previously had to make do with a limited number of expensive, and often barely legible manuscripts, they now could make use of rapidly growing personal libraries, having all necessary information at their fingertips. The information explosion led to the need of systematisation, and it was during these generations that interest grew, and the need was seen to systemize the entire body of Jewish knowledge, including the Kabbalah.

It was during this period that the era of *Rishonim* (early codifiers) came to a close, and that of *Acharonim* (later codifiers) began. While the Rishonim were considered to be primary sources, the Acharonim were merely secondary sources, who dealt mainly with clarifying and writing commentaries on the works of the Rishonim. While the Rishonim studied and published manuscripts, the Acharonim studied and published printed books.

The second major event was Columbus' discovery of the New World in 1492. As a result of the change in world view, much of earlier philosophy had to be re-examined, and the philosophical schools, which had opposed the Kabbalah, were significantly weakened. The discoveries of that time expanded man's horizons, and people began to seek similar expansion of their spiritual lives. This led many to explore the mind-expanding systems taught by the Kabbalah.

Most explosive, however, was the Spanish Inquisition, culminating with the expulsion of all Jews from Spain, also in 1492. Spain had been an important center of Jewish learning in general, and Kabbalah in particular, for many centuries, and with the expulsion, its leaders were forced to find a new center. We shall encounter a few individuals who left Spain as youths, most notably Joseph Caro, who was four at the time, and Jacob Berab, who was eighteen. But most important for the initial development of Safed were two mature Kabbalists, both named Joseph: Rabbi Joseph Saragossi and Rabbi Joseph Taitatzak.

Until this time, Safed had been a small Jewish community, not exerting any known influence. In the early 1490's, its spiritual leader, Rabbi Peretz Colobo, had to maintain a small grocery in order to support himself, the community being too small to pay him. All this, however, was changed with the arrival of Rabbi Joseph Saragossi.

Born in Saragossa, Spain, the birthplace of Abulafia, Rabbi Joseph fled with his correligionist in 1492. Possibly following Abulafia's path, he settled for a while in Sicily. From there, he emigrated to Beirut, and in 1496, described as an "absolute saint," we find him moving to Sidon, where he accepted te post of chief rabbi.[5] From there, he assumed the role of rabbi in Safed, which he began to build up as a center for Kabbalah. One of his first tasks as rabbi was to start an academy, where both the Talmud and Kabbalah were taught.

Saragossi was respected by Jew and Moslem alike for his appeasing spirit, and he was loved and revered like an angel of peace. The author of *Sefer Cheredim,* a younger contemporary, writes, "Joseph Saragossi, teacher of the Radbaz, always brought peace between man and his neighbors, and between husband and wife, even among the gentiles. He was worthy of seeing the prophet Elijah."[6]

The Radbaz mentioned here was Rabbi David abu Zimra (1470—1572), who had also been exiled from Spain. Together with his father, he had settled in Safed, and he soon became an important disciple of Rabbi Joseph. Although the Radbaz later gained fame as one of the greatest authorities on Jewish Law, he also wrote numerous books on Kabbalah. He was aware of Abulafia's writings, and in at least one place mentions his *Chayay Olam HaBah.*[7]

It is highly significant to note that Rabbi Judah Albotini, author of *Sulam Aliyah* (Ladder of Ascent) and one of the most important teachers of Abulafia's methods, was still alive at the time. He was rabbi in Jerusalem, and continued to teach until 1519. It would appear highly probable that the Radbaz made his acquaintance, and there was possibly also communication between Albotini and Saragossi. Albotini had also lived on the Iberian Peninsula, in Portugal, and was most probably known to the Spanish Kabbalists.

The Radbaz emigrated to Egypt in 1514, and three years later, Egypt was overrun by the Turks. Abraham Castro, who had been appointed master of the mint, elevated the Radbaz to the position of Chief Rabbi of Cairo. The two were undoubtedly very close, and the Radbaz taught Castro the mysteries of the Kabbalah, informing him of the schools in Jerusalem and Safed. Later, in 1538, we find Castro as a patron and disciple of Rabbi Joseph Tzayach, who had succeeded Albotini as the leader of the Jerusalem school of Kabbalah. It is also known that Tazyach and the Radbaz corresponded with each other.

An important disciple of the Radbaz in Egypt was Rabbi Betzalel Ashkenazi, renowned as the author of the *Shitah Mekubetzet,* a most important Talmudic commentary. But beyond this, along with the Radbaz, Rabbi Betzalel was the one who introduced the Ari into the mysteries of the Kabbalah.

The second important Joseph who had been exiled from Spain was Rabbi Joseph Taitatzak (1477—1545), who settled in Salonica. Renowned as one of the greatest sages of his time, he counted among his disciples such luminaries as Rabbi Samuel di Modina (the Maharashdam), Isaac Adrabi and Joseph Caro. A younger contemporary, Rabbi Eliahu di Vidas, writes in his *Reshit Chokhmah*, "I heard that the sage, Rabbi Joseph Taitatzak, of blessed memory, did not sleep in a bed for forty years, except on the Sabbath. It is told that he used to sleep on a box, with his feet hanging down, and that he would get up at midnight. No one knew about this, and it was only revealed by his wife after he died."[8]

One of Taitatzak's most important disciples in Kabbalah was Rabbi Shlomo AlKabatz (1505—1584), a native of Solinica, best known as the author of the Friday night hymn, *Lecha Dodi*. It was he who was destined to initiate the Ramak into the mysteries of the Kabbalah.

In 1522, the year of the Ramak's birth, another event took place that had a profound effect on the Jewish community. This was the pilgrimage of David Reuveni, a cryptical messianic figure from Kheybar on the Arabian peninsula, who was able to stand up before popes and kings. Travelling through Egypt in 1523, Reuveni reports seeking an audience with Abraham Castro, and it is also possible that he met with the Radbaz.[9] A year later, Reuveni gained an audience with Pope Clement VII (1478-1534), who was apparently very impressed with his visitor from Arabia.

During Reuveni's travels, he arrived in Portugal, where he was accepted in the court of King John III. It was there that he met the king's scribe, Shlomo Molcho, (1501—1532), a Marrano who had been baptized under the name of Diogo Pires. Like many Marranos of that period, he had studied Judaism secretly, and was proficient in Bible and Talmud. Portugal had been the site of a great Kabbalistic school, producing such luminaries as Rabbi Judah Chayit and Judah Albotini, and it is quite possible that Molcho had also come into contact with a remnant of this school that had survived the expulsion and had gone into hiding. Upon meeting Reuveni in 1525, Molcho circumcised himself and fled to Solinica.

What happened next is somewhat vague. In Salonica, Molcho was drawn into the circle of Rabbi Joseph Taitatzak, and apparently learned much Kabbalah from him. On the other hand, Molcho seemed much more adept in the meditative Kabbalah than Taitatzak, possibly on the basis of mysteries he had learned while still in Portugal. By means of meditative devices that we shall discuss, Molcho was able to communicate with a Maggid, a kind of angelic spokesman. Apprised of these methods, Taitatzak also made use of them, and before long he was also in communication with a Maggid.

There are reports that Molcho also travelled to the Holy Land, possibly communicating with the Kabbalists of Jerusalem and Safed. He met with Pope Clement VII in 1530, and, having gained respect in the Vatican, was adored by the Jews of Rome. A dangerous trap in meditation is that it often makes one feel that he has superhuman powers when these powers are actually nonexistent, and it appears that Molcho fell into this trap.

In 1532, Molcho sought an audience with Charles V (1500—1558), King of Spain and Holy Roman Emperor. As a leader who had engaged in many religious battles, Charles was unimpressed with this upstart, and had him handed over to the Inquisition. Since Molcho had been baptized as a Catholic in Portugal, he was tried as a renegade, and burned at the stake for heresy. Years later, Molcho's example was taken as a warning for those who would venture too far into the mysteries of the meditative Kabbalah.[10]

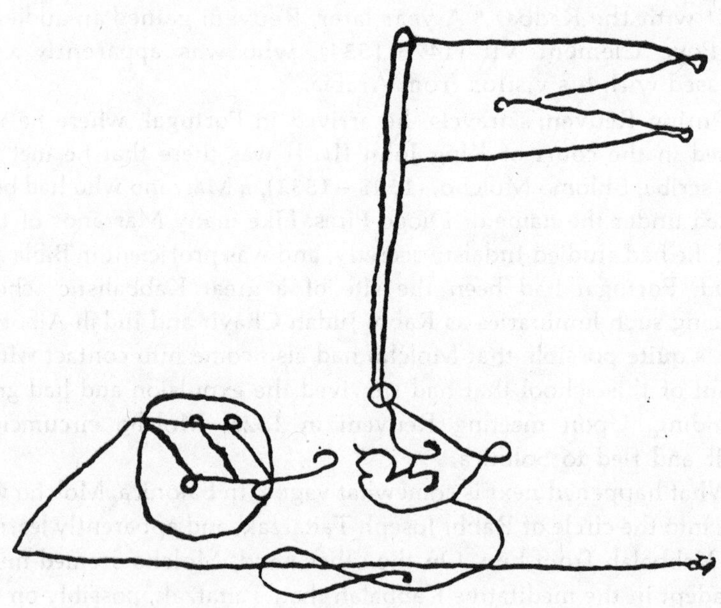

Autograph of Rabbi Shlomo Molcho

A few years later, in the mid 1530's, three individuals came to Safed, and these were to make the city a center of scholarship and mysticism. The first was the thirty-year-old Shlomo AlKabatz of Solinica, a disciple of Rabbi Joseph Taitatzak, who had already earned a reputation as a brilliant Kabbalist. The young Moshe Cordevero, who had recently celebrated his Bar Mitzvah, looked upon him with awe, never realizing that he would some day become his most famous disciple.

The second individual was Rabbi Jacob Berab (1474—1546), a native of Castile, who had been expelled from Spain as a teenager. After spending a number of years in Portugal, Morocco and Algiers, he settled in Egypt in 1523, where he came under the influence of the Radbaz. It is also possible that he had met David Reuveni, who had passed through Egypt around that time. Already renowned as an important sage, Berab was almost fifty when he settled in Safed in 1535. A year later, upon the death of Rabbi Joseph Saragossi, he was appointed chief rabbi of the community.

The third new arrival was Rabbi Joseph Caro (1488—1575), author of the *Sulchan Arukh* (Set Table), the recognized Code of Jewish Law. Born in Toledo, he was only four years old when his family was expelled from Spain and emigrated to Portugal. Recognized as a prodigy even at this tender age, he studied together with Rabbi Jacob Berab, who was fourteen years his senior, while they both were in Lisbon. With the expulsion of Jews from Portugal in 1498, he emigrated to Constantinople, and from there to Adrianople, in European Turkey.

By the time he was twenty, Caro was recognized as a leading expert in Jewish law. In 1522, the year of the Ramak's birth and David Reuveni's emergence, he began his *magnum opus,* the *Bet Yosef* (House of Joseph). This book brought together, for the first time, in a single volume, virtually every decision that had ever been rendered in Jewish Law. Caro worked at this task for twenty years, and this monumental work later became the basis for his better known *Shulchan Arukh.*

While in Adrianopolis, Caro met Shlomo Molcho and was very much impressed with him. The two became close, and it was from Molcho that the great legalist learned the meditative techniques involved in communicating with a Maggid.

In 1533, a year after Molcho's execution, Caro moved to Salonica, where he established a major Talmudical academy. He became close friends with Rabbi Joseph Taitatzak, and apparently reviewed the techniques for summoning a Maggid with him. It was on the festival of

Shavuot (Pentecost), probably in 1535, that a Maggid first revealed itself to Caro, and the revelations of this Maggid are recorded in a most interesting book *Maggid Mesharim*.

At the urging of his Maggid, Caro emigrated to the Holy Land, settling in Safed in 1537.[11] There he found a community that had grown to over a thousand Jewish families, and he rapidly established himself as a leading figure in the academy of Rabbi Jacob, his older tutor from Lisbon. It was not long before the two brilliant minds devised a scheme that, if successful, would alter the entire structure of Jewish life, and possibly also hasten the coming of the Messiah.

What they had in mind was nothing less than to re-establish the ancient rite of ordination. This ordination had far-reaching legal consequences, and had been handed down from master to disciple from the time of Moses until the Fourth Century. Then, as a result of persecutions in the Holy Land, the chain had been broken.

The great Moses Maimonides had written that this *Semichah*-ordination would have to be re-established before the coming of the Messiah. He also wrote that even if there was no master to confer it, it could be granted to any sage by the mutual consent of all the rabbis in the Holy Land.[12] Since the majority of such rabbis resided in Safed at the time, Berab and Caro felt that the other communities would go along once the project was initiated. In 1538, the Rabbis of Safed unanimously decided to confer this ordination on Rabbi Jacob Berab. There was one rabbi, however, who refused to accept this ordination. That was the Ralbach (Rabbi Levi ibn Chabib: 1480—1541), chief rabbi of Jerusalem, and a result of his opposition, the question of ordination erupted into a major controversy.

As a result, Berab was forced to leave his post and flee to Damascus. Before leaving, he conferred this special *Semicha*-ordination on four of his most outstanding disciples. This *Semicha* was the highest academic honor that could be conferred on an individual, and it indicated that he had mastered all areas of Talmudic and legal scholarship. Three of the recipients were mature rabbis, who were already renowned as the leading luminaries of that period. These were Rabbi Joseph Caro, Moshe of Trani, and Joseph Sagis. The fourth was a sixteen-year-old youth — the Ramak.

Rabbi Jacob Berab died in 1541 and was succeeded as rabbi of Safed by Rabbi Joseph Caro. A year later, Caro completed his monumental *Bet Yosef*, a work that would establish him for all times as a leading authority in Jewish law.

That same year, at the age of twenty, the Ramak heard a voice urging him to begin studying Kabbalah with Rabbi Shlomo AlKabatz. He was thus initiated into the mysteries of the Zohar, and mastered the text completely. This failed to satisfy him, however, since the teachings of the Zohar are often vague, and its system does not have a discernible structure. In order to clarify this in his own mind, the Ramak began writing two books. The first, which has only recently been published, was *Or Yakar* (The Precious Light), a huge commentary on the Zohar.[13] It was the second book, however, that was his *magnum opus.*

Known as the *Pardes Rimonim* (Orchard of Pomegranates), or simply as the *Pardes,* it was a systematization of all Kabbalistic thought up to that time. Especially important was the fact that the Ramak reconciled many early schools with the teachings of the Zohar, demonstrating the essential unity of Kabbalah. Using the same close logic that Caro had used in his legal works, the Ramak shows how the Kabbalistic system has a self-consistent philosophical basis. Were it not for the fact that philosophy and Kabbalah are usually considered to be antagonistic, the *Pardes* would be considered a classic of philosphical analysis, as well as one of Kabbalah.

Soon after the completion of the *Pardes* in 1548, The Ramak began engaging in *Gerushin* meditation, together with other members of AlKabatz's group. This was also the same year in which Rabbi Joseph Tzayach completed his *Sheirit Yosef* in Jerusalem. The Ramak was familiar with Tzayach's methods, as well as those of Abulafia, but he apparently preferred a different method, known as *Gerushin,* which was apparently related to that used to evoke a Maggid.

An Excerpt From

Maggid Mesharim

[The Maggid declared:]

Whenever you are in a pure place, constantly think about Torah, fear [of God] and my Mishnah. Do not abandon Torah and fear, even for a second, even when you eat and speak. Your tongue should be the heaviest limb of your body, like it was for the last few days. All your limbs must constantly be unified toward my service, fear, and Torah. Recall what [the Talmud] says about Rav, that he never spoke an idle word, all his life.

This is what a person must do: He must integrate all of his

thoughts toward the fear of God and His worship. It is thus written, "My son, give Me your heart, let your eyes observe My ways" (Proverbs 23:26). This means that when you keep a commandment or study Torah, your heart should be unified to God, and you should not think about anything else....

This should certainly be true when you pray. Nullify every thought that enters your heart. [Banish] the Evil Urge and its host, as well as the forces of Samael and the Serpent, which accompany this. Unify your heart constantly, at all times, so that every instant you will think of nothing other than God, His Torah and His worship.

This is the mystery of Unity, through which a person literally unifies himself with his Creator. The soul attachs itself to Him, and becomes becomes one with Him, so that the body literally becomes a dwelling place of the Divine Presence. This is what the Torah means when it says, "You shall fear God your Lord, and you shall serve Him and attach yourself to Him" (Deuteronomy 10:20).[14]

Therefore, my son, complete a perfect Unification. If you do so, then "I will give you a place to walk among those [angels]who stand here" [15] I will make you worthy to go to the Land of Israel, and to come together with my beloved Shlomo [Molcho].

Maggid Mesharim[16]

2. COLORS

We have already discussed the method of ascending through the Sefirot using the names of God, especially as elucidated in Rabbi Joseph Gikatalia's *Shaarey Orah* (Gates of Light). The Ramak echoes this, and in his *Pardes* states that the main reason why the Sefirot were created was to provide a ladder upon which one could climb to the highest spiritual levels.[17] The method taught by the Ramak and other members of the Safed school, aims at a greater degree of unification than that embraced by Gikatalia's school.

This system, based on the Zohar, makes use of no other name than the Tetragrammaton. The Sefirot are represented by ten different vowel points.[18] One can then meditate on the Tetragrammaton with these different vowel points, and in this manner, bind himself to whichever Sefirah he desires.

Although one can simply meditate on the Names as they would be written in a book, this technique is greatly enhanced when colors are used. When each Name is colored with a shade appropriate to that Sefirah, one can bind himself to that Sefirah all the more intimately. The system of colors is discussed at length in the works of Rabbi Joseph Tzayach, and the Ramak was apparently aware of these writings.[19] But, while Tzayach makes no attempt to relate his system to that of the Zohar, the Ramak shows that the two are both an identical tradition.

Excerpts From

Pardes Rimonim

The Ninth Gate:
The Gate of Colors

In many places in Kabbalistic texts and the Zohar, we find that various colors parallel the Sefirot. One must be very careful and not imagine that this is to be taken literally. Color is something physical, used to describe the physical world, and [the Sefirot], which are spiritual should not be described with physical properties. If a person thinks that these are literally the colors of the Sefirot, he destroys the entire system, and oversteps the boundaries set by the ancients. One who delves into this should therefore be most careful not to assume that anything physical is implied.

But actually, these colors allude to the results that are transmitted from the highest Roots. Thus, for example, Gevurah-Strength is responsible for victory in war. Since this involves bloodshed, where red blood is spilt, it is fitting to ascribe the color red to this Sefirah. The color red likewise expresses hatred, anger and rage. This is obvious.

We therefore ascribe the color red to the place of Judgment. Furthermore, everything that is red is derived from the power of this Root. This has been discussed in detail in the "Gate of Essence and Function."[20]

Likewise, the color white indicates mercy and peace. This is because people with white [hair] are usually merciful. Thus, for example, the elders and aged do not usually fight in armies. Therefore, if you wish to depict peace and the Sefirah of Chesed-Love, you depict it with the color white.

There is no question that things that are white emanate from the power of this Root. This too has been explained in the above mentioned Gate.

This, then, is the proper interpretation of the relationship between the colors and the Sefirot. The colors are used allegorically to allude to their functions and results.

[The Sefirot] do not exist in a spatial continuum, and therefore, it is impossible to differentiate them except through allegory. This can only be done when we use colors to allegorically represent [the Sefirot. We can then imagine the Sefirot as] being differentiated, ascending, or increasing, according to the relation between one color and another. The dynamics of the Sefirot can therefore be alluded to completely through the interplay of colors. All this is to "ease the physical ear,"[21] allowing the verbal expression of these concepts.

There is no question that the colors can thus serve as a door to the dynamics of the Sefirot. They are also useful in transmitting influence from a given Sefirah.

Thus, if you wish to transmit the influence of mercy from the

Colors and the Sefirot	
Sefirah	*Color*
Keter-Crown	blinding invisable white
Chokhmah-Wisdom	a color that includes all colors
Binah-Understanding	yellow and green
Chesed-Love	white and silver
Gevurah-Strength	red and gold
Tiferet-Beauty	yellow and purple
Netzach-Victory	light pink
Hod-Splendor	dark pink
Yesod-Foundation	Orange
Malkhut-Kingship	Blue

Sefirah of Chesed-Love, [meditate on] the color associated with this Sefirah. Depict the color of the attribute [that you desire]. If you wish pure mercy, then this color will be pure white. If your request involves a lesser degree of mercy, depict a softer white, like that of the "mortar of the Temple."[22] We will discuss this further in the "Gate of Kavanah."

Therefore, if an individual wishes to accomplish something through the transmission of Judgment, he should wear red vestments. He then meditates on the Tetragrammaton, depicting it in red [letters]. Similarly, in any activity where one wishes mercy, and desires to transmit the power of Chesed-Love, he should wear white vestments.

This is clearly seen from the Cohen-priests. Their function was to transmit power from the side of Chesed-Love. They therefore wore white vestments, which indicate peace. On Yom Kippur (the Day of Atonement), the High Priest would likewise remove his golden vestments and wear white. The entire service that day was performed in white vestments, and the reason given is that ""an accuser does not become an advocate,"[23] [since gold denotes Judgment. The white, however] indicates the [mercy] that the High Priest was seeking.

The same principle holds true for amulets. When one makes an amulet (*kameya,* קָמֵעַ) to transmit Chesed-Love, he should draw the necessary Name in brilliant white [letters]. This will enhance the effectiveness of the Name. Likewise, when one seeks Judgment, he should draw the Name associated with Judgment in red. Goat's blood is often used for this purpose, since both its color and source then allude to Judgment.[24] These things are well known and are obvious to those who write amulets, even though we have no portion in these practices.

It is thus known that when Names are drawn on amulets, those which involve Judgment are drawn in red, those involving Love, in white, and those pertaining to Mercy, in green. This is all known through Maggidim, who taught the methods of writing amulets.[25]

All this teaches that the colors can serve as a channel for the forces that are transmitted from on high.

This also closely parallels the rites of some idolators. When they offer incense, they know how to influence the power of a particular sign of the Zodiac. While performing these rites, they would wear vestments [whose color] was associated with their actions.

Clear evidence to this concept can be seen in the Breastplate of the High Priest.[26] This contained twelve precious stones, each one [being a different color], alluding to the transmission of power from the spiritual source of each of the Twelve Tribes.

Do not reject this concept. The alchemists teach that when a person gazes at running water, the White Bile is aroused in him. Thus, when a person has insomnia and cannot sleep, they set pipes with running water in front of him, in order to arouse the White Bile. This increases the moisture in his body, and he is able to sleep.

The same is true in our case. When an initiate flies with his mind, he finds this invaluable. Colors that are visible to the eye, or which are depicted in the mind, can have an effect on the spiritual, even though the colors themselves are physical.

The Nefesh (lower soul) can motivate the Ruach (middle spirit), and the Ruach in turn motivates the Neshamah (upper soul). The Neshamah then ascends from one essence to the next, until it reaches its Source. It can then be motivated by what it imagines.

These [thoughts] are like a mirror to the [Divine] Countenance. Through [the thoughts transmitted to] the Source [of the Neshamah], the Countenance can [be made to] appear red. It then transmits [an influence associated with the color] red [back to this Source].[27] The same can be true of the color white. This is explained in the "Gate of Pipes," Chapter 1. All influence on the Lower Countenance is the result of human action, as explained in the "Gate of Essence and Function," Chapter 18.

The Thirty-Second Gate: The Gate of Kavanah

Chapter 1

In the previous Gate, we have discussed how man is a "portion of God from on high." If one is pure and upright in deed, and if he grasps the cords of love, which exist in the holy roots of his soul, he can ascend to every level in all the [supernal] Universes. All this has been discussed in the previous Gate.

When a person is upright and righteous, he can meditate *(kaven)* with appropriate thoughts , and ascend through the levels of the transcendental. He must unify the levels of his soul, joining one part to another, bringing the different levels of his soul to vest themselves in each other. It then becomes like a single candelabrum, made of different parts joined together.

The individual must then unify the Sefirot, bringing them to bind themselves together with a powerful knot. He and his soul then become a channel through which the Sefirot can exert influence. [All of them], from the highest to the lowest [then act in concert] through the powerful cord that binds them together. For when a person binds his soul to the [Supernal] Soul through his Mishnah,[28] it causes the Roots to be bound together with a strong knot. . . .

Chapter 2

We must now explain the idea of meditating on the Sefirot, since there is some confusion in this area.

Commenting on the verse, "[Who is a great nation that has God close to them,] like the Lord (YHVH) our God, whenever we call Him" (Deuteronomy 4:7), the *Sifri* states, "[We call to] Him, and not to His Attributes." [29]

This is also logical. Why should we approach the King's servants rather than the King himself? It is certainly fitting that we pray only to the Master of all Treasuries. This being true, why are all our prayers associated with the various Sefirot?

The question becomes even stronger when we realize that every word alludes to a different Sefirah. Therefore, if one keeps his mind [on the inner essence of his words], it comes out that all his prayers allude to the Sefirot. We are left with nothing that is directed to the Source of Sources.

Besides this, how is it possible to meditate on the Sefirot. If a person attempts to depict any Sefirah in his mind, it is inevitable that he will delineate it and depict it as something physical. The mind can only depict physical things, so how can he imagine a purely spiritual concept? The mind's eye cannot imagine spiritual entities without making them finite and physical. It is therefore impossible to meditate on a Sefirah.

There is also a third difficulty. When a person thinks about any one of the Attributes, it is inevitable that he will separate it [from the rest]. In his mind, he imagines a separate Attribute, distinct from all the others. This is certainly not proper, since they all must be unified. This is well known.

We will now explain the meaning of this, and clarify all these concepts.

It is necessary to realize that the Infinite Being (*Ain Sof*), the blessed King of Kings, cannot be encompassed by any name or word.[30] It is not correct to speak of any attributes in this Essence, since it does not change, and cannot be described. It cannot be altered, first having one desire and then another, or first engaging in one activity and then in another.

Therefore, when one meditates on the Infinite Being, he should not call It *El*, or *Elo'ah*, or *Elohim*, or any other name or appelation. All of these names only pertain to the Sefirot.

But, as we have already said, one should not direct his intent toward the Sefirot, heaven forbid, since one who does so falls into a deep pit. It is with regard to this that the *Sifri* says, "To Him, and not to His Attributes." The true intent, however, is as we have explained in the "Gate of Essence and Vessels."

God is called "Mighty" through the Attribute of Gevurah-Strength. This is because it is He who gives [the Sefirah of] Gevurah-Strength the power to act. [The same is true of "Greatness," which is associated with the Sefirah of Chesed-Love.][31]

Therefore, when a person says, "The Great God" [in the Amidah], he should meditate on the fact that this alludes to "Greatness" [the Sefirah of Chesed-Love], and that the word itself is in "Greatness." Still, his intent should [not be directed to the Sefirah itself, but to the Infinite Being, which is] the Essence that permeates "Greatness." The Same is true of Gevurah-Strength and the other Sefirot.

The words are therefore appellations [for the various Attributes] in the Sefirot, and they are adjectives pertaining to God. The intent,

Sefirot and the Tetragrammaton

Sefirah	*Vowel*			*Tetragrammaton*	
Keter	*Kametz*	a	אָ	YaHaVaHa	יָהָוָהָ
Chokhmah	*Patach*	a	אַ	YaHaVaHa	יַהַוַהַ
Binah	*Tzeré*	e	אֵ	YeHeVeHe	יֵהֵוֵהֵ
Chesed	*Segol*	e	אֶ	YeHeVeHe	יֶהֶוֶהֶ
Gevurah	*Sheva*	ʼ	אְ	Y'H'V'H'	יְהְוְהְ
Tiferet	*Cholem*	o	אֹ	YoHoVoHo	יֹהֹוֹהֹ
Netzach	*Chirek*	i	אִ	YiHiViHi	יִהִוִהִ
Hod	*Kibbutz*	u	אֻ	YuHuVuHu	יֻהֻוֻהֻ
Yesod	*Shurek*	u	אוּ	YuHuVuHu	יוּהוּווּהוּ
Malkhut	*No Vowel*			YHVH	יהוה

The Four Letters and the Sefirot

Apex of Yod	*Keter*
Yod (י)	*Chokhmah*
Heh (ה)	*Binah*
Vav (ו = 6)	*The Six Sefirot: Chesed, Gevurah, Tiferet, Netzach, Hod, Yesod*
Heh (ה)	*Malkhut*

however, is directed only toward the Infinite Being, who is clothed in [the Sefirot] and makes use of them.

In the *Tikuney Zohar*, Rabbi Shimon bar Yochai says, "Whenever one pronounces a word, he must keep in mind that speech is *Adonoy* (אֲדֹנָי), and voice is YHVH (יהוה). One must bring them together, unifying them in the Concealed Unity (*Ain Sof*), which binds them together and makes them as one. One's intent must be directed to this alone. This is not voice or speech, but thought."[32]

It is explicitly taught that the Tetragrammaton (YHVH) is associated with the Sefirah of Tiferet-Beauty. Since the voice that emanates from [God's] "mouth" is also associated with Tiferet, it is related to [the Tetragrammaton]. Similarly, speech is related to the name Adonoy, which is associated with the Sefirah of Malkhut-Kingship.

Thought, however, is the Infinite Being (*Ain Sof*), through which these two Attributes are unified.

In the entire worship service, there is no allusion to the Infinite Being (*Ain Sof*), other than the thought that the worshipper directs toward It. This, however, is everything. It unifies all the Attributes and Influences. This is the mystery of the Basic Essence that infuses all the Sefirot, through which the Sefirot have power to function. Due to this, the action itself is also ascribed to [this Essence]. This is explained in detail in the "Gate of Essence and Vessels."

This does not mean that one should meditate on the Sefirot or try to imagine them, since this is impossible, as we have already explained. Rather, it means that the Sefirot are associated with ten names, [spelled with the four letters] of the Tetragrammaton. These names are only differentiated by their vowels, as explained in the "Gate of the Tetragrammaton."[33] . . . (The Names are given in the Table).

One who meditates should concentrate on these Names. He should keep in mind that nothing can allude to the Attribute that he seeks other than the Tetragrammaton that is depicted in his mind. These consist of the Four Letters, vocalized in the appropriate manner. If he does this, he can procede without fear.

One should also keep in mind that these Four Letters themselves allude to the Ten Sefirot. This denotes the fact that all Ten Sefirot agree to the action desired of any single Sefirah.

It is best if one can depict each Tetragrammaton in the color [associated with the particulr Sefirah]. His prayer will then help all the more. The only condition is that he should keep in mind that nothing in this world can depict the action of that Attribute, other than the color associated with it.

3. RABBI CHAIM VITAL

It would appear appropriate to place the chapter dealing with Rabbi Chaim Vital after that dealing with the Ari, since he was a disciple of the latter. But Chaim Vital was more closely associated with the older schools of Kabbalah, while the Ari used the Zohar to blaze a completely new trail. The disciple will therefore be discussed first.

The output of Chaim Vital was prodigious. If not for him, very little if any of the Ari's teachings would even be known. But even though Rabbi Chaim was strongly influenced by the Ari, he was only a disciple for less than two years. Within a decade after his master's death, he was showing increased signs of independence, and began delving into the teaching of the older schools once again. At one point, the Ari came to him in a dream and asked, "Why have you forgotten me?"[34]

One of the most remarkable books about the meditative Kabbalah, and one of the very few ever printed, was Chaim Vital's *Shaarey Kedushah* (Gates of Holiness). Although the author states that he learned these methods from the Ari, nuch of the material comes from older sources. Indeed, the unpublished Fourth Section of this book consists almost entirely of quotations from older texts.

Rabbi Chaim Vital was a most unusual individual. Possessing an extremely brilliant mind, he was acknowledged as an expert in Kabbalah even before he met the Ari. At the time of this first meeting, he was engaged in writing a commentary on the Zohar.[35] Although only twenty-seven at the time, he was already an outstanding expert in alchemy, astronomy, astrology, Kabbalistic magic, and all the occult arts. When Chaim Vital first heard of the Ari, he hesitated to visit him, considering himself a far superior Kabbalist.

It did not take long before Rabbi Chaim became aware of the Ari's superior vision and insight, but the Ari also saw his main disciple in this lofty soul. On one occasion, he tells Chaim Vital that he had come to Safed especially to teach him, and at another time, he told his disciple that he had been born into this world only to teach him.[36] The disciple himself was an expert in all Kabbalistic meditations, and was aware of all schools. In many ways, his *Shaarey Kedushah*, especially the Fourth Part, is an anthology of these teachings.

Rabbi Chaim was born in 1543 in Safed to Rabbi Joseph Vital, who was also known as Calabrese, since his family originated in Calabria, the toe of Italy's boot. Rabbi Joseph was a scribe who specialized in making Tefillin, and the Tefillin capsules that he made were famed as the finest available.[37] Chaim's childhood in Safed must have been fascinating, since this city had become one of the most important hubs of Jewish thought, both Kabbalistic and otherwise. He was a child of five when the Ramak completed his great *Pardes Rimonim*, and at the age of seven, he saw the first printed copies of Rabbi Joseph Caro's monumental legal work, the *Bet Yosef*. As a ten year old lad, he witnessed the return to Safed of the great Radbaz, who had served as chief Rabbi of Cairo for over forty years.

Safed was a city steeped in Kabbalah, not only in its theoretical and philosophical forms, but also in its most occult aspects. The city abounded with chiromancers, oil drop readers and fortune tellers, and Rabbi Chaim even associated with Arab mystics who were involved in crystal gazing and geomancy.[38] Although the Ari disapproved of these practices, soon after his master's death, Chaim Vital renewed his interest in them.

Shortly after his Bar Mitzvah, Chaim became a student of Rabbi Moshe AlShech (1508—1600). "The AlShech," as he is usually called, is best known as the author of *Torat Moshe*, which is considered to be the most important homiletic commentaries ever written on the Bible. A native of Adrianople, he studied there under Rabbi Joseph Caro, and later in Salonica, under Joseph Taitatzak. In Safed, Caro was told by his Maggid to speak to AlShech, and instruct him to pay attention to the young Chaim Vital, since he was an extraordinary soul and would someday be an important leader.

In 1558, when Vital was fifteen years old, an event took place that would permanently change the entire status of the Kabbalah. This was the first printing of the Zohar in Mantua, Italy. There had been considerable dispute regarding the propriety of openly publishing a text that dealt with the highest mysteries, but a leading authority, Rabbi Isaac de Lattes (1502—1571), rendered a decision permitting it. The

Zohar would now not just be the province of those well enough connected to procure a manuscript copy, but would be available for all who wished to purchase it.

Rabbi Chaim was married at the age of twenty-two, but for some reason, could not consummate the marriage for nine months, during which time he was led into very serious temptations.[39] It was around this time that he also became a disciple of the Ramak in Kabbalah, and his brilliant mind mastered the complex system with relative ease. Before long he had begun his own commentary on the Zohar, following the Ramak's principles. Still, he was hounded by temptations, and for some two years, abandoned his studies almost completely.

Seeking advice from the ancient Radbaz, Vital was informed of the Kabbalistic school in Damascus, possibly that of Rabbi Joseph Tzayach, who was still teaching there at the time. Rabbi Chaim went to damascus in 1569, continuing his work on the Zohar commentary. He was soon to be brought back to Safed by an event that would make the city a citadel of Kabbalah: the arrival of the Ari.

The relationship between the Ari and Chaim Vital is most significant, and will be discussed at length in the next chapter. In all, Vital was the Ari's disciple for only twenty-two months, but during this time, he was able to absorb a prodigious amount. He became the leading expounder of the Ari's system, writing over a dozen large volumes on the subject.

After the death of the Ari in 1572, Chaim Vital frequently saw him in dreams, but as the years passed, these nocturnal visits became increasingly infrequent. Rabbi Chaim soon began giving his own lectures in Kabbalah, and in 1576 went to Egypt, possibly to link up with the Kabbalistic school founded by Abraham Castro, which used Tzayach's methods. From there, he returned to Jerusalem, where in 1590, he received the *Semichah*-ordination from Rabbi Moshe AlShech, who had in turn received it from Joseph Caro.[40] Rabbi Chaim Vital settled in Damascus in 1594, and with the exception of occasional visits to Safed, remained there until his death in 1620.

4. GATES OF HOLINESS

Rabbi Chaim Vital's *Shaarey Kedushah* (Gates of Holiness) stands alone as being the only textbook of Kabbalistic meditation ever printed. Indeed, the Fourth Section, which deals with the specific methods, was never published. The printer of the first edition, which came out in 1738, states that it is for this reason that this section must remain unpublished, as we have discussed in the introduction. Although this remarkable book has gone into over thirty editions, the Fourth Section has never been published.

It is not known precisely when this book was written, but it was obviously written a number of years after the Ari's death, when his influence no longer overwhelmed Chaim Vital.[41] Missing from this book is the kaleidoscopic style that distinguishes Vital's earlier writings, where he is basically expounding the teachings of the Ari. Furthermore, very little is mentioned of the method of Yichudim (Unifications), which, as we shall see in the next chapter, was the main meditative technique advocated by the Ari.

Still, even though he is clearly his own man in this book, the author does not forget his indebtedness to his master. He writes, "In [this book] I will explain mysteries that were not grasped by earlier generations. These I received from the lips of the holy man, the angel of the Lord of Hosts, the Godly Rabbi Isaac Luria, of blessed memory." [42]

Although this would seem to indicate that the methods discussed in *Shaarey Kedushah* were taught by the Ari, there is considerable evidence to the contrary. In all the voluminous literature that is attributed to the Ari, we find no evidence of these methods, especially those discussed in the Fourth Section.

Rabbi Chaim, however, leaves very little doubt that he himself made use of these methods. He writes, "In the Fourth Section, [I will speak] of the methods themselves, through which one attains *Ruach HaKodesh.* I myself have tried and tested them, and found them to be authentic."[43]

Although the Fourth Section was never published, it exists in a number of manuscripts, some in private hands, and a few in library collections.[44] One of the greatest surprises in this unpublished section is the fact that it begins by advocating the methods of Rabbi Abraham Abulafia, as taught in his *Chayay Olam HaBah* (Life of the Future World). After a discussion of this method, Vital goes on to quote a long portion from the Abulafia's *Sefer HaCheshek* (Book of Passion), without actually quoting it by name.[45]

This advocacy of Abulafia's methods may have been one of the underlying reasons why this Fourth Section was never printed. Such highly respected authorities as the Rashba, Rabbi Judah Chayit, and Yashar of Candia had denounced Abulafia's works in no uncertain terms. If it had become publicly known that Rabbi Chaim Vital had advocated these methods, the entire status of his teachings may have been undermined.

A good deal of the material in this Fourth Section has been published elsewhere, and this includes quotations from the works of the Ramban, Rabbi Menachem Recanti (1223—1290), and Rabbi Judah Chayit.[46] Of particular interest is the context in which he quotes the Ramban's *Iggeret HaMussar* (Epistle of Admonishment), which the latter had sent to his son in Barcelona.[47] Although this is usually cited merely as an inspirational text, here it is quoted as an important method for attaining enlightenment.

Here can also be found a number of quotations from the works of Rabbi Isaac of Acco. The most important of these is his discussion of stoicism, taken from his *Meirat Eynayim,* which we have already quoted. Also to be found here are a number of other quotations from Rabbi Isaac of Acco which are also included in Rabbi Eliahu di Vidas' *Reshit Chokhmah* (Beginning of Wisdom).[48] Rabbi Chaim Vital also provides the complete text of the "Gate of Kavanah," which we have also discussed earlier, as well as a similar text that appears to advocate a very similar method.[49]

One of the most significant things that we find in this Fourth Section is some insight into Rabbi Joseph Caro's Maggid, the angelic "spokesman" who came to him and taught him. It is well-established that this Maggid was closely associated with Caro's intense study of the Mishnah (the earliest codification of the Oral Torah).[50]

In this context, it is important to say something about the nature of the Mishnah. The original Jewish tradition consisted of two parts, often referred to as two Torahs. The first was the "Written Torah," which consisted of the well-known scroll. The second, however, was called the "Oral Torah," and it consisted of the unwritten tradition given to Moses on Sinai. This Oral Tradition was handed down by word of mouth until the harsh Roman persecutions threatened to extinguish it completely. Finally, around the year 205, Rabbi Judah the Prince compiled it into a written code. It is significant to note that while not included in the Mishnah, the main body of the Kabbalah was also part of this same Oral Tradition.

Here, in the Fourth Part of *Shaarey Kedushah*, the author also speaks about a type of *Hitbodedut* meditation where one meditates on a passage from the Mishnah, often simply called "a Mishnah." The initiate is instructed to seclude himself in a room, wrap himself in his Prayer Shawl, and sit with his eyes closed. He is then to depict himself leaving behind his body and ascending to heaven.

When the initiate reaches this state, he is to take a passage from the Mishnah, and repeat it over and over like a mantra. This produces a very high meditative state, where one can actually clothe himself in the soul of the Sage of the Mishnah. If one does this correctly, that Sage will actually speak through the initiates mouth. Alternatively, he may visualize a mystical message.[51]

Although it is not definite that this was the method used by Caro, it is certainly very closely related. In one place, Caro mentions that he communicated with his Maggid after reading several chapters from the Mishnah.[52] Even if he did not repeat the same text over and over, he was so familiar with the Mishnah that reciting any part could be used as a technique for clearing his mind.

It is also significant to note that Rabbi Chaim Vital also made use of this method. In his diary, he speaks of inducing a state of *Hitbodedut*-meditation by repeating a Mishnah three times.[53] Although this took place shortly after he came under the influence of the Ari, from the context, it is evident that he was aware of this method even earlier. There is a distinct possibility that he may have learned it from Rabbi Joseph Caro. It is also important to note the apparent similarity between this method and that of *Gerushin* used by the Ramak.

Also very significant in this Fourth Section is the discussion of how to do meditation involving *Yichudim* (Unifications). Although this

The Hebrew Alphabet in Ashurit Script

אבגדהוזחטי
כך למם נןס ע
פף צץקרשת

According to Rabbi Joseph Caro:

אוחעצץש ט

Variations according to the Ari:

is discussed at length in the teachings of the Ari, as we shall see in the next chapter, there is no mention there of the precise techniques. Here in *Shaarey Kedushah,* however, a very similar method is discussed, and the technique is spelled out in detail.[54]

The initiate is to spend the entire day in preparation, immersed in Torah study, not speaking any unnecessary words, and concluding with actual immersion in the *Mikvah.* He is then to seclude himself, wear white garments, and divest himself of all physical sensation. Mentally, he then ascends from one firmament to the next, until he reaches the highest one, which is called Aravot.[55]

When one reaches this level, he is to depict the firmament as a tremendous white curtain. Upon this curtain is the Name or letter combination upon which he is meditating. The letters are written in *Ashurit,* the script to write a Torah. Each letter appears brilliantly white, but at the same time, it is shaded with the color appropriate to the particular Sefirah with which it is associated.

After depicting the letters in this manner, one must expand them, until they fill the entire mind. Each letter should apper as a dazzling white mountain, filling the entire field of vision. One can then combine the letters or Names, or, alternatively, permute the letters through the methods of *tzeruf.*

This method provides important insight into the method of *Yichudim,* as well as techniques involving meditation on Divine Names, as taught by Rabbi Joseph Gikatalia and the Ramak. But what is also highly significant is the close parallels to these methods found in other systems of Kabbalah meditation. Thus, in his *Chayay Olam Habah,* Abulafia speaks of a very similar technique. He says, "The letters are without question the root of all wisdom and knowledge, and they themselves are the substance of prophecy. In a prophetic vision, they appear as if they were solid bodies, actually speaking to the individual. They appear like pure living angels . . . and sometimes the individual sees them as mountains." [56]

A very similar idea is also found in the teachings of Rabbi Isaac of Acco. In his *Otzar Chaim,* he speaks of the proper methods of meditating on Names and prayers. He writes, "One must imagine that before his eyes is a book made entirely of white fire. The letters, words, and combinations that he is reading are written in this book with letters of black fire. As he reads, his physical eyes should be on the words, while his mind's eye should be on the . . . Infinite Being (*Ain Sof*)." [57] This is very reminiscent of the Talmudic teaching that the original Torah was written with "Black fire on white fire." [58]

The earlier sections of *Shaarey Kedushah* deal at length with the preparation that one must undergo before involving oneself in the higher forms of meditation. Thetext also speaks about trhe prophetic state at length, as well as that of the *Hekhalot*, and we have presented most of this material elsewhere.[59]

Excerpts From

Shaarey Kedushah

The Seventh Gate: Ruach HaKodesh in our Times

In the previous gate, we have warned the initiate regarding the pitfalls that lie in the road leading to enlightenment. Still, he should not give up. Commenting on the verse, "Deborah was a prophetess" (Judges 4:4), the prophet Elijah taught his disciples, "I call heaven and earth to witness, that any individual, man or woman, Jew or gentile, freeman or slave, can have *Ruach HaKodesh* (Holy Spirit) come upon him. It all depends on his deeds." [60]

Our own eyes have seen, and our own ears have heard distinguished individuals who have attained the level of *Ruach HaKodesh,* even in our times. Some of these individuals can predict the future. Others have mastered wisdom that had never been revealed to previous generations.

In order that those who wish to enter the Sanctuary not be discouraged, I will explain a few concepts, opening the door like the eye of a needle. "For God will not withhold good from those who walk uprightly."[61] First, I will explain a few general principles involving enlightenment. Then, in the Eighth Gate, I will discuss a number of specific practices.

The best way of all is that taught by Elijah. This was the way of the early saints *(Hasidim Rishonim),* also known as the Pharisees.[62] The technique is as follows:

One must first repent every sin he has ever done, rectifying all the spiritual damage he has caused. He must then perfect his soul through keeping the positive Commandments, as well as through complete concentration in prayer and diligent Torah study without ulterior motive. He must continue like an ox under its yoke, until the physical becomes weak. This should also include such disciplines as minimizing the amount of food one eats, waking up at midnight, shunning all unworthy traits, separating oneself from other people, and not speaking unnecessary words. One must also constantly purify his body through immersion in the *Mikvah.*

After this, one should meditate (*hitboded*) occasionally on the fear of God. He should mentally depict the letters of the Tetragrammaton. At this time, he should be careful to keep his thoughts away from all worldly vanities, binding himself to the love of God with great passion.

Through this, one can be worthy of *Ruach HaKodesh* in one of the following aspects:

The first aspect consists of a transmission to the individual's soul of the Highest Light, from the Root of the highest levels of his soul. Such a revelation is *Ruach HaKodesh* in its purest form.

The second aspect comes about through the study of Torah or observance of some commandment. Our sages taught, "When a person keeps a commandment, he earns an Advocate [Angel]."[63] This actually means that an angel is created through one's actions. If this individual does this consistently according to the law, with great *Kavanah,* then this angel will reveal itself to him. This is the meaning of those angels called *Maggidim* which are mentioned in various writings. But if the commandment is not kept according to the Law *(halakhah),* then this angel will be made up of good and evil, combining truth and falsehood.

The third aspect is that as a result of one's piety, Elijah will reveal himself to him. The greater one's piety, the greater will be his enlightenment.

The fourth aspect is greater than [the previous two]. This involves the revelation of the soul of a Tzadik (saint), who has already passed away. This Tzadik may share the same root with the individual's soul, or may come from other roots. This aspect can come about through the proper observance of a commandment, just like the previous aspects. People who are worthy of this attain a level where they gain knowledge of high wisdom and the hidden mysteries of the Torah. This, too, depends on one's deeds.

The fifth aspect is the lowest of them all. This involves dreams where the future and other knowledge is revealed to the individual. This is also close to *Ruach HaKodesh*.

The method discussed earlier brings one on a straight path. The individual does not use mystical oaths to bind the Supernal Beings, but only resorts to the power of his good deeds and sanctification of the self. He can then be assured that the *Ruach HaKodesh* that he attains will be pure, without any admixture of evil whatsoever.

This, however, is not true when a person attempts to coerce [the Supernal Beings. It is true that one may have success] through methods involving mystical oaths, specific actions, prayers and *Yichudim*. But if one makes the slightest error, it is possible that his revelation will be inermingled with Outside Forces.

There are also other methods involving specific techniques, which will be discussed in the Fourth Section. These can bring the above-mentioned aspects to a person, even when they do not come automatically Those methods, however, require great holiness and purity, since otherwise they will give rise to a mixed revelation, as mentioned above.

The first way that we have discussed, however, is the path taken by the earlier generations. It is the path referred to by the Ramban in his commentary on the Torah.[64] This is also the significance of Ben Azzai's experience, when he would [simply] study, and would be surrounded by burning flames, as the Ramban explains in his *Iggeret HaKodesh* (Holy Epistle).[65]

The Eighth Gate: Methods of Sanctifying Oneself

One must purify himself in four ways:

First, one must repent all of his sins,wether they involve violating the Torah's prohibitions, neglecting its positive commandments or even transgressing rabbinical laws or adhering to unworthy traits. Such repentance must include a resolve never to repeat the sin or return to the bad trait. Such repentance is especially important for sins for which the Torah prescribes a penalty of being [spiritually] "cut off," or those which involve a desecration of God's Name.[66] This includes violation of the Sabbath, the menstrual rules, sexual pollution, oaths — even if they involve the truth — gazing at forbidden members of the opposite sex, malicious gossip, talebearing, mockery and idle chatter. One must also keep himself from pride, anger, oversensitivity, and depression, behaving with modesty and humility and rejoicing in his portion.

The second purification involves the meticulous observance of all 248 commandments of the Torah [which parallel the 248 parts of the human body], as well as the legislated commandments. Particularly, it involves keeping set times for Torah study, praying with *Kavanah* reciting all blessings and grace after meals with *Kavanah,* loving one's fellow man, and honoring the Sabbath in every detail. One should also wake up each night at midnight to study Torah and mourn for Jerusalem. Whatever one does should be with love, for the sake of heaven.

The third and fourth purifications involve specific preparations through which one sanctifies himself for *Ruach HaKodesh*.

The first of these involves purification of the body, through immersion in the *Mikvah* and clean clothing.

The second should be done when one actually prepares to receive *Ruach HaKodesh,* after the other good traits have become part of his nature.[67]

You should be in a room by yourself, after immersion and sanctification. It should be a place where you will not be distracted by the sound of human voices or the chirping of birds. The best time to do this is shortly after midnight.

Close your eyes and divest your thoughts of all worldly things. It should be as if your soul had left your body, and you should be as devoid of sensation as a corpse. Then strengthen yourself with a powerful yearning, meditating on the supernal universe. There you should attach yourself to the Root of your soul and to the Supernal Lights.

It should seem as if your soul had left your body and had ascended on high. Imagine yourself standing in the supernal universes.

If you make use of a *Yichud* (Unification), have in mind that through it you are transmitting Light and Sustenance to all universes. Keep in mind that you, too, will receive your portion in the end.

Meditate (*hitboded*) in thought for a short time, and attempt to sense if Spirit had rested on you.

If you do not feel anything, it can be assumed that your are not fit and ready for it. You should therefore strengthen yourself all the more with worship and holiness. After a few days, you should meditate again in this manner, until you are worthy that the Spirit should rest upon you.

When the spirit rests on you, you must still discern if it is pure and clean, or from the Other Side, a mixture of good and evil. Keep in mind what happened to Ben Zoma and Ben Azzai when they ascended to the Orchard.[68] You can discern this through what is revealed. It can consist completely of truth, or it can be truth mixed with falsehood. Occasionally, the revelation will consist of idle concepts, dealing with worldly vanities, or ideas that do not conform to the teachings of the Torah. When this occurs, you must repel yourself from it. You must then continue to fortify yourself with worship, until the revelation is faithful, based on the fear of heaven.

At first, the spirit [of *Ruach HaKodesh*] will rest on you occasionally, at distant intervals. The revelation will only involve simple concepts, and not deep ideas. Very little will be revealed, but as you progress, your power will likewise increase.

CHAPTER SIX

The Ari

1. A HUMAN ANGEL

There are a select number of individuals who live on a plane so high above the rest of humanity that it seems as if they are a completely different, higher species of being. They teach, but we grasp but little, and from the few crumbs that we glean, we can build mountains. Such a person was Rabbi Isaac Luria (1534—1572), renowned as the greatest Kabbalist of modern times.

Rabbi Isaac Luria is commonly known as the Ari (אֲרִ״י), an acronym standing for *Elohi Rabbi Isaac* (אֱלֹהִי רַבֵּינוּ יִצְחָק) — the Godly Rabbi Isaac. No other master or sage ever had this extra letter, standing for — *Elohi* — Godly — prefaced to his name. This was a sign of what his contemporaries thought of him. Later generations, fearsome that this appelation might be misunderstood, said that this Alef stood for *Ashkenazi,* indicating that his family had originated in Germany, as indeed it had. But the original meaning is the correct one, and to this day among Kabbalists, Rabbi Isaac Luria is only referred to as the "Holy Ari."

It is relatively easy for a great leader to become a legendary figure centuries after his death. There are even cases where people become legends in their time, especially to the masses who never get too close to them. But usually, the closer one gets to the legend, the more it wanes, until those closest to him see the legendary character as little more than a gifted human being, if that. In the case of the Ari, the exact opposite is true. His closest disciple, Rabbi Chaim Vital, who spent days and nights with him, saw him as nothing less than a human angel.

In one place there is a responsum that Rabbi Joseph Caro sent to the the Ari.[1] The Ari is inquiring about an involved legal problem involving a quasi-partnership where one partner dies and the merchandise is lost. The great Joseph Caro answers like a student before his master, hanging on to every word of the Ari's question. One must remember that at this time, Caro's momumental code, the *Bet Yosef*, had already been printed, and he was considered one of the foremost leaders of that period. Characteristically, he writes with the greatest of authority, even to the foremost luminaries of that generation. Yet before the Ari, he is totally subjected, both spiritually and intellectually. There are also legends that Caro wished to enroll as a disciple of the Ari in Kabbalah, but was discouraged. The Ari said that Caro was meant to be an authority in Law, and not in mysticism.[2]

The teachings of the Ari were afforded status as a primary authority, on the same level as the Zohar itself. Every custom of the Ari was scrutinized, and many were accepted, even against previous practice. The great Polish codifier, Rabbi Abraham Gombiner (1635—1683), author of the *Magen Avraham* (Shield of Abraham), takes the Ari's personal customs as legally binding precedents. In deciding disputes that had remained unresolved for centures, he often cites the Ari's custom as the final authority. The fact that the Ari had acted in a certain manner was enough to convince this tough-minded legalist that this was the correct opinion.

The Ari was born in Jerusalem in 1534, and it is said that Elijah himself attended his circumcision ceremony. By the time he was eight, he was recognized as a wonder child, a prodigy who already outshone the greatest minds of Jerusalem. At this tender age, when most children are just beginning to read, he had already mastered the intricasies of the Talmud, and had committed dozens of volumes to memory. Had he remained nothing more than a Talmudic scholar, he would have joined the ranks of the greatest of all times.

The Ari's father died while he was still a young child, and since she was unable to support the family, his mother went to Egypt, where they lived with her brother, Mordecai Frances, a wealthy tax agent. The young prodigy was placed under the tutelage of Rabbi Betzalel Ashkenazi (1520—1592), best known for his important Talmudic commentary, the *Shitta Mekubetzet* (Embracing System). There is also evidence that the young lad also studied under the great Radbaz, who was then the chief rabbi of Cairo.[3] According to a reliable account, the Ari himself also wrote a large Talmudic commentary around this time.[4]

Having thoroughly mastered the maze of Talmudic thought, the Ari discovered the Zohar when he was seventeen, obtaining his own manuscript copy. But even more important were the fifteen years that he spent in meditation, first with Rabbi Betzalel and then by himself. It is not certain what methods he used, but it is known that both the

Radbaz and Rabbi Chaim Vital were aware of Abulafia's works and speak highly of them.

Another interesting link that needs exploration involves Rabbi Joseph Tzayach, whom we have already discussed at length. It is known that at least two of Tzayach's major works were dedicated to Abraham Castro, who was master of the mint in Egypt. From the wording of his dedication, it appears that besides being a major philanthropist, Castro was looked upon as a saint and a Kabbalist of major proportions. There are also indications that Castro had founded a secret school in Egypt based on Tzayach's teachings.

When we couple this with the fact that it was Castro who gained the Radbaz's appointment as chief rabbi of Cairo, and that the Radbaz corresponded with Tzayach, we see an important link. The Ari was associated with the Radbaz's school, and he studied with his major disciple, Rabbi Batzalel Ashkenazi. This school, however, seemed to have an intimate relationship with Joseph Tzayach.

It would certainly be very significant to discover a link between the Ari and Tzayach, but no direct evidence exists. While the style of the Ari exhibits the same detailed intricacy as Tzayach, the Ari's system is built entirely upon the Zohar, while Tzayach apparently avoids the Zohar completely. Still, the Ari almost certainly knew of Tzayach's teachings, and the connection between the two should be further explored.

The most important meditative practice of the Ari involved the Zohar itself. Rabbi Chaim Vital presents evidence that the Ari would spend days, and sometimes weeks, engrossed in a single passage in the Zohar, remaining with it until he had grasped its deepest meaning.[5] While it is entirely possible that this was a purely intellectual exercize, it is also highly possible that the Ari used passages of the Zohar like a mantra, just as others used passages from the Bible and Mishnah. The states induced by such meditation would have resulted in precisely the Zohar consciousness that is evident throughout the Ari's teachings.

The Ari spent two years meditating alone in a hut near the Nile, and at the end of this period he received a command to go to the Holy Land, according to legend, from the lips of Elijah the Prophet. Without discounting this legend completely, we can also speculate that the Radbaz also exerted some influence in this area. This ancient sage had left for the Holy Land in 1553, and was already in Safed at the time. There is no question that he knew both the Ramak and Rabbi Chaim Vital, both of whom were among the world's leading Kabbalists.

Perhaps the Radbaz realized that bringing the Ari together with these forces would have the effect of raising the Kabbalah to unprecedented heights, as indeed it did.

In any case, the Ari arrived in Safed during the summer of 1570, and began by concealing his gifts completely. He was only there a short time when the Ramak died on June 26, 1570 (23 Tammuz, 5330). According to legend, the Ramak had already decided that the Ari would succeed him as leader of the Safed school, and this was pointed out by a pillar of fire that followed the Ramak's beir

There are clear indications that around this time, Rabbi Chaim Vital was deeply involved in his commentary on the Zohar, and was not aware of the Ari at all.[6] Rabbi Chaim might have been in Damascus at the time, aware neither of the Ari's coming nor of the Ramak's demise. He writes that he did not see the Ari until six months after he had arrived in Safed, and that one reason was that he initially thought that his own knowledge of the Kabbalah was superior to that of the Ari.[7] All that it took, however, was a single meeting, and Rabbi Chaim was convinced of the Ari's awesome stature. It was not long before he begged to become the latter's disciple.

According to our best estimates, the initial meeting between the Ari and Rabbi Chaim Vital took place in February of 1571.[8] It was at this time that the Ari informed him that he had come from Egypt specifically to teach him, and that this was one of the most important tasks in life. From that time on, the two were inseparable.

It is difficult to imagine the amount of information that passed between the two. According to his own accounts, Rabbi Chaim was a disciple of the Ari for less than eighteen months, and during this period, he gained a complete mastery of the Ari's system. The writings that Chaim Vital produced in this field encompass over a dozen large volumes, each one intricately compiled and written in an extremely terse style. It is from this that we can understand the genius of these two individuals, as well as their high spiritual level.

The Ari passed away on July 15, 1572 (5 Ab, 5332), barely two years after he had arrived in Safed.[9] During his brief stay there, he had assembled a group of approzimately a dozen disciples, with Chaim Vital at their head, and they continued to review his teachings. For the most part, it was Rabbi Chaim who put them into writing. The main works are the *Etz Chaim* (Tree of Life) and *Pri Etz Chaim* (Fruit of the Tree of Life), as well as the Eight Gates, which deal with everything from Bible commentary to divine inspiration and reincarnation.

Chiromancy of the Ari

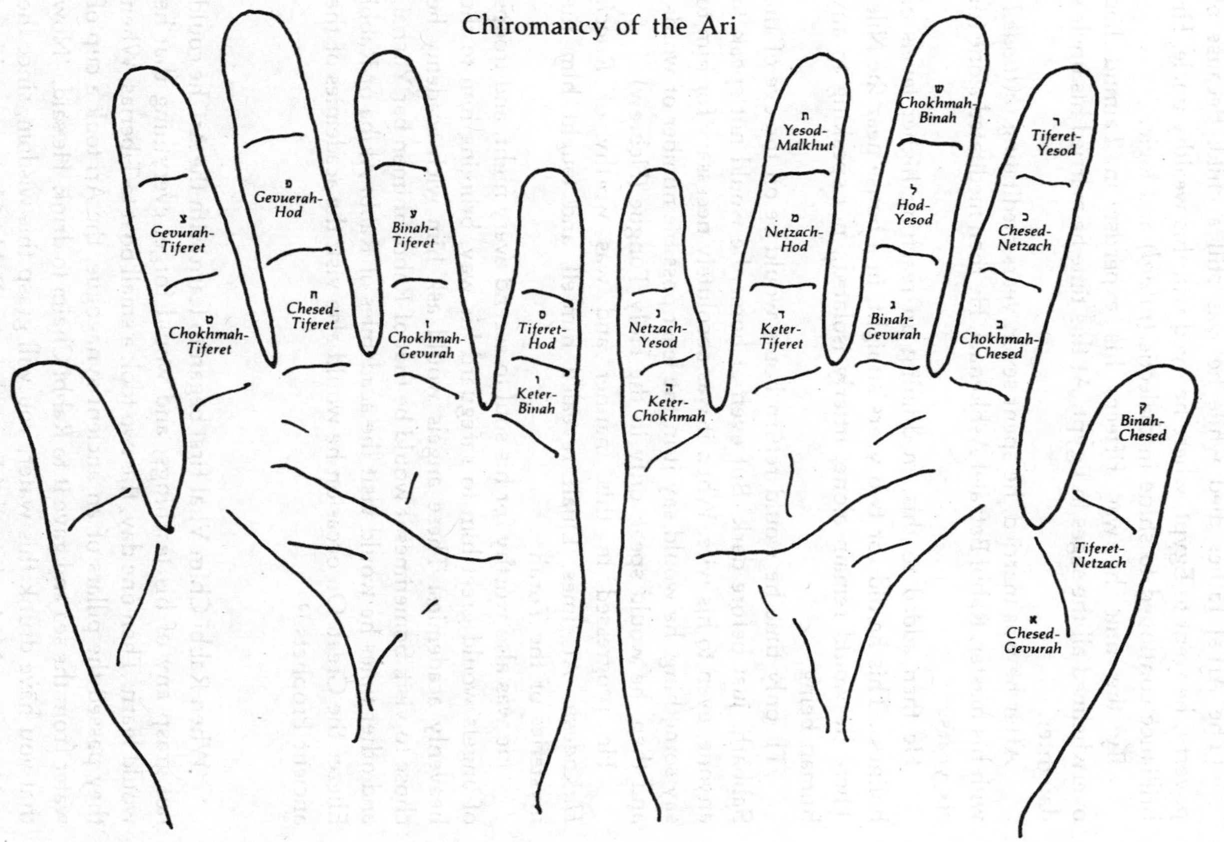

SOURCES

[The Ari's] father died while he was still a child. Because of poverty, he went to Egypt, where he lived with his wealthy uncle. His brilliance continued to shine in dialectic (*pilpul*) and logic.

By the time he was fifteen, his expertise in Talmud had overwhelmed all the sages in Egypt. At this time he married his uncle's daughter.

After he was married, he spent seven years meditating (*hitboded*) with his master, Rabbi Betzalel Ashkenazi. He then meditated alone for six years.

He then added to this, meditating an reaching higher levels of holiness. This he did for two years straight, in a house near the Nile. There he would remain alone, utterly isolated,, not speaking to any human being.

Th only time he would return home would be on the eve of the Sabbath, just before dark. But even at home, he would not speak to anyone, even to his wife. When it was absolutely necessary for him to say something, he would say it in the least possible number of words, and then, he would speak only in the Holy Tongue (Hebrew).

He progressed in this manner and was worthy of *Ruach HaKodesh*. At times, Elijah revealed himself and taught him the mysteries of the Torah.

He was also worthy for his soul to ascend every night, and troops of angels would greet him to safeguard his way, bringing him to the heavenly academies. These angels would ask him wich academy he chose to visit. Sometimes it would be that of Rabbi Shimon bar Yochai, and other times he would visit the academies of Rabbi Akiba or Rabbi Eliezer the Great. On occasion he would also visit the academies of the ancient Prophets.[10]

When Rabbi Chim Vital first began to learn with the Ari, he could not grasp any of his teachings, and would forget everything that he would learn. Then one day, the two took a small boat to Tiberias. When they passed the pillars of an ancient synagogue, the Ari took a cup of water from the sea and gave it to Rabbi Chaim to drink. He said, "Now that you have drunk this water, you will grasp this wisdom, since the water is from Miriam's well." From then on, Rabbi Chaim was able to grasp the Ari's teachings.[11]

In every generation, there were exceptional individuals who were worthy of *Ruach HaKodesh*. Elijah revealed himself to these individuals and taught them the mysteries of this Wisdom (Kabbalah). This is found many places in the books of the Kabbalists.

In his discussion of the Priestly Blessing, [Rabbi Menachem] Recanti (1228—1290) writes, "Elijah had revealed himself to Rabbi [David], head of the Rabbinical Court, and had taught him the wisdom of the Kabbalah. He taught this to his son, the Raavad (Rabbi Abraham ben David of Posqueres: 1120—1198), and he also experienced a revelation of Elijah. The tradition was passed to his son, Rabbi Isaac the Blind, who was blind from birth, and to him Elijah also revealed himself. He gave the tradition to his two disciples, the first being Rabbi Ezra, who wrote a commentary on the Song of Songs, and the second was Rabbi Azriel. From them, it was given over to the Ramban." [12]

In his commentary on Maimonides' Code, the Raavad himself writes, "*Ruach HaKodesh* has been revealed in our Academy for many years. . . ." [13] Elsewhere he likewise writes, "This was revealed to me, as a mystery of God to those who fear Him." [14]

But I must also sing praise, for in each generation God's love is with us. . . . In this generation too, God of the first and last did not withhold such a leader . . . He sent us an angel . . . the great Godly pious Rabbi, my master and teacher, our mentor, Rabbi Isaac Luria Ashkenazi, of blessed memory.

[The Ari] was overflowing with Torah. He was thoroughly expert in the Bible, Mishnah, Talmud, Pilpul, Midrash, Agadah, Workings of Creation, and Workings of the *Merkava*. He was expert in the conversation of trees, the conversation of birds, and the speech of angels.[15] He could read faces in the manner outlined in the Zohar.[16] He could discern all that any individual had done, and could see what they would do in the future. He could read people's thoughts, often before the thought even entered the individual's mind. He knew future events, and was aware of everything happening here on earth, and what was decreed in heaven.

He knew the mysteries of reincarnation, who had been born previously, and who was here for the first time. He could look at a person and tell him how he was connected to the Supernal Man, and how he was related to Adam. He could read wondrous things in the light of a candle or in the flame of a fire.

With his eyes he gazed and was able to see the souls of the righteous, whether those who had died recently, or those who had lived in ancient times. With these he studied the true mysteries. By a person's odor he was able to know all that he had done, an ability that the Zohar attributes to the Holy Child.[17]

It was as if all these mysteries were lying in his bosom, ready to be used whenever he desired. He did not have to meditate (*hitboded*) to seek them out.

All this we saw with our own eyes. These are not things that we heard from others. They were wondrous things, that had not been seen on earth since the time of Rabbi Shimon bar Yochai.

None of this was attained through the Practical Kabbalah, heaven forbid. There is a strong prohibition against using these arts.

Instead, it came automatically, as a result of his piety and asceticism, after many years of study in both the ancient and newer Kabbalistic texts. He then increased his piety, asceticism, purity and holiness until he reached a level where Elijah would constantly reveal himself to him, speaking to him "mouth to mouth," and teaching him these mysteries.

This is the same thing that had happened to the Raavad, as Recanti states. Even though true prophecy no longer exists, *Ruach HaKodesh* is still here, manifest through Elijah. It is as the prophet Elijah taught his disciples, commenting on the verse, "Deborah was a prophetess" (Judges 4:4): "I call heaven and earth to bear witness, that any individual, man or woman, Jew or Gentile, freeman or slave, can have *Ruach HaKodesh* bestowed upon him. It all depends on his deeds." [18]

Rabbi Chaim Vital.[19]

There was no one like [the Ari] since the days of Rabbi Shimon bar Yochai. Furthermore, he revealed to us that he was a reincarnation of Rabbi Shimon bar Yochai, and that his disciples were reincarnations of those of Rabbi Shimon.

It is for this reason that when he went to [Rabbi Shimon's cave in] Meron, he would place them in an appropriate order. He himself would sit in the place of Rabbi Shimon bar Yochai, Rabbi Chaim Vital would be set in the place of Rabbi Eliezer, son of Rabbi Shimon, and Rabbi Benjamin Cohen, in the place of Rabbi Abba. The other seven disciples would be set in the places of the "seven Eyes of God," each one in his proper place according to his incarnation.[20]

He revealed to us more than any prophet or seer. Even Ezekiel only revealed the mystery of the *Merkava* in the Universe of Beriyah. But the Ari revealed the mysteries of Atzilut, even reaching to the Universes of the Infinite, which are "Bonds, Dots and Stripes." [21] "How great is the good that You have hidden for those who fear You" (Psalms 31:20).

His level was high above any angle or Maggid. He knew all that was on high and below, as well as what was decreed in the Tribunal on High — and he could annul these decrees.

In many cases, he was able to indicate where the earlier Kabbalists had been mistaken. An example of this is with regard to the seven Sabbatical Years.[22]

Even the Maggid that was revealed to Rabbi Joseph Caro did not know the inner meaning of the Zohar, and was occasionally mistaken. This is because an angel or Maggid is only from the Universe of Yetzirah, while the soul is from the Universe of Beriyah. . . . The sould of a Tzaddik (saint), however, can also be from the Universe of Atzilut.

The soul of our Master (the Ari) was from a level of the Partzuf of Arikh Anpin [which is the level of Keter-Crown, the highest of Atzilut].

Rabbi Mosheh of Prague (1630—1705).[23]

The Supernal Universes

Universe	*Inhabitants*	*Counterpart*
Adam Kadmon (First "Man")	Tetragrammatons	Apex of Yod
Atzilut (Nearness)	Sefirot, Partzufim	Yod (י)
Beriyah (Creation)	The Throne, Souls	Heh (ה)
Yetzirah (Formation)	Angels	Vav (ו)
Asiyah (Making)	Forms	Heh (ה)

2. THE SYSTEM

The Ari's Kabbalistic system covers literally thousands of pages, and pervades virtually every area of thought. It is utterly impossible to adequately summarize it, and attempts to do so are most often one-sided and unsuccessful. Still, there are a number of general principles that are dominant, and these are particularly important in understanding the Ari's system of meditation.

The basic elements of the Ari's system are the Ten Sefirot, the Four Universes, and the Five levels of the Soul. These concepts are discussed widely in the Zohar, and play an important role in the teachings of such masters as the Ramak. It is upon these older systems that the Ari builds.

Three of the most opaque books of the Zohar are the *Sifra DeTzeniuta* (Concealed Book) and the Greater and Lesser *Idras.* In these books, we find ideas that in other Zoharic literature are only alluded to in the vaguest terms. While other sources speak primarily about the Sefirot, here the discussion revolves different spiritual entities — the *Partzufim* (Archetype Personas). The Ari clarifies the significance of these by revealing the one-to-one relationship that exists between the Partzufim and the Seifirot. (See Table).

While the simpler Kabbalah involving the Sefirot appears to speak of the statics of the highest Universes, the system of Partzufim involves their dynamic interactions. When they were first created, the Sefirot were simple points, which could not interact with each other. They could therefore not give anything to each other. All they could do was receive from the Infinite Being (*Ain Sof*), and for this reason, at this stage, they are called "vessels"

In order to receive God's Light, however, a Vessel must in some way be connected to God. The basic difference between the spiritual and the physical is the fact that space does not exist in the spiritual realm. Hence, there is no way in which the Sefirot can be physically connected to God. The only possible relationship is therefore resemblance. In order to receive God's Light, the Vessel must, at least to some degree, resemble God.

This, however, presents a difficulty. If God is the ultimate Giver, then the Vessel is the ultimate receiver, and the two are then absolute opposites. In order for a Vessel to properly receive, it must also give.

What is therefore needed is a "vessel" that can give as well a receive. The ultimate expression of such a vessel is man. If man is to receive God's light, he must first resemble God by being a giver. This is accomplished through keeping God's commandments, thus providing spiritual sustenance to the spiritual Universes. Before man can do this, however, he must also resemble God by having both free will and free choice. This is only possible when both good and evil exist.

The first stage of creation is called the Universe of Chaos (*Tohu*). This is a state where the Vessels, which were the primitive Ten Sefirot, could receive God's Light, but could neither give nor interact. Insofar as they did not resemble God, these Vessels were incomplete, and therefore, they could not hold the Light. Since they could not fulfil their purpose, they were overwhelmed by the Light and "shattered." This is the idea of the "Breaking of Vessels."

The original Vessels were in what is now the Universe of Atzilut. When they were shattered, the broken pieces fell to a lower spiritual level, which became the Universe of Beriyah. It is at this level that evil begins to manifest, and its source is in the fragments of the Broken Vessels.

The reason the Vessels were originally created without the ability to hold the Btght was that Evil should come into being. This in turn would give man freedom of choice, which, as we have seen, was necessary for the rectification of the Vessels. Furthermore, since Evil originated in the highest original Vessels, it can be rectified and re-elevated to this level.

This "Breaking of Vessels" is alluded to in the Midrash, which states that "God created universes and destroyed them."[24] It is also alluded to in the Torah, in the account of the Kings of Edom, at the end of Genesis 36. The death of each of these Kings is said to infer the shattering of a particular Vessel and its falling to a lower level, such a fall being referred to as "death."

After having been shattered,the Vessels were then rectified and rebuilt into the Partzufim. Each of these Partzufim consists of 613

The Partzufim

Partzuf		*Sefirah*	
Atika Kadisha	The Holy Ancient One	Upper Keter	
Atik Yomin	Ancient of Days		
Arikh Anpin	Long Face	Lower Keter	
Abba	Father	Chokhmah	Yod
Imma	Mother	Binah	Heh
Zer Anpin	Small Face (Male)	The Next Six	Vav
Nukva	Female	Malkhut	Heh

The Four Tetragrammatons

Value			*Name*		*Level*
72	*Ab*	עב	*YOD HEH VYV HY*	יוד הי ויו הי	*Chokhmah*
63	*Sag*	סג	*YOD HY VAV HY*	יוד הי ואו הי	*Binah*
45	*Mah*	מה	*YOD HA VAV HA*	יוד הא ואו הא	*The Six*
52	*Ben*	בן	*YOD HH VV HH*	יוד הה וו הה	*Malkhut*

Levels of Expression

Universe	*Expression*	
Asiyah-Making	*Otiot*	Letters
Yetzirah-Formation	*Tagin*	Orniments
Beriyah-Creation	*Nekudot*	Vowel Points
Atzilut-Nearness	*Ta'amim*	Cantellation Notes

parts, paralleling the 613 parts of the body, as well as the 613 commandments of the Torah. These Partzufim were then able to interact with each other. More important, they then resembled both man and the Torah. They were therefore able to interact with man through the Torah, and they therefore become givers as well as receivers.

In their rectified state as Partzufim, the Vessels are then adequate to receive God's Light. In the Ari's terminology, this state is called the Universe of Rectification (*Tikkun*). He said that the other Kabbalists had only spoken of the Universe of Chaos, while he was the first to reveal the mysteries of the Partzufim, which are in the Universe of Rectification. These Partzufim constantly interact with each other in an anthropormorphic manner. It is for this reason that the symbolism of sex, birth, and growth play such an important role in the Ari's system.

The earlier Kabbalists spoke of four Universes, Atzilut, Beriyah, Yetzirah, and Asiyah, paralleling the four letters of the Tetragrammaton (see table). There were also hints of a universe above these four, corresponding to the apex of the Yod in the Tetragrammaton. The Ramak speaks of this fifth universe and calls it the Universe of *Tzachtzachim* (Splendors), but is hard-pressed to find any reference to it in the Zohar.[25]

The Ari, however, identified this fifth Universe as the realm of another mysterious Partzuf mentioned in the Zohar — *Adam Kadmon* (First Man) — the primary Partzuf. Within this fifth Universe there are another four levels, again paralleling the four letters of the Tetragrammaton. These are the four expansions of the Tetragrammaton, usually referred to by their numerical value: Ab (עב = 72), Sag (סג = 63), Mah (מה = 45), and Ben (בן = 52). (See Table).

It is these four levels that ultimately manifest themselves in the four letters of the Tetragrammaton, the four lower Partzufim of Atzilut, and ultimately, in the Four Universes themselves. In written language, we again find these four levels, this time represented by the accent marks, the vowel points, the letter decorations (*tagin*), and by the letters themselves.

3. *KAVANOT*

Although the bulk of the Lurianic writings deal with the theoretical Kabbalah, his teachings were by no means confined to theory. An important meditative aspect of the Ari's system involved Kavanot, which are specific meditations related to particular practices. These can involve dressing, putting on the Tallit or Tefillin, or the various holiday practices, such as eating Matzah on the Passover, or taking the Four Species on Succot. Since a person was constantly involved in these religious observances, the Kavanot would bring him to a meditative state throughout his daily activities. Particularly important is the formal prayer service, where each word has Kabbalistic significance, and is the focus of an entire system of meditations.

Many Kavanot are discussed among the older Kabbalists, and most of these are based on the Zohar, even though the Zoharic allusions are often very vague. But an important part of the Ari's greatness was his ability to extract the fullest meaning from each word in the Zohar, and therefore, where the Zohar only hints, the Ari is able to present a fully-structured meditation. For the most part, these Kavanot fit closely into the Ari's theoretical system.

To a large degree, these Kavanot bring a person into the upper Universes, and involve combinations of Divine Names and many gematriot (numerology). They fill two large volumes, the *Pri Etz Chaim* (Fruit of the Tree of Life), and the *Shaar HaKavanot* (Gate of Kavanot), as well as several smaller texts. These Kavanot involve virtually every aspect of life, both religious and mundane.

To take only one of thousands of examples, we shall present here the Ari's system of meditations when immersing in the Mikvah (ritual pool) before the Sabbath. As we have seen, such immersion played an important role in virtually all the meditative systems, being an essential

Expansions of the Name Ehyeh			
The Name *Ehyeh* (אהיה) is spelled Alef (א) Heh (ה) Yod (י) Heh (ה).			
Value	*Expansion*		*Letter*
161	*ALePh HeY YOD HeY*	אלף הי יוד הי	Yod
151	*ALePh HeH YOD HeH*	אלף הה יוד הה	Heh
143	*ALePh HeA YOD HeA*	אלף הא יוד הא	Alef

step in attaining spiritual purity. This meditation can also be compared with a similar one that we shall present from the Baal Shem Tov in the next chapter.

Meditation for Immersion[26]

This is a meditation for immersing before the Sabbath:

After entering the lake, river or Mikvah, but before immersing, meditate on the word Mikvah:

MKVH מקוה

Meditate that the Mikvah is the mystery of the Name Ehyeh (אהיה) expanded through the letter Heh (ה):

ALePh HeH YUD HeH אלף הה יוד הה

This expansion has a numerical value of 151, and this is also the numerical value of the word Mikvah. [Just as water is gathered together in a Mikvah,] the expansions of the Name Ehyeh are gathered [into the above expansion].

Now meditate on the word *Nachal* (נחל), meaning stream.

This supernal Stream consists of [seven Names]. These are the four expansions of the Tetragrammaton, Ab, Sag, Mah, and Ben, together with the three expansions of Ehyeh, respectively with the Yud, the Heh, and the Alef. (Ehyeh is AHYH, אהיה).

Bring the Mikvah into this Stream.

Meditate on these seven Names when they are not expanded:

YHVH	יהוה
YHVH	יהוה
YHVH	יהוה
YHVH	יהוה
AHYH	אהיה
AHYH	אהיה
AHYH	אהיה

Each of these contains a single Yod. Therefore, in the Seven Names, there are a total of seven Yod's.

These Seven Names are the mystery of the Seven Names of the Sabbath.

This is the mystery of the seven letters AHYH YHV (אהיה יהו), mentioned in the Zohar.[27]

You must meditate on the simple spelling of the Seven Names, which contain seven simple Yod's. At the same time, you must also meditate on the expanded forms.

[To the Seven Names,] ,now add the name YaH (יָה). This Name is the mystery of the Sabbath itself. You have a total of eight Yod's.

These eight Yod's [each having a numerical value of ten] add up to 80. This is the numerical value of the letters Nun and Lamed (נל) from the word *Nachal* (נחל), the Stream. Then include [the letter Chet (ח), which represents] the eight Yod's themselves. You now have *Nachal* (נחל), the Stream.

Now meditate on the Yod's in groups. There are two such groups, [those of YHVH, and those of AHYH]. You must therefore meditate on the number two.

[The word *Nachal* (נחל) has a numerical value of 88.] Add this to the two and you have [90. This is the numerical value of] *Mayim* (מַיִם), meaning Water.

In this manner, you have brought Water into the Mikvah.

Now meditate that all of this should be "in honor of the Sabbath" (*LiKevod Shabbat*, לִכְבוֹד שַׁבָּת). [Meditate on these two words.]

We have used eight Names. These are the four Tetragrammatons, the three expansions of Ehyeh, and Yah. [The original Seven Names, each having four letters, contain a total of 28 letters. Add this to the two letters of YaH, and] you have a total of 30 letters. [This is the numerical value of the letter Lamed.] This is the Lamed (ל) of the word *LiKevod* (לכבוד), meaning "in honor of."

Sum of the Eight Names	
Expansions of the Tetgragrammaton:	Ab = 72
	Sag = 63
	Mah = 45
	Ben = 52
Expansions of Ehyeh:	161
	151
	143
Yah (יה)	15
	702

Now divide the eight into two groups, the original Seven Names and the added name, YaH. [This yields the number two. Add this to the number 30 above, and you have 32.] This is the numerical value Kavod (כבוד), meaning "honor."

[Now take the expansions of the Seven Names, together with YaH.] The sum of all eight Names is [702, which is the numerical value of the word] Shabbat (שַׁבָּת), the Sabbath.

[Now immerse.] When you emerge from the water, say the verse, "If you rest your foot for the Sabbath" (Isaiah 58:13).[28]

Im Tashiv MiShabbat Raglecha אִם תָּשִׁיב מִשַּׁבָּת רַגְלֶךָ

4. YICHUDIM

The essence of the Ari's meditative system consists of *Yichudim* (Unifications), where one manipulates the letters of various names of God. The word itself indicates a unification, and in general, these meditations consist of unifying two or more names. Sometimes the names are intertwined and various vowel points are added. Since the various divine Names reflect spiritual forces, and these forces have their counterparts in different parts of the human mind, these Yichudim can have powerful effects in integrating the psyche. At times, this can also be extremely traumatic.

As in the case of the Kavanot, many of these Yichudim are alluded to in the Zoharic literature, but little or no indication is provided that these manipulations are actually meditative techniques. It took the genius and inspiration of the Ari to reveal explicitly how they should be used.

The idea of unifying God's Name is a most ancient one. The *Sh'ma,* the declaration of faith, "Hear O Israel, the Lord is our God, the Lord is One" (Deuteronomy 6:4), is often spoken of as the "Unification of the Name." [29] As we have seen, the Zohar provides a specific Yichud associated with this verse.[30] On the verse, "[You shall] attach yourself to [God]" (Deuteronomy 30:20) an ancient Midrash states that this is a "Unification of the Name," indicating that it is through such unification that one binds himself to the Divine.[31] Among the earlier Kabbalists, there are specific references to Yichudim involving combinations of Divine Names, a clear example being in the writings of Rabbi Isaac of Acco.[32]

We have also seen how the Ramak advocates meditating on the various names of God, especially on the Tetragrammaton with different vowel points paralleling the Ten Sefirot. In the Ari's system, the Sefirot are no longer seen as independent entities, but as complex interacting Partzufim. His system of meditation therefore involves manipulating these names in a manner corresponding to these interactions on high.

The exact method of depicting these Names is not discussed, but we have spoken of this in the previous chapter. The mind is completely emptied, and the letters are then seen as huge solid bodies, completely filling the mind. Gematriot involving the numerical value of letters also plays an important role.

The Ari saw the method of Yichudim meditations as being most important to attain true enlightenment. Although other methods exist, the only one specified, if only by allusion, in the Zohar was that of Yichudim, and it was therefore the purest and most effective of them all. While other meditative systems involved the pronunciation of Divine Names, the system of Yichudim was completely mental, and therefore did not involve the dangers inherent in actually pronouncing names.

Still, Yichudim can produce very high meditative states and channel powerful currents of spiritual energy. If improperly used, they can produce effects that are both traumatic and dangerous. Even someone as spiritually advanced as Rabbi Chaim Vital was often overwhelmed by these experiences.

SOURCES

This happened in Tammuz, 5331 (August, 1571). I had asked my master (the Ari) to teach me a Yichud so that I should gain enlightenment. He replied that I was not ready. I continued to press him until he gave me a short Yichud, and I got up at midnight to make use of it.

I was immediately filled with emotion, and my entire body trembled. My head became heavy, my mind began to swim, and my mouth became crooked on one side. I immediately stopped meditating on that Yichud.

In the morning, my master saw me, and he said, "Did I not warn you? If not for the fact that you are a reincarnation of Rabbi Akiba, you would have [become insane] like Ben Zoma. There would have been no way to help you."

He then touched my lips, making use of a Kavanah that he knew. He did this each morning for three days, and I was healed.

On the day before the New Moon in Elul (September), he said to me, "Now you are ready." He then [gave me a Yichud and] sent me to the cave of Abbaye [(278—338), an important sage of the Talmud].[33]

On the day before the New Moon in Elul, 5331 (September, 1571), my master sent me to the cave of Abbaye and Rava. I fell on the grave of Abbaye, and meditated with the Yichud involving the mouth and nose of Atika Kadisha (The Holy Ancient One).[34]

I fell asleep, and when I woke up, I could see nothing. I then fell on Abbaye's grave once again, and made use of another Yichud that I found in a manuscript actually written by my master.[35] This Yichud involved intertwining the letters YHVH (יהוה) and Adonoy (אדני), as is well known. When I did this, my thoughts became so confused that I could not integrate them. I immediately stopped meditating on this coupling.

It then appeared as if a voice in my mind was saying to me, "Return in you! Return in you!" over and over, many times. I thought to myself, "These are the words that Akavya ben Mehalelel said to his son." [36] Then I once again began meditating on this juxtaposition of letters, and I was able to complete the Yichud.

It then appeared in my mind as if a voice was quoting to me the verse, "God will provide Himself a sheep for the burnt offering my son" (Genesis 22:8). It seemed as if this voice was explaining the meaning of that verse. I had been worried that the first Yichud that I had used had not accomplished anything, and this voice was telling me that I had completed it successfully, and had benefitted from it. This was the significance of the verse, "God will provide Himself a sheep."

It then appeared in my mind as if this voice was explaining that this verse alluded to the first Yichud that I had used. [This Yichud involved the names] YHVH (יהוה) and Ehyeh (אהיה), and the sum of these two names is 47. The initial letters of the verse, "God will provide Himself a sheep" (*Elohim yireh lo ha-seh*, אֱלֹהִים יִרְאֶה לוֹ הַשֶּׂה), [אילה], add up to 46 [and adding an extra unit yields the same number 47].

The initial letters of, "A sheep for a burnt offering my son" (*Ha-seh le-olah b'ni*, הַשֶּׂה לְעֹלָה בְּנִי) spell out *Hevel* (הֶבֶל) a Breath. This is the mystery of the supernal Breath upon which I had meditated.

It also appeared as if the initial letters of "For Himself a sheep for a burn offering" (*Lo ha-seh le-olah*, לוֹ הַשֶּׂה לְעֹלָה) spelled out the name Hillel (הִלֵּל), [the leading sage of the First Century b.c.e]. I did not understand the meaning of this, however.

All this I imagined in my mind. I then began to tremble and all my limbs shuddered. My hands vibrated toward each otehr, and my lips also vibrated in an unusual manner. They trembled very strongly and rapidly.

It seemed as if a voice was sitting on my tongue, between my lips. Very rapidly it repeated the words, "What does he say? What does he say?" These words were repeated over a hundred times. I tried to force my lips not to vibrate, but I could not stop them.

Then I thought to inquire about wisdom. The voice literally exploded in my mouth and on my tongue, and over a hundred times it repeated, "The Wisdom! The Wisdom!" Then it began repeating over and over, "Wisdom and Science! Wisdom and Science!" Then the voice repeated the phrase, "Wisdom and Science are given to you," and then, "Wisdom and Science are given to you from Heaven, like the knowledge of Rabbi Akiba." Then it said, "And more than Rabbi Akiba!" Then it said, "Like Rabbi Yebi the Elder!" Finally the voice said, "Peace to you," and then, "From heaven they wish you peace."

All of his happened very quickly while I was wide awake. It was a wondrous phenomenon. I then fell on my face, prostrate on the vault of Abbaye.

When I related this to my master, he told me that I had benefitted greatly because I had meditated on these two Yichudim in succession, since this was the proper procedure. The reason that I had not been answered after the first Yichud was that they had waited until I had finished them both.

My master later told me that as I walked home that day, he had seen the soul of Benaiah ben Yehoiada accompanying me. He explained that he did not share the same soul-root with me, but that he reveals himself to everyone who completes a lofty Yichud. This was what he did while he was alive, as we have discussed elsewhere.[37]

Rabbi Chaim Vital.[38]

5. GATE OF THE HOLY SPIRIT

The greatest portion of the Ari's teachings are included in a set of eight volumes called the "Eight Gates." These were written down by Rabbi Chaim Vital and redacted by his son, Samuel Vital.

Of these "Gates," the seventh is the one that explains the Ari's system of Yichudim. This is the *Shaar Ruach HaKodesh* (The Gate of the Holy Spirit). As discussed earlier, the term *Ruach HaKodesh* (Holy Spirit) is a general term for enlightenment and inspiration. It is this volume that describes the Yichudim taught by the Ari through which *Ruach HaKodesh* could be attained.

For the most part, the Yechudim presented in this book were not taught in general terms, but were given to specific individuals. These were usually the Ari's disciples, most often Rabbi Chaim Vital himself. Besides the Yechudim themselves, a general system of disciplines is presented and these must be fulfilled before one can successfully use the Yechudim.

Many of the Yichudim in this book are for specific purposes, such as the rectification of sins, or for such esoteric rites as exorcism. In general their purpose was to channel spiritual power toward specific ends. This is also true when one seeks enlightenment, since one is then channeling spiritual energy into oneself. The other uses of Yichudim will not be presented here, since they are outside the scope of this book. Here, we will deal specifically with Yichudim designated specifically for enlightenment.

A very interesting concept discussed here at length is that of the Maggid, the angelic spokesman that we have discussed previously. Here, we not only find a description of a Maggid, but also an explanation of the general framework in which it functions.

Equally important is the idea of binding oneself to saints who lived in ancient times. It is for this reason that many Yichudim are best accomplished near the graves of such saints, as in the example cited in the previous section. The theory behind this is discussed at considerable length.

Excerpts From

The Gate of the Holy Spirit

We will begin by explaining the concept of Prophecy and *Ruach HaKodesh* and their various levels.[39]

When a person is righteous and pious, studying Torah and praying with Kavanah, this must certainly produce something substantial. As the Zohar states, even the sound of one banging a stick is not without effect.[40] One's good practices are certainly not without effect, but result in the creation of angels nd holy spirits. These survive and endure, as mentioned in the Zohar.[41] The Talmud likewise teaches, "Whoever does a good deed earns an Advocate."[42]

Both good and evil angels are created from a person's speech, depending on his words, as mentioned in the *Tikkuney Zohar.* When a person studies Torah, the words and breath that emanate from his mouth become a vehicle for the souls of the early saints. These can descend and teach that person mysteries, as discussed in the Zohar.[43]

All of this, however, depends on one's intent. If a person studies Torah without ulterior motive, then the angel created as a result of such study will be very holy and elevated, and can be trusted to speak the absolute truth. If one reads without error, the angel will also be without error and absolutely reliable.

The same is true of the observance of a commandment. If it is done correctly, a very holy angel is created... Whatever is lacking in one's observance, however, will also be lacking in that angel.

It is certain that the power of an angel created from the study of Torah is much greater than that created through an observance. But one should not discuss these details at length.

These angels are the Maggidim mentioned in a number of books. They reveal themselves to individuals, teaching them mysteries and informing them of future events. These are angels created from the individual's own observance and study of Torah.

These angels are the Maggidim mentioned in a number of books.

Most of the time, these Maggidim do not reveal themselves to the individual, but sometimes they do. This depends on the nature of the person's soul, as well as his deeds. There is no need to dwell upon this at length.

Some Maggidim are absolutely true, these being created from torah and observances done with perfection. Other Maggidim occasionally speak falsely, mixing truth and falsehood. The reason for this is that when there is some falseness or ulterior motive in an observance, the angel created from it consists of both good and evil. The good aspect of such an angel speaks the truth, while the evil in it speaks falsehood.

Some Maggidim are created from the Universe of Asiyah alone. These are created through deeds involving action, done without Kavanah. Others are from the Universe of Yetzirah, created from the study of Torah. There are also Maggidim from the Universe of Beriyah, and these are created from a person's meditations and thoughts, when he is involved in studying the Torah and observing the Commandments. In every Universe there are many different details, but there is no need to discuss this at length.

My master (the Ari) gave a sign [through which one can recognize a proper Maggid]. It must constantly speak the truth, motivate one to do good deeds, and not err in a single prediction. If it can explain the secrets and mysteries of the Torah, it is certainly reliable. From its words, one can recognize its level.

The mystery of *Ruach HaKodesh* is this: It is a voice sent from on high to speak to a prophet or to one worthy of *Ruach HaKodesh.* But such a voice is purely spiritual, and such a voice cannot enter the prophet's ear until it clothes itself in a physical voice.

The physical voice in which it clothes itself is the voice of the prophet himself, when he is involved in prayer or Torah study. This voice clothes itself in his voice and is attached to it. It then enters the prophet's ear so that he can hear it. Without the physical voice of the individual himself, this could not possibly take place.

The explanation is as follows: First there is an earlier voice, from which the angel or holy spirit was created. This itself is the voice of prophecy. When this voice then comes to reveal the prophecy, it must clothe itself in that individual's present physical voice. This must be a voice expressed by the individual at the very moment that he is experiencing the prophecy.

This is the mystery of the verse, "The spirit of God speaks in me, and His word is on my tongue" (2 Samuel 23:2). The "spirit" and "word" are the original voice, created through his deeds. This is now resting on his tongue. It is literally emanating from his mouth, expressed in his speech, and therefore, it literally speaks with his mouth.[44] It is only then that he can hear it. This involves many details.

This can also occur in another manner. This supernal voice can clothe itself in the voices of other saints, from earlier generations. The two voices then come together and speak to the individual...

It is impossible for the voice of such a saint to speak to the individual unless the two share the same soul root. Sometimes, however, it can also occur when the individual has done some deed that is associated with that saint in particular...

When the voice is clothed in the individual's own speech, this is certainly a much higher level than when it is clothed in the speech of another saint. When one needs another saint, this is an indication that his own speech does not have the power to induce prophecy.

This explains the difference between Prophecy and *Ruach HaKodesh.* Prophecy is from the Male aspect, while *Ruach HaKodesh* is from the Female.

. . .

The lower soul *(nefesh)* is from the Universe of Asiyah, which is associated with the name Adonoy. One should therefore meditate on the name Adonoy (אדני) binding it to the name YHVH (יהוה) in the Universe of Asiyah. He should then bind this to the name Ehyeh (אהיה) in the Universe of Asiyah.[45]

He should then meditate on this, elevating the name Ehyeh of Asiyah, and binding it to Adonoy of Yetzirah. Adonoy of Yetzirah should then be bound to YHVH of Yetzirah.

[One proceeds in this manner through the Universes of Yetzirah, Beriyah and Atzilut], step by step, until he reaches Ehyeh of Atzilut. He should then bind Ehyeh of Atzilut to the very highest level, which is the Infinite Being *(Ain Sof).*[46]

. . .

There is another Yichud that you must constantly keep before your eyes. Meditate on the name Elohim (אלהים), with the letters spelled out, [and the Heh spelled] with a Yod (י), הי:

ALePH LaMeD HeY YOD MeM　　אלף למד הי יוד מם

This has a numerical value of 300. This is the same as the numerical value of MTzPTz (מצפץ), which is YHVH (יהוה) transformed by the Atabash (אתב״ש) cipher.

א ב ג ד ה ו ז ח ט י כ ל מ נ ס ע פ צ ק ר ש ת
ת ש ר ק צ פ ע ס נ מ ל כ י ט ח ז ו ה ד ג ב א

The Atbash Cipher

Meditate that Malkhut-Kingship is called Elohim and includes thirteen attributes. These parallel the thirteen letters in the expansion of Elohim.

The Thirteen Attributes are introduced with the Tetragrammaton (YHVH), as they are spelled out, "YHVH, YHVH, a merciful and loving God . . ." (Exodus 34:6).[47] The letters YHVH are then transformed into MTzPTz (מצפץ)[48]

(These are the qualities that a person must cultivate in order to attain enlightenment.)[49]

When a person prays, studies Torah, or observes a Commandment, he must be happy and joyful. He must have more pleasure than if he had reaped a great profit or had found a thousand gold coins. The Talmud thus teaches that the sage, Abbaye was standing before Rava and was very joyous because he had just put on Tefillin.[50]

The Torah states [that the people were punished], "Because you did not serve the Lord your God with joy and gladness of heart, because of the abundance of all things" (Deuteronomy 28:47).[51] You must rejoice in serving God more than when you profit with "the abundance of all" the money in the world.

The trait of sadness is a very bad quality, especially for one who wishes to attain wisdom and *Ruach HaKodesh*. There is nothing that can prevent enlightenment more than depression, even for those who are worthy. We find evidence for this from the verse, "And now bring a minstrel, and when the minstrel played, the hand of God came upon him" (2 Kings 3:15). [The music was needed to dispel his sadness].[52]

The same is true of anger, which can prevent enlightenment completely . . . The sages thus teach, "If a person becomes angry, if he is a prophet, his prophecy is taken away." [53]

. . .

Very important is the study of Torah. My master, of blessed memory, told me that one's main intent when studying Torah should be to bring enlightenment and the highest holiness to himself. Depend on this.

One must therefore concentrate on binding his soul to its highest root through the Torah and attaching it there. His intent should be that through this, the rectification of the Supernal Man should be completed. This was God's ultimate intent when He created man and commanded him to study the Torah.

There are other qualities that one must cultivate. These include humbleness, humility and the fear of sin. These three traits should be cultivated to the ultimate degree.

There are also traits that should be avoided to the ultimate degree. These include pride, anger, temper, frivolity, and malicious gossip. Even if one has good reason to display his temper, he should avoid it.

One should also avoid idle chatter, although it is not as serious as the five things mentioned above. One should not display temper, even to members of his family.

Keep the Sabbath in action and speech, with all its particulars. This is very helpful for enlightenment.

Sit in the synagogue with awe and trembling. The special meditation for this is of great help in attaining *Ruach HaKodesh.*[54]

My master also taught that prime path of *Ruach HaKodesh* is through care and Kavanah is the blessing over food. In this manner, one dispels the power of the Husks (*Klipot*) that have a hold on food and attaches themselves to the person who eats it. When a person recites a blessing over food with Kavanah, he removes these [evil spiritual] Husks. In this manner, an individual purifies his body, making it [spiritually] transparent, prepared to receive holiness. My master stressed this very much.

It is also important to wake up at midnight and recite the 111th Psalm. While reciting this, one should meditate on the letters MNTzPKh (מנצפך) , as discussed elsewhere.[55] This is very helpful for enlightenment. . . .

When you wear Tefillin, meditate that the four parchments of the head-Tefillin parallel the four letters of the Tetragrammaton. . . .

It is also important to have a set order of study each day and not miss it. This should include Bible, Mishnah, Talmud and the Kabbalah, together with the proper meditations, as discussed elsewhere.[56] It is important to be very careful regarding this.

My master also said that it is good for a person to live in a house with windows open to the heavens, so that he can always lift his eyes to the heavens and gaze at them. He can then meditate on the miracle of God's creation, as it is written, "When I look at Your heavens, the work of Your fingers . . ." (Psalms 8:4). The Zohar also says this about Nebuchadnezzar, who stated, "At the end of the days, I Nebuchadnezzar lifted my eyes to heaven, [and my understanding returned to me, and I blessed the Most High]" (Daniel 4:31).[57] It is therefore good for a person to constantly gaze at the heavens. This is something that will bring him wisdom, holiness and fear of God.

My master also told me that the root of all when it comes to enlightenment, is the study of Law (*Halakhah*). He gave me this reason:

When a person delves deeply into a question of Law, he should meditate how the shell (*Klipah*) of a nut covers the kernel. The kernel is the concept of Holiness. The Shell consists of the questions that one has with regard to that question of Law. This Shell surrounds the Law and does not permit the person to understand it.

When he then resolves the question, he should have in mind that he is breaking the power of that Shell, and removing it from the Holiness. The kernel, which is the Law, is then revealed.

If a person does not study the Law, and thereby break the Shells, how can he come to the kernel, which consists of the Wisdom of Kabbalah and the secrets of the Torah? One must therefore strive very much, studying and meditating in the above manner.

I also heard that my master would always interpret each Law in six ways. Then he would give it a seventh interpretation which would involve its hidden mystery. This is related to the myster of the six week days ahich precede the sventh, which is the Sabbath. . . .

Rabbi Jonathan Sagis also told me in the name of my master that nothing is more important for a person who seeks enlightenment than immersion [in the Mikvah], since one must be pure at all times. However, I noticed that my master generally did not immerse during the six winter months. He had a rupture and was subject to sickness, and his mother did not allow him to immerse. Of this I am certain. But as a result of this, he did not lose any enlightenment whatsoever. . . .

Rabbi Abraham HaLevi [Berukhim] told me that my master once gave him advice regarding enlightenment. He was told to avoid idle conversation, to rise at midnight, and to weep regarding his lack of knowledge. He was also instructed to go through the Zohar, hesitating only to understand the text, but not probing it in depth. In this manner, he was to cover forty or fifty pages a day, until he had gone through the entire Zohar many times.

I once asked my master why he was worthy of all this wisdom. He replied that he had worked very hard at it. I countered, "The Ramak and I, Chaim, also worked very hard." He answered, "Yes, you worked very hard, more than anyone else in this generation, but you did not work as hard as me."

On many occasions, he would stay up all night, pondering a single passage in the Zohar. Sometimes he would spend an entire week meditating (*hitboded*) on a single teaching of the Zohar. At such times, he would virtually go without sleep completely.

Rabbi Samuel Uceda told me that he heard my master say that if a person does not engage in any mundane speech whatsoever for forty days, he will attain wisdom and enlightenment.

I also heard from my master the mystery of "entrusting the soul." This involves the ascent of the soul at night in the mystery of, "Into Your hand I entrust my spirit" (Psalms 31:6).[58] There is no question that if a person is a Tzadik (saint), and is perfect in all his deeds, then his soul will ascend on high each night. This stated explicitly in the Zohar.[59]

But even if a person is not perfect, there are some practices that have the specific power to elevate his soul at night. One need not do them all; only one done properly is sufficient. If one does this, then his soul will ascend on high for that night alone. The only time that this will fail is if he has some major [unrepented] sin, which prevents him from ascending. But we are only speaking about the individual who walks in the ways of God and does not sin purposefully.

There are six methods, and each one is sufficient by itself if done properly.

The first method is that on that particular day, the individual should have perfect Kavanah in his prayers. If he does this, then in the 'Falling on the Face" in the morning prayer, he will bring about the supernal coupling.[60] This is the mystery of the verse, "Who shall ascend to God's mountain" (Psalms 24:3). The verse is speaking of the person who can ascend at night to the Upper Garden of Eden, this being "God's Mountain." The verse itself then replies, "He of clean hands and pure heart, who does not lift his soul in vain." This is speaking of the person who "lifts his soul" through the mystery of the Feminine Waters in the "Falling on the Face," when he says [in that prayer] , "To You O God I lift my soul" (Psalms 25:1). The individual [who does this with Kavanah] does not "lift his soul in vain." He is literally lifting his soul, and through this, bringing about the supernal coupling.

Such an individual can certainly have his soul rise at night, ascending to "God's mountain, His holy place." This is because he had brought about the supernal coupling between Jacob and Leah, which takes place each night after midnight. Then, through the mystery of the Feminine Waters, his soul also ascends to this place, as we have explained elsewhere.[61]

The second method involves giving charity properly on that day. This means that he should not know to whom he is giving, and the recipient should not know from whom he is receiving it. It is also necessary that such charity be given to a proper individual, one who is truly in need and worthy of it.

The third method involves wearing Tefillin the entire day. One must not take his mind off from them during this entire period. While wearing them, he should meditate on the "short meditation" for Tefillin, which we have presented elsewhere.[62]

The fourth method involves "bringing merit to the guilty." On that day, one should prevent a wicked person from committing some sin, and bring him to repent that one sin. Alternatively, he should speak to that person about repenting. This will bear fruit that will be of great benefit.

The fifth method involves concentrating and recalling every sin that one has done the entire day. This should be done when the individual is lying in bed. All of his sins should be before his eyes, and he should repent them all. After saying the bedtime Sh'ma, he should also confess them verbally, as explained in our writings . . . the Zohar speaks of individuals who use this method, calling them "masters of nightly reckonings."

It is important not to omit even a single sin or fine point that one transgressed on that particular day. When going to sleep, he should confess them all [before God] and not forget even a single one. It appears that I heard from my master, however, that it is not necessary to review all that one had done that day, since this would be an endless task. But one must strive to do so, setting his heart to remember all that he had done wrong that day. This is sufficient.

. . .

My master also taught me a meditation that can be used with [any observance, such as]charity and prayer. [This involves meditating on the Tetragrammaton (YHVH, יהוה), and] uniting te name YH (יה), which is separated from VH (וה).

Before any observance, one should say, "[I am doing this] to unite the Name of the Blessed Holy One (Male) and His Divine Presence (Female), with reverence and love, love and reverence, in the name of all Israel."

He should then meditate that he is combining the letters YH (יה), which represent love and reverence, with the letters VH (וה), which represent the Blessed Holy One (*Zer Anpin*, the Male) and His Divine Presence (*Shekhinah,* the Female).

When a person gives charity, he takes in his hand a coin, which in Hebrew is a *Perutah* (פרוטה). He should meditate on this word, and contemplate that the letters of *Perutah* and *PRaT VH* (פרט וה, a detail of VH) are the same.

The root of all Judgments is the 288 Sparks [which fell from Atzilut to Beriyah when the Vessels were shattered].[63] Add to this [a unit representing] the whole, and you have 299, [the numerical value of PRaT (פרט)].

These Judgments themselves are in Malkhut-Kingship (the Female), which is the final Heh (ה) of the Tetragrammaton. When a person binds this Heh to the Vav (ו) [which represents Zer Anpin, the Male], then these Judgments are ameliorated in every detail (*P'rat,* פְּרָט). This is accomplished through charity.

When a person wishes to repent, it is good to read the 20th Psalm and meditate on the mystical name YBK (יבק) that appears twice in this Psalm. The first such reference is in the initial verse, "God will answer you in a day of trouble" (*Ya'ankha YHVH B'Yom Tzara,* יַעַנְךָ יהוה בְּיוֹם צָרָה), were the initial letters [are YYBTz (ייבצ). These] add up to [112, the numerical value] of YBK (יבק). The second such reference is more explicit, in the last verse of this Psalm, "[the King] will answer us in the day we call" (*Ya'ane'nu B'Yom Kare'nu,* יַעֲנֵנוּ בְיוֹם קָרְאֵנוּ). Here the initial letters themselves spell out YBK (יבק).[64]

(Regarding the Practical Kabbalah.)[65]

I once asked my master the reason why the Practical Kabbalah is forbidden in all the later Kabbalistic texts. How did Rabbi Ishmael, Rabbi Akiba and the other sages of the *Hekhalot* make use of fearsome Names to open their hearts

He replied that at that time, the ashes of the [Red] Heifer were available, through which they could purify themselves of all defilement. Now, however, we are all defiled by the dead, and we do not have the ashes of the [Red] Heifer, which is the only means of removing this defilement. It does not help when we purify ourselves from other defilement when that resulting from contact with the dead remains as it was. We are therefore no longer permitted to make use of these Holy Names, and one who does so can be punished very severely.[66]

Rabbi Eliahu di Vidas told me that he had also asked my master this question, "How did earlier generations make use of the Divine Names?" He replied that one my use them if he can fulfil in himself the verse, "Maidens (*Alamot*) love you" (Song of Songs 1:3). The Talmud says, do not read *Almot* (maidens), but *Al mot* (over death), [making the verse read, "The one over death loves you."] This means that one must be so righteous that he is even loved by the Angel of Death.[67]

If a person does not have any sin, the Accuser cannot come before the Blessed Holy One and say, "Behold this person is making use of Your Names, and on that day, he committed such a sin." [68] [When such an accusation is made] that person is punished from heaven for making use of God's Names. But if he is totally without sin, then there is no way in which he can be denounced. The Angel of Death [who is identified with the Accuser] becomes his friend. Such a person can make use of Divine Names and not be punished.

This is alluded to in the *Hekhalot,* which states that one should not enter the Orchard (*Pardes*) unless he has never violated any negative commandment of the Torah.

We also see a case when Rabbi Nehunia ben HaKana was meditating (*hitboded*) and gazing into the Orchard (*Pardes*). Rabbi Ishmael and Rabbi Akiba touched him with the gown of a woman who was only questionably unclean, and he was dismissed immediately from before the Throne of Glory.[69]

We therefore see proof to both of my master's replies.

On another occasion, this same [Rabbi Eliahu di Vidas] received a somewhat different reply from my master. He said that the names and amulets that are now found in various manuscripts all contain errors. Even names and amulets that have been tested and found effective are still full of errors. It is therefore forbidden to make use of them. If we knew the names correctly, however, then we would also be permitted to use them.

[One who makes use of the Practical Kabbalah therefore blemishes his soul.] His penitence is to roll nine times in the snow. He must undress completely, and while totally nude, roll back and forth in the snow. This must be done nine times. [It should be done in a totally secluded place.]

This is alluded to in the verse, "When the Almighty is articulated, Kings are in her, [it will snow in deep shadows]" (Psalms 68:15). It is speaking of a person who articulates the Almighty's Names, which are called Kings. It is for this reason that the initial letters of the words, "When the Almighty is articulated, Kings" (*B'Paresh Shaddai*

M'lakhim, בְּפָרֵשׂ שַׁדַּי מְלָכִים), spell out *BaShem* (בְּשֵׁם), meaning "with the Name."

When a person articulates such Divine Names and pronounces them with his lips, then he is punished in the Genihom of Snow. It is known that Gehinom has two chambers, one of snow, and the other of fire.[70] The verse therefore concludes, "It will snow in deep shadow," indicating that this person will be condemned to the Gehinom of Snow. It is for this reason that his penitence must also be through snow.

When a person makes use of Divine Names, he causes great evil for himself. [Through these Names,] he binds angels by an oath, coercing them to do his will. These same angels then come and cause him to sin, destroying him completely. [Since he uses God's name incorrectly,] they will cause him to take God's name in vain in other matters, such as blessings, since one sin brings on another.

INTRODUCTIONS FOR THE USE OF YICHUDIM[71]

First Introduction

When a person meditates through a Yichud, souls of the righteous attach themselves to him, and reveal themselves. Soetimes a soul will do this because it comes from the same Root as the person who is meditating. At other times, it is because the individual does some good deed that pertains particularly to that saint. The saint then comes to him through the mystery of Nativity (*Ibbur,* עִבּוּר).

One such saint who reveals himself is Benaiah ben Yehoiada.[72] He comes particularly when one meditates with a Yichud that elevates the Feminine Waters, [which consists of spiritual energy that ascends from below].

This is his mystery. There are many saints who meditated with Yichudim during their lifetime, and they knew how to time this so that it would be accepted by the Supernal Will. At such times they would make use of Yichudim and transmit great benefit to themselves.

Usually, when a person makes use of a Yichud, he can only do so through the aspect of his Soul Root. But if one uses the Yichud at an auspicious time, he can then bring all the Supernal Roots together, and this is a very great advantage.

In general, when a saint dies, he causes all the universes to unite. But there are saints who knew how to use Yichudim at auspicious times, and they could do this even during their lifetime. What other saints could accomplish only after death, they could do while they were still alive.

One such saint was Benaiah ben Yehoiada. It is for this reason that he was called "son of a Living Man" (2 Samuel 23:20), even after his death. This indicates that even when he was alive he was able to unify all universes. He was therefore said to be "from Kabtziel," [which means "Gathering of God."] This is because he gathered and united all universes.

He was called Benaiahu (בְּנָיָהוּ) because of the Yichud through which he meditated and elevated the Feminine Waters. His name can be read as Ben (בֵּן) and YHV (יהו). The letters YHV denote the Sefirah of Tiferet-Beauty (*Zer Anpin*, the Male), who gives Ruach (spirit) to the Feminine Waters. The Feminine Waters themselves are called Ben, [which is the fourth expansion of the Tetragrammaton], when they are in the Female [Partzuf]. It is for this reason that he is called *Benaiah* — Ben YHV.

He is also called "Son of a Living Man" (*Ben Ish Chai*). "Ben" (בן) denotes the Tetragrammaton expanded with Heh's, which is called Ben (52). This Tetragrammaton is derived from the Sefirah of Yesod-Foundation, which is called *Ish Chai* ("A Living Man," or "A Man of Life").

There were other saints who resembled him in this respect. They included Moses, Rabbi Hamnuna the Elder, Rabbi Yebi the Elder, and others like them.

These saints were worthy of a very high level during their lifetime. Therefore, even after they died, whenever they see sages studying the Torah and meditating on higher Yichudim, they join them and reveal themselves. Sometimes they are there, but they remain concealed.

Such saints can bind themselves to people even if they do not share the same Soul Root. The reason is that they bound together all universes, and therefore include them all.

These saints reveal the mysteries of the Torah to certain individuals. The general concept explains how Rabbi Hamnuna the Elder and Benaiah ben Yehoiada revealed themselves to Rabbi Eliezer [son of Rabbi Shimon] and Rabbi Abba, as mentioned in the Zohar. [It also explains why the Elder said,] "Whenever I find sages, I follow them." [73]

When the soul of a saint reveals himself to an individual who shares the same Soul Root, then this individual gains very great enlightenment. Even though they can also reveal themselves to one who does not share their Soul Root, the influence is all the greater when they do share it, since they are then rectified through his rectification.

If a person begins meditating with a particular Yichud and then stops, he can cause himself great harm. "If he abandons it for one day, it will abandon him for two." [74] The souls that wish to bind themselves to him will then abandon him and repel him.

Do not say that the study of Torah is greater, and it is not fitting to neglect it [in order to meditate on Yichudim]. For the Yichudim that are mentioned here are more important than the study of Torah. Through them one can unify the Supernal Universes. This is considered to be a combination, including both Torah study and meditation.

Even if souls do not reveal themselves to you, do not be concerned, and do not stop meditating. Your intent should not be to bring souls to yourself, but to rectify the Supernal Universes.

Second Introduction

It is very beneficial to meditate on a Yichud while lying prostrate on the grave of a saint. When you do so, contemplate that through your own position, you are causing the saint to prostrate his soul and infuse the bones in his grave. This causes him to come to life in a sense, since his bones become like a body for the soul that infuses them. This soul is that which remains in the grave, this being the mystery of the verse, "His soul mourns for him" (Job 14:22). At this time, [as a result of your Yichud], it is as if both the body and soul of the saint were alive.

If you are not on a grave, but meditate on Yichudim at home, you need not have this intent. But at all times, whether on a grave or at home, it is beneficial to contemplate that your soul and that of the saint are bound together, with your soul included in his, and that the two of them are ascending together.

You should also meditate on the Root where your soul and that of the saint are bound to Adam. Contemplate on arousing that place, which is the limb where the saint is bound to Adam. As a result of that limb, you can elevate the saint's soul through the mystery of Feminine Water.

Thus, for example, imagine that the root of the saint is in the right arm of Adam, and that you also share this same root. After the saint died, he ascended from the arm to the head. Your soul, however, is still in the arm.

Each and every such root is a complete *Partzuf* (human form). If,

Levels of the Soul

Soul Level		Universe		Letter
Yechidah	Unique Essence	*Adam Kadmon*	First Man	
Chai	Living Essence	*Atzilut*	Nearness	Yod
Neshamah	Pneuma	*Beriyah*	Creation	Heh
Ruach	Spirit	*Yetzirah*	Formation	Vav
Nefesh	Soul	*Asiyah*	Making	Heh

for example, your soul is derived from the heel of that Partzuf, contemplate that you are elevating it from the heel to the head. Your soul will then bind itself to that of the saint. The two souls together are then motivated, and you, too, can ascend through the mystery of the Feminine Waters.

If you have reached the level of Neshamah, you should motivate your Neshamah to ascend with that of the saint. If you have attained only Ruach, you should motivate only your Ruach. The same is true if you have only the level of Nefesh. . . .

The most important thing is that you must do this with powerful yearning and joy. Your soul should be completely divested from the physical.

YICHUDIM[75]

The First Yichud

This is a Unification of Chochmah-Wisdom and Binah-Understanding.

Meditate on the name YHVH (יהוה) in Chokhmah-Wisdom.

Then meditate on the name Ehyeh (אהיה) in Binah-Understanding.

Now bind the two names together, meditating on the combination, which is YAHHVYHH (יאההויהה). This is the Upper Union.

Then meditate on the Name that unites the two. This is Ab (72), the Tetragrammaton expanded with Yod's:

YOD HY VYV HY יוד הי ויו הי

This expansion [has a numerical value of 72] the same as that of Chesed-Love (חֶסֶד). This is the upper Chesed, which brings about the Higher Union. It is called Destiny (*Mazla*, מַזָּלָא), and it is created through the Neshamah of the saint, when he ascends on high in Binah-Understanding. This involves the Feminine Waters of Binah-Understanding. It is the mystery of the statement, "Thus has it arisen in Thought,"[76] [since Thought is Binah-Understanding].

Now meditate on YHVH (יהוה) in Tiferet-Beauty. Then meditate on Adonoy (אדני) in Malchut-Kingship.

Bind the two names together, and then meditate on the combination, which is YAHDVNHY (יאהדונהי). [This is the Lower Union.]

Then meditate on the Name that unites the two. [This is Mah (45),] the Tetragrammaton expanded with Alef's:

YOD HA VAV HA יוד הא ואו הא

This is made through the Ruach of the saint. The Nefesh of the saint provides the Feminine Waters [for this Union].

Thus, the Lower Union requires the Ruach and the Nefesh. The Ruach motivates the Union, while the Nefesh provides the Feminine Waters.

For the Upper Union, however, all that is required is Neshamah. This is because Neshamah also includes the Neshamah of the Neshamah [which is the Chayah]. The Neshamah of the Neshamah, which is associated with Chokhmah-Wisdom motivates the Union. The Neshamah itself, which is associated with Binah-Understanding, is the mystery of the Feminine Waters.

It therefore resembles the Lower Union. In the Lower Union, Ruach, which is associated with Tiferet-Beauty motivates the Union. The Nefesh, which is associated with Malkhut-Kingship then stimulates the Feminine Waters.

There are four ways to expand the Tetragrammaton.
It can be expanded with Yod's [to form Ab, having a numerical value of 72] like this:

YOD HY VYV HY יוד הי ויו הי

It can be expanded [to form Sag, which has a numerical value of 63] like this:

YOD HY VAV HY יוד הי ואו הי

It can be expanded with Alef's [to form Mah, having a numerical value of 45] like this:

YOD HA VAV HA יוד אה ואו הא

And it can be expanded with Heh's [to form Ben, having a numerical value of 52] like this:

YOD HH VV HH יוד הה וו הה

The Tetragrammaton expanded wth Yod's, adding up to 72 (Ab), motivates the union of Chokhmah-Wisdom (Father) and Binah-Understanding (Mother), through the Neshamah of the Neshamah of the saint. It is associated with Chokhmah-Wisdom.

The Tetragrammaton adding up to 63 (Sag) then elevates the Feminine Waters through the Neshamah of the saint. This is associated with Binah-Understanding.

The Tetragrammaton adding up to 45 (Mah) then motivates the union between Tiferet-Beauty (Male) and Malkhut-Kingship (Female) through the Ruach of the saint. [It is associated with Tiferet-Beauty (*Zer Anpin*)].

The Tetragrammaton adding up to 52 (Ben) then elevates the Feminine Waters through the Nefesh of the saint. This is associated with Malkhut-Kingship (the Female Partzuf).

Review all of this carefully and understand it well.

In short, place the four letters of the Tetragrammaton (יהוה) before your eyes and meditate on them. Contemplate that you are uniting the Blessed Holy One (Male) with His Divine Presence (Female). this is the union of the letters Vav Heh (וה) [of the Tetragrammaton]. This union takes place through Love and Reverence, which are the letters Yod Heh (יה).

Then meditate on YHVH in Chokhmah-Wisdom, where it has the vowel point Patach (a, אַ):

YaHaVaHa יַהַוַהַ

Then meditate on the name Ehyeh (אהיה) in Binah-Understanding. Then bind them together:

YAHHVYHH יאההויהה

This is done through [Ab, which is] the Tetragraomaton expanded with Yod's, and is motivated by the Neshamah of the saint. This is associated with Chokhmah-Wisdom, which is the first letter (י) of the Tetragrammaton.

Then contemplate that you are elevating the Feminine Waters from Binah-Understanding, which is a motivation from below.

This is done through the Tetragrammaton expanded as Sag, and it is motivated by the Neshaman of the saint. This is associated with Binah-Understanding, which is the second letter (ה) of the Tetragrammaton.

Then meditate on YHVH in Tiferet-Beauty, where it has the vowel point Cholam (o, אֹ):

YoHoVoHo יֹהֹוֹהֹ

Then meditate on the name Adonoy (אדני) in Malkhut-Kingship. Then bind them together:

YAHDVNHY יאהדונהי

This is done through [Mah, which is] the Tetragrammaton expanded with Alef's, and is motivated by the Ruach of the saint. This is associated with Tiferet-Beauty, which is the third letter (ו) of the Tetragrammaton.

Then contemplate that you are elevating the Feminine Waters from Malchut-Kingship.

This is done through [Ben, which is] the Tetragrammaton expanded with Heh's, and is motivated by the Nefesh of the saint. This is associated with Malkhut-Kingship, which is the fourth letter (ה) of the Tetragrammaton.

When you meditate on a Yichud involving the saint's Neshamah, have in mind to bind your Neshamah to his. The same is true with regard to the Ruach and Nefesh.

If you do this, you will be completely bound to the saint, and you will be worthy of knowing all that you desire and receiving answers to all that you ask.

This, however, requires great concentration. You must clear your mind of all thought, and divest your soul from your body. If you do not do this correctly, you can be guilty of death, heaven forbid.

If you are yourself worthy of Neshamah of Neshamah as well as the lower levels of Neshamah, Ruach and Nefesh, then all four levels will be bound to those of the saint. You will then attain an extremely high level of enlightenment. If you have only the lower levels of the soul, your enlightenment will be correspondingly less. Through your devotion, you can increase your attachment and enlightenment. Through this, God will reveal to you the wonders of His Torah, and bring you close to Him in worship, love and reverence.

The Zohar teaches that a saint's Nefesh remains in the grave, his Ruach is in the Garden of Eden, while his Neshamah is under the Throne of Glory. This, however, is only speaking of a person whose Nefesh is from Asiyah, whose Ruach is from Yetzirah, and whose Neshamah is from Beriyah.

There are saints, however, who are worthy that all three levels of their soul, Nefesh, Ruach and Neshamah, are all from Atzilut. In such a case, there is no question that his Nefesh ascends to Malkhut-Kingship [in Atzilut], his Ruach ascends to Tiferet-Beauty, and his Neshamah ascends to Binah-Understanding. This is because all things return to their Root.

The Nefesh that remains in the grave is therefore only the Nefesh of Asiyah.

The *Tikkuney Zohar* states that the Tetragrammaton expanded as Sag is the mystery of the Feminine Waters of Binah-Understanding. Through this, the Son (*Zer Anpin*) ascends upward to [the Partzuf of] Father.[77]

The souls of saints are the Feminine Waters of Malkhut-Kingship [the Female Partzuf]. In a similar manner, [Zer Anpin and the Female, which are] the Children of Binah-Understanding (Mother), serve as Her Feminine Waters.

Tiferet-Beauty (Zer Anpin) then ascends through the mystery of Daat-Knowledge to unite Chokhmah-Wisdom and Binah-Understanding through [Ab,] the Tetragrammaton expanded with Yod's. Malkhut-Kingship then remains in the mystery of the Feminine Waters of Binah-Understanding, through the Tetragrammaton expanded as Sag. Understand this well.

I copied all of this from an actual manuscript written by may master.[78]

What follows was heard from him orally.

The Third Yichud[79]

The name Mah is the Tetragrammaton expanded with Alef's. When this is "squared" it has a numerical value of 130.

The Square of Mah

Mah itself, having a numerical value of 45, is:

YOD HA VAV HA יוד הא ואו הא

Its "Square" is:

YOD	יוד =	20
YOD HA	יוד הא =	26
YOD HA VAV	יוד הא ואו =	39
YOD HA VAV HA	יוד הא ואו הא =	45
		130

This is the Mouth of Atika Kadisha (The Ancient Holy One). [Atika Kadisha is the Partzuf that parallels the upper part of Keter-Crown, and it is the highest Partzuf in Atzilut]

This is the mystery of the verse, "Who placed a Mouth in Man (Adam)" (Exodus 4:11). The name Mah has a numerical value of 45, the same as that of Adam (אָדָם), meaning "man."

The "square" of Mah is 130. Subtract from this 45, which is the numerical value of Mah itself. You then have 85, which is the numerical value of Peh (פֶּה), meaning "mouth." Therefore, if you add "muth" (85) to "man" (45), you have 130.

This is the Outer Essence [of this Mouth].

The Inner Essence of the Mouth, however, is the Tetragrammaton expanded as Sag.

From our other teachings, you already know that there is a Union in the mouth itself. This involves the Throat, which gives rise to the letters AHChE (אהחע), and the Palate, which produces the letters GYKhK (גיכק). This then produces the other three phonetic groups, making a total of 22 letters.

The Inner Essence of the Nose of Atika Kadisha is the Tetragrammaton expanded as SAG.

Its Outer Essence consists of the three names Ehyeh (אהיה). These emanate from the three Alef's that are in the name Mah.

The name Mah is in the mouth of Atika Kadisha, as mentioned above. The three Alef's are transmitted upward and become the Outer Essence of the Nose.

THE PHONETIC GROUPS
(According to Sefer Yetzirah)

Gutterals	אחהע	*Alef Chet Heh Eyin*
Labials	בומף	*Bet Vav Mem Peh*
Palatals	גיכק	*Gimel Yod Kaf Kof*
Dentals	דטלנת	*Dalet Tav Lamed Nun Tav*
Sibilants	זסשרץ	*Zayin Samekh Shin Resh Tzadi*

We can now write the Yichud in brief. This is how you should meditate:

First meditate on the name Mah, the Tetragrammaton expanded with Alef's:

YOD HA VAV HA יוד הא ואו הא

This is the Mouth of Atika Kadisha. Then meditate on the three Alef's in this Name and draw them upward

YOD H^{A} V^{A}V H^{A} יוד ה^{א} ו^{א}ו ה^{א}

Now form each of these Alef's into the name Ehyeh (אהיה).

AHYH AHYH AHYH אהיה אהיה אהיה
YOD H V V H יוד ה ו ו ה

Draw these three names upward, and form the Outer Essence of the Nose of Atika Kadisha.

Meditate on these three names Ehyeh (אהיה) [with the vowel point of Kametz (אָ). Kametz corresponds to Keter-Crown, which is the parallel of Atika Kadisha.]

AaHaYaHa AaHaYaHa AaHaYaHa אָהָיָהָ אָהָיָהָ אָהָיָהָ

Contemplate that the name Ehyeh (אהיה) [has a numerical value of 21]. The three names therefore have a numerical value [of 63, the same as that] of *Chotem* (חוטם), which means Nose.

[The Kametz has the form of a Vav and a Yod. The Vav has a value of 6 and the Yod has a value of 10, so therefore the value of the Kametz is 16.]

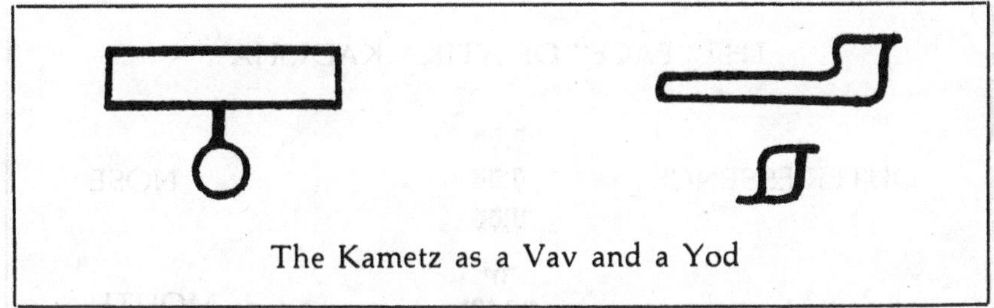

The Kametz as a Vav and a Yod

Meditate on the Kametz's in the names Ehyeh (אהיה). Since there are four such vowels in the name, their total numerical value is 64. This is the numerical value of Chotem (חוטם), plus a unit for the word itself.

Meditate on the vowels and contemplate that from this Nose there emanates great life force to the Male and Female.

From the right nostril, there emanates spiritual essence (*ruach*) to Zer Anpin (the Male). From the left nostril, spiritual essence emanates to the Female. This motivates their Union.

This motivation of the Female, however, will only take place in the Messianic Age. At that time, She will be motivated by the essence from the Left Nostril. Now, however, She must be motivated by the souls of the righteous.

These two essences, the right and the left, are alluded to in the vowel points. The four vowels Kametz in each of the three names have a numerical value of 64.

Meditate on this, and contemplate that it alludes to the expansion of the Tetragrammaton as Sag [which has a value of 63] plus an additional unit for the whole. This motivates spiritual essence for Zer Anpin (the Male).

Now meditate again on the four vowels Kametz, which have a numerical value of 64. Add to this a unit representing the whole, and you have 65, the numerical value of Adonoy (אדני), the name associated with the Female. This alludes to the fact that from these vowels a life spirit is transmitted to the Female of Zer Anpin.[80]

Then meditate on the Inner Essence of this Nose, which is the name Sag

YOD HY VAV HY יוד הי ואו הי

The first HY (הי) of this expansion is the Female of the right Nostril. The Heh (ה) [in this pair] conceals the Yod (י) because [Heh is feminine and] all of this takes place in an aspect of the Feminine Waters.

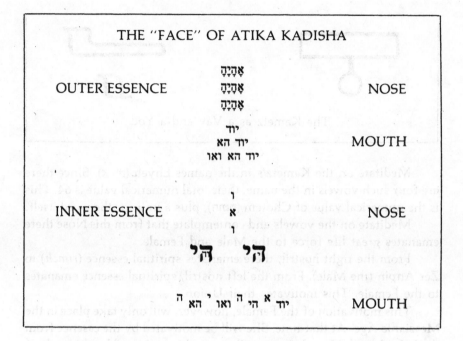

THE "FACE" OF ATIKA KADISHA

	אָהָיָהָ	
OUTER ESSENCE	אָהָיָהָ	NOSE
	אָהָיָהָ	
	יוד	
	יוד הא	MOUTH
	יוד הא ואו	
	ו	
INNER ESSENCE	א	NOSE
	ו	
	הי הי	
	יוד א הי ה ואו י הא ה	MOUTH

The second HY (הי) in Sag is the Female of the left Nostril.

The VAV (ואו) is the Septum that separates these two orifices.

All that now remains is YOD (יוד). This represents the two Yod's which are concealed in the two Nostrils.

The [initial] letter Yod (י) [in YOD (יוד)] is the spiritual essence which is concealed in the Right Nostril. [It is the Yod (י) concealed] inside the first HY (הי). From this comes the life force that motivates Zer Anpin (the Male) toward the Union.

The two letters OD (וד) in YOD (יוד) also have a numerical value of 10. This is [the second Yod (י)] concealed in the Left Nostril, which is the final HY (ה). From this comes life force to the Female, [the Bride] of Zer Anpin to motivate the Union.

Meditate in this manner so as to complete the Inner Essence and Outer Essence [of the Nose].

Then meditate to bring about the Union in the Mouth of Atika Kadisha in this manner.

First contemplate that the Inner Essence of the breath of this Mouth is the name Sag:

YOD HY VAV HY יוד הי ואו הי

Then intertwine this with the name Ehyeh (אהיה) in this manner:

YOD A HY H VAV Y HY H יוד א הי ה ואו י הי ה

Contemplate the fact that [Sag has a value of 63 and Ehyeh has a value of 21, making a total of 84]. This is the numerical value of [all the gutterals] AChHE (אחהע).

These letters are sounded with the throat, which corresponds to the Female.

Then meditate on the Palatals, GYKhK (גיכק). These are sounded with the palate, which corresponds to the Male.

[Meditate on GYKhK (גיכק) and] intertwine them with AChHE (אחהע), like this:

GAYChKhHKE גאיחכהקע

Contemplate on the fact that [AChHE (אחהע) has a value of 84 and GYKhK (גיכק) has a value of 133, making a total of 217]. Subtract a unit for the whole and you have 216. This [is three times 72, and it] gives rise to the other three phonic groups, [the dentals, the labials, and the sibilants].

The first group are [the Dentals] DTLNTh (דטלנת), which are pronounced with the Tongue. This parallels the Union of Father (Chokhmah) and Mother (Binah), YHVH (יהוה) and Ehyeh (אהיה). This takes place through Daat-Knowledge, which is the Tongue.

Then take the Sibilants, ZShSRTz (זשסרצ), which are produced by the Teeth. These parallel the union of YHVH (יהוה) and Elohim (אלהים). [Elohim has five letters, paralleling the] Five Strengths, and these are the five Sibilants.

Then take the Labials, BVMPh (בומף), which are produced with the lips. They represent the mystery of the Union of YHVH (יהוה) and Adonoy (אדני). This is the external Union opposite the Mouth, produced by the Union of the [two] lips.

Now meditate that each of these three categories corresponds to the name YHV (יהו):

DTLNTh — YHV דטלנת — יהו
ZShSRTz — YHV זשסרצ — יהו
BVMPh — YHV בומף — יהו

[Each of these three names YHV (יהו) has a numerical value of 21. The three of them together therefore have a numerical value of 63] which is the numerical value of the name Sag. But as we have seen, this is the Inner Essence of the Mouth, and this is from where these sounds emanate.

Now contemplate on each of the three names YHV (יהו), and expand each one in the same manner that Sag is expanded:

YOD HY VAV יוד הי ואו

[This expansion has a numerical value of 48, which is] the sum of YHVH (יהוה = 26) and Ehyeh (אהיה= 21), adding a unit for the whole. Thus, we are constantly uniting the two names, YHVH (יהוה) and Ehyeh (אהיה).

[Now meditate on these three names:]

YOD HY VAV	יוד הי ואו
YOD HY VAV	יוד הי ואו
YOD HY VAV	יוד הי ואו

[Also meditate on the gutterals AChHE (אחהע) and the palatals GYKhK (גיכק), which have a numerical value of 216, as above.]

When these three names emanate from 216, they are drawn into the Mouth. They then become the Vapor (Hevel, הֶבֶל) that emanates from the mouth.

At this point, however, they cannot yet emanate, but are only drawn to the mouth.

You must therefore meditate on each of the three abovementioned Names, YHV (יהו) expanded with Yod's [like Ab].

YOD HY VYV	יוד הי ויו

Now place under each letter, the two vowel points, Kametz (ָ) and Shva (ְ):

Y'aU'aD'a H'aY'a V'aY'aV'a	יְָוְָדְָ הְָיְָ וְָיְָוְָ

[You should have before your eyes a column of three such names.]

Now meditate that the two letters HY VYV (הי ויו) in each of these names have a numerical value of 37. This is the numerical value of Hevel (הבל), meaning Vapor. This is because they represent the Vapor that emanates from the Mouth.

[The Shva (ְ) consists of two dots, and each of these two dots can be seen as a Yod. The Shva therefore consists of two Yod's. As mentioned earlier, the Kamatz (ָ) consists of a Yod and a Vav.] The vowel point of each letter is a Shva and a Kametz, and this consists of three Yod's and a Vav. This has a numerical value of 36, and adding a unit for the whole, it yields 37. This, too, is the numerical value of Hevel (הבל) meaning Vapor, for the same reason given above.

Now meditate on these three names:

Y'aO'aD'a H'aY'a V'aY'aV'a	יְָוְָדְָ הְָיְָ וְָיְָוְָ
Y'aO'aD'a H'aY'a V'aY'aV'a	יְָוְָדְָ הְָיְָ וְָיְָוְָ
Y'aOa'D'a H'aY'a V'aY'aV'a	יְָוְָדְָ הְָיְָ וְָיְָוְָ

Bring them into the Mouth of Atika Kadisha and bind them there. Now meditate that the essence of this mouth, the "square" of the name Mah, YOD HA VAV HA (יוד הא ואו הא), from which Mah itself is subtracted

YOD	יוד
YOD HA	יוד הא
YOD HA VAV	יוד הא ואו

This has a numerical value of 85, which is the same as that of *Peh* (פֶּה) meaning Mouth. As mentioned at the beginning of this Yichud, this is the Outer Essence of the Mouth.

You should now meditate on the Inner essence of the Mouth, which is the Tetragrammaton expanded as Sag:

YOD HY VAV HY יוד הי ואו הי

Add this Name, which has a numerical value of 63, to the 22 letters of the alphabet. The total will then be 85, which is the numerical value of *Peh* (פה) meaning Mouth.

Now meditate to bring these three names YHV (יהו) from inside the mouth to the outside. This is the mystery of the Vapor *(Hevel)* that emanates from the Mouth. It is also an aspect of Enveloping Light *(Or Makif).* It is well-established that all Vapor that comes from the Mouth is Enveloping Light.

Do not draw it all outside, however. One name YHVH (יהוה) must remain inside the Mouth. This is made from all three names YHV (יהו) in the following manner:

Yod (י) is taken from the first name YHV (יהו).
Heh (ה) is taken from the second name YHV (יהו).
Vav Heh (וה) is taken from the third name YHV (יהו).

[This remains inside.] The rest emanate in the mystery of Vapor *(Hevel).* The letters that emanate are:

HV (הו) that remains from the first name YHV (יהו).
YV (יו) that remains from the second name YHV (יהו).
Y (י) that remains from the third name YHV (יהו).

[All of these letters, HV YVY (הו יו י) together have a numerical value of 37. This is the numerical value of *Hevel* (הבל) meaning Vapor.]

Now meditate on these letters, HV YV Y (הו יו י). They should be expanded [with Yod's], together with the vowel points shva (ְ) and Kametz(ָ):

H'aY'a V'aY'aV'a Y'aO'aD'a V'aY'aV'a Y'aOa'D'a

הָ֑יְ וָ֑יְוָ֑ יָ֑וְדָ֑ וָ֑יְוָ֑ יָ֑וְדָ֑

Contemplate that you are bringing these out through the mystery of the Vapor that emanates from the Mouth, which is the Enveloping Light. This then encompasses the Nose.

Both the Inner Essence and Outer Essence [of the Nose] are drawn to this place, which is outside the Mouth of Atika Kadisha. The Essence of the Nose then becomes the Inner Light (*Or Penimi*), which is clothed in the Vapor from the Mouth, which is its Enveloping Light.

Now meditate that you are bringing about the following three Unions:

YHVH (יהוה) and Ehyeh (אהיה).
YHVH (יהוה) and Elohim(אלהים).
YHVH (יהוה) and Adonoy (אדני).

The first Union, [YHVH (יהוה) and Ehyeh (אהיה)] is that of Father and Mother. Meditate on these names in the following manner:

Father: Y'aH'aV'aH'a יְָהְָוְָהְָ
Mother: AaHaYaHa אֲהֲיֲהֲ

Now meditate on the two expansions

H'aY'a V'aY'aV'a הְָיְָ וְָיְָוְָ

These come from the first name YHV (יהו). Meditate that you are bringing down these two expansions from the Vapor of the Mouth, which is the Encompassing [Light]. All letters should have the vowel points Kametz (ָ) and SHVA (ְ).

Bring down these two expansions and draw them into the name YHVH (יהוה), which represents Father, since this will motivate Him toward the Union. It is for this reason that when you meditate on the name YHVH (יְָהְָוְָהְָ) representing Father, each letter has the vowel points Kametz and Shva. These vowel points represent Vapor *(Hevel)*, as discussed earlier.

Now meditate that you are bringing down the Inner Essence of this Vapor, which is the Outer Essence of the Nose.

[As discussed earlier, the Outer Essence of the Nose consists of three names Ehyeh (אהיה) with the vowel point Kametz.] Meditate on the first of these three names:

AaHaYaHa אָהָיָהָ

Bring this name down and draw it into the name Ehyeh (אהיה) which represents Mother, since this will motivate Her toward Union. When you meditate on the name Ehyeh (אָהָיָה) representing Mother, it should have the vowel point Kametz.

Now meditate on the expansion

H'a Y'a V'a Y'a V'a הָי וָיָו

This is derived from the first name YHV (יהו). This is the Vapor of the Mouth.

Meditate how these letters represent the Vapor *(Hevel)*. The letters themselves [HY VYV (הי ויו) have a numerical value of 37,] the same as that of Hevel (הבל) meaning Vapor. The vowel points, Kametz and Shva also have the numerical value of Hevel, as discussed earlier.

Meditate that from these two Vapors [the Internal and the External], motivation is transmitted to Father and Mother, which are YHVH (יהוה) and Ehyeh (אהיה), so that they come together in Union.

MOTIVATING THE UNION OF FATHER AND MOTHER	
The Vapor of the Mouth	הָי וָיָו
is transmitted to Father	יָהָוָהָ
The Light of the	
External Essence of the Nose	אָהָיָה
is transmitted to Mother	אָהָיָה

Now contemplate that you are elevating the Neshamah of the saint with whom you desire to commune, through the mystery of the Feminine Waters. Contemplate that you are arousing the place in Adam's body to which this Neshamah' soul is bound. Bind your soul to his soul, in the manner described earlier.

Now meditate in the two names representing Father and Mother:

Y'aH'aV'aH'a AaHaYaHa יָהָוָהָ אָהָיָה

Intertwine these two names in the following manner:

Y'aAaH'aHaV'a YaH'aHa יָאהָהָוָ יָהָה

Now you are ready to bring about the second Union. Meditate on the two names YHVH (יהוה) and Elohim (אלהים) like this:

Y'aH'aV'aH'a AaLaHaYaMa יְהָוָה אָלָהָיָם

Then meditate on the letters YOD VYV (יוד ויו) from the second name YHV (יהו) like this:

Y'aO'aD'a V'aY'aV'a יְוָד וְיָו

This is the Vapor of the Mouth that is the Enveloping [Light]. Bring this down to the name YHVH (יהוה) in Tiferet (Zer Anpin). When you meditate on this name YHVH, its vowels should be Shva and Kametz:

Y'aH'aV'aH'a יְהָוָה

This motivates [Zer Anpin] toward the Union.

Contemplate to draw the Inner Essence of this Vapor, which is the Inner Essence of the Nose. Meditate that you are bringing this from the Yod in the Right Nostril, mentioned above, to this name YHVH in Tiferet (Zer Anpin), motivating Him toward Union.

Then meditate to bring down the Inner Essence of this Vapor which is the Outer Essence of the Nose. Contemplate the second of the three names Ehyeh (אהיה) [that comprise the Outer Essence of the Nose] with the vowel Kametz:

AaHaYaHa אָהָיָה

Draw this down to the name Elohim (אלהים), meditating on this name with the vowel Kametz:

AaLaHaYaMa אָלָהָיָם

Then meditate to draw the Inner Essence of the Nose from the letters OD (וד) in the Left Nostril. Bring this into the name Elohim (אלהים) so as to motivate the Female [Partzuf] toward Union.

Then meditate to elevate the Ruach-spirit of the saint, along with your own Ruach-spirit, in the same manner mentioned above with respect to the Neshamah.

Then intertwine the two names YHVH (יְהָוָה) and Elohim (אָלָהָיָם):

Y'aAaH'aLaV'aHaH'aYaMa יְאָהָלָוָהָהָיָם

You are now ready to bring about the third Union. Meditate on the two names, YHVH (יהוה) and Adonoy (אדני) like this:

Y'aH'aV'aH'a AaDaNaYa יְהָוָה אָדָנָי

Then meditate on the letter YOD (יוד) from the third name YHV (יהו), like this:

Y'aU'aD'a יָוָדָ

This is the Vapor of the mouth that is the Enveloping [Light]. Bring this down to the name YHVH (יהוה) [representing Zer Anpin] as above. When you meditate on the name YHVH, its vowels should all be Kametz Shva:

Y'aH'aV'aH'a יְָהְָוְָהְָ

Contemplate to draw the Inner Essence of this Vapor, which is the Outer Essence of the Nose. Contemplate the third of the three names Ehyeh (אהיה) [that comprise the Outer Essence of the Nose] with the vowel Kametz:

AaHaYaHa אָהָיָהָ

This draws it into the name Adonoy (אדני), as mentioned, so as to motivate [the Female Partzuf] to Union.

Then meditate to elevate the Nefesh-soul of the saint, along with your own Nefesh, in the manner discussed earlier with regard to the Neshamah.

Then intertwine the two names YHVH (יְָהְָוְָהְָ) and Adonoy (אֲדֹנָי) like this:

Y'aAaH'sDaV'aNaH'aYa יְָאָהְדָוְָנָהְָיָ

Finally meditate on the two letters OD (וד) which have been drawn down to the Female from the Left Nostril. [Take the Vav (ו) and form it into the left leg of the Heh. Then draw it under the Dalet (ד)] so as to form a Heh (ה). This indicates that the [Female Partzuf] has become pregnant from this Union.

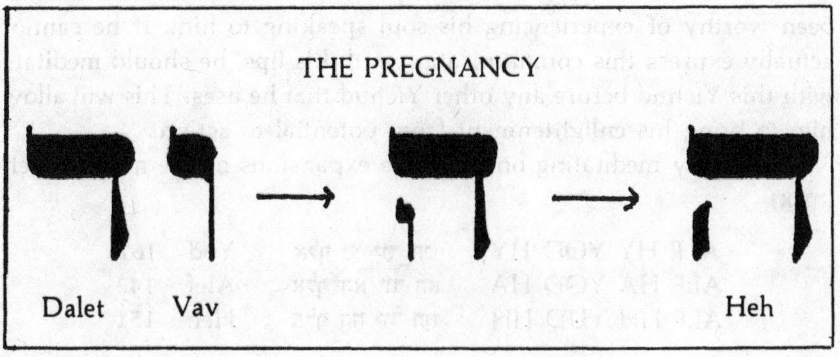

The Fifth Yichud

The purpose of this Yichud is to repel and banish the Outside Forces. You may meditate on it after another Yichud.

Meditate on the two names Elohim Elohim like this:

ALHYM ALHYM אלהים אלהים

Then intertwine the two names with the following vowels:

AeAe LeLe HeHe YeYe MaMa אֵאֵ לֵלֶ הֵהֵ יֵיֵ מַםַ

Contemplate [that each name Elohim (אלהים) has a numerical value of 86, and therefore the two names have a value of 172]. Add to this an additional 10 for the ten letters in both names, and you have 182, which is the numerical value of Jacob (יַעֲקֹב).

Also contemplate that the vowel points have the same numerical value as Jacob. The first eight letters all have the vowel point Tzeré (ֵ), except for the second Lamed, (ל), which has a Segol (ֶ). [The Tzeré consists of two dots or Yod's, and thus has a numerical value of 20. The Segol consists of three dots or Yud's and has a value of 30. The seven Tzerés therefore have a total value of 140, and together with the 30 of the Segol] this yields 170. This is the value of AC (עק) of Jacob.

The two letters Mem (מ) have the vowel Patach (ַ). [This has the form of a (headless) Vav (ו), and therefore has a numerical value of 6. The two therefore have] a numerical value of 12. This is the value of JB (יב) of Jacob.

Combining AC (עק) and JB (יב) then yields Jacob (יעקב).

The Sixth Yichud

This Yichud is designated for a person who has meditated and has been worthy of experiencing his soul speaking to him. If he cannot actually express this communication with his lips, he should meditate with this Yichud before any other Yichud that he uses. This will allow him to bring his enlightenment from potential to action.

Begin by meditating on the three expansions of the name Ehyeh (אהיה).

ALF HY YOD HY	אלף הי יוד הי	Yod	161
ALF HA YOD HA	אלף הא יוד הא	Alef	143
ALF HH YUD HH	אלף הה יוד הה	Heh	151

The first of these is expanded with Yod's [and has a numerical value of 161]. The second is expanded with Alef's [and has a numerical value of 143]. The third is expanded with Heh's [and has a numerical value of 151].

Then meditate on the triangulation of Ehyeh (אהיה):

AHYH	אהיה	= 21
AHY	אהי	16
AH	אה	6
A	א	1
		44

Contemplate that this has a numerical value of 44. Add this to the 455 obtained earlier from the expansions, and you have a total of 499.

Now meditate on the name Tzevaot (צְבָאוֹת), [meaning "Hosts," as in "the Lord of Hosts."] This name is in Yesod-Foundation, in its aspect as the "Covenant of the Tongue." [81]

Contemplate that the numerical value of the name Tzevaot (צבאות) is also 499.

After you complete this, you can make use of any Yichud that you desire.

The Seventh Yichud

This is very similar to the previous one. If you begin to perceive something with your mouth through a Yichud, but can only move your lips without expressing sounds, make use of this Yichud. First meditate with this, and then make use of any other Yichud that you desire.

First meditate on the names Ehyeh (אהיה), YHVH (יהוה), and Adonoy (אדני). Intertwine them in direct order like this:

AYADHHNVYYHH איאדההנוייהה

Then meditate on the same three names combined in reverse order:

AYAHHDYVNHHY איאההדיונההי

Contemplate this well, and then you can make use of any other Yichud that you may desire.

The Tenth Yichud

Begin by closing your eyes and holding them tightly shut. Meditate (*hitboded*) in this manner for one hour. Then make use of the following Yichud.

Meditate on the name [of the angel] Metatron (מְטַטְרוֹן). Divide the name into three parts like this:

MT TR ON מט טר ון

Contemplate that the numerical olue of the first pair of letters, MT (מט) is 49. These are the Forty-Nine Gates of Understanding (Binah). This is the total essence of Metatron.

Meditate that this relates to the combination of the two names, YHVH (יהוה) and Ehyeh (אהיה), intertwined like this:

YAHHVYHH יאההויהה

[The name YHVH (יהוה) has a value of 26, while Ehyeh (אהיה) has a value of 21] making a total of 47. Adding two for the two names themselves then yields 49, the numerical value of MT (מט).

Then meditate on the second pair, TR (טר).

This is associated with the two combinations, one of YHVH (יהוה) and Elohim (אלהים), and the other of YHVH (יהוה) and Adonoy (אדני). These must be intertwined in the following manner

YAHHVHHYM יאהההוהים
YAHDVNHY יאהדיהני

All of these names have a numerical value of 203. This is the numerical value of Be'er (בְּאֵר), meaning "a well."

[The numerical value of TR (טר) is 209,] so an additional six are required. These six are the first six letters, YAHHVY (יאההוי), of the above-mentioned combination of YHVH (יהוה) and Ehyeh (אהיה).

Two letters HH (הה) are then left over from the original eight of that combination. Contemplate on these together with the final two letters [of Metatron], ON (ון).

Elsewhere, we have discussed how the letters ON (ון) are related to the mystery of Judgment.[82] [There are five letters that change their form at the end of a word:] MNTzPKh (םןץףך). Taken together, these five letters have a numerical value of 280. This is five times 56, where 56 is the numerical value of ON (ון). These are the Five Strengths [of Judgment].

This is the significance of the two letters HH (הה). The numerical value of Heh (ה) is five, denoting the Five Strengths of Judgment. [The first Heh (ה) denotes the Five Strengths represented in MNTzPKh (מנצפך), while the second Heh (ה) represents those of the five combinations ON (ון).]

The Twenty-First Yichud

This includes three beneficial Yichudim, along with six good meditations.

(The scribe writes: These are the Yichudim upon which a person should constantly meditate.)

It is very good for a person to depict the letters of the name YHVH (יהוה) before the eyes of his mind. This brings a person's heart to fear his Creator, and also purifies the soul. This is the significance of the verse, "I have placed YHVH (יהוה) before me at all times" (Psalms 16:8).[83]

Always meditate how you were created in the "Form of God." This is its significance.

In the physical man, there is Inner Essence and Outer Essence. This also has a counterpart in the Supernal Man (Zer Anpin). The Inner Essence consists of the Mentalities (*Mochin*), while the Outer Essence is the flesh.

The Mentalities permeate the entire body. This relates to the "Form (*tzelem*) of YHVH."

The two letters YH (יה) parallel the two Mentalities in man's head. The letter V (ו) is man's body, which is pervaded by the Mentalities. The final H (ה) is the "Coronet of the Foundation," which is man's mate.

The Outer Essence alludes to the "Form (*tzelem*) of Elohim (אלהים)." ([Chaim Vital writes:] I forgot the precise concept, but this is my best recollection.)

The Alef (א) [of Elohim (אלהים)] represents [the counterpart of the Sefirah of] Keter-Crown in man. This is his Skull.

The Skull contains two cavities, in which the Mentalities (brains) rest. This is the Alef, which is Keter-Crown.

The Lamed (ל) [in Elohim (אלהים) has a numerical value of thirty. Since we assign a value of ten to each Mentality,] this represents the three Mentalities, Chokhmah-Wisdom, Binah-Understanding, and Daat-Knowledge.

The Heh (ה) [in Elohim (אלהים) has a numerical value of five.] This represents the five "corners" in man, from Chesed to Hod. [Chesed is the right arm, Gevurah is the left, Tiferet is the Body, while Netzach and Hod are the two legs.]

The Yod (י) [in Elohim (אלהים)] represents Yesod-Foundation.

The final Mem (ם) [in Elohim (אלהים)] is Malkhut-Kingship. It is the Coronet of Foundation, the Female, who is the man's mate.

This is the mystery of the verse, "God (Elohim) created man in His form, in the form of God (Elohim), He created him" (Genesis 1:27). [The word "form" occurs twice in this verse,] alluding to the two Forms. The first is the "Form of YHVH," which is alluded to in the word *Tzalmo* (צַלְמוֹ), translated as "His form." This can also be read as *Tzelem O* (צֶלֶם ו), that is, the Form of Vav. The letter Vav (ו)[has a numerical value of six, representing the Six Sefirot that form] the Partzuf of Zer Anpin. This is YHVH, and hence "His Form" is the "form of YHVH." The second form, is mentioned explicitly, and this is the "form of Elohim."

THE SEFIROT AND MAN

Mentalities

Keter-Crown	Skull	YaHaVaHa	יָהָוָהָ
Chokhmah-Wisdom	Right Brain	YaHaVaHa	יַהַוַהַ
Binah-Understanding	Left Brain	YeHeVeHe	יֵהֵוֵהֵ
(Daat-Knowledge)	Middle Brain		

Body

Chesed-Love	Right Arm	YeHeVeHe	יֶהֶוֶהֶ
Gevurah-Strength	Left Arm	Y'H'V'H'	יְהְוְהְ
Tiferet-Beauty	Torso	YoHoVoHo	יֹהֹוֹהֹ
Netzach-Victory	Right Leg	YiHiViHi	יִהִוִהִ
Hod-Splendor	Left Leg	YuHuVuHu	יֻהֻוֻהֻ
Yesod-Foundation	Sexual Organ	YuHuVuHu	יוּהוּווּהוּ
Malkhut-Kingship	Mate	YHVH	יהוה

You must constantly meditate, making yourself into a vehicle for the Holy Atzilut. It is thus written, "In the form of God He made [man]" (Genesis 5:1), and "In the form of God He made man" (Genesis 9:6).

It is especially fitting and necessary that you meditate in this manner when you pray. Through this, your prayers will be accepted and you will be answered. Through such meditations, you bind all the Universes together, and the Highest Holiness then rests on you and pertains to you.

This is how you should meditate.[84]

Prepare your head so that it should be a Throne for the Name YHVH with the Vowel Kametz	יָהָוָהָ
The mentality of Chokhmah-Wisdom in it should be YHVH:	יַהַוַהַ
The mentality of Binah-Understanding should be YHVH:	יֵהֵוֵהֵ
The right hand should be with a Segol:	יֶהֶוֶהֶ
The left hand should be with a Shva:	יְהְוְהְ
The torso should be with a Cholem:	יֹהֹוֹהֹ
The right leg should be with a Chirek:	יִהִוִהִ
The left leg should be with a Kibbutz:	יֻהֻוֻהֻ
The Yesod-Foundation should be with a Shurek:	יוּהוּווּהוּ
Its Coronet does not have any vowel at all:	יהוה

Then contemplate that your ear is the Tetragrammaton expanded as Sag, with the final Heh left out, like this:

YOD HY VAV Y   יוד הי ואו י

The reason for this is that the final Heh descends to the Nose. The expansion Sag [has a numerical value of 63, but removing the Heh takes away five, leaving 58.] This is the numerical value of *Ozen* (אֹזֶן), meaning Ear. Through this meditation, you may be worthy that your ear should hear some lofty holiness when you pray.

Then meditate on your nose, contemplating that it is the expansion of Sag:

YOD HY VAV HY   יוד הי ואו הי

This has a numerical value of 63, the same as that of *Chotem* (חוֹטֶם), meaning Nose, as discussed elsewhere in detail.[85] Through this, you may be worthy of sensing the fragrance of Holiness.

Then meditate on your mouth, contemplating that it is the expansion of Sag, together with the 22 letters that are expressed by the mouth. [Sag has a value of 63, and together with 22,] the sum yields 85, the numerical value of *Peh* (פֶּה), meaning Mouth. In one's prayers, one may then be worthy of the level mentioned by King David, when he said, "The ruach-spirit of YHVH speaks in my mouth, and His word is on my tongue" (2 Samuel 23:2).

This is the meditation for the eyes:

If one is in the Universe of Asiyah . . . he should meditate on five simple Tetragrammatons:

YHVH	יהוה
YHVH YHVH YHVH	יהוה יהוה יהוה
YHVH	יהוה

[Each Tetragrammaton has a value of 26, so the five of them have a value of 130] the same as that of *Eyin* (עַיִן), meaning Eye.

If you are in the Universe of Yetzirah . . . meditate on these same five simple Tetragrammatons. Then expand them with Alef's to form the expansion of Mah.

If you are in the Universe of Beriyah, expand them as Sag. If you are in Atzilut, expand them with Yud's as Ab.[86]

When you walk in the street, meditate that your two feet are the Sefirot Netzach and Hod. When you look at something with your eyes, meditate that your eyes are Chokhmah and Binah. Meditate in this manner with regard to every part of your body. Also contemplate that you are a vehicle for the Highest Holiness. This is the meaning of the verse, "In all your ways know Him" (Proverbs 3:6).

There is no question that if you constantly make use of these meditations, you will become like an angel of heaven. You will gain an enlightenment so that you will be able to know all that you desire. This is especially true if you do not interrupt this meditation, thinking of this constantly, and not separating your mind from it. Everything depends on your intensity of concentration and attachment on high. Do not remove this from before your eyes.

The Fifth Kavanah

On Monday and Thursday, you should meditate on the Universe of Yetzirah, making use of the name of El Shadai (אל שדי).

You should also meditate on the Name of Forty-Two Letters, since

The Name of Forty-Two Letters

1. ABG	YThTz	אבג יתץ	Sunday
2. KRE	ShTN	קרע שטן	Monday
3. NGD	YKhSh	נגד יכש	Tuesday
4. BTR	TzThG	בטר צתג	Wednesday
5. ChKB	TNE	חקב טנע	Thursday
6. YGL	PZK	יגל פזק	Friday
7. ShKV	TzYTh	שקו צית	Sabbath

this name is in Yetzirah. This name consists of seven parts. Meditate on these seven parts, and through them, you can elevate your Nefesh-soul from Asiyah to Yetzirah.

On Monday, meditate that the [second] group, KRE ShTN (קרע שטן) should dominate the other letters. Through this group you can then ascend.

On Thursday, meditate that the [fifth] group, ChKB TNE (חקב טנע), should dominate.

It is then necessary to bind the group associated with the final one, ShKV TzYTh (שקו צית). This name pertains to the Sabbath, and your intent in meditation is to attain [a level of enlightenment which is] the Sabbath Increase.

On Monday, you must intertwine the associated name KRE ShTN (קרע שטן) with ShKV TzYTh (שקו צית) like this:

KShRKEVShTzTYNTh קשרקעושצטינת

On Thursday, you must intertwine the associated name ChKB TNE (חקב טנע) with ShKV TzYTh (שקו צית) like this:

ChShKKBVTTzNYETh חשקקבוטצניעת

When you do this, it will enable the name associated with that particular day to receive illumination from the name pertaining to the Sabbath.

The Sixth Kavanah

This is a meditation through which you can elevate your Nefesh-soul from Asiyah to the Universe of Yetzirah.

Contemplate on the mystery of Wings.[87] Through Wings, man can fly and ascend on high. A bird cannot fly except with its wings. Paralleling the wings of a bird are the arms of man.

There are five loves *(Chasadim)*. These permeate the Six Directions of the Body [which parallel the six Sefirot, Chesed, Gevurah, Tiferet, Netzach, Hod, and Yesod].

In the arms and the upper third of the torso, these Loves are concealed. In the lower part of the body, they are revealed.

It is for this reason that man flies with his arms, which are his Wings, and not with his legs or other limbs.

The Loves in the arms are concealed and cannot expand or escape. They therefore exert pressure and oscillate in their effort to escape. This causes the arms to vibrate.

The upper Root of these Loves is Daat-Knowledge, and this is their source. The Loves that permeate [the body] are lights that are produced by [the ones in Daat-Knowledge].

[The Loves that pervade the body] therefore attempt to fly upward. Since they cannot escape, however, they elevate the man along with them. It is for this reason that the Wings parallel the arms more than any other limbs.

This is the Kavanah upon which you should meditate. Every ascent is through this Name of Forty-Two.

Meditate on your right arm (Chesed). Contemplate that this is the name ABG YThTz (אבג יתץ).

Then meditate on your left arm (Gevurah). Contemplate that this is the name KRE ShTN (קרע שטן).

Finally, meditate on the upper third of your torso, where [the Loves are] hidden. Contemplate that this is NGD YKhSh (נגד יכש).

Through these three names, the Loves [that are in the arms and upper torso] fly upward to their root, which is Daat-Knowledge. When they ascend they also take along the man and elevate him to the Universe of Yetzirah. You will then be like a bird, flying in the air.

If you wish to strengthen your power of light, meditate to bring down new Loves from the Daat-Knowledge of the Partzuf of Zer Anpin for the purpose of Union. Through this, you will add strength to the Loves. This will bring you to fly with greater strength, and you will be able to ascend from Asiyah to Yetzirah.

CHAPTER SEVEN

The Hasidim

1. THE BAAL SHEM TOV

Of all mystical movements, none captured the popular imagination as did Hasidism. At its peak, this movement literally had millions of followers. Although much has been written on Hasidism, its meditative aspects are usually ignored or missed. One reason for this is that this is a side that is not readily apparent unless one has explored the earlier methods of Kabbalah meditation. Actually, however, it was its meditative practices more than anything else that gave Hasidism its great impetus, and drew into its ranks many important Kabbalists.

The Hasidic movement was founded in the mid 1700's by Rabbi Israel, known as the Baal Shem Tov (1698—1760). By the time the movement was fifty years old, it commanded the allegiance of a majority of Eastern European Jewry, and Hasidic rabbis dominated many important communities. Many Kabbalah texts were printed under the aegis of this movement, often for the first time. Important changes took place in community life, and entire countries changed their worship habits so as to conform to the Kabbalistic norm. Where Kabbalah had previously been the province of only the greatest scholars, it had now become part of the popular folklore, and even the simplest individuals had become familiar with its terminology.

This was a period when the theoretical Kabbalah had been on the ascendancy. The Ramak and others of his school had earlier succeeded in expressing the Kabbalah as a tightly reasoned philosophy, and the Ari expanded this system, greatly enriching it. In Europe, such giants as Rabbi Joseph Ergas (1685—1730) and Rabbi Moshe Chaim Luzzatto (1707—1747) had lifted the Kabbalah to a level where it could compete with rival philosophical systems on their own logical ground. But with the great concentration on the theoretical and philosophical aspects of the Kabbalah, its mystical and meditative aspects had virtually been forgotten. It was this gap that Haidism had come to rectify, and it did so with remarkable success.

Even during the time of the Ramak and the Ari, the Kabbalah had already gained considerable popularity in Europe. Besides sending a significant number of great thinkers to the Holy Land, the expulsion from Spain had also greatly enriched Jewish life in Eastern Europe, particularly in Poland and Bohemia. While Rabbi Joseph Caro had written his *Shulchan Arukh* as the authoritative code of Jewish Law, his European contemporaries, the Rama (Rabbi Moshe Israelish, 1520—1572) and the Maharshal (Morenu HaRav Sh'lomo Luria, 1510—1573) had challenged him, and had eventually written their own versions of the Code. It was around this time that community life in Eastern Europe became strong, and such cities as Lublin, Cracow and Prague became important centers of intellectual activity.

At the same time, there were also a good number of important Kabbalists in Eastern Europe. The Maharal of Prague (Rabbi Judah Liva, 1512—1609) write a number of important books, largely based on the Kabbalah. For the most part, however, the Maharal's fame came from his creation of the legendary Golem (גֹלֶם). A Golem is a sort of android, formed of clay and brought to life through the mysteries of the *Sefer Yetzirah*. The making of a Golem requires the channeling of intense spiritual energy through powerful meditative techniques, that bear more than a superficial resemblance to those of Rabbi Abraham Abulafia. In 1653, the Frankfort Kabbalist, Rabbi Naftali Bacharach, had the courage to include the formula in a printed edition of one of his Kabbalistic books.[1]

Another important Kabbalist of that period was Rabbi Isaiah Horowitz (1560—1630), who is frequently also cited as an authority on Jewish Law. He spent ten years of his life in the Holy Land, where he became familiar with the teachings of the Ari and the Safed School. It is also possible that he was aware of the writings of Rabbi Joseph Tzayach. In his main work, *Sh'nei Luchot HaB'rit* (Two Tablets of the Covenant), we find an important discussion of magic squares.[2]

In 1594, Rabbi Matathias Delecreta, a native of Italy who was then living in Cracow, published an important commentary on Joseph Gikatalia's *Shaarey Orah* (Gates of Light). His main disciple in Kabbalah was Rabbi Mordecai Jaffe (1530—1612), best known as the author of the *Levush* ("Garment"). This was also written as an alternative to Caro's Code, and, while it did not supplant the *Shulchan Arukh*, it did become an important standard source in Jewish Law. Rabbi Mordecai also wrote a major commentary on Kabbalistic exegesis of Rabbi Menachem Recanti (1223—1290). During this period in general, many important rabbis of major communities were also well-known Kabbalists. Most, however, dealt only with theory, and not with practice.

Although very little is known of the origin of the Baal Shem Tov's system of Hasidic meditation, there are traditions, particularly well-preserved by the Lubavitcher dynasty, that trace the history of the movement to this period.[3] Although there has been some question as to the authenticity of these traditions, and they have been generally ignored by historians, they do have enough historical consistency to merit serious consideration. Most important here is a tradition regarding the Nistarim, a secret society of Kabbalists. Even the existence of this society was totally unknown to outsiders until it finally surfaced under the leadership of the Baal Shem Tov.

According to this tradition, the Society of Nistarim (hidden ones) was founded in 1621 or 1623, shortly after the death of Rabbi Chaim Vital. Its founder was Rabbi Eliahu of Chelm (1537—1653), known as Eliahu Baal Shem. He is know historically as the great-grandfather of Chacham Zvi (1660—1718), who writes that his ancestor had created a Golem.[4] Eliahu Baal Shem was a contemporary and friend of the Maharal of Prague, and it is possible that the two of them together were involved in the building of the Golem.

Eliahu Baal Shem was born in Cracow to Rabbi Joseph Jospa, who had escaped Spain during the Expulsion of 1492. At the age of seven, he already had a reputation as a wonder child, and he would accompany his father to the study hall, drinking in the words of the sages as they taught. Shortly after his Bar Mitzvah in 1550, his father died, and he left home. He was not heard from again for forty years. Suddenly, in 1590, he emerged in Worms, where he rapidly gained a reputation as a miracle worker.

From there, Rabbi Eliahu moved to Chelm in Eastern Poland, where he founded a major academy. One of the most famed students was Rabbi Yom Tov Lipman Heller (1579—1654), best known as the author of the *Tosefot Yom Tov,* who was also a disciple of the Maharal. Around 1624, Rabbi Eliahu moved to Prague, where he remained until he died in 1653, having lived for over 116 years.

Leadership of the Society of Nistarim was then taken over by Rabbi Joel of Zamoshtch, another cryptic figure of the time, whose biography is also known only from this tradition. His father, Rabbi Israel Joseph, had been a disciple of Rabbi Mordecai Jaffe, discussed earlier. It was in 1613, a year after Rabbi Mordecai's death that Rabbi

Joel was born. At a very young age, he was sent to study in the academy in Brisk, under his namesake, Rabbi Joel Sirkes (1561—1640), best known as the author of the *Bet Chadash* ("New House"). When he was twenty, his father sent him to Eliahu Baal Shem's academy in Prague, where he became the leading disciple. When Rabbi Eliahu died in 1653, Rabbi Joel took over the leadership of the Society of Nistarim, and he remained its head for fifty years, until his own death in 1703. He made his seat in Zamoshtch, and is generally known as the Baal Shem of Zamoshtch.[5]

The title *Baal Shem* literally means "master of the Name," and in general, seems to have been used for those who knew how to make use of Divine Names in the practical Kabbalah.[6] In later times, however, this title seems to have been used particularly by the leader of the Society of Nistarim, perhaps because they alone had the authority to decide when these Names could be used. All during this period, the activities of this Society were kept absolutely secret, and almost nothing is known of them, except for the bits and pieces that have come down by tradition.

The methods of these two Baal Shems would be equally cryptic if not for a remarkable little book, *Toledot Adam* (Generations of Adam), which is attributed to them. Here we find all sorts of mystical remedies clearly influenced by the school that produced *Shoshan Yesod Olam,* discussed in Chapter Four. In *Toledot Adam,* use is made of magic squares, discussed at length by Rabbi Joseph Tzayach, and it is here that we find one of the few printed versions of the Seven Mystical Seals, discussed earlier in relations to Rabbi Isaac of Acco.[7] One gets a distinct impression that, while most European Kabbalists were concerned with the theoretical aspects of their discipline, this group was primarily engaged in its practical and meditative aspects.

An important activity of the Society of Nistarim was to raise the status and educational level of women. During this period, most Jewish women were not even taught how to read. On the rare occasions that women came to the synagogue, the *Zagaka,* an older woman who knew the service by heart, would lead them in worship. Members of the Society set up the first rudimentary educational system for girls, a system that would eventually encompass most of Europe. The wives and daughters of the Nistarim were encouraged to study, and many became distinguished scholars and mystics in their own right.

Under Rabbi Joel's leadership, the Society met some of its greatest challenges. The first was the rise of the Cossack leader, Bogdan

Chmielnitsky (1593—1657), who led the infamous massacres of 1648, where hundreds of Jewish communities in Poland were annihilated. For a decade the Polish community was in complete ruins. Those who were not killed outright were driven from their homes, penniless. Libraries, accumulated over centuries, were put to the torch, and the treasures of the past were destroyed without mercy. At a time when spiritual life was disintegrating, the Society of Nistarim was very strongly involved in rebuilding the crushed communities of Eastern Europe.

A second challenge threatened the very existence of the Society, since its enemies took every opportunity to associate it with the false Messiah of Izmir. As a very young man, Sabbatai Zvi (1626—1676) had become very deeply involved in the meditative shools of Kabbalah, and it is speculated that he even came in contact with some disciples of Elihu Baal Shem. It is well known that one of the dangers of meditation without proper training and supervision is that one can get illusions of power. Apparently this is what happened to Sabbatai Zvi. Reaching very high levels, he began to speculate that he might be the promised Messiah, and during the Chmielnitsky massacres, he announced that he would be the one to redeem Israel.

Sabbatai Zvi gave the impression of being on a very high spiritual level, and many people began to accept his claim. At first he hesitated, but finally, in 1654, he announced that he was the promised one. He gathered followers from all over Europe, and in hundreds of synagogues, prayers were introduced on his behalf. The would-be Messiah had set his residence in Abydos, near Constantinople, and Sultan Mahomet IV felt that he could be politically dangerous. In 1666, Sabbatai Zvi was imprisoned and given the choice of either converting to Islam or being put to death. Not willing to accept martyrdom, he left the fold of Judaism. The result was shattering to the world Jewish community, and Sabbatai Zvi's name became a curse among his people.

Still, many of Sabbatai Zvi's followers refused to believe that their leader had done wrong, and they continued to believe in his mission. Mercilessly hounded by the rabbinical leadership, these followers went underground, setting up a worldwide network. A number of prominent rabbis were discovered to be closet members of this cult.

As a result, anything even remotely associated with Sabbatai Zvi became suspect. Since he was strongly involved in Kabbalah meditation, all those who made use of these techniques came under scrutiny. The Society of Nistarim were one of the main schools that taught these methods, and was particularly vulnerable. The Society had many opponents, and they lost no time in associating the group with the False Messiah, claiming that he had been a disciple of Eliahu Baal Shem. In some cases, letters and correspondence was even forged, lending credence to these accusations. With many of its members under dire suspicion and its very foundations under attack, the Society began to make its work all the more secretive.

It was during this period that leadership of the Society passed to its most cryptic master, Rabbi Adam Baal Shem of Ropshitz (1655—1734). Other than the traditions, there is absolutely no historic record of this individual, and his only public appearance seems to have been in Slutzk in 1710.[8] He left absolutely no writings, and because of this lack of direct evidence, some historians have even doubted his existence.

Another reason for these doubts was that of his unusual name. Up until that time, there are no cases where Adam was used as a Jewish name, and some earlier authorities had even forbidden its use.[9] The same, however, was also true of the name Noah, and we also find no use of this name until the middle 1600's. By the 1700's, Noah had become a fairly common name, and there is also evidence that the name Adam was also in use.[10]

There may well be an important reason for this. According to our best calculations, Adam Baal Shem was born in 1655, a year after Sabbatai Zvi had announced his Messiahship, but over a decade before he was exposed as a fraud. Even among those who rejected Sabbatai Zvi, this was a period of new hope, where people saw the rebuilding of Europe after the Chmielnitski massacres. If the Messiah had not arrived, he would not be far off. Anticipating a new age, people began to make use of such names as Adam and Noah, since both of these individuals saw the beginning of a new world. In the case of Noah, the name has remained in use until today.

This is in no way meant to imply that Rabbi Adam himself was ever in any way associated with the false Messiah. Quite to the contrary, as a young man, he was a disciple of Rabbi Solomon Samuel of Polotzk, a vigorous opponent of all mysticism. He kept an open mind, however, and was particularly impressed by Joel Baal Shem's famed exorcism, which took place in Posen in 1682.[11] His curiosity grew, and finally, in 1688, at the age of 33, Adam visited Rabbi Joel to see for himself. He was so impressed that he remained there in the academy for fifteen years, until Rabbi Joel's death in 1703.

Upon the death of Joel Baal Shem, leadership of the Society passed on to his favorite disciple, Rabbi Adam. At that time, however, it was not the only secret society in existence. An important group that had gone underground were the followers of Sabbatai Zvi, who by this time had become very influential. Although the false Messiah had become an apostate, they taught that his unfortunate experience was necessary in order to bring about the final true redemption. Although the ban of excommunication had been pronounced against the followers of Sabbatai Zvi a number of times, the underground groups were still highly successful in attracting recruits. The religious leaders of the time therefore kept a very sharp eye open for any hint of association with these heretic groups.

This posed a grave danger for the Society of Nistarim. If their opponents could in any way associate them with the followers of the false Messiah, their effectiveness would be destroyed completely. The only way in which they could avoid this, however, was to keep the very existence of their Society a closely guarded secret. Thus, during his period of leadership, Rabbi Adam Baal Shem allowed absolutely no publicity whatsoever, neither with regard to himself, nor with regard to the Society's activities. Nothing was published in the name of Rabbi Adam, and his name itself was never uttered outside the company of the elect.

The Society was not to publicize its existence until it came under the leadership of its last master, Rabbi Israel, usually referred to simply as *The* Baal Shem Tov. He had been born on August 25, 1698 (18 Elul, 5458) in Okop, a small village on the Polish-Russian border. Like many other small villages, it has been obliterated by time, or has had its name changed — in any case, historians are hard-pressed to identify its exact location. Israel's parents, Eliezer and Sarah, were quite old when he was born, and they died while he was still a very young child.

Adopted by the synagogue, Israel was given the education common to Jewish communities at the time. He had a brilliant mind as well as a deep spiritual nature, but at an early age, he learned to keep his gifts a secret. He could not hide, however, from the true mystics, and he was contacted by the Society of Nistarim when he was ten years old. By the time he was fourteen, Rabbi Adam sent his son to teach him and initiate him into the mysteries of the Society. When he was eighteen, Rabbi Israel had already assumed a leadership role in the Society, but to all outward appearances, he was nothing more than a simple synagogue caretaker.

From Okap, Rabbi Israel moved to a town near Brody, where he was employed as a teacher of young children. He became acquainted with Rabbi Ephraim of Brody, who, almost inadvertently, became aware of the young man's unique gifts. Shortly before his death, Rabbi Ephriam arranged the engagement of Rabbi Israel to his daughter Hannah.

Rabbi Ephriam's son, Gershon of Kitov (1696—1760) was a leading rabbi in Poland, and was very much taken aback when Israel came to him, asking for his sister's hand in marriage. Taking the young man to be an ignorant boor, Rabbi Gershon was about to throw him out, when Israel produced a letter of engagement, signed by the girl's father. Although the famed scholar was very much against the match, he begrudgingly acquiesed, sending the couple away with a horse and wagon as a wedding present.

Along with his bride, Rabbi Israel lived in a small mountain town between Kitov and Kasov in the Carpathean mountains. Supported by his wife, he spent his days and nights in study, worship, and meditation, coming home only on the Sabbath. Like the Ari, he spent seven years in such secluded meditation, while at the same time studying a set of mystical writings that had been entrusted to him by Adam Baal Shem.

There has been considerable speculation as to the nature of these writings, but in part at least, it is almost certain they consisted of *Sefer HaTzoref* (Book of the Smith), which had been written by Rabbi Heschel Tzoref (1623—1700). Although there is no mention of him in the Society's traditions, it appears that Rabbi Heschel had been a disciple of Elihau and Joel Baal Shem, and was a leading figure among the Nistarim. He was known as a saint, working as a silversmith by day, while spending his nights in worship, meditation and Kabbalah study.

Rabbi Heschel maintained that the Society should go above-ground and openly refute the accusions of its detractors. Emphasizing this point, in 1666, the year of Sabbatai Zvi's apostacy, he began to publicly teach Kabbalah in Vilna. From there, he moved to Cracow, where his reputation as a saint grew. In the records of the burial society of Cracow, we find a note that states, "May God remember the soul of . . . Rabbi Joshua Heschel Tzoref, who knew how to blend *(tzaref)* the letters of the Torah. His soul left him with literal holiness and purity. He died as if by the Kiss [of God] on 27 Iyar, 5460 (May 16, 1700)," His teachings are also quoted in *Kav HaYashar* (The Straight Measure), one of the most popular devotional texts, first published in 1705.[12]

Along with many mystics of that time, Tzoref was accused of having associations with the followers of Sabbatai Zvi, and correspondence was even forged to prove these allegations. Such witchhunts, however, were very common at the time, and everything dealing with the Kabbalah was suspect. There is a manuscript of Abulafia's *Chayay Olam HaBah* (Life of the Future World) that attributes the authorship to Sabbatai Zvi, and his name also appears in an important manuscript of *Shoshan Yesod Olam*[13] Since Rabbi Heschel's *Sefer HaTzoref* followed the methods of *tzeruf* advocated by Abulafia, it, too, became suspect.

This *Sefer HaTzoref* still exists in manuscript, in the hands of the Karliner Hasidim. It is some 1400 pages long, and consists of revelations, like those of Rabbi Isaac of Acco, as well as considerable word manipulation, reminiscent of Abulafia's methods. This manuscript has an interesting history. Upon the death of the Baal Shem Tov, it found its way into the hands of his grandson, Rabbi Aaron of Tutiev. A copy was made by Rabbi Isaiah Dinovitz, a disciple of the Mezricher Maggid, and it was eventually given over to the Karliner dynasty.

After ending his period, Rabbi Israel served for a while as teacher and ritual butcher in Koslowitz. In 1734, upon the death of Rabbi Adam, he was chosen by the Society to be its new leader. Announcing to his brother-in-law, Rabbi Gershon, that the time had come for him to reveal himself, he settled in Talust, where his fame quickly spread. From there, he moved to Medzyboz, in the western Ukrain, where he remained until his death in 1760.

It was in Medzyboz that his teachings began to spread, and it was also here that he gained his main disciples. Attracting not only the common man, his disciples soon included some of the greatest minds of Eruope. Most important of these were Rabbi Dov Baer, the Mezricher Maggid (1704—1772), and Rabbi Jacob Joseph of Polonoye (1703—1794), the most faithful recorder of the Baal Shem Tov's teachings.

It is well established that the Baal Shem Tov was highly involved in meditation and spiritual ascent. One of the most remarkable documents regarding this is an epistle written to his brother-in-law, Rabbi Gershon, who was then in the Holy Land. While it does not describe his methods, it does provide a good idea of the type of spiritual levels reached by the Baal Shem Tov.

The Epistle[14]

On Rosh HaShanah 5507 (September 15,1746), I made an oath and elevated my soul in the manner known to you. I saw things that I had never before witnessed since the day I was born. The things that I learned and saw there could not be communicated, even if I would be able to speak to you in person.

When I returned to the lower Garden of Eden, I saw innumerable souls, both living and dead, some whom I knew and others whom I did not. They were fleeting back and forth, going from one universe to another through the Column that is known to those who delve in mysteries. They were in a state of joy that was so great that the lips cannot express it, and the physical ear is too gross to hear about it.

There were also many wicked people who were repenting, and their sins were forgiven since this was a special time of grace. Even to my eyes it was wondrous how many were accepted as penitents, many of whom you know. There was great joy among them, too, and they also ascended in the above-mentioned manner.

All of them beseeched and petitioned me unceasingly: "Go higher with the glory of your Torah. May God grant you greater understanding to perceive and know these things. Ascend with us, so that you can be our help and support."

Because of the great joy that I saw among them, I decided to ascend with them. Due to the great danger involved in ascending to the supernal Universes, I asked my Master to come with me.[15] From the time that I began, I had never before ascended to such a high level.

Step by step I ascended until I entered the chamber of the Messiah. There the Messiah studies Torah with all the sages and saints, as well as with the Seven Shepherds.[16]

I saw great joy there, but I did not know the reason for it. At first I thought that the reason for this joy was that I had passed away from the physical world, heaven forbid. Later, they told me that I had not died, since they have great pleasure on high when I bring about Unifications through the holy Torah down below. But to this very day, I do not know the reason for that joy.

I spoke to the Messiah himself and asked him, "When is your majesty coming?"

He replied, "This shall be your sign. It will be at a time when your teachings become widespread in the world, and 'your springs overflow abroad.'[17]

"It will be when the things which I have taught you, and which you have yourself perceived, become known, so that others can also bring about Unifications and elevate themselves like you do. All the Husks will then be annihilated, and it will be a time of grace and salvation."

I was very surprised, and distressed, since it would take a long time for this to be possible. But when I was there, I learned three specific remedies and three holy Names, and they are easy to learn and explain. My mind was then set at ease, and I realized that it would be possible for people in my generation to reach the same level and state as I did. They would then be able to ascend, learn and perceive, just like myself.

All during my lifetime, I was not granted permission to reveal this. For your sake, I made a request that I might be allowed to teach this to you, but permission was denied. I am still bound by this oath, but this I can tell you, and let God be your help:

Let your path be toward God.[18]

When you pray and study let [my words] not forsake you.[19]

With every word and expression that leaves your lips, have in mind to bring about a Unification. Every single letter contains universes, souls and godliness, and as they ascend, one becomes bound to the other and they become unified. The letters then become unified and attached to form a word. They are then actually unified with the Divine Essence, and in all these aspects, your soul is included with them.

All universes are then unified as one, and immeasurable joy and delight results. Consider the joy of a bridegroom and bride in this lowly physical world, and you will understand how great is this delight.

God will certainly help you. Wherever you turn you will succeed and prosper. "Give wisdom to the wise, and he will become still wiser."[20]

2. MEDITATION

An important part of the Baal Shem Tov's teachings involved Hitbodedut meditation. This was an integral part of his personal life as well, and it is reported that, as a young child, he would miss his lessons, going off to meditate (*hitboded*) in the forests.[21] During his seven years of seclusion, he would meditate in the mountains, as well as ain a special cave.[22] When he studied together with the son of Rabbi Adam, he did so in a special "Meditation Room" (*Bet Hitbodedut*), and it was in this room that they engaged in meditation in an attempt to commune with the Angel of the Torah.[23] Later, when he was a famed leader, he would also spend much time in such a "Meditation Room." [24]

Most of the Baal Shem Tov's general teachings regarding meditation are found in the writings of his greatest disciple, Rabbi Dov Baer, the Mezricher Maggid. A few of these are also included in the Baal Shem's ethical will.

SOURCES

In our generations, we have limited intelligence and must strengthen our love and reverence of God.

In your mind, you must therefore constantly meditate (*hitboded*) on the love and reverence of God. Even when you are studying, it is good to pause occasionally and to meditate in your mind. This is true even though it may take time from your sacred studies.[25]

In your mind, constantly meditate (*hitboded*) on the Divine Presence. Have no other thought in your mind other than your love, seeking that [the Divine Presence] should bind itself to you. Constantly repeat in your mind, "When will I be worthy for the Light of the Divine Presence to dwell with me." [26]

You can lie in bed and appear to be sleeping, but at that time, you can actually be meditating (*hitboded*) upon God.[27]

When you wish to enter a [high] state of meditation (*hitbodedut*), you should have someone else with you. When a person does this while alone, he can be in great danger. Two people should therefore be together, and one should meditate, [mentally secluded] with his Creator.[28]

3. A YICHUD

Very important in the Baal Shem Tov's meditative methods were the system of Yichudim as taught by the Ari. Besides these, the Baal Shem also had his own system of Yichudim, but very little of this has been preserved. In other cases, the Baal Shem Tov made use of the Ari's Methods, but greatly expanded upon them.

One of the very few samples of the Baal Shem's Yichudim that are known involve a meditation for the Mikvah. We have quoted the Ari's Kavanah for immersion earlier, and it is instructive to compare it to the meditation of the founder of Hasidism.

A Yichud for Immersion[29]

When you enter the Mikvah meditate on the name KNA (קנא). [This is the number 151, and is] the name Ehyeh (אהיה) expanded with Heh's, like this:

ALF HH YUD HH אלף הה יוד הה

This has a numerical value of 151, the same as that of Mikvah (מִקְוֶה). It is important that you contemplate that the physical Mikvah in which you are immersing in itself is actually the name KNA, through the sequence of spiritual descent.

Immerse once, and while you are under water, meditate on the name KNA.

Now meditate on the name AGLA (אגלא). This is the name that is related to the Strengths. It emanates from [the initial letters of the phrase in the Amidah], "You are strong for the world O Lord" (*Atah Gibor LeOlam Adonoy*, אַתָּה גִּבּוֹר לְעוֹלָם אֲדֹנָי).

Immerse a second time and meditate on this name.

Then meditate on the name ALD (אלד) [which is the tenth triplet in the Name of Seventy Two. This name can be read as *Eled (אֵלֵד)*, meaning "I will give birth," indicating that one is born anew when he emerges from the Mikvah.]

Contemplate that in the name AGLA (אלד), [the Alef (א) has a value of one, while the Gimel (ג) has a value of three. Added together, these two letters have a value of four, the numerical value of Dalet (ד).]. The Alef and Gimel of AGLA (אגלא) therefore combine to form the Dalet of ALD (אלד).

Immerse a third time and meditate on the name [ALD (אלד)].

Then immerse a fourth time, and while your head is under water, meditate on the two names, ALD (אלד), and the expansion of Ehyeh (אהיה), intertwining the two together like this:

ALF A HH L YOD D HH אלף א הה ל יוד ד הה

Now meditate on the subject of your prayer. Contemplate that it is inside this name, and is being attended to as you elevate it.

Then immerse a fifth time, and meditate on the two names, ALD (אלד) and the simple name Ehyeh (אהיה), intertwining the two like this:

AAHLYDH אאהלידה

Then meditate that you are elevating the subject of your prayer to the highest level of Binah-Understanding. Everything is then transformed into pure love and mercy.

4. STATES OF CONSCIOUSNESS

Although the earlier meditative Kabbalists occasionally discuss their experiences, they provide very little theory regarding states of consciousness. One of the first to speak specifically of states of consciousness appears to be the Baal Shem Tov.

The two states of consciousness that he discusses are *Mochin DeGadlut* and *Mochin DeKatnut,* or more commonly, simply *Gadlut* and *Katnut.*

These terms are somewhat difficult to translate. The word *Mochin* literally means "brains," and in the Ari's terminology, refers to "mentalities." In the context used by the Baal Shem, however, the term *Mochin* actually should be translated, "states of consciousness."

Gadlut means "maturity" or "greatness," while *Katnut* means "immaturity" or "smallness." Actually, then, the best way to translate *Mochin DeGadlut* would be "expanded consciousness," while *Mochin DeKatnut* would be "constricted consciousness." Within the general theory of meditation, it is known that an important goal of this practice is to bring a person to a state of expanded consciousness.

These are actually borrowed terms. When the Ari speaks of the Partzuf of Zer Anpin, he expands upon its development which is outlined in the most mysterious Zoharic texts, the Greater and Lesser *Idras.* In its development, the Partzuf of Zer Anpin goes through stages of birth and growth. Like a human being, this Partzuf can thus be in a state of immaturity, as well as one of maturity. The immature state is called *Katnut,* while that of maturity is called *Gadlut.*

As the Partzuf matures, so does its mentalities. It is in this context that we find the terms *Mochin DeKatnut* and *Mochin DeGadlut,* in their original meaning. *Mochin DeKatnut* denotes the immature mentalities of Zer Anpin, while *Mochin DeGadlut* denotes the mature mentalities.

This anthropomorphism is to be taken symbolically rather than literally, and the states of immaturity and maturity do not exist in different time spans. Both states exist at all times, and are responsible for different effects in the lower world. The Ari expresses it in this manner:[30]

> The power of forgetfulness in man is a result of these Immature Mentalities (*Mochin DeKatnut*).
>
> One must transmit Mature Mentalities (*Mochin DeGadlut*) [to Zer Anpin]. When this is accomplished through one's deeds, he causes [the Immature Mentalities] to descend to [the Female Partzuf. The Immature Mentalities which are derived from the name] Elohim is thus expelled and removed completely from Zer Anpin.
>
> If a person can do this, he will then have a wondrous memory, and will comprehend all the mysteries of the Torah.

Since Zer Anpin is the "Supernal Man," everything in this Partzuf also has a counterpart in man. The Baal Shem Tov therefore taught that these states of immaturity and maturity in Zer Anpin parallel different states of consciousness in the human mind.[31] In man these are the states of expanded and constricted consciousness.

When a person is in a state of expanded consciousness, he is enlightened in all walks of life. He has realized the vanity of the mundane world and the greatness of the spiritual. Everything that he does is with a different awareness, whether it is eating and drinking, worship or study. The idea is discussed often in the teachings of the Baal Shem Tov.

SOURCES

Expanded and Constricted Consciousness can be explained in the following manner. When a person learns something, but does not understand it in depth, this is a state of Constricted Consciousness, since his mental picture is not complete. But when he grasps something with enthusiasm and full understanding, then he is on the level of Expanded Consciousness, bound to the highest levels.

Similarly, there are states of Expanded and Constricted Consciousness in prayer and all other observance.[32]

When a person is in a state of Exanded Consciousness, he has great joy in the study of Torah and worship of God.[33]

When a person is in a state of Constricted Consciousness, he cannot worship with reverence and love, but must force himself to do so, without joy. This state is the mystery of Constricted Consciousness.[34]

When a person follows his desires and the ways of his heart, then he is in a state of Constricted Consciousness. This is the mystery of the verse, "I have made you small (constricted) among nations, you are very despised" (Obadiah 1:5).

Expanded Consciousness is when one involves himself in the great mysteries of the Future World and despises all worldly things.[35]

Even when a person falls from his level, he should try to remain attached to God with a small thought. For sometimes there is a level of Constricted Consciousness on high, even in Zer Anpin. But through this Constricted Consciousness, one can attain Expanded Consciousness.

This is like a coal. If even a small spark remains, one can fan it into a large flame. But when the spark is extinguished, fanning no longer helps. Similarly, if one does not remain attached [on high] at all times, at least with a small thought, [the fire in] his divine soul can be completely extinguished.

Sometimes the holy spark of the Divine Presence in a person's soul expands until it can literally place words in his mouth. He does not speak voluntarily, but words are automatically expressed from his mouth. This is a very high level.

This phenomenon, however, can also come from the Other Side. When this occurs, the person becomes insane.[36]

Sometimes you can only worship with Constricted Consciousness. Then you do not enter into the supernal worlds at all. Still, you can realize that God is close and that "the whole earth is filled with His glory" (Isaiah 6:3).

At such a time, you are like a small child, whose intellect has just begun to develop. But even though you are worshipping while in a state of Constricted Consciousness, you can still worship with great ttachment.

Even though you are in a state of Constricted Consciousness, if you bind yourself closely to the Divine Presence you can instantly transport your thoughts to a supernal universe. You are then actually in that supernal universe, since a person is where his thoughts are. If you were not in that supernal universe, then your thoughts would also not be there.[37]

Man consists of matter and form, body and soul.

The soul constantly has a burning desire to attach itself to God. It is enveloped by a physical [body] however, which acts as a barrier to such attachment.

Man's physical self desires such material things as sex and food. These things, however, are also required on high, in order to accomplish such things as the separation [and elevation] of the [holy] Sparks.

There are certain times, however, when form can totally overwhelm matter, and attach itself to God.

This is the mystery of, "The Living Angels (Chayot) ran and returned" (Ezekiel 1:14).

There are two levels, Expanded Consciousness and Constricted Consciousness. ["Running" denotes the state of Expanded Consciousness, while "returning" refers to that of Constricted Consciousness.]

I heard from my master [the Baal Shem Tov] that this is the mystery of the Constriction, which was "from Him and in Him." [38]

ברוך יא להוריד י' דהויה ולהעלות א דאדני.

יכוין להמשיך ו"ק דאחור דאחור דחכמה דכתר דבינה (בחזרה דחכמה) דנה"י דתבונה עם ו"ק דצלמי המו' יו"ד ה"י דקס"א עם הנרנח"י לו"ק דאחור דאחור דחכמה דכתר דבינה (בחזרה דחכמה) דנה"י דבינה דז"א. והם אות ך דהויה.

ו'

(א) אהיה אהיה אהיה אהיה

יהוה יהוה יהוה יהוה

אהיה אוהויוהו אוהויוהו אהיה

יהוה יוהוווהו יוהוווהו יהוה

(ב) יו ד ז' דקס"א

נג' כלי חסד דז"א	נג' כלי ת"ת דז"א	נג' כלי גבורה דז"א
		י ד ו
א אל אלו אלוה	יוד הא ואו הא	אלף אלף למד אלף למד הי אלף למד הי יוד אלף למד הי יוד מם
א ל ו ה	י יה יהו יהוה	י ה ו ה
אלף למד	י ה ו ה	

אהיה אוהויוהו אוהויוהו אהיה

יהוה יוהוווהו יוהוווהו יהוה

י ד ו דקס"א

נג' כלי נצח דז"א	נג' כלים דיסוד	נג' כלי הוד דז"א
יהוה	יאהדונהי	א ד נ י
צ צב צבא	שין שין דלת שין דלת יוד	א צבאו צבאות
צבא	שין דלת יוד	א ו ת

ומשם לחב"ד חג"ת דחכמה דכתר דבינה או דחכמה דבינה דרחל דאחור דאחור אות ה אחרונה דהויה שורש הכ' של הנוק' העומדת באחורי היסוד דז"א (א)

אהיה אהיה אהיה

יהוה יהוה יהוה

אהיה אוהויוהו אוהויוהו אהיה

יהוה יוהוווהו יוהוווהו יהוה

יוד הי דקס"א

י"כ דמוחין עם ו"ה סכס הו"ם ני' מ"ז לכמשיך מילוי דמ"ב זה מאבא ומחכמה דז"א לנוקבא

י ה ו ה

יוד הי וה

וד י ין י

Rabbi Shalom Sharabi's *Kavanot* on the First Word of the *Amidah*

5. THE WAY OF PRAYER

One of the Baal Shem Tov's most important accomplishments was to reveal a safe method of meditation, which could be used by even the simplest person. Earlier methods involved Divine Names and could release potentially dangerous spiritual forces. The Way of Prayer, as taught by the Baal Shem Tov, involved nothing more than the regular prayer service, uttered three times daily by every Jew.

The focal point of the prayer service is the *Amidah* or *Shemonah Esreh,* a collection of eighteen (or nineteen) blessings, which is repeated three times each day. This prayer was composed by the Great Assembly just before the close of the prophetic period. There is considerable discussion as to why a single prayer was prescribed to be repeated over and over each day. There is considerable evidence, however, that the entire Amidah was meant to be used as a meditative device, very much like a long mantra.

After a person has repeated the Amidah every day for a few years, he knows the words so well that they become an integral part of his makeup. It takes no mental effort on his part to recite the words, and thus, it is not very different than repeating a single word or phrase over and over. If a person clears his mind of all other thoughts, then simply repeating the Amidah can produce a very high mental state. This is borne out in practice. The same is true of other parts of the prayer service that are recited daily.

In an important teaching, the Talmud states, "One who prays must direct his eyes downward, and his heart on high." [39] One of the important early commentaries, Rabbi Jonah Gerondi (1196—1263), explains that, "this means that in one's heart he should imagine that he is standing in heaven. He must banish from his heart all worldly delights and bodily enjoyments. The early sages taught that if one wishes to have true Kavanah, he must divest his body from his soul." [40]

A few decades later, this very same concept was pressed even more explicitly by Rabbi Jacob ben Asher (1270—1343). In his *Tur*, a major early code of Jewish Law, he writes:

> It is taught that when one prays, he must concentrate his heart . . . This means that one must concentrate fully on the words that are expressed with his lips. One must have in mind that the Divine Presence is before him, as it is written, "I have placed God before me at all times" (Psalms 16:8).
>
> One must arouse his concentration and banish all disturbing thoughts, so that his thoughts and intentions in prayer should be pure. . . .
>
> This was the practice of the saints and men of deed. They would meditate (*hitboded*) and concentrate in their prayers until they reached a level where they divested themselves from the physical. The transcendental spirit would be strengthened in them until they would reach a level close to that of prophecy.[41]

It is significant to note that this passage is quoted verbatim by Rabbi Joseph Caro in his *Shulchan Arukh,* and is also mentioned in the teachings of the Baal Shem Tov.[42]

The idea of using the prayer service as a meditative device did not originate with the Baal Shem. Many of the older Kabbalists speak of the importance of concentrating in prayer, and many devised extensive Kavanot associated with the various parts of the service. This plays a particularly important role in the Ari's system, and many prayer books incorporate the Kavanot that he devised.

This system of Kavanot reached its zenith among the Sefardic Jews under the leadership of the renowned Kabbalist, Rabbi Shalom Sharabi (1702—1777). He devised elaborate charts, looking almost like mandalas for many key words in the prayer service, greatly expanding upon the Ari's system. His methods are still used by members of the Bet El Academy in Jerusalem, who often spend as much as four hours in the daily morning service.

Much simpler than this was the method of the Baal Shem Tov. It could be used by anyone, from the greatest Kabbalist to the simplest individual. Rather than concentrate on the various Kabbalistic concepts during prayer, one must use the prayer itself as a mantra, focusing his entire mind on the words. While praying, one then rises mentally from one universe to the next, from chamber to chamber, until he reaches the highest level. Although this system is not presented in any one place, it is discussed at length, both in his own teachings, and in those of his disciples.

Levels of Prayer

Universe	*Portion of the Service*
Asiyah	Sacrificial Readings (*Korbanoth*)
Yetzirah	Biblical Songs of Praise (*Pesukey DeZimra*)
Beriyah	The Sh'ma and its Blessings (*Birkat Sh'ma*)
Atzilut	The Amidah

When you pray, you should be totally divorced from the physical, not aware of your existence in the world at all. Then, when you reach the level where you are not cognizant whether or not you are in the physical world, you should certainly not have any fear of extraneous thoughts. When you are divested from the physical, extraneous thoughts cannot come to you.[43]

When you want to pray, it should be with awe. This is the gate through which one enters before God.

Say to yourself, "To whom do I wish to bind myself? To the One who created all worlds with His word, who gives them existence and sustains them." Think about His loftiness and greatness and you will then be able to enter the supernal worlds.[44]

Attachment means that when you say a word, you draw it out and do not want to let it go. Because of your attachment to each word, you draw it out.

If you have extraneous thoughts when you worship, then the Husks are riding on your words. For thought rides upon each word. . . .[45]

Do not pray for your own needs, for your prayer will then not be accepted. But when you want to pray, do so for the heaviness of the Head. For whatever you lack, the Divine Presence also lacks.

This is because man is a "portion of God from on high." Whatever any part lacks also exists in the Whole, and the Whole feels the lack of the part. You should therefore pray for the needs of the Whole.[46]

Place all your thoughts into the power of your words, until you see the light of the words. You can then see how one word shines into another, and how many lights are brought forth in their midst.

This is the meaning of the verse, "Light is sown to the righteous, and joy to the upright in heart" (Psalms 97:11).

The lights in the letters are God's chambers, into which He transmits His emanations.[47]

Separate your soul from your body. Your soul can then be clothed in the thought that is contained in the words that you pronounce. You will then be able to perceive many universes on high.

You have many powers, one required for one universe, and another for the next. When your soul ascends to all the worlds that you must elevate, it is examined in each universe to see if it is fit to go higher. If it is not, it is cast outside.

When an extraneous thought comes to you, this is a sign that you are being cast out. But if you are wise, you can use that thought itself to bind yourself to God all the more. The thought consists of letters that are part of the Divine Presence's body, but they fell as a result of the Breaking [of Vessels]. The combination of these letters therefore becomes bad, intermingled with the Husks.

This is like sweetmeats intermingled with other things. Each thing is good by itself, but mixed together they are vile and disgusting. This likewise becomes evil.

But when you understand the idea of the thought [that falls into your mind, you can then elevate it]. If it involves desire and lust, it has fallen from the Universe of Love, if it is a debilitating phobia, it is from the Universe of Fear, and if it involves pride, it is from the Universe of Beauty. The same is true of all other such thoughts, since [the attributes paralleling] all seven days of creation have fallen.

When you bind these thoughts to God through love and fear of the Creator, you then return them to their Root. The same is true of other attributes, and each thought can be elevated to the Attribute from which it fell. You can once again bind it to that Attribute, and transform the Husks that fell from it into a good combination. . . .

God has great delight when you do this. It is like a royal prince who is kidnapped. The king has great delight when he is returned, even more than from a son who has never left his side.[48]

It is actually very surprising that a mortal human being should be able to attach himself to God. Besides his physical body, many Husks separate him from God. Even though, "the whole earth is filled with His glory," God is still hidden behind many barriers.

But all the barriers that separate and restrain can be torn down by the word that you utter. Your words should therefore be attached to God. This means that you must intimately feel that you are actually speaking to God.

If we could speak just one line, or even two or three words, to God in each service, in the above-mentioned manner, it would be sufficient.[49]

The reason why both love and fear are required is this. If a person only had love for God, he would grow accustomed to be with God, and this would become part of his nature. But as a result of his fear, he does not dare to come too close.[50]

The Talmud speaks of "things that stand in the highest places of the universe, and are taken lightly by people." [51]

The Baal Shem Tov explained that the results of prayer are often manifest in the "highest places of the universe," and not in the physical world. It is for this reason that prayer is "taken lightly by people," since they think that their prayer is in vain.

The truth, however, is that all prayer has an effect.[52]

Our main link to God is through words — words of Torah and prayer.

Every single letter [in these words] has an inner spiritual essence. You must attach your thought and innermost being to this essence.

This is the mystery of, "Let Him kiss me with the kisses of His mouth" (Song of Songs 1:2) — the attachment of spirit to spirit.[53] It is also the mystery of, "If you lie between the lips" (Psalms 68:14)[54]

When you draw out a word, and do not want to let it go, then you are in such a state of attachment.[55]

Every word is a complete concept, and you must place all of your strength into it. If you do not, then it remains incomplete.[56]

You can sometimes pray very fast. This is because the love of God is burning in your heart very strongly. The words then leave your mouth of their own accord when you pray silently.

When you attach yourself on high, you can be worthy of being lifted still further by the very same prayer. Our sages thus teach us, "When one comes to purify himself, he is helped from on high."[57] Through prayer, you can attach your thoughts on high. From the power of such prayer, you can then reach even higher levels. Then, even when you are not praying, you can be attached to the spiritual.[58]

Sometimes you must worship in thought, with your soul alone.

Sometimes you can pray with love and awe and with great intensity without moving at all. Another person looking on can think that you are merely reciting the words without any feeling. For when you are very closely bound to God, you can serve Him with great love, with the soul alone.

This is the best type of worship. It moves quickly, and can bring you closer [to God] than prayer whose intensity is visible outside through your body. Such prayer is all inside, and therefore, the Husks cannot grasp on to it.[59]

Rabbi Israel Baal Shem Tov said that a person can read the Torah and see lights on the letters, even though he does not understand it fully. Since he is reading with great love and enthusiasm, God does not pay attention to the fact that he may not be reading correctly.

This is very much like a child who is very much loved by his parents. Even though it cannot speak well, its parents have great enjoyment when it asks for something.

The same is true when a person recites words of Torah with love [and devotion]. God has great delight, and does not pay attention to the fact that he does not read it correctly.[60]

When you want to pray to God for something, think of your soul as part of the Divine Presence, like a raindrop in the sea. Then pray for the needs of the Divine Presence.

You can have faith that your prayer will benefit the Divine Presence. Then, if you are properly attached to the Divine Presence, this influence will also be transmitted to you.

When a person is happy, he unconsciously claps his hands. This is because his joy spreads through his entire body.

The same is true of the Divine Presence. Each influence is transmitted to each of its parts.[61]

There are times when you feel that you cannot pray. Do not give up even trying that day. Instead, strengthen yourself all the more, and arouse your awe of God.

This is very much like a king in battle, who must disguise himself [so as not to be recognized by the enemy]. Those who are wise are able to recognize the king by his motions. Those who are less wise can still recognize the king, since he is always surrounded by extra guards.

The same is true when you cannot pray with devotion. You should know that the King is there and you are encountering his additional Guards. The only reason why you cannot come close to the King is because of this great protection surrounding Him.

You must therefore fortify yourself with reverence, great strength, and additional intensity in order [to break through this barrier] and come close to God. If you are successful, you will then be able to pray with the greatest possible feeling.[62]

It is found in the writings of the Ari that the concept of one day's prayers is not the same as that of the next day. [The concept of our daily service therefore changes every day] until the arrival of the Messianic Age. Our sages therefore say, "If one's prayers are fixed, this is not a supplication." [63]

I heard from my master [the Baal Shem Tov] that this can be proven through the extraneous thoughts that enter one's mind during worship. These thoughts come from the Broken Vessels, and the 288 Sparks that one must separate each day.[64]

[These extraneous thoughts enter one's mind during prayer in order that] he rectify and elevate them.

The extraneous thoughts of one day, however, are not at all the same as those of the next. This evidence should be obvious to one who considers it.[65]

When extraneous thoughts come to you during study or prayer, you should break these thoughts down and attach yourself to God. In this manner, you can rectify the Holy Spark that is in each particular thought.

This is like a person who is counting money while his children are being held for ransom. They come to him and say, "You have money! Ransom us!"[66]

We are taught, "When one comes to purify himself, he is helped from on high."[67]

This is somewhat difficult to understand, for it does not seem to apply to all who want to purify themselves.

Sometimes you may want to pray with great enthusiasm before God. You make many preparations [so your prayers should be just right]. Still, when you are in the depths of prayer, you are disturbed by extraneous thoughts.

You may then wonder, where is this help from on high? You have made every possible preparation, cleansing your thoughts so that you should pray in purity. [Why then are you disturbed by these extraneous thoughts?]

Actually, however, this itself is God's help. . . . God sends you these thoughts in order that you should elevate them. . . . These thoughts do not come by chance, but in order that you should elevate them to their Root.

Thus, for example, you may have an extraneous thought involving some evil love or fear. You must then push aside this thought and attach yourself to the love and fear of God, completing your prayers with great enthusiasm. You can then elevate the Spark [of holiness] out of the Husk [of evil in that thought].

This itself is the help that is given to you from on high.[68]

I heard from my master [the Baal Shem Tov] that even after Rabbi Nehunia ben HaKaneh knew all the [Kabbalistic] meditations associated with prayer, he would still pray like a small child,[69]

Accustom yourself to pray and recite the Psalms in a very low voice. Scream quietly, saying the words with all your strength. This is the meaning of the verse, "All my bones shall say [God, who is like

You]" (Psalms 35:10). A scream that results from complete attachment [to God] is absolutely silent.[70]

There is a "burning sword that rotates, to guard the way of the Tree of Life" (Genesis 3:24).

When you wish to attach your thoughts to the Creator in the supernal worlds, the [Evil] Husks (*K'lipot*) do not allow you. But even though you are not able, you must exert yourself with all your strength over and over again, even during a single prayer. Eventually you will bind yourself to God and enter the supernal Universes.

The faith with which you should strengthen yourself is the fact that "The whole earth is filled with His glory" (Isaiah 6:3). One must have perfect faith, as it is written, "The righteous man lives by his faith" (Habakkuk 2:4).

Even if you fall from a high level during a prayer, continue to recite the words with concentration to the best of your ability. Then strengthen yourself to return to your level. You may do this many times during a single prayer.

First pronounce the word itself. This is the body. Then place a soul in the word.[71]

At first, you should arouse your body with all your might. Only then will the power of your soul shine for you.

The Zohar thus teaches, "If fire does not burn brightly, tap the wood, and it blazes forth. If the light of the soul does not burn brightly, tap the body, so that the light of the soul should blaze forth." [72]

When a person does this successfully, he can worship in thought alone, without any motion on the part of his body.

When a person is attached to God in a Supernal Universe, he must be careful not to allow his body to move, since this will destroy his attachment.[73]

Sometimes you may be praying in a state of Constricted Consciousness. Then in an instant, the light of your soul blazes forth, and you ascend to one of the upper Universes. It is very much like climbing a ladder.

The supernal Light is alluded to in the verse, "Send forth Your light and truth, they will lead me" (Psalms 43:3).[74]

In silent prayer, you can attach yourself on high. Then, if you are worthy, you can be elevated still higher in that same prayer. This is the meaning of the teaching, "When one comes to purify himself, he is helped."[75]

Through a prayer, you can be worthy of attaching yourself on high. Then, from this power, you can rise to a still higher level. When you reach this higher level, you can be attached on high even when you are not praying.[76]

6. SPIRITUAL ASCENT

Although prayer was the primary vehicle for spiritual ascent, the Hasidic masters often discussed the concept in more general terms. One could climb the spiritual ladder, from one chamber to the next, from one Universe to the one above it. One would thus go through the four universes, Asiyah, Yetzirah, Beriyah and finally to Atzilut, the Universe of the Sefirot.

Using these universes for spiritual ascent and attaching one's mind on high plays an important role in the Baal Shem's system. The general level which one attains through such ascent is called *Devekut* (דְבֵקוּת), which literally means "attachment." Here it refers to a particular attachment to the spiritual.

SOURCES

I heard from my master [the Baal Shem Tov] that a person is like the "ladder standing on the ground, with its top in the heavens" (Genesis 28:12). He can do worldly, physical things here on earth, but "its top is in heaven," since he meditates on lofty concepts. The person then binds the deed to his thought, and this in itself is a Yichud (Unification).[77]

My master [the Baal Shem Tov] once explained this in more detail. He said that a person must place his mind on each physical thing, elevating it and binding it on high. . . .

He also taught that when a person studies a difficult subject and does not understand it, then he is on the level of Malkhut-Kingship. But when he places his mind on it, understanding it and probing its depths, he then binds Malkhut-Kingship to Binah-Understanding, and attaches the two together.[78]

My master [the Baal Shem Tov] revealed to me that when a person has pain, whether physical or spiritual, he should meditate that even in this pain, God can be found. He is only concealed in a garment in this pain. When a person realizes this, then he can remove the garment. The pain and all evil decrees can then be nullified.[79]

Rabbi Israel Baal Shem Tov said that when he is attached to God and a thought falls into his mind, this is a minor level of *Ruach HaKodesh*.[80]

Think of yourself as a resident of the Supernal Universes, and you will not consider the people of this world important. For the physical world is like a mustard seed compared to the Supernal Universes. Meditate on this and it will make no difference to you whether people love you or hate you. Their love and hate will be nothing to you.[81]

When you are attached to one of the Supernal Universes with no extraneous thoughts, you can then receive a thought very much like prophecy. This thought comes because of an announcement on high regarding the same subject.

Sometimes you hear a voice speaking. This is because the Supernal Voice is attached to the voice of your prayer and Torah study. You then hear the likeness of a voice speaking, and it can reveal future events.[82]

If you wish to ascend on high, you must go from one step to the next.

First, you should have in mind that you are ascending only to the first Firmament, which is a journey of 500 years. In your mind, expand this firmament on all sides. It should not appear small and narrow in your mind, but broad, filling the entire mind.

Once you stand there, you must strengthen your mind to go higher, and then still higher. You must go step by step, however, since you cannot ascend through all Seven Firmaments [at once].

The only time that it is possible to do this is in the middle of prayer. If you attach yourself [on high] properly at the very beginning, then you can ascend to all Seven Firmaments at once.[83]

When you come to the First Firmament in your ascent from level to level, you must see to two things. First, you must see to it that you do not fall down again, and second, you must see to it that you should ascend still higher.

Since in your mind you are literally in the First Firmament, you can then ascend to the next Firmament. [You can climb from one Firmament to the next] until you reach [Yetzirah], the world of Angels. You then climb to [Beriyah], the world of the Throne.

Finally all that remains is the Universe of Atzilut. When you reach this level, you can bind your thoughts to God.[84]

When you desire to ascend, you will first see the form of a man and an image of dogs. These are the [Evil] Husks (*Klipot*), which are in the Universe of Asiyah. You must strengthen yourself and not be afraid.

Sometimes you can speak on high with your soul alone, without your body. This is when you separate yourself from your body, and it is called "divestment of the physical" *(Hit-pashtut HaGashmiut).* In such a state you feel no bodily sensation and are totally unaware of the physical world. Your entire mind depicts only the Supernal Universes, with their angels and archangels.

When you reach the Universe of Atzilut, you are devoid of all sensation. All that you experience is the most etherial feeling, which is nothing other than God's closeness.

On this level, you can know future events. Occasionally, you can also become aware of future events in the lower [three] Universes, since it is there that they are announced.

Sometimes you will have to make many attempts, just to ascend from one Firmament to the next. This interval is a journey of 500 years, and sometimes you can fall in the middle.[85]

Regarding this, Rabbi Israel Baal Shem Tov said, "When I bind my thoughts to God, I let my mouth say anything that it desires. I have bound my speech to its highest Root in the Divine, and every word has a Root on high in the Sefirot."

He also said, "Sometimes I sit among people engaged in idle talk. I attach myself to God properly, and I can bind all their words on high."[86]

When you are properly attached to God, you can engage in any activity that you wish. It appears that you are gazing at the subject of your activity, but actually, you are gazing at nothing other than God.[87]

When your thoughts ascend on high to the Supernal Universes, you must strengthen your mind. You will then be able to stroll through these Universes just like a person strolls from one room to the next.[88]

I heard this from my master [The Baal Shem Tov]. Wherever a person places his thoughts, that is where all of him is.[89]

It is written, "Send Your light and Your truth, they will direct me" (Psalms 43:3). The whole earth is filled with the glory of the Divine Presence, and this is what brings your thought from the lower world to the transcendental. With that great power, your soul ascends and with your thoughts, you break through the Firmaments. It is as if they are opened before you.

You are thus brought to the Universe of Yetzirah, then to the Universe of Beriyah, and finally to the Universe of Atzilut.

You must first bring your thoughts down below, and then you can ascend on high. In your thoughts, you must descend and ascend many times. This is because you must come down before you can go up.

When you descend, that is when you gain power. When you go up once again, you are then able to ascend to a still higher level. This is like a person throwing a rock [where he must lower his hand before he throws it].

When you ascend mentally to the Universe of Asiyah or Yetzirah, you should have in mind [the entities] in that world are speaking, and that their speech is being expressed by your mouth in that Universe. You should also meditate that God is in front of you in the Ten Sefirot of that Universe, and that His greatness is infinite.

Wherever you ascend on high, keep in mind that you are bringing yourself closer to God, and binding yourself to Him on a higher level. The Zohar thus says, "The King's feet are not the same as the King's head."[90]

At all times during the day, even when you are not praying, you should mentally elevate your thoughts on high. This takes great effort.

Strengthen yourself with all your power of concentration, even if at first you do not ascend very high.

Do not attempt to ascend too quickly. First attempt the Universe of Asiyah, then Yetzirah, then Beriyah, and finally Atzilut.[91]

The supernal universes are really very great, but because the soul is clothed in the body, they seem very small. But when a person divests himself of his physical bodily nature, then with his mind he can see that these universes are very great.[92]

When you bind yourself to God, then through you, all the worlds under your hand are bound to God.

Through eating and wearing clothing, you have the power to include in yourself the concepts of animal, vegetable and mineral in all universes, and through you, they can all be bound to God. But this is possible only when you attach yourself to God.

When a person does not believe with absolute faith that through his words and attachment to God he can accomplish such things, then nothing at all is actually accomplished on high.

It is therefore written [that the angel who wrestled with Jacob] "touched the hollow of his thigh" (Genesis 32:26) This means that [the angel] took away his faith.[93]

Faith is all-important. Many people love and fear God, but still, they accomplish nothing on high because they lack absolute faith.[94]

It is written, "The Living Angels ran and returned" (Ezekiel 1:14). I heard the following explanation of this from my master [the Baal Shem Tov].

Every thing has a burning desire and longing to return and attach itself to its root. The soul therefore also constantly desires to attach itself to its Root on high.

[The soul would thus want to constantly satisfy] this longing through worship and Torah study.

If the soul were to constantly experience this ardor, it would totally nullify itself. [Totally swallowed up in God, it would revert to the state that existed] before the World of Rectification came into being.

This is the mystery of the "Graves of Desire" [where out of

longing and desire, the people were totally nullified in the Infinite Essence, and thus ceased to exist] as discussed in *B'rit Menucha*. . .[95]

God therefore arranged that man should have to occasionally engage in his worldly needs. He must eat, drink, and earn a livelihood to some degree, even though he is willing to make do with little. At these times, he is prevented from worshipping God, and the soul can rest.

The individual's mental faculties are then [renewed and] strengthened, so that he can once again engage in worship.

This is the mystery of, "The Living Angels ran and returned." [96]

7. NOTHINGNESS

In classical meditation, the most difficult path is undirected meditation. This is a path where one must totally clear one's mind of all thought and sensation, whether physical or spiritual. All that one experiences on this level is absolute nothingness.

It is significant to note that in classical Kabbalah, the highest spiritual levels are also referred to an *Ayin* (אַיִן) — literally, "nothingness." Thus, the Universe of Beriyah literally refers to the level that is called "creation." Creation, however, is defined as bringing forth "Something from Nothing." The level above Beriyah, from which it emanates, must therefore be considered "Nothing." It is in this context that the universe of Atzilut is often referred to as "Nothingness."

This term is also used to denote Keter-Crown, the highest of the Sefirot in Atzilut. With regard to Chokhmah-Wisdom, the second highest Sefirah, it is written, "Wisdom comes into being from Nothing (*Ayin*)" (Job 28:12). Thus, Keter-Crown, the level from which Chokhmah-Wisdom emanates is also called "Nothingness." While Atzilut in general is nothingness in a conceptual sense, Keter-Crown is nothingness in even a spiritual sense.[97]

This is also suggested by the term *Ain Sof* (אֵין סוֹף), an appelation often assigned to God in the Kabbalah. Literally, *Ain* (אֵין) means "without" and *Sof* (סוֹף) means "end." *Ain Sof* is therefore usually translated to mean "The Endless One," the "Infinite Being," or simply, "The Infinite."[98] The term "Ain Sof," however, also has the connotation as "The Nothingness End" or "The Ultimate Nothingness." In this context, it refers to the ultimate level in Nothingness to which one ascends.

Undirected meditation on Nothingness is one of the most dangerous methods in classical meditation, and should not be attempted except under the guidance of a master. Prior to the Hasidic masters, there is virtually no mention whatsoever of this method. Even in the Hasidic writings, it is only mentioned occasionally and obliquely, but the few references are highly significant. It is discussed most often by the Mezricher Maggid, and by his most illustrious disciple, Rabbi Levi Yitzchak of Berdichov (1740—1809).

SOURCES

The many levels of the mind include the thinker, thought and speech. One is influenced by the other.

Speech exists in time. Thought is also in time, since a person has different thoughts at different times.

There is also an essence that binds the thinker to thought. This is an essence that cannot be grasped. It is the attribute of Nothingness. It is often referred to as the Hyle [the state between potential and realization].

An egg becomes a chicken. There is, however, an instant when it is neither chicken nor egg. No person can determine that instant, for in that instant, it is a state of Nothingness.

The same is true of the transition of thinker to thought, or of thought to speech. It is impossible to grasp the essence that unites them. . . .

In order to bind them all together, one must reach the level of Nothingness.

Moses thus said, "If Nothingness, erase me" (Exodus 32:32). [The Israelites had bowed down to the Golden Calf and] had been blemished by idolatry. What Moses wanted to do was elevate them back to their original level. He therefore brought himself to the level of Nothingness, and [wishing to go still higher,] he prayed, "erase me." [99] When he reached the highest level, he was able to bind all things on high.[100]

Think of yourself as nothing, and totally forget yourself when you pray. Only have in mind that you are praying for the Divine Presence.

You can then enter the Universe of Thought, a state that is beyond time. Everything in this realm is the same, life and death, land and sea.

Levels of Existence		
Universe	*Manifestation*	*Sefirah*
Atzilut	Nothingness	Chokhmah
Beriyah	Thought	Binah
Yetzirah	Speech	The next six
Asiyah	Action	Malkhut

. . . But in order to enter the Universe of Thought where all is the same, you must relinquish your ego, and forget all your troubles.

You cannot reach this level if you attach yourself to physical worldly things. For then, you are attached to the division between good and evil, which is included in the seven days of creation. How then can you approach a level above time, where absolute unity reigns.

Furthermore, if you consider yourself as "something," and ask for your own needs, then God cannot clothe Himself in you. God is infinite, and no vessel can hold Him at all, except when a person makes himself like Nothing.[101]

In prayer, you must place all your strength in the words, going from letter to letter until you totally forget your body. Thinking how the letters permute and combine with each other, you will have great delight. If this is a great physical delight, it is certainly a great spiritual delight.

This is the Universe of Yetzirah, [the world of Speech].

The letters then enter your thoughts, and you do not even hear the words that you pronounce. This is the Universe of Beriyah, [the world of Thought].

You then come to the level of Nothingness, where all your [senses and] physical faculties are nullified. This is the Universe of Atzilut, [which parallels] the Attribute of Chokhmah-Wisdom.[102]

Nothing can change from one thing to another [without first losing its original identity]. Thus, for example, before an egg can grow into a chicken, it must first cease totally to be an egg. Each thing must lose its original identity before it can be something else.

Therefore, before a thing is transformed into something else, it must come to the level of Nothingness.

This is how a miracle comes about, changing the laws of nature. First the thing must be elevated to the Emanation of Nothingness. Influence then comes from that Emanation to produce the miracle.[103]

When a person gazes at an object, he elevates it into his thought. If his thought is then attached to the supernal Thought, he can elevate it to the supernal Thought. From there it can be elevated to the level of Nothingness, where the object itself becomes absolute nothingness.

This person can then lower it once again to the level of Thought, which is somethingness. At the end of all levels, he can transform it into gold.[103]

God is boundless. This means that there is nothing physical that can hinder His presence. He fills every element of space in all universes that He created, on all levels, and there is no place devoid of Him.[104]

When a person ascends from one level to the next, but still wants to attain more, then he has no limits and is literally like the Infinite. This person then has the attribute with which to grasp the seed transmitted from the Infinite Being.

But when a person says, "That which I can grasp is sufficient for me," he then only aspires to the straw and chaff, which are the Husks.[105]

Man is primarily his mind. It would be natural for something which is mind to only bind itself to mental concepts.

One should therefore keep in mind this thought: "Why should I use my mind to think about physical things? When I do this I lower my mind by binding it to a lower level. It would be better for me to elevate my mind to the highest level, by binding my thoughts to the Infinite."

Even physical things must serve the Creator in a spiritual manner. It is thus taught, "They are My slaves, and not slaves of slaves."[106]

Love is not restricted by limitations. For love does not have any bounds, being an aspect of the Infinite Love.

If one has love for something physical, then this physical thing becomes a vessel [that limits] his love.

But when one has love for the Infinite Being, then his love is clothed in the Infinite. Both the love and its vessel are then boundless. The same is true of all other attributes.[107]

When a person repents and directs his love toward God, his thought is, "Why did I expend my love for physical things? It is better for me to love the Root of all Roots." His love is then rectified, and he draws the Sparks of Holiness out from the Husks.[108]

[God is called] the Endless One (*Ain Sof*), and not the Beginningless One.

If He were called the Beginningless One, it would be impossible to even begin to speak about Him. But to some extent, it is possible to comprehend Him through His creation. This is a beginning, but it has no end.[109]

Rabbi Levi Yitzchak:

The most important thing to realize is that God created all and that He is all.

God's influence never ceases. At every instant, He gives existence to His creation, to all the universes, to the heavenly chambers, and to all the angels....

We therefore say [in the prayer before the *Sh'ma*], "He *forms* light and creates darkness" [in the present tense], and not "He *formed* light and created darkness" [in the past tense]. We say that God "creates" in the present tense because every second he creates and gives existence to all that is.

Everything comes from God. He is perfect and He includes all things.

When a person attains the attribute of Nothingness, he realizes that he is nothing, and that God is giving him existence. He can then say that God "creates" — in the present tense. This means that God is creating, even at this very moment.

When a person looks at himself and not at Nothingness, then he is on a level of "somethingness" [and independent existence]. He then says that God "created" — in the past tense. This means that God created him earlier [but that he now has independent existence].

We therefore say the blessing, "[Blessed are You, O God . . .] who *created* man with wisdom." [We use the past tense,] since Wisdom is on a level of "somethingness."

We therefore find in the writings of the Ari that the expression, "God is King," is an aspect of Nothingness. For when we say that "God *is* King" [in the present tense] it means that He is presently giving us existence. This is the aspect of Nothingness — we are nothing, and it is God who is giving us the power [to exist.].

On the level of Nothingness, everything is above the laws of nature. On the level of "somethingness," on the other hand, all things are bound by nature.

The way in which we bind "somethingness" to Nothingness is through the Torah and commandments. This is the meaning of the verse, "The Living Angels ran and returned" (Ezekiel 1:14) — [that is, from a level of Nothingness to one of "somethingness."]

The Zohar teaches that the commandments and Torah are both hidden and revealed.[110] "Hidden" alludes to Nothingness, while "revealed" applies to "somethingness." They thus bind something to Nothingness, and Nothingness to somethingness.

This is the meaning of the word *Mitzvah* (מִצְוָה), meaning "commandment." When we reverse the Hebrew alphabet through the Atbash (אתב"ש) cipher, then Alef (א) becomes Tav (ת), Bet (ב) becomes Shin (ש), and so on. [Through this cipher, the Mem (מ) of *Mitzvah* (מצוה) becomes a Yod (י), while the Tzadi (צ) becomes a Heh (ה).

[The first two letters of *Mitzvah* therefore] are Yod Heh (יה), the first two letters of the Tetragrammaton, YHVH (יהוה).[111]

This is an aspect of Nothingness.

The last two letters of the word *Mitzvah* are Vav Heh (וה), [the last two letters of the Tetragrammaton].

This is an aspect of somethingness.

The letters Yod Heh (יה) [in the word *Mitzvah*] are hidden, just like the concept of Nothingness. [The letters Vav Heh (וה), on the other hand, are written directly, and are revealed, just like somethingness.]

The commandments thus have a hidden part and a revealed part. The hidden part is our bringing pleasure to God through our observance of the commandments, since we have no way of detecting this. [The revealed part is] when we benefit ourselves, since this is visible.

This is the meaning of the verse, "Hidden things belong to the Lord our God, [but revealed things belong to us and to our children forever]" (Deuteronomy 34:22).

"Hidden things" allude to the hidden part of the commandment, and these "belong to the Lord our God." What we accomplish with relation to God is hidden from us.

"Revealed things belong to us and to our children," however, since the divine influence that we bring about is revealed to us.[112]

At every instant, all universes receive sustenance and Life Force from God. Man, however, is the one who motivates this sustenance and transmits it to all worlds.

When a person wants to bring new sustenance to all universes, he must attach himself to the level of Nothingness. This is the level in all universes that were not constricted.

When man nullifies himself completely and attaches his thoughts to Nothingness, then a new sustenance flows to all universes. This is a sustenance that did not exist previously.

A person must fear God so much that his ego is totally nullified. Only then can he attach himself to Nothingness. Sustenance, filled with all good, then flows to all universes. . . .

The individual thus attaches the Life Force of all universes to Nothingness, which is higher than all worlds. . . . On the level where this [Life Force] had not yet been constricted into the universes, it is attached to the Nothingness, which is called the Hyle. . . .[113]

8. RABBI NACHMAN'S WAY

The classical word for meditation is *Hitbodedut,* which literally means mental self-seclusion. Although this term has been used in this context for a thousand years, the name with which it is most often associated is Rabbi Nachman of Breslov (1772—1810). Where other masters speak of *Hitbodedut* only occasionally, Rabbi Nachman has provided us with an entire literature.

The *Hitbodedut* meditation taught by Rabbi Nachman would be called inner directed meditation in classical terminology. That is, rather than concentrating on some external thing, such as a name or a mantra, one concentrates on the thoughts that arise in his mind. In Rabbi Nachman's system, one does so in the context of prayer, expressing, these spontaneous thoughts as prayers before God. Although it is often referred to as spontaneous prayer, Rabbi Nachman's *Hitbodedut* is actually one of the classical methods of meditation.

Rabbi Nachman was the last master of Kabbalah meditation, and it is with him that we conclude this discussion. Looking at the entire field of meditation from a historical viewpoint, we find that the closer one gets to the present, the less dangerous and more universal the methods become. The techniques of the *Hekhalot* and Abulafia are highly advanced and dangerous, and should be used only after many, many years of preparation. The Ari's Yichudim and Kavanot, on the other hand, involve only thought and are much gentler in their effect. The Baal Shem Tov made use of the prayer service almost as a mantra, making the method accessible to all who could recite the service. But still, Rabbi Nachman's method was the most universal, and could be used by literally everybody.

Besides being a great master of a major meditative school, Rabbi Nachman has attained great fame as a story teller, and his tales have taken their place among the classics of world literature. He was also a major Kabbalist, according to some, on a level as great as that of the Ari and the Baal Shem Tov.

A great-grandson of the Baal Shem Tov, Rabbi Nachman was born in the founder's house in Medzeboz on *Rosh Chodesh* Nissan, 5532 (April 4, 1772). His father, Reb Simcha, was the son of Rabbi Nachman Horodenker, a leading disciple of the Baal Shem Tov. Feiga, his mother, was the daughter of Udel, who in turn was the only daughter of the Baal Shem. Rabbi Nachman's birth occurred at a time when Hassidism was in deep trouble, and it was on the day of his circumcision that the dread *Cherem* or ban was pronounced against the entire Hassidic movemnt.

In many ways, Rabbi Nachman's childhood resembled that of his illustrious great-grandfather, and he also spent hours meditating in the fields and mountains, hiding his brilliance and piety from those around him. He married at an early age, and settled with his father-in-law in Ossatin, in the Western Ukraine. When his mother-in-law died and his father-in-law remarried, the new mistress of the house made things difficult for the young Tzaddik, and he moved away to take a post in Medvedevka, several miles away. Renowned as a direct descendent of the Baal Shem Tov, Rabbi Nachman had no difficulty in attracting a following, but as he matured, he became a brilliant leader in his own right.

It was from Medvedevka that Rabbi Nachman set out on his pilgrimage to the Holy Land in the spring of 1798. After a long delay in Istanbul due to Napolean's Egyptian Campaign, he finally set foot on the Holy Land a day before Rosh HaShanah (September 10, 1798). There he met Rabbi Avraham Kalisker, leader of the Holy Land Hassidim, and a strong bond of friendship developed between the two. Upon his return, he made a valiant attempt to subdue the dispute which had been raging between Rabbi Avraham and Rabbi Schneur Zalman of Liadi, even making a 700-mile trip to see the latter.

In the fall of 1800, Rabbi Nachman moved from Medvedevka to Zlatipolia, just a few miles from Shpola. Rabbi Leib, the Shpola Zeida (Grandfather), was obviously annoyed at the intrusion of this young "upstart," and after a number of false accusations on the part of his followers, began a heated controversy against Rabbi Nachman. Things became so bad that Zeida tried to enact a ban of *Cherem* against the Young Rebbe, and it was only the intervention of Rabbi Levi Yitzchok of Berdichov and his uncle, Rabbi Baruch of Medzeboz, that prevented it. This controversy, however, was not to abate, and it led to great persecutions of the Breslover Hassidim after Rabbi Nachman's death.

Not being able to bear the pressure of this controversy, Rabbi Nachman moved to Breslov in the central Ukraine, arriving there on 10 Elul, 5562 (September 7, 1802). It was here that he attracted his major disciple and Boswell, Rabbi Nathan of Nemerov. Most of the teachings of Rabbi Nachman that have survived were written down by Rabbi Nathan, and the master himself said, "If not for my Nathan, no memory of my teachings would have remained."

Early in 1805, Rabbi Nachman instructed Rabbi Nathan to begin arranging his teachings in order, compiling what was to become his *magnum opus*, the *Likutey Moharan* (Anthology of Our Master, Rabbi Nachman). A little over a year later, Rabbi Nachman's infant son, Sh'lomo Ephriam, died. Stricken by grief—and perhaps out of a need to rectify his son's death—Rabbi Nachman set out on a long mysterious journey in the winter of 1807. It was during this journey that his wife died, and he contracted the tuberculosis that was to take his life.

Suffering from consumption, Rabbi Nachman journeyed to Lemberg (Lvov) where he sought medical treatment. It was during this period that he sent *Likutey Moharan* to be printed, and it was completed in the late summer of 1808.

After a fire burned Rabbi Nachman's house in the spring of 1810, he relocated in Uman (a city half way between Kiev and Odessa), scene of the great massacre of 1768, where tens of thousands of Jews had been slaughtered by the Haidmacks. Rabbi Nachman said that he now had the task of rectifying these souls with his own death. It was also his desire to be buried in Uman's martyr-filled cemetery.

While in Uman, Rabbi Nachman became quite friendly with a number of secularized Jewish intellectuals who lived there. He declared that it was an important task to bring these "lost souls" back to the truth. One of the leaders of the anti-religious "enlightenment" of Uman declared that if Rabbi Nachman had not died prematurely, he would have made him into a religious Jew.

With tuberculosis sapping away his strength, Rabbi Nachman barely made it through the High Holy Days. He passed away during Sukkot, on 18 Tishrei, 5571 (October 16, 1810). Early the next day, he was laid to rest in the old cemetery in Uman, and his grave remains a shrine to Breslover Hassidim to this very day.

After his master's death, Rabbi Nathan worked diligently to keep the group together. Gathering penny by penny, he printed the second part of *Likutey Moharan*, as well as the *Sichot HaRan* and *Sichot Moharan*, compilations of Rabbi Nachman's sayings. Mercilessly hounded by Rabbi Moshe of Savran because of false accusations, the group barely survived the next few decades. It was only Rabbi Nathan's tremendous dedication and strength of character that kept the Breslover Hassidim alive as a group. Despite the persecutions, a synagogue was built in Uman, numerous books published, and the group eventually grew to number in the thousands.

Although Rabbi Nachman's teachings comprise a good number of volumes, his ideas regarding meditation are collected in a remarkable book called *Hishtapchut HaNefesh* (Outpouring of Soul).

SOURCES

You must include yourself in God's unity, which is the imperative Existence. You cannot be worthy of this, however, unless you first nullify yourself. It is impossible to nullify yourself, however, without Hitbodedut-meditation.

When you meditate and express your spontaneous thoughts before God, you can be worthy of nullifying all desires and all evil traits. You will then be able to nullify your entire physical being, and become included in your Root.

The main time to meditate is at night. This is a time when the world is free from mundane concerns. Since people are involved in the mundane by day, you will be held back and confused, so that you will not be able to attach yourself to God and include yourself in Him. Even if you yourself are not so involved, since the world is concerned with worldly vanities, it is difficult for you to nullify yourself.

It is also necessary that you meditate in an isolated place. It should be outside the city, or on a lonely street, or some other place where other people are not found. For wherever people are found, they are involved in the mundane world. Even though they may not be in this place at that time, the very fact that they are usually there can confuse one's meditation, and then one cannot nullify himself and include himself in God.

You must therefore be alone, at night, on an isolated path, where people are not usually found. Go there and meditate, cleansing your heart and mind of all worldly affairs. You will then be worthy of a true aspect of self-nullification.

Meditating at night in an isolated place, you should make use of many prayers and thoughts, until you nullify one trait or desire. Then make use of much meditation to nullify another trait or desire. Continue in such a time and place, proceeding in this manner, until you have nullified all. If some ego remains, work to nullify that. Continue until nothing remains.

If you are truly worthy of such nullification, then your soul will be included in its Root, which is God, the Necessary Existence. All the world will then be included in this Root along with your soul.[114]

Hitbodedut-meditation is the best and the highest level of worship.

Set aside an hour or more each day to meditate, in the fields or in a room, pouring out your thoughts to God. Make use of arguments and persuasion, with words of grace, longing and petition, supplicating God and asking that He bring you to serve Him in truth.

Such meditation should be in the language that you normally speak. It is difficult to express your thoughts in Hebrew, and the heart is therefore not drawn after the words. We do not normally speak Hebrew, and are not accustomed to expressing ourself in this language. It is therefore much easier to express yourself in your native language. . . .

In your everyday native language, express all your thoughts to God, speaking of everything that is in your heart. This can involve regret and repentance for the past, or requests and supplications asking that you should truly come close to God in the future. Every person can express his own thoughts, each according to his level.

You should be very careful with this practice, accustoming yourself to do it at a set time each day. The rest of the day can then be joyous.

This is a very great practice. It is the best possible advice, including all things. It is good for everything that may be lacking in your relationship with God. Even if you are completely removed from God, you should still express your thoughts to Him, and ask [that He bring you back].

Even if your words are blocked, and you cannot open your mouth to God, you can still prepare yourself to do so. Even getting ready to speak to God is in itself very good. Even though you cannot speak to Him, you long and yearn to do so — and this itself is very good.

You can even make a prayer out of this itself. You can cry out to God that you are so far from Him that you cannot even speak. You can ask Him to have mercy on you and open your mouth so that you should be able to express your thoughts to Him.

You should know that many great, famous saints (*Tzaddikim*) said that they only reached their high level through this practice of Hidbodedut-meditation. If you have wisdom, you will understand the importance of this practice, and how it brings one higher and higher. Yet, it is something that can be done equally by every individual, great and small alike. Everyone can observe this practice and reach the highest levels. Happy is he who does so.[115]

You should be consistent in your meditation, expressing your thoughts before God each day.

Even if you cannot speak at all, you should simply repeat a single word, and this, too, is very good. If you can say nothing else, remain firm, and repeat this word over and over again, countless times. You can spend many days with this one word alone, and this will be very beneficial. Remain firm, repeating your word or phrase countless times. God will eventually have mercy on you and open your heart so that you will be able to express all your thoughts.

Speech has great power. It is even possible to prevent a gun from firing. Understand this.[116]

You must be worthy to be able to meditate for a given time each day, [thinking about your life] and regretting what you must. Not every one can have such mental tranquility each day. The days pass and are gone, and you find that you never once had time to really think.

You must therefore make sure to set aside a specific time each day to calmly review your life. Consider what you are doing, and ponder whether it is worthwhile for you to devote your life to it.

A person who does not meditate cannot have wisdom. He may occasionally be able to concentrate, but not for any length of time. His power of concentration remains weak and cannot be maintained.

If a person does not meditate, he also does not realize the foolishness of the world. But when an individual has a relaxed and penetrating mind, he can see that it is all meaningless.[117]

It is best to meditate in the meadows outside the city. Go to a grassy field, and the grass will awaken your heart.[118]

Know that when you pray in the fields, all the grasses come into your prayers. They help you and give you strength to pray.

It is for this reason that prayer is called *Sichah*. This shares a root with the word for grass, as in, "All the grass (*Si'ach*) of the field . . ." (Genesis 2:5).

It is thus written, "And Isaac went out to meditate (*Suach*) in the field" (Genesis 24:63). His prayer was helped and strengthened by the field, since all the grasses fortified and aided his prayer.[119]

Rabbi Nachman said that the main time that King David would meditate upon God was at night, under the covers in bed. Hidden from the sight of all others, he would pour out his heart before God. He therefore said, "I meditate every night on my bed in tears" (Psalms 6:7).[120]

It is very good to have a special room, set aside for Torah study and prayer. Such a room is especially beneficial for secluded meditation and conversation with God.

Rabbi Nachman said that it is very good even to sit in such a special room. The atmosphere itself is beneficial, even if you sit there and do nothing.

Even if you do not have a special room, you can still meditate and express your thoughts to God.

Rabbi Nachman said that you can create your own "special room" under your Tallit. Just drape your Tallit over your eyes and express your thoughts to God as you desire.

You can also meditate with God in bed under the covers. This was King David's custom, as he said, "I meditate every night on my bed in tears" (Psalms 6:7).

You can also converse with God while sitting before an open book. Let others think that you are merely [reading or] studying.

There are many other ways in which you can accomplish this if you truly want to meditate and express your thoughts to God. Above all else, this is the root and foundation of holiness and repentance.[121]

Elijah was an ordinary human being, living in this world. But through secluded meditation, he reached such a high level that he never tasted death.

From Rabbi Nachman's words, it was obvious that Elijah reached his high level only through this practice. The same is true of all the other great saints.[122]

There are many prayers, supplications and petitions that have already been composed. The Destroyers and Denouncers know of them and therefore lay in the way to ambush these prayers.

You can travel on a path that is well-trod, known and publicized to all. But murderers and robbers also know of this road, and lay in wait there. But when you travel on a byway, taking a route that is as yet unknown, robbers are also ignorant of it.

The same is true here. Your personal prayers before God are like a new route. They are prayers that have been composed in your heart, and are not being expressed for the first time. Therefore, no Denouncers lie in wait for these prayers.

Nevertheless, [your own prayers are not enough]. You should also be very careful to say the other [standard] supplications and prayers.[123]

בנל״ך ולאע״י

תושלב״ע

ל״ג לעומר תשל״ו

Notes

Chapter One: Meditation

1. This is discussed at length in the companion volume, *Meditation and the Bible.*

2. This method is mentioned by Maimonides in *Yad, Avodat Kokhavim* 11:6.

3. *Be'er Hetiv, Orach Chaim* 1:3. See below, Chapter Six, note 83. Also see Chapter Four, note 76.

4. This is described at length by Rabbi Dov Baer of Lubavitch in his *Kuntres HaHitpa'alut.* This has been published in English as *A Tract on Ecstasy.*

5. *Yad, Yesodey HaTorah* 2:1 See also *Yad, Tshuvah* 10:3.

6. *Moreh Nevuchim* 3:51. This "kiss" is mentioned in the Talmud, *Berakhot* 8a, *Moed Katan* 28a, *Bava Batra* 17a; *Devarim Rabbah* 11:10. See Commentaries on Psalm 91:14.

7. *Mishnah, Succah* 5:4.

8. *Yerushalmi, Succah* 5:1 (22b).

9. *Taanit* 1:30; *Yerushalmi, Megillah* 2:4 (20b), *Moed Katan* 3:7 (17b). See also *Tanchuma, Shemini* 11.

10. There are many places where the word *Hitbodedut* is used unambiguously to denote meditation. See Hai Gaon, quoted in commentary of R. Moshe Botril on *Sefer Yetzirah* 4:2; Ibn Ezra, commentary on Exodus 20:8, Isaiah 44:25, Micah 2:1, Psalms 92:5, *Yesod Moreh* 8; Maimonides, *Yad, Yesodey HaTorah* 7:4, *Moreh Nevuchim* 1:8, 3:51, *Iggeret HaMussar* (in *Iggerot HaRambam,* Warsaw, 1927) p. 7; *Perush HaAgadot* of Rabbi Azariah of Goronda (in Scholem, *Kitvey Yad BaKabbalah,* Jerusalem, 1930), p. 197, quoted in Recanti on *VaYechi* (Lvov, 1880) p. 37d, quoted in *Minchat Yehudah* (Chayit) on *Maarekhet Elokut* 10 (Mantua, 1558) p. 143b; Ramban on Deuteronomy 13:2, *Tur, Orach Chaim* 98, *Sefer HaChinuch* 510; Rabbi Shem Tov ibn Shaprut, *Pardes Rimonim* (Sabbioneta, 1554) p. 4a; Ralbag on Exodus 4:10, 24:11, 1 Samuel 28:8, 2 Kings 9:1, *Or HaShem* 2:4:4 (Vienna, 1860) p. 16a, *Sefer HaIkkarim* 2:25 (Warsaw, 1871) p. 90b; R. Simon ben Tzemach Duran, *Magen Avot* 2:2 (Livorno, 1785) p. 16a, Sforno on Exodus 3:1, R. Meir ibn Gabbai, *Avodat HaKodesh, Sitrey Torah* 27 (Warsaw, 1894) p. 135c,d; Abarbanel, commentary on Exodus 19:3, 24:11, 1 Samuel 3:3, 10:5, 19:10, 19:18, 28:7, 1 Kings 18:42, 2 Kings 9:11, *Nachalat Avot* on *Avot* 1:1, 3:4; *She'elot U'Tshuvot haRadbaz* 3:532; R. Moshe Cordevero, *Pardes Rimonim* 21:1, 30:3, *Shiur Komah* 13 (Warsaw 1883) p. 9d, 15a, 16, p. 30d; *Sefer Cheredim, Tshuvah* 3 (Jerusalem, 1958) p. 214, 215; *Kav HaYashar* 12; R. Chaim Yosef David Azzulai (Chida), *Avodat HaKodesh, Tziporen Shamir* 51, *Midbar Kadmut,* Heh 13; Yaakov Emdin, *Migdal Oz, Bet Midot* 9 (Warsaw, 1886) p. 63a, Malbim on Genesis 24:63. *Shalshelet HaKabbalah* p. 51.

11. In its earliest use, it has this sense, see *Ekhah Rabbah,* introduction 20. See also *Chovot HaLevavot, Shaar Cheshbon HaNefesh* 3, #17 (53a), *Shaar HaBechinah* 6, *Shaar HaYichud* 8; Radak, *Sefer Shereshim, YaRaD, EChaD; Otzar Nechemad,* on *Kuzari* 3:1 (3a). It is also apparently used in this sense in *Mesilat Yesharim* 15, 26. See also *Chovot HaLevavot, Shaar HaPerishut* 2.

12. *Shaarey Kedushah,* Part Four (British Museum, Ms. #749) p. 15b. A similar expression is found in *Shaarey Kedushah 3:8; Likutim Yekarim* (Jerusalem, 1974) #29, 38.

13. *Milchemat HaShem* 2:6 (Riva di Trento, 1506) p. 19a.

14. *Otzar Chaim* (Guenzburg, Ms. 775) p. 7a.

15. *Sefer HaMaspik LeOvdey HaShem* (Jerusalem, 1965) p. 177 ff. This is a translation from the Arabic *Kefayah Al-e'abdin,* done by Yosef ben Tzalach Dori.

Chapter Two: Talmudic Mystics

1. *Chagigah* 14b, *Tosefta* 2:1. See *Mishnah* 2:1 (11b). See note 16.

2. Ezekiel 10:5, *Chagigah* 13b; Ibn Ezra, Radak, on 1 Chronicles 28:18, Ramban, Recanti, Tzioni, on Exodus 25:21. For an extensive discussion, see *Meditation and the Bible* 2:2,3.

3. *Shaar Ruach HaKodesh* (Ashlag ed, Tel Aviv, 1963) p. 41. The text is reproduced below, pp. 231, 232.

4. *Hekhalot Rabatai* 21. See below, p. 49.

5. *Chagigah* 13a.

6. *Nedarim* 10a, *Bava Kama* 30a, *Niddah* 38a, *Simachot* 3:10, *Bereshit Rabbah* 62:2.

7. *Shaarey Kedushah,* Introduction. Quoted in *Meditation and the Bible.* 2:8.

8. *Berakhot* 5:1 (30b), 32b.

9. See especially *Shaar HaKavanah LeMekubalim HaRishonim,* reproduced below, p. 122. See also *Sefer Cheredim, Tshuvah* 3 (Jerusalem, 1958) p. 215.

10. *Avot* 1:13.

11. *Avot Rabbi Nathan* 12:13, *Shulchan Arukh, Yoreh Deah* 146:21 in *Hagah.*

12. *Chagigah* 14b. In *Brit Menuchah* (Warsaw, 1884) p. 2b, however, we find that Rabbi Akiba received this tradition from Rabbi Eliezer.

13. *Mekhilta ad loc.*

14. *Succah* 28a, *Bava Batra* 134a.

15. *Megillah* 3a.

16. *Chagigah* 14b, *Tosefta* 2. See note 1.

17. Ibid. See *Shoshan Sodot* 57b. *Cf.* note 51.

18. See *Chagigah* 12b. *Cf.* Chapter 5, note 55.

19. *Hekhalot Rabbatai* 26:2, quoted below, page 53. In our editions, the wording is somewhat different. This is also cited in the next two quotations with some differences.

20. This is the *Ispaklaria,* the "glass" or "mirror" into which one gazes to see a spiritual revelation. The Talmud thus teaches, "All other prophets saw through a dull *Ispaklaria,* while Moses saw through a clear *Ispaklaria.*" *Yebamot* 49b, Rashi, Ramban, ad loc, *Sanhedrin* 97b, *VaYikra Rabbah* 1:14, *Zohar* 1:171a,

Rashi, Sforno to Numbers 12:6, Ramban on Genesis 18:2, *Yad, Yesodey HaTorah* 7:6, *Ikkarim* 3:17. The Midrash states, "All other prophets looked through nine *Ispaklariot*, while Moses looked through only one," *VaYikra Rabbah loc. cit. Tosefot Yom Tov* on *Kelim* 30:2 interprets *Ispaklaria* as a lens. Rashi, *Succah* 45b likewise writes that it is a barrier between man and the Divine Presence. Also see Rashi, *Sanhedrin* 97b. We likewise find that *Zekhukhit* (glass) is rendered *Ispaklaria* in the *Targum* to Job 28:17. Bertenoro and *Tiferet Yisrael* on *Kelim*, however, interpret *Ispaklaria* to mean a mirror. See *Targum Yonathan* on Exodus 38:8. The Ari relates the term to various Sefirot, see *Shaar Ruach HaKodesh*, p. 12, *Etz Chaim, Shaar HaYareach* 2. In *Adir BaMarom* (Warsaw, 1886) p. 78a, Rabbi Moshe Chaim Luzzatto states that a "shining *Ispakleria*" is a lens, while a "dull *Ispaklaria*" is a mirror. See also below, p. 123.

21. See notes 10, 11.

22. *Arukh*, s.v. *Avney Shayish Tahor*.

23. See *Shabbat* 15b, *Yerushalmi, Shabbat* 6:2, *Eruvin* 10:11, *BaMidbar Rabbah* 12:3, *Tanchuma, Nasa* 27, *Midrash Tehillim* 91:1. *Cf. Shaarey Orah* 1 (3b).

24. This belief is part of the Zoroasteran religion, prevalent in Babylon at the time.

25. See *Berakhot* 5:5 (34b).

26. As quoted in *HaKotev* on *Eyin Yaakov* #11. See also *Otzar HaGaonim, Chagigah* 14b, *Chelek HaTshuvot* p. 14; *She'elot U'Tshuvot HaGaonim* (Lyck, 1864) #99. See *Otzar Chaim*, p. 165a.

27. *Chagigah* 14b.

28. The *Chabura Kadmaah*, mentioned in *Zohar* 3:219b. See *Kisey Melekh* on *Tikuney Zohar* (Jerusalem, 5723) #7, "*BeAgada*" p. 7b; *Sichot HaRan* 278. The final edition of the Zohar was apparently written by Rabbi Abba, see Rabbi David Luria, *Kadmut Sefer HaZohar* 5:2.

29. This is the angel Metatron.

30. The Doe is the Divine Presence *(Shekhinah)*.

31. The number 613 is the number of Commandments in the Torah. It is also the number of parts in the body, consisting of 248 limbs, and 365 veins. See *Makkot* 24a. *Targum J.* on Genesis 1:27. The Ari discussed the 370 lights in detail, see *Shaar HaHakdamos* (Ashlag Ed., Tel Aviv, 1961) p. 235, *Etz Chaim, Shaar Klipat Nogah* 4. In general, the numerical value of the word *Chashmal* is 378, and this is closely associated with the 370 Lights.

32. Ahiyah the Shilonite is mentioned in 1 Kings 11:29, 14:2. He was said to be from the generation of the Exodus, and was the teacher of Elijah, see *Baba Batra* 121b, Introduction to *Yad*, *Zohar* 3:309a, *Zohar Chadash* 19a. Ahiyah was said to be the master of the Baal Shem Tov, see Chapter 7, note 15.

33. The verse continues, "and he sent them to the East." See *Sanhedrin* 91b, *Be'er Sheva ad loc.*, R. Yehudah of Barcelona on *Sefer Yetzirah* (Berlin, 1885) p. 159; *Zohar* 1:133b, 1:233a.

34. The *Sefirot* are the Divine Eminations which God created so as to direct the universe. They all come together in the lowest one which is Malkhut-Kingship, which is associated with the Divine Presence *(Shekhinah)*.

35. See *Zohar* 3:25a. Also see *Toledot Yaakov Yosef, Shlach* (Koretz, 1780), p. 138c.

36. See *Shaarey Orah* 3, 4 (Warsaw, 1883) p. 37b. This is quoted below, pp. 131, 132.

37. *Bava Batra* 10b.

38. *Bahir* (Margolies Ed., Jerusalem, 1951) #150. *Cf. Chagigah* 14a.

39. *Bahir* #88.

40. *Shevuot* 26a. See *Bahir* #32.

41. See *She'elot U'Tshuvot HaGaonim* (Lyck, 1864) #116, *Or Zerua, Keriat Sh'ma* 8 (Zitomer, 1862), p. 11b; Rabbi Yehudah of Barcelona on *Sefer Yetzirah* (Berlin, 1885), p. 20, 22, 257; Pardes Rimonim 6, *Malakhey Elyon, Akatriel.*

42. See Ibn Ezra on Exodus 3:4.

43. *Sanhedrin* 38b.

44. *Berakhot* 51a.

45. It is thus stated that a disciple of Rabbi [Judah the Prince] expounded on the Merkava. *Yerushalmi, Chagigah* 2:1 (9a top).

46. See *Chagigah* 13a.

47. *Berakhot* 7a. See *Shoshan Sodot* 52b.

48. *Sefer HaPardes,* quoted in *Shalshelet HaKabbalah* (Jerusalem, 1962) p. 64, *Seder HaDorot* 5 (Munkatch, 1896) p. 118a. *Cf. Bet HaMidrash,* Volume 3, p. XLVII.

49. In *Merkava Shlemah* (Jerusalem, 1922) p. 2b.

50. *Yoma* 9b.

51. *Chagigah* 14b. This has been discussed earlier. See note 17 ff.

52. *Cf. Chagigah* 25a. Also see Chapter 6, note 66.

53. Paraphrase of Proverbs 22:5.

54. *Shaarey Kedushah* 3:6.

55. See *Etz Chaim, Shaar HaTzelem* 3 (Ashlag Ed., Tel Aviv, 1960) p. 51, *Shaar HaChashmal* 1, p. 291, *Shaar Kitzur ABYA* 6, p. 401; *Mavo Shaarim* 6:2:3; *Shaar HaKavanot, Inyan Levishat Begandim* (Tel Aviv, 1962) pp. 12, 13; *Pri Etz Chaim, Shaar HaTefillah* 3 (Tel Aviv, 1966), p. 19. *Cf. Shaarey Kedushah* 3:6.

56. We have primarily used the Hekhalot text in Wertheimer, *Batey Midrashot* (Jerusalum, 1968) Volume 1, p. 67 ff. This has been corrected according to other versions, most notably, that in A. Jellinek, *Bet HaMidrash* (Leipzig, 1856), Volume 3, page 83 ff. This is also in *Otzar Midrashim* (New York 1915), Volume 1, page 107 ff. Also see *Pirkey Hekhalot,* Shklav, 1785, Berdichov, 1817, Zalkiev, 1837, Lvov, 1824. Also in *Chayay Nefesh* (with commentary, *Otzar HaChakhmah*), Jerusalem 1891; *Arzey Levanon* (Venice, 1601) #6, *Amudey Shesh* (Lvov, 1785) #5.

57. A similar formula is repeated 120 times in *Razo Shel Sandelfon, Merkava Shlemah* 4b.

58. For a further description of these seals, see *Shoshan Yesod Olam* (Sasoon, Ms. 290) #1010 (p. 384b).

59. Wertheimer reads *Yituk* (יתוק), and states that he does not know the meaning of the word. Although it is not definite that platinum was known at the time this was written, the word was chosen because it fits the sense of the text. Jellinek has the reading *Litik* (ליתיק). At the end of *Otzar Midrashim,* Dr. Solomon Horowitz identifies this with the Greek *Lithios,* meaning stone.

60. This is Jellinek's reading. Wertheimer has ADSTAN and AYRN ADSTAR and KhPYNO ShMNUSh EKhShNH. In the Jerusalem edition, it is "ARSTAN, and some say ARSTAD and KhNPYShT TzMNShERGH."

61. This is Wertheimer's reading. Jellinek has "TARS and bar - MShGYYH." In the Jerusalem edition, it is, "TADM and BRMNYGYYH and KhEShPTYSh."

62. These are taken from Jellinek. Other editions appear confused. Wertheimer has, "Churpaniel Zehpataryay, Abirzehyay Cabapel, Atagiel, Chatrogiel, Banagel, Hash, Sastitiel, Anafiel." The Jerusalem edition has, "Haypanyarav, Abarazyay, Ataringel, Narudiel, Sastatiel, Anpiel."

63. This is Jellinek's reading. Wertheimer has, "ATRTS, the Great Master, APYMYAL ShMCh BRTzE." The Jerusalem edition has, "ATNKh SRBZHG KhOPY LShKhTh KhHTzE."

64. This is also taken from Jellinek.

65. The Talmud says the same about Metatron, see note 43. See *Megalah Amukim* #217, *Avodat HaKodesh, Yichud* 16.

66. See Targum J., Rashi, on Ezekiel 1:6.

67. Alternatively, "A large sieve of branches." See *Bikurim* 3:8, *Kelim* 20:2.

68. This is the chant, *"Melekh abir, Melekh Adir, Melekh Adon,"* etc. This is an alphabetical chant, where each letter is repeated three times. In *Merkava Shlemah,* p. 34b, a similar chant is found where each letter is repeated six times.

69. An allusion to Ezekiel 1:25.

70. A number of chants are presented here. Among them is the song, *"HaAderet VeHeEmunah,"* which is said in Yom Kippur by the Ashkenazim, and on Sabbath (or daily) by the Seferdim.

Chapter Three: Rabbi Abraham Abulafia

1. *Chayay Olam HaBah* (Jewish Theological Seminary, Ms. 2158) p. 4b, quoted in Scholem, *Kitvey Yad BaKabbalah* (Jerusalem, 1930) p. 25; *Otzar Eden HaGanuz,* see below note 102. Also see *Shaarey Tzedek* (Jerusalem, Ms. 8° 148) p. 66b, 67a, quoted in *Kiryat Sefer* 1:135; *Sulam HaAliyah* 10 (Jerusalem, Ms. 8° 334) p. 98a, quoted in *Kitvey Yad BaKabbalah,* p. 228. *Cf.* Psalms 23:5, 45:8, 109:18, 133:2.

2. *Tshuvot Rashbash* 189. See also *Tshuvot Rivash* 157. Compare this to Abulafia's statement in *VeZot LeYehudah,* in Jellinek, *Ginzey Chakhmat HaKabbalah* (Jerusalem, 1969) p. 19.

3. *Metzaref LeChakhmah* 12.

4. This is reproduced below, see notes 105, 112. See chapter 5, notes 2 and 3. The Ramak's master in Kabbalah, Rabbi Shlomo AlKabatz also mentions Abulafia's teachings, see *Brit HaLevi* (Lvov, 1863)p. 13c.

5. *Magen David, Vav* (Munkatch, 1912) p. 13c. See Chapter 5, note 7.

6. *Tshuvot Rashba* 548. See *VeZot LeYehudah,* p. 18.

7. *Bava Batra* 12b.

8. In one manuscript of *Chayay Olam HaBah,* the text is actually written within a series of circles. Jewish Theological Seminary, Ms. 2165.

9. *Minchat Yehudah* on *Maarekhet Elokut,* end of Introduction (Mantua, 1558) p. 3b. This is quoted in full in *Metzaref LeChakhmah loc. cit.* Chayit also quotes the *Tshuvot HaRashba.*

10. *Shem HaGedolim, Sefarim, Chayay Olam HaBah* (*Chet* 76). In *Devash LePhi, Alef* 1, the Chidah writes that the final letters of the patriarch's names, when transformed by the AtBash code, spell out the divine name Shaddai. The source of this is obviously Abulafia's *Chayay Olam HaBah* (Jewish Theological Seminary, Ms. 2158) p. 7a.

11. See *Bet HaMidrash,* Volume III, p. XL, note 6. In the beginning of *Ginat Egoz,* Gikatalia appears to indicate that he was initiated into the mysteries in the year *Keter Torah* (כתר תורה) of his life. In its "minor numerical value" *(Mispar Katan), Keter Torah* has a value of 25, indicating that this is the age when he began. It is also significant to note that the same expression, *Keter Torah,* in a similar context can be found at the beginning of *Sefer HaTzeruf,* which is usually attributed to Abulafia. However, this begins to raise the possibility that this was also written by Gikatalia. Further evidence is from the expression "Know my brother, may God watch you," which is found in the same manner in *Sefer HaTzeruf* and in *Ginat Egoz.* It is very possible that *Sefer HaTzeruf* was written by Gikatalia while under the influence of Abulafia. In many manuscripts, *Sefer HaTzeruf* is followed by *Perush HaNikkud* (cf Paris, Ms. 774, p. 38b), and the system of the latter is not that of Abulafia at all. Regarding the expression *Keter Torah,* see also *Get HaShemot* (Oxford, Ms. 1658) p. 101a.

12. *VeZot LeYehudah,* p. 12.

13. *Sefer HaCheshek* (Jewish Theological Seminary, Ms. 1801) p. 12b.

14. See *Sheva Netivot HaChakhmah* (in Jellinek, *Philosophie und Kabbalah,* Leipzig, 1854) p. 22. He also mentions having mastered *Emunot VeDeyot* by Rabbi Saadia Gaon, *Chovot HaLevavot* by R. Bachya ibn Pakuda, and the works of R. Abraham Ibn Ezra. See *VeZot Le Yehudah* p. 18. He was also familiar with *Tikkun HaMiddot,* by R. Solomon ibn Gabriel. See *Otzar Eden HaGanuz* (Oxford, Ms. Or. 606) p. 44b.

15. This was published in Lyck, 1874.

16. *Otzer Eden HaGanuz* p. 131a. He also mentions *Otiot Rabbi Akiba* there. Among other kabbalah texts that he mastered were *Shimushey Torah* and *Shimushey Tehillim,* Ibid. p. 48b. These two books are mentioned by the Ramban in *Torat HaShem Temimah* (in *Kitvey Ramban,* Jerusalem, 1964) p. 168. *Sefer HaTemunah* is mentioned in *Chayay Olam HaBah* p. 6b. In *Sheva Netivot HaChakhmah,* p. 21, he mentions having mastered *Pirkey Rabbi Ishmael* (the *Hekhelot), Otiot Rabbi Akiba, Sefer HaRazim, Sefer Raziel,* and *Mishmerot HaElyonim VeHaTachtonim.*

17. In *VeZot LeYehudah,* p. 17, he uses the term *Avir Kadmon.* This is a Zoharic term, see *Idra Rabbah, Zohar* 2:135b. *Cf. Etz Chaim, Shaar HaNesirah* 7 (p. 81).

18. *VeZot LaYehudah,* p. 15.

19. *VeZot LaYehudah,* p. 15. These are listed in *Otzar Eden HaGuanuz,* p. 16a, and the list is published in *Bet HaSefer,* Volume III, p. XLII.

20. *Ibid.* This book is existant in manuscript, Paris, Ms. 771, Jewish Theological Seminary, Ms. 835. The entire text is published in G. Scholem, *HaKabbalah shel Sefer HaTemunah VeShel Abraham Abulafia* (Jerusalem, 1965) p. 229ff. He is mentioned in commentary of Moshe Botril on *Sefer Yetzirah* 4:2,

4:4. See Ben Yaakov, *Otzar Sefarim, "Choshen Mishpat"* (Chet 861). Also see below, Chapter 3, notes 53,54. Abulafia also mentions another of his masters, a certain Rabbi Joseph, see *Mafteach HaRayyon* (Vatican, Ms. 291) p. 31b.

21. *Or HaSekhel* 4:4 (Vatican, Ms. 233) p. 53a, *Chayay Olam HaBah,* p. 21b, *Otzar Eden HaGanuz,* p. 131b. The expression, "The Satan was on my right hand," alludes to Zechariah 3:1.

22. *Or HaSekhel* 4:1, p. 41b. On p. 53b, he also states that *Satan* (שטן) has the same numerical value as *Diabolos* (דיאבולוש, Devils), and that this word has the connontation of *Dio Bolos* (Two Balls). This piece is deleted from many manuscripts of *Or HaSekhel.*

23. This introductory poem is in *Ginzey Chakhmat HaKabbalah,* after *Sefer HaOt,* p. 23.

24. Genesis 38:9, *Niddah* 13a.

25. See *Zohar* 1:19a, 1:57a, 1:69a, 1:219b.

26. *Sichot HaRan* 141.

27. *Cf. Or HaSekhel* 4:4 (53b). He also makes several gematriot with the word "Demons," see *Chayay Olam HaBah,* p. 10b (in *Kitvey Yad BaKabbalah,* p. 26); *Otzar Eden HaGanuz,* pp. 20b, 153a.

28. *Otzar Eden HaGanuz,* pp. 21a.

29. *Mafteach HaChakhmot* (Jewish Theological Seminary, Ms. 1686) p. 107b. Here it states explicitly that he is speaking of the Christians. In Ms. Parma De Rossi 141, p. 16b, quoted in Scholem, *Major Trends in Jewish Mysticism* (New York, 1941) p. 379, note 33, this reference is missing.

30. *Sefer HaCheshek,* p. 26b. This is discussed in *HaKabbalah shel Sefer HaTemunah VeShel Abraham Abulafia,* p. 185.

31. See note 42.

32. *Or HaSekhel* 7:3, p. 92a. *Cf. Chayay Olam HaBah* 7b.

33. *VeZot LeYehudah,* p. 19. See *Mafteach HaChakhmot* la, and *Mafteach HaShemot* (Jewish Theological Seminary, Ms. 1897) p. 79a, where this Achitov is counted among Abulafia's closest disciples.

34. The Sambation is a mystical river, beyond which the Ten Lost Tribes were exiled. It is reputed to boil and toss up stones every day but the Sabbath. See *Sanhedrin* 65a, Targum J. on Exodus 34:10, *Yerushalmi* 10:5 (53b), *Bereshit Rabbah* 73:6.

35. It is to him that *VeZot LeYehudah* was written. Since he lived in Barcelona, the place of the Rashba, it is possible that Abulafia meant him to be an adovcate.

36. He is the author of a commentary on *Asara Sefirot HaOmer,* Leipzig, Ms. 12.

37. In *Mafteach HaChokhmot,* Abulafia ennumerates his disciples in Mesina: Saadia ben Yitzchak Segalmaas, Abraham ben Shalom Komti, and Nathan ben Saadia Charar. In Palermo (Paldes?) his disicples were Achitov, son of Yitzchak the physician, his brother, David the physician, Sholomo Chazan, son of Yachin, and Shlomo the physician, son of David Yitzchak. See note 33. *Or HaSekhel* was dedicated to Nathan and Abraham, while *Sefer HaCheshek* was written for Saadia and Yaakov, son of Abraham.

38. Paraphrase of Deuteronomy 28:34.

39. The word *Mikreh* used here also often refers to a noctural emmission.

40. *Otzer Eden HaGanuz*, p. 164a. This is published in full in *Bet HaMidrash*, Volume III, page XL, and in *HaKabbalah Shel Sefer HaTemunah VeShel Abraham Abulfaia*, p. 193.

41. The Hebrew word for "these," *Eleh*, has a numerical value of 41. This might be an allusion to the year 5041, or 1280.

42. Munich, Ms. 285, published in MGWJ 36:558, and in *HaKabbalah Shel Sefer HaTemunah VeShel Abraham Abulafia*, p. 197. He writes that he was captured on the Fast of Gedalia, which is the day after the New Year.

43. Paraphrase of Deuteronomy 28:61.

44. An allusion to Exodus 3:15.

45. Published in Jellinek, *Ginzey Chakhmat HaKabbalah*, pp. 12-14.

46. *VeZot LeYehudah*, p. 17.

47. *Imrey Shefer*, quoted in *HaKabbalah Shel Sefer HaTemunah VeShel Abraham Abulafia*, p. 126.

48. *Sefer HaCheshek*, p. 13b.

49. *Otzar Eden HaGanuz*, pp. 96b, 101a, 125a, *Sefer HaCheshek*, p. 34b, *Chayay Olam HaBah*, p. 10b.

50. *Mafteach HaChakhmot*, p. 1a

51. *Otzar Eden HaGanuz*, p. 25a.

52. *Sheva Netivot HaTorah*, in *Philosophie und Kabbalah*, p. 23. This was written to Abraham ben Shalom Comti, one of his disciples in Messina, to whom *Or HaSekhel* was also dedicated.

53. See above, pp. 68-69.

54. *Sefer HaCheshek*, p. 31a, *VeZot LeYehudah*, p. 15.

55. *Mafteach HaShemot*, p. 58b. *Cf.* Recanti, Bachya, *ad loc.*

56. *Sefer Yetzirah* 6:4. See *Otzar Eden HaGanuz*, p. 81a. *Cf. Sefer Yetzirah* 2:2.

57. Rabbi Yehudah ben Barzilai, Commentary on *Sefer Yetzirah* (Berlin 1885), p. 226. Abulafia virtually quotes this verbatim in *Get HaShemot* (Oxford, Ms. 1658), p. 90a. See also *Otzar Eden HaGanuz*, pp. 16a, 17a. A very similar idea is found in Baruch Targomi's *Maftechot HaKabbalah*, in *HaKabbalah shel Sefer HaTemunah VeShel Abraham Abulafia*, p. 234.

58. *VeZot LeYehudah*, p. 14, 15.

59. *Berakhot* 55a. Betzalel was the one who constructed the Tabernacle under Moses' authority (Exodus 35:30). See Raavad on *Sefer Yetzirah* 6:4. *Cf. Otzar Eden HaGanuz* 26b, *Sefer HaCheshek* 31b. Abulafia discusses the concept of *Tzeruf* in detail in *Or HaSekhel* 7 (p. 89a ff).

60. See *Likutey Amarim* (Tanya), *Shaar HaYichud VeEmunah* 1, *Chesed LeAvraham* 2:11.

61. *Sefer HaCheshek, loc. cit.* See Psalms 12:7, 119:140, Proverbs 30:5.

62. See *Meditation and the Bible* 3:7.

63. *Otzar Eden HaGanuz*, p. 161a. Text is below, p. 84.

64. *Shaarey Tzedek* (Jerusalem, Ms. 8° 148), p. 64b. See *Chayay Olam HaBah*, quoted below, p. 96.

65. These include *Sefer HaTzeruf*, *Shaarey Tzedek*, and *Sulam HaAliyah*. Regarding the authorship of *Sefer HaTzeruf*, see note 11.

66. *Hekhelot Rabatai* 1:1. *Bahir* 88; *Otzar Eden HaGanuz* 8a, *Sefer HaCheshek* 31b, *Sheva Netivot HaTorah* (in *Philosophie und Kabbalah*) p. 11.

67. *Otzar Eden HaGanuz, loc. cit.* Regarding seeing one's own face, see *Shoshan Sodot,* quoted below, p. 109. See note 42.

68. *Otzar Eden HaGanuz,* loc cit.

69. *Sefer Yetzirah* 1:6. *Otzar Eden HaGanuz, loc cit.*

70. *Otzar Eden HaGanuz,* p. 7a, *Gan Na'ul* (Munich, Ms. 58) p. 322b, quoted in *HaKabbalah Shel Sefer HaTemunah VeShel Abraham Abulafia,* p. 153. See below, pages 105, 106, 132.

71. *VeZot LeYehudah* 19a. See note 2.

72. *Brit Menuchah* 2a. *Cf.* Malbim on Genesis 4:26.

73. *Minachot* 43b, *Bahir* 96.

74. *Sefer HaCheshek* 35a.

75. *Mafteach HaChakhmot* 90a.

76. *Sefer HaTzeruf* (Paris, Ms. 774), p. 1a.

77. *Ibid. Cf. Maftechot HaKabbalah,* p. 230. See Chapter 4, note 124.

78. *Sefer HaTzeruf,* p. 1b.

79. See Chapter 2, note 18.

80. *Sefer HaTzeruf,* p. 2b.

81. See *Sefer Yetzirah* 4:3, *Bahir* 70, 117, 154, *Tikuney Zohar* 18 (32a).

82. *Sefer HaTzeruf,* p. 2b.

83. *Ibid.* 3a. *Cf. Bahir* 1.

84. *Ibid.* 4a.

85. *Ibid.* 4b, *Chayay Olam HaBah,* p. 5b. See above, Chapter 1, note 6. Also see *Perush HaAgadot* of Rabbi Azariah of Goronda, Recanti, quoted in Chapter 1, note 10.

86. *Sulam HaAliyah* 10 (Jerusalem, Ms. 8° 334), p. 98a, in *Kitvey Yad BaKabbalah,* p. 228.

87. *Sefer Yetzirah* 1:8. See *Otzar Eden HaGanuz,* p. 9a. See notes 68, 111.

88. *Or HaSekhel* 10:4, p. 125b, *Chayay Olam HaBah,* p. 21a f.

89. *Otzar Eden HaGanuz,* p. 147a. See *HaKabbalah shel Sefer HaTemunah VeShel Abraham Abulafia,* p. 179.

90. *Otzar Eden HaGanuz,* p. 61a, *Or HaSekhel* 1:4 (p. 20a).

91. *Kiddushin* 71a.

92. *Mekhilta* on Exodus 12:1, *Sifri* on Deuteronomy 18:15, *Tanchuma, Bo* 5, *Midrash Tehillim* 132.3, Rashi, Radak, on Jonah 1:3, Ramban on Deuteronomy 18:15, *Zohar* 1:85a, 1:121a, 2:170b, *Emunot VeDeyot* 3:5, *Kuzari* 2:14, Ibn Ezra on Joel 3:1, *Tshuvot Radbaz* 2:842.

93. *Sefer HaCheshek,* p. 32a.

94. *Sefer Yetzirah* 4:12. One multiplies all numbers up to and including the number in question to attain the result. In mathematics, this is called a factorial.

95. *Or HaSekhel* 7:1, p. 90a, *Sulam HaAliyah* 1. See *Pardes Rimonim, Shaar HaTzeruf* 1.

96. *Sefer HaCheshek,* p. 20b; *Or HaSekhel* 6:1, p. 79a.

97. *Otzar Eden HaGanuz,* Bodleian Library, Oxford, Ms. Or. 606, pp. 160-162. I would like to acknowledge the Curators of the Bodleian Library for permission to reproduce this portion of their manuscript.

98. See *Ibid.* p. 30b, where this is discussed at length.

99. The word *tzeruf* usually means to purify. Here Abulafia uses it in the same sense as the Talmud uses it with regard to Betzalel. See notes 59, 61.

100. See *Moreh Nevuchim* 2:30, Ramban on Genesis 1:2. In many places the *Zohar* speaks of a *Butzina DeKardenita,* and according to many commentaries, this means "the Lamp of Darkness," *Cf.* HaGra on *Tikuney Zohar* 5 (Vilna, 1867) p. 20c. Also see *Shaarey Kedushah* 3:2, where the author speaks of a "Light of Darkness."

101. The word *Otiot* here is normally translated as "things to come," from the root *Ata* (אתא), meaning to "come." Usually, however, the word means letters, although it is never found to have this meaning in the Bible.

102. See note 1.

103. See *Rosh HaShanah* 21b, *Zohar* 2:115a, 3:216a.

104. See *Bahir* 139, 140, 142.

105. *Or HaSekhel* 8:3, p. 108b f., quoted in *Pardes Rimonim* 21:1. It is also quoted in *Sulam HaAliyah* 9, p. 95a ff, quoted in *Kiryat Sefer* 22:167 ff. The Ramak writes regarding Abulafia's teaching, "This is either a direct tradition, given over from mouth to mouth, or else it was revealed by a *Maggid* (Angelic Spokesman)."

106. This *Sefer HaNikkud* is mentioned in the commentary of Moshe Botril on *Sefer Yetzirah* 1:1 (14b). He is also cited as the author of a book called *HaPardes.*

107. See *Or Yakar* on Zohar, *Shir HaShirim* (Jerusalem, Ms. 4° 74), quoted in *Kitvey Yad BaKabbalah,* p. 232. Here, the Ramak states, "The method of pronouncing the Name is found in the book *Or HaSekhel* by Abraham Abulafia, and this method is the secret of *Sefer Yetzirah.*" See note 109.

108. See *Minchat Yehudah* on *Maarekhet Elokut* 14, p. 197b. *Cf Pardes Rimonim* 21:2.

109. See *Emek HaMelekh* (Amsterdam, 1653) p. 9c. See note 107, Chapter 7, note 1.

110. Cf. Genesis 17:3, Joshua 5:14.

111. See note 87.

112. See note 105. See *Shoshan Sodot,* p. 72b.

113. *Bahir* 110, *Zohar* 2:270. *Cf. Sefer Hakanah* (Cracow, 1894) p. 88a, *Pardes Rimonim* 21:5.

114. *Pesikta Zutrata* on Exodus 14:21, Rashi, *Succah* 45a, "*Ani.*"

115. The same system is found in *Shaar HaKavanot* (Lvov, 1856), p. 18a. Also see *Shaar HaKavanot,* p. 89 *Adam Yashar* (Lvov, 5616) p. 5b, *Shmirot U'Segulot Niflaot* (New York, 1968) 4b. Also see *Shemirah LeChaim* (Bagdad, 1898), *Seder Pitum HaKetores* (Prague, 1615). *Cf. Shnei Luchot HaBrit* (Jerusalem, 1960), Volume 2, page 141b.

116. Paraphrase of Amos 4:12.

117. Paraphrase of Isaiah 48:17, Psalms 94:10.

118. Metatron adds up to 314, and adding six for the six letters of the word, this yields 320.

119. This two together add up to 314, like Metatron.

120. This verse refers to Metatron, *Sanhedrin* 38b.

121. See Rashi on Exodus 23:21.

122. See *Or HaSekhel,* quoted above, page 91.

123. See *Sefer HaCheshek,* p. 4b, where the author writes that the name does not contain Gimel, since the numerical value of this letter is three, and

the essence of this name is threefold. It is therefore not necessary to also include the letter itself. *Cf. Magalah Amukot* 179.

124. *Eduyot* 2:10, *Shabbat* 152b, *Rosh HaShanah* 17a.

125. Cf. Exodus 25:18.

126. These are the only places in the Torah where the verse *"Lo TeChayah"*—"Do not let live," is found.

127. Paraphrase of *Yerushalmi, Peah* 1:1, from Deuteronomy 32:47.

128. This is taken from Jewish Theological Seminary, Ms. 2158, pp. 19a ff. I would like to acknowledge the Jewish Seminary of America for permission to publish portions of their manuscript in translation. Parts of this section have already been published in the original in Jellinek, *Philosophie und Kabbalah*, pp. 44, 45; *Kitvey Yad BaKabbalah*, p. 27; *HaKabbalah shel Sefer HaTemunah VeShel Abraham Abulafia*, p. 210 ff. A small part is translated in Scholem, *Major Trends in Jewish Mysticism*, p. 136 ff.

129. Four manuscripts of this are known, Jerusalem, Ms. 8° 148, Columbia University, Ms. X 893 - Sh. 43, Leiden, Ms. Warner 24, 2; British Museum, Ms. Gaster 954. Only the first two manuscripts contain the autobiographical sketch. See *Kitvey Yad BaKabbalah*, p. 34, *Kiryat Sefer* 1:127 ff.

130. It should be compared with *Or HaSekhel* and *Sefer HaTzeruf*.

131. Scholem, *Major Trends in Jewish Mysticism*, p. 147 ff.

132. *Shaarey Tzedek* (Jerusalem, Ms. 8° 148), p. 59b; quoted in *Kiryat Sefer*. See Chapter 7, note 99.

133. Rabbi Abraham Maimonides also speaks about the Moslem Sufis, see *Sefer HaMaspik LeOvdey HaShem*, p. 185.

134. *Shaarey Tzedek*, pp. 60a, 60b.

135. See Chapter 4, note 61.

136. *Shaarey Tzdek*, p. 62b, 63a.

137. See Chapter 5, note 56.

138. See note 1.

139. *Shoshan Sodot* (Koretz, 1784) p. 69b. A manuscript version has been published by G. Scholem, MGWJ 77:287. The author of *Shoshan Sodot* is R. Moshe ben Yaakov of Kiev (1449-1518).

140. Most probably Nathan ben Saadia Charar of Mesina, to whom *Or HaSekhel* was dedicated. See note 37.

141. *Bereshit Rabbah* 27:1.

142. Ibn Ezra on Daniel 10:21. The Talmud likewise says that God spoke "with the voice of Moses," See *Berakhot* 45a, *Midrash Tehillim* 18:29, 24:11, *BaMidbar Rabbah* 14:21, *Tanchuma, Ki Tisa* 15. This is discussed in *Chayay Olam HaBah*, p. 1b. This is also discussed by R. Isaac of Acco, see *Otzar Chaim*, p. 163a. See Chapter 6, note 44.

143. See Recanti, beginning of *VaYera*.

144. R. Moshe of Narbonne, *Commentary on Moreh Nevuchim* 1:46 (Vienna, 1852) p. 5a.

145. He is the author of the *Malechet Shlemah* on the Mishnah. This is found in the Vilna, Rom, edition of the Mishnah, at the beginning of *Taharos* (with *Yachin U'Boaz)*.

146. The name of this commentary is *Yesod Mishnah Torah*, British Museum, Ms. Add. 19.783, Jewish Theological Seminary, Ms. Deinard 398.

147. See *Shemen Sason* (Jerusalem, 1869) Volume I, p. 6a. Also see *Kitvey Yad BaKabbalah,* p. 33, *Kiryat Sefer* 2:272.

148. The important library manuscripts are Jerusalem, Ms. 8° 334, discussed in *Kitvey Yad BaKabbalah,* p. 32. Another manuscript is Jerusalem, Ms. 8° 1302, and Jewish Theological Seminary, Ms. 1816, which are actually two halves of the same manuscript. See Marx, PAAJR 4:161. The introduction and table of contents were published in *Kiryat Sefer* 2:138-141; chapters 7 to 9, in *Kiryat Sefer* 22:161 ff., and chapter 10 in *Kitvey Yad BaKabbalah,* pp. 79a-100b.

149. *Sulam HaAliyah* 9 (Jerusalem, Ms. 8° 1302) p. 13b. See Chapter 4, note 69.

150. *Sulam HaAliyah* 3 (Jewish Theological Seminary, Ms. 1816) p. 10b.

151. *Sulam HaAliyah* 10 (Jerusalem, Ms. 8° 334), in *Kitvey Yad BaKabbalah,* pp. 229, 230.

152. *Pardes Rimonim* 30.

153. See *Chayay Olam HaBah,* p. 9b, beggining of *Sefer HaTzeruf.*

154. *Sulam HaAliyah* 8 (Jerusalem, Ms. 8° 1302) p. 8b.

155. Ibid. Chapter 10, in *Kitvey Yad BaKabbalah,* p. 226.

156. *Sefer HaCheshek,* p. 38a.

157. *Sulam HaAliyah* 7 (Jerusalem, Ms. 8° 1302), p. 8a. *Cf. Sefer HaCheshek,* p. 22a. Also see *Shaarey Tzedek,* p. 73b, with regards to the Urim and Thumim.

159. *Sulam HaAliyah* 9, p. 16a.

160. *Ketubot* 111a. The entire first section of *VaYoel Moshe* discusses this.

161. *Sulam HaAliyah* 9, p. 16b.

162. *Ibid.* See Chapter 4, note 28.

Chapter Four: Other Early Schools

1. Commentary to *Yad, Lulav* 8:5, *Bet HaBechirah* 6:14, Introduction to commentary on *Eduyyot.* Also see introduction to *Sefer HaEshkol* (Halberstadt, 1868) p. xv. *Cf. Shem HaGedolim, Alef* 10. See below, Chapter 6, notes 13, 14.

2. *Bachya* on *Genesis* 32:10. See *Avodat HaKodesh* 2:13 (33d), 3:18 (81b), *Shomer Emunim (HaKadmon),* Introduction 2, #2, *Metzaref LeChakhmah* 13, *Minchat Yehudah* on *Maarekhet Elokut* 14 (198b). See Chapter 6, note 12.

3. See note 6.

4. The lights called *Zohar, Bahir,* and *Tov* are alluded to in the *Bahir* 147. See note 161 in my translation.

5. Regarding the four colors of the fire, see *Zohar Chadash* 39b, *Tikuney Zohar* 31 (50a). Also see *Zohar* 1:41b, 3:33b, *Tikuney Zohar* 6 (22a), 19 (41a).

6. This is taken from Jewish Theological Seminary, Ms. 1822:9, p. 43a,b. I would like to acknowledge the Jewish Theological Seminary for granting me permission to publish portions of their manuscript in translation. This is also found in Florence, Ms. 41, p. 222a,b; Vatican, Ms. 31, p. 37; Munich, Ms. 240:8; British Museum, Ms. 777:4; Perma, Ms. 86:7. It is also quoted in the Fourth Part of *Shaarey Kedushah,* (British Museum, Ms. 749) p. 18b. The text has been published, together with a German translation by G. Scholem, MGWJ 78:511 (1934).

7. *Cf.* Ezekiel 1:4,27, Proverbs 4:18. See *Hekhalot Rabatai* 21, quoted above, page (65).

8. *Cf.* Genesis 1:4. This is spoken of as the light stored away for the righteous in the Future World.

9. *Cf.* Job 37:21; *Bahir* 1.

10. See Ezekiel 8:2, Daniel 12:3. *Cf. Kitvey Yad BaKabbalah,* p. 209.

11. The reading in *Shaarey Kedushah* is *MeUkam* (מעוקם), meaning "crooked." Other manuscripts, however, have the reading *Melkaro* (מעקרו), meaning, "from the principle path."

12. These words are only in *Shaarey Kedushah.*

13. This is an important concept discussed at length among later Kabbalists, see *Avodat HaKodesh, Avodah* 10, *Toldot Yaakov Yosef, Sh'lach,* p. 133b; *Maggid Devarav LeYaakov* (Jerusalem, 1971) #66, 159; *Likutim Yekarim* (Jerusalem, 1974) #224, *Tzavaat HaRivash* (Kehot, New York, 1975) #73. *Cf. Midrash Tehillim* 20:1.

14. Wisdom, Understanding and Knowledge *(Chakhmah, Binah, Daat),* are the upper three Sefirot. The word *Havayot* (הוית) can mean "existences," but here it means Tetragrammatons, since the word *Havaya* (הויה) is often used for the Tetragrammaton. In the very next quotation in *Shaarey Kedushah* (p. 19b), a system is presented, where each of these "Lights" parallels the Tetragrammaton with different vowel points. The table of correspondence between the Lights and Sefirot is based on this. See p. 119.

15. *Mishnah, Berakhot* 5:1 (30b). The discussion here is very similar to that found in *Sefer Cheredim, Tshuvah* 3 (Jerusalem, 1958) p. 215. See above, Chapter 2, note 9.

16. *Berakhot* 32b.

17. Most manuscripts end here. *Shaarey Kedushah* includes an additional section regarding how to complete this.

18. Paraphrase of Daniel 12:3.

19. *Cf. BaMidbar Rabbah* 12:8, *Zohar* 2:241a. See note 5.

20. The term *Marot Tzavaot* occurs in Exodus 38:8.

21. See Chapter 2, note 20.

22. Thus, even though the prophets saw through a "dull glass," still what they saw was actually the Glory itself. See *Derekh HaShem* 3:3:5.

23. This is the "light that receives Zohar."

24. *Shekkel HaKodesh* (London, 1911) pp. 123,124.

25. See *Maftechot HaKabbalah* (in *HaKabbalah shel Sefer HaTemunah VeShel Abraham Abulafia)* p. 230.

26. *Shaarey Kedushah,* Part Four, p. 20a. The two selections are from *Shaarey Orah,* Chapter 3,4, p. 37b and Chapter 9, p. 96a.

27. See above, pages 105, 106.

28. See Chapter 3, note 162.

29. *Shaarey Orah,* Introduction (Warsaw, 1883) p. 1a. In a number of places, I have ammended the text according to Oxford, Ms. 1658, p. 165 ff., where the reading clarifies numerous difficult passages.

30. Both Adonoy (אדני) and *Hekhal* (היכל), meaning "palace" having the numerical value of 65.

31. *Shaarey Orah* 1, p. 4b. See above, Chapter 3, notes 113,114.
32. *Ketubot* 111b.
33. *Ibid.* The allusion is to Deuteronomy 4:24.
34. *Shaarey Orah* 1, p. 14b.
35. This is the end of the prayer *Yishtabach* in the morning service.
36. *Shaarey Orah* 2, p. 18a.
37. *Moed Katan* 28a. *Cf. Zohar* 1:181a, 2:5a, 3:25a, 216b, 292b.
38. *Tikuney Zohar* 8b. A similar expression is found in *Pesikta,* end of 31 (p. 201a); *Otiot DeRabbi Akiba, Yud* (Bet HaMidrash, volume 3, p. 32; *Batey Midrashot,* volume 2, p. 372.
39. *Shaarey Orah* 3,4, p. 39b. This is quoted from *Shaarey Kedushah.*
40. *Ibid.* 5, p. 40b.
41. *Ibid.* 42b.
42. *Ibid.* 46a.
43. *Ibid.* 67b.
44. *Sefer Yetzirah* 1:7.
45. *Shaarey Orah* 5, p. 68b.
46. *Ibid.* 8, p. 84b.
47. *Ibid.* 9, p. 93a.
48. *Ibid.* 96a. This is quoted in *Shaarey Kedushah.* See above, Chapter 2, note 39.
49. See *Shem HaGedolim, Yud* 353; *Midbar Kadmut, Chakhmah* #11.
50. *Meirat Eynayim* (Jerusalem, 1979), p. 318. Also see *Otzar Yisrael* 2:285a.
51. *Otzar Chaim* (Moscow, Ms. Guenzburg #775) p. 183a.
52. Moscow, Ms. Guenzburg #775, 32nd (unnumbered folio at beginning) side b. (P. 64 in my manuscript). On (unnumbered) p. 32a, these are attributed to R. Nohaniel Gaon, but no record of such a Gaon exists. See *Toldot Adam* #158, where these seals are also drawn, and attributed to the Ramban. They are also found in *Shoshan Yesod Olam* (Sasoon, Ms. 290) pp. 268, 322, 460.
53. Ms. Guenzburg, p. 32b (unnumbered).
54. *Meirat Eynayim,* p. 240. He is also mentioned in commentary of R. Moshe Botril on *Sefer Yetzirah* 4:2, 4:4. See *Otzar Sefarim, "Choshen Mishpat" (Chet* 861).
55. *Otzar Chaim,* p. 94a. Regarding Abulafia, see above, chapter 3, note 93.
56. *Otzar Chaim,* p. 5b. See *Chayay Olam HaBah,* p. 22b.
57. *Otzar Chaim,* p. 16b. See *Sefer HaCheshek,* p. 10b.
58. *Otzar Chaim,* p. 131b. See *Chayay Olam HaBah, p. 18b, quoted above, page 000.*
59. *Otzar Chaim,* p. 123b. See *Shaarey Tzedek,* p. 58a.
60. See Chapter 3, note 134.
61. *Otzar Chaim,* p. 36a. *Cf. Shoshan Yesod Olam* #545, p. 241.
62. See Chapter 3, note 155.
63. See note 83.
64. *Megillah* 28a. This is called *Maavir al Midotav* in the Talmud.
65. *Kiddushin* 71a. Elijah says that he only reveals himself to such a person, see *Mesechta Kallah Rabatai,* end of Chapter 5; *Shaarey Kedushah,* Part Four, p. 15a, *Reshit Chakhmah, Shaar HaAnavah* 3 (p. 220a).

66. *Taanit* 25a.
67. *Yoma* 23a. See below, note 80.
68. *Shaarey Kedushah,* Part Four, p. 17a. See note 78.
69. *Otzar Chaim,* pp. 128a, 136a.
70. See note 49.
71. *Meirat Eynayim* is found in a number of manuscripts, notably Oxford, Ms. 1619, Munich, Ms. 14, and it was published in Jerusalem, 1979. The most complete manuscript of *Otzar Chaim* is Moscow, Ms. Guenzburg 775. Selections from it are in *Leket Shoshanim,* Neubauer, Cat. no. 1911, and many extracts are in such manuscripts as Sasoon, Ms. 919, and Adler, Ms. 1589.
72. The commentary on *Sefer Yetzirah* is in Jerusalem, Ms. 8° 404, pp. 15b-33a, and in British Museum, Ms. Gaster 956, pp. 13a-16a. It has been published by G. Scholem in *Kiryat Sefer* 31:379 ff (1956). It is part of a collection called *Avney Zikaron,* p. 83; *Kiryat Sefer* 6:259-276 (1930), 7:457-465 (1931). Also see British Museum, Ms. Gaster 720. The commentary on *Pirkey Rabbi Eliezer* is found in Jewish Theological Seminary, Ms. Enelow 2316, and in translation into Arabic in the commentary of R. Judah ben Nissim ibn Malka on *Pirkey Rabbi Eliezer,* Sasoon, Ms. 919b. It has been published in *Revieu Etudes Juifs* (REJ) 115:27:71 (1956).
73. *Otzar Chaim,* 22a, 49b, 57a.
74. *Ibid.* 22a.
75. This piece is quoted in MGWJ 78:500.
76. See Chapter 1, note 3, Chapter 6, note 83.
77. This Rabbi Abner may have been the disciple of the Ramban mentioned in *Emek HaMelekh,* p. 4a, Seder HaDorot 4954.
78. *Meir Eynayim, Ekev* (Munich, Ms. 14) p. 140b. This has been published by Jellinek in *Philosophie und Kabbalah,* p. 48. It is also quoted in the Fourth Part of *Shaarey Kedushah,* see note 68.
79. *Reshit Chakhmah, Ahavah* 3 (p. 59a). Also quoted in Fourth Part of *Shaarey Kedushah,* p. 15a. *Cf. Reshit Chakhmah, Ahavah* 10 (p. 87d).
80. See note 67.
81. *Reshit Chakhmah, Anavah,* 3 (119d). Also quoted in Fourth Part of *Shaarey Kedushah,* p. 15a.
82. Ibid. Also see *Anavah* 5 (228b).
83. *Chovot HaLevavot, Shaar Yichud HaMaaseh* 4 (Warsaw, 1875) p. 12a.
84. *Maggid Mesharim, BeShalach* (Jerusalem, 1960) p. 57a.
85. *Likkutim Yekarim* #179, *Keter Shem Tov* 220, *Tzavaat HaRivash* 2; *Or Torah* on Psalm 16:8 (Kehot, New York, 1974) p. 67a. *Cf.* Hirsch on Psalms 119:30, 131:2.
86. Alluding to Zechariah 3:7. This refers to the angels.
87. *Reshit Chakhmah, Anavah* 3 (p. 222b).
88. It is thus quoted in *Moshal HaKadmoni* by R. Isaac ibn Abu Saulah, published in many editions. It is also found in *Otzar HaKavod* by R. Todros Abulafia, see *Kadmut Sefer HaZohar* 1:3. See *Tarbitz* 3:181-183 (1932), *Kiryat Sefer* 6:109-118 (1930).
89. *Shem HaGedolim, Sefarim, Zayin* 8.
90. *Zohar* 2:9b.
91. *Sefer HaYuchesin* (Constantinople, 1510) p. 42. The entire text is quoted

in Tishbi, *Mishnat HaZohar* (Jerusalem, 1971), Volume 1, p. 29. Also see *Sefer Yuchasin HaShalem* (London-Edinberg, 1857) pp. 88, 89; *Otzar HaSefarim, Zayin* 61; *Jewish Quarterly Review* (JQR) 4:361-368 (1892).

92. See Rabbi David Luria, *Kadmut Sefer HaZohar* 1 (New York, 1951) p. 27 ff.

93. *Otzar Chaim*, p. 95a.

94. *Ibid.* 65b, 66a.

95. *Ibid.* 60a, 102a, 215a. Also see *Ibid.* 183a, and compare this to Jewish Theological Seminary, Ms. Adler 1589, p. 123b, quoted in Scholem, *Major Trends in Jewish Mysticism*, p. 394, note 127.

96. See note 73.

97. This most probably refers to the *Otzar Chaim*, which, according to this, was written in the year 5096 (1336). Toward the end of the book (p. 238b), the author speaks of a revelation that came to him on a Sabbath, 16 Elul, when the portion *Ki Tavo* was read. Such a Sabbath did occur on 16 Elul in the year 5096!

98. Paraphrase of Psalm 36:10.

99. See note 93.

100. Paraphrase of *Betza* 27a, *Bava Batra* 31b, *Avodah Zarah* 7b.

101. Rabbi Todros HaLevi [Abulafia] was the author of the *Otzar HaKavod*. He often quotes the *Zohar*, see note 88.

102. *Moreh Nevuchim* 1:42.

103. *Otzar Eden HaGanuz*, p. 147 ff. See *HaKabbalah Shel Sefer HaTemunah VeShel Abraham Abulafia*, p. 177 ff.

104. See *Otzar Chaim*, pp. 116b, 139a, 140b.

105. See *Shivechey R. Chaim Vital (Sefer Chazyonot)* (Brooklyn, 1971) pp. 6, 11, 23, etc.

106. See *Sheirit Yosef*, p. 45a. Also see *Evven HaShoham*, p. 177b.

107. See *Shoshan Yesod Olam* #538 (p. 239), #743 (p. 283), #1726 (p. 495), #1744 (p. 502). See *Temirin* 1:204.

108. *Shaarey Kedushah* 3:6 (quoted above, p. 40); *Toldot Yaakov Yosef, Schlach*, p. 133b.

109. *Shoshan Yesod Olam* #715 (p. 280).

110. *Ibid.* #381 (p. 156). This is erased in the text, but it can be found in the table of contents.

111. *Ibid.* #467 (p. 205). Also see #1109 (p. 427), #582 (p. 264).

112. *Ibid.* #1004 (p. 382), #1017 (p. 386).

113. *Charba DeMoshe (The Sword of Moses)* was published by M. Gaster (London, 1896). *Sefer Hakasdim* was also published by Gaster as "Wisdom of the Chaldeans, and old Hebrew Astrological Text," in the *Procedings of the Society of Biblical Archeology* 22:329-351 (December, 1900). *Sefer HaRazim* was published in Jerusalem, 1967. Another text, *Shimusha Rabbah* has been published by G. Scholem, Tarbitz 16:197-203 (1945). See *Temirin* 1:202, 203.

114. This has been published in a number of editions, most notably Zolkieve, 1720; Lvov, 1805; Willhelmsdorf, 1734. Similar books include *Amtachot Binyamin*, and *Refua VeChaim*.

115. Sasson, Ms. 190. This is described in detail in Meir Benayahu, *Temirin* 1:187-269, where the entire table of contents is also published. Also see Sasoon Collection, *Descriptive Catalogue* #290 (1932) pp. 443-446; *Catalogue*,

Sotheby and Co., Zurich, November 5, 1975, #1 (where this manuscript is labeled as *Charba DeMoshe).* The following owners are recorded: David ben Mehalel (p. 21), Yechiel ben Mehalalel (p. 21), Yechiel ben Shalom ben Mehalelel (p. 21), Eliahu ben Yosef (p. 59), Shabbatai Zvi (p. 522), Aaron Altaras (pp. 1, 437). See below, Chapter 7, note 13.

116. See *Temirin* 1:197. A list is found in Sotheby's Catelogue.

117. See *Ta'am Zekenim* (Frankford a Mein, 1855) p. 54-56, Commentary on *Sefer Yetzirah* of R. Yehudah of Barcelona, p. 104; Ibn Ezra on Exodus 14:19, 28:9; Bachya on Deuteronomy 29:28; R. Moshe Botril, Commentary on *Sefer Yetzirah* 4:3; *Brit Menuchah* (Warsaw, 1889) pp. 49d, 55a; *Raziel HaMalach* (Amsterdam, 1701) pp. 31c, 40a; *Lekutey HaShas MeHaAri* (1783) p. 29a. See Reuven Margolies, *She'eLot U'Tshuvot Min HaShamayim* (Jerusalem, 1957) p. 15 ff. See *Minachot* 67a; *Bava Metzia* 107b, Rabenu Chananel, *Shita Mekubetzet ad loc., Arukh, Davar* 2; *Yerushalmi, Kelayim* 9:3.

118. See *Tshuvot MaBit* 246, *Tshuvot Mahari BeRab* 2:202, *Korey HaDorot* (Berlin, 1865) pp. 36b, 37a. He might also be identified with the Joseph Tzayag mentioned in *Shivechey R. Chiam Vital,* p. 17, since the Gimel and Chet can easily be interchanged. Note that here, Joseph Tzayag is mentioned before R. Joseph Caro, and hence may be said to have been a greater Kabbalist. Also see S. Assaf, *Kiryat Sefer* 11:492 (1935), C. Hirschensohn, *HaMisderonah* 1:192-201, 1:255-259; Frumkin-Rivlin, *Toldot Chakhamey Yerushalayim* (1929) 1:67-68; Shlomo A. Rozanis, *Divrey Yemey Yisrael BeTogarma* (Husyatin, 1911) Volume 2, p. 124; M. Benayahu, *Sefunot* 7:103-117 (1963).

119. *Avkat Rochel* 10, 54, 58, 115, 139, 186, 188, 189.

120. *Evven HaShoham* is extant in Jerusalem, Ms. 8° 416, see *Kitvey Yad BaKabbalah,* p. 90. According to a note at the end of the manuscript, it was completed in 5298 (1538). *Tzaror HaChayim* is a commentary on the *Otzar HaKavod* of R. Todros Abulafia, and is extant in London, Jews College, Ms. 318. On page 85a of the manuscript, there is an indication that it was written in 5299 (1539). *Evven HaShoham* is mentioned in this second manuscript on pp. 12a, 57b, see *Kitvey Yad BaKabbalah.*

121. This is extant in Vienna, Ms. 260; see A.Z. Schwarz, *Die hebraeischen Handschriften in Oesterreich* (1931), 203, #260. It is also mentioned in *Shem HaGedolim, Yud* 163; *Midbar Kadmut, Ch'khmah* 11 (as the book written in 5309); J. Emden, *Torat HaKenaot* (Lemberg, 1870) p. 69. At the end of the manuscript there is a note that it was completed on 14 Sivan, 5309 (1549).

122. See *Tzaror HaChaim,* p. 63b. This might be the book mentioned in the beginning of *Evven HaShoham,* p. 2a, that had previously been given to Abraham Castro.

123. See Mordechai Margolies, *Encyclopedia LeToldot Gedoley Yisrael* (Tel Aviv) Volume 3, page 798.

124. *Evven HaShoham,* p. 177b, *Sheirit Yosef,* p. 168a, *Tzaror HaChaim,* p. 10a. See Chapter 3, note 77.

125. *Tzaror HaChaim,* p. 77a; *Or HaSekhel* 6:2, p. 79a. Regarding a Gematria interpretation of the word *HaSneh,* see *Evven HaShoham,* p. 10b, and compare this to *Sefer HaCheshek* p. 12a. *Cf. Sheirit Yosef,* p. 169b.

126. *Evven HaShoham,* pp. 3b, 4a, where there are clear quotations from the *Bahir,* even though the book itself is not mentioned.

127. *Tzaror HaChaim,* p. 38a.

128. See *Zohar* 2:74b, *Tikuney Zohar* 132b, *Midbar Kadmut, Chakhmah* 13; R. Yisrael ben Aaron, *Or Yisrael* (Frankfort de Adar, 1702). *Cf. Kitvey Yad BaKabbalah.* See Chapter 6, note 16.

129. See Exodus 28:20, Targum J. *ad loc., Sh'mot Rabbah* 25:11, *BaMidbar Rabbah* 2:7.

130. A good example of this involves the prophetic position, see below.

131. *Evven HaShoham,* p. 12a. Cf. Bachya on Leviticus 8:23; *Sheveiley Emunah* 4.

132. *Cf. Sefer Yetzirah* 2:3. See below, p. 242.

133. *Evven HaShoham,* p. 5a.

134. *Ibid,* p. 2b.

135. This may be alluded to in Exodus 33:22,23. See *Shaarey Tzedek,* p. 57b, 58a, that *Kapai* (כפי), "may hand," has the numerical value of *Dimyon* (דמיון), meaning an "image."

136. *Evven HaShoham,* p. 33a ff., *Sheirit Yosef,* p. 18a ff. See especially *Evven HaShoham,* p. 119b, 137b ff. In a marginal note in *Sheirit Yosef loc cit.* there appears to be a marginal note telling how this can be used practically. Compare *Shoshan Yesod Olam* #344 (p. 147), #505 (p. 221, 222), #1730 (p. 499), #1736 (p. 501); *Toldot Adam* #29, 80, 109, 131. A 4×4 magic square is found at the end of *Shaar Ruach HaKodesh.*

137. *Shnei Luchot HaBrit, Mesechta Shavuot* (Lvov, 1860), Volume 2, p. 98b.

138. *Evven HaShoham,* p. 119b. Note that the order of the numbers is from left to right, rather than from right to left as one would expect in Hebrew.

139. They are discussed in the words of Abbot John Trithemius (1462-1516), Pietro d'Abano, Henry Cornelius, and Agrippa von Nettenscheim (1468-1535). They are also used in *The Magus* by Francis Barrett. Also see Israel Regardie, *How to Make and Use Talismans.* For a mathematical discussion, see W.S. Andrews, *Magic Squares and Cubes* (Open Court, 1917).

140. *Evven HaShoham,* p. 29ff, *Sheirit Yosef,* p. 46a ff.

141. Thus a tenth order square is presented in *Evven HaShoham,* p. 33a, and a corrected version is on p. 111b. In *Sheirit Yosef,* p. 46a, the corrected version is found.

142. *Sheirit Yosef,* p. 140a.

143. *Evven HaShoham,* p. 33b.

144. *Ibid.* p. 42a.

145. See below, p. 275.

146. *Evven HaShoham,* p. 1b,2a. Regarding Ben Zoma, see above p. 240.

147. See above, p. 26.

148. *Evven HaShoham,* p. 1b. "Vision and not allegory" is a paraphrase of Numbers 12:8.

149. *Sheirit Yosef,* p. 168a.

Chapter Five: Safed

1. *Elemah Rabatai* 1:1:16 (Lvov, 1881) p. 6b.
2. See Chapter 3, notes 4, 105.

3. *Ibid.* note 107.

4. *Sefer Gerushin* was published in Venice, 1600; Sklov, 1796, Jerusalem, 1962. It is discussed in his *Or Ne'erav* 5:2.

5. *Michtav Masa* 2, in *Otzar Masaot* (New York, 1927) p. 125.

6. *Sefer Cheredim* 8 (Jerusalem, 1958) p. 49.

7. See Chapter 3, note 5.

8. *Reshit Chakhmah, Kedushah* 7 (154c).

9. *Nesiyat David HaReuveni* 6, in *Otzar Hasaot,* p. 154a.

10. See *Shaarey Kedushah* 3:6 (Bnei Brak, 1967) p. 109.

11. See *Maggid Mesharim, Toldot,* p. 21a. This was said on a Sabbath, 4 Kislev. The only year that 4 Kislev occured on a Sabbath, however, was in 1537 (5277).

12. *Yad, Sanhedrin* 4:11; Commentary on *Sanhedrin* 1:3, *Bekhorot* 4:3.

13. This is mentioned a number of times in the *Pardes Rimonim,* for example 4:7 (Munkatch, 1906) p. 21a. It is currently being printed. A summary of this commentary is found in *Or HaChamah.*

14. See Chapter 4, note 33. Following this is the section quoted above, on page 145.

15. Paraphrase of Zechariah 3:6.

16. *Maggid Mesharim, BaShalach,* 15 Shevat, p. 56c.

17. *Pardes Rimonim* 2:6 (p. 10a).

18. See note 33.

19. See *Evven HaShoham,* p. 93a. In *Tzaror HaChaim,* p. 25a, Tzayach apparently describes how to climb the Sefirot through the colors.

20. *Pardes Rimonim, Shaar Mahut VaHanhagah* 8.

21. *Cf. Mekhilta* on Exodus 19:18, *Tanchuma, Yitro* 13. See *Etz Chaim, Shaar AChaP* 2.

22. *Cf. Negaim* 1:1.

23. *Berakhot* 59a, *Rosh HaShanah* 26a.

24. The word *Ez* (עז) meaning goat has the same letters as *Az* meaning strong or brazen. This alludes to judgement, see *Pardes Rimonim* 23:16.

25. See *Sefer Chasidim* 205, 206; Introduction to *Shaarey Kedushah.*

26. See Exodus 28:17 ff.

27. The Source of Souls is the Sefirah of Malkhut-Kingship, while the Countenance is Tiferet-Beauty (Zer Anpin).

28. This might refer to meditating on a Mishnah, see note 51.

29. This is quoted in Bachya *ad loc.*, but it is not in our editions. Regarding the strong prohibitions against worshipping the Sefirot, see *Tshuvot Rivash* 157, *Elemah Rabatai* 1:1:2; Radbaz, *Metzudot David* 2; *Shomer Emunim (HaKadmon)* 2:64,65; *Kisey Melekh* on *Tikkuney Zohar* 22 (p. 94, #50). The *Tshuvot HaRivash* is found in the manuscript of *Otzar Chaim,* p. 121, but it is obviously a later insertion, since the Rivash (Rabbi Isaac ben Sheshet Barafat: 1326-1408) lived after R. Isaac of Acco. The *Sifri* is an ancient Midrash, written a generation after the Mishnah.

30. The question regarding how such a term as Ain Sof can be used is discussed by the author in *Pardes Rimonim* 3:1.

31. See *Zohar* 2:42b. *Tikuney Zohar* 17a.

32. *Tikuney Zohar,* Introduction 3a (#50 in Sulam).

33. *Pardes Rimonim* 19. See *Tikuney Zohar* 70 (126a).

34. *Shivechey R. Chaim Vital* (Brooklyn, 1971) p. 13.

35. *Shivechey HaAri* (Warsaw, 1875) p. 9a.

36. *Ibid.* 3a. Cf. *Shaar HaGilgulim* (Ashlag Ed., Tel Aviv, 1963) p. 125.

37. *Tshuvot R. Menachem Azariah Fano #38.* Here we see that the surname Vital also was used by the father, and was not merely a Latinization of Chaim, which means "life."

38. See *Shivechey R. Chaim Vita,* pp. 6, 18, 21, 25, 37.

39. *Ibid.* p. 30. *Shaar HaGilgulim,* p. 127.

40. *Shem HaGedolim, Chet* 21.

41. In Part Four of *Shaarey Kedushah* (p. 15b), Rabbi Eliahu di Vidas is cited as the author of *Reshit Chokhmah.* This was not written until 1575, and not printed until 1579. The Ari died in 1572. It also appears to have been written after Rabbi Eliahu had also died.

42. *Shaarey Kedushah,* Introduction, p. 9.

43. *Ibid.*

44. We have used British Museum, Ms. 749. Another manuscript is Moscow, Ms. Guenzburg 691 (formerly Coronel 129).

45. *Shaarey Kedushah,* Part Four, p. 12a-13b. This is found in *Sefer HaCheshek* (Jewish Theological Seminary, Ms. 1801) pp. 9a-11a. There are some variations between the texts, but that in *Shaarey Kedushah* appears more accurate. The name quoted in *Shaarey Kedushah* is the ordinary name of 72, with the letter rearranged, while that in *Sefer HaCheshek* is the name found in *Chayay Olam HaBah,* p. 12a.

46. From the Ramban: On p. 14a, a quote from *Shaar HaGamul (Kitvey HaRamban,* Vol 2, p. 299); on p. 14b, quotations from commentary on Deuteronomy 13:2 and Genesis 18:2; on p. 18a, the same quote from *Shaar HaGamul;* on p. 18b, the same quote from the commentary on Genesis; on p. 19b, a quotation from *Iggeret HaKodesh,* chapter 5. On p. 18a, there is a quotation from *Minchat Yehudah* on *Maarekhet Elokut* 10 (p. 143b), and from Recanti on *VaYechi* (p. 37d). It is to be noted that this last section is from the commentary of R. Azriel on the *Agadot,* in *Kitvey Yad BaKabalah,* p. 197.

47. On pp. 14b, 15a. This *Iggeret HaMusar* has been printed in Mantua, 1623; Cracow, 1625; Amsterdam, 1652. It is also found in *Reshit Chakhmah, Anavah* 6 (235a), *Kall Bo* 66 (Furth, 1783) p. 56a, *Kitvey Ramban,* Volume 1, p. 374; *Anthologya Shel HaSafrut HaIvrit SheAcharey HaTanach* (Philadelphia, 1921) Volume 1, pages 133-136. In *Kitvey Ramban,* R. Chaim Dov Chavel wonders where the tradition originated that the Ramban sent this letter from the Holy Land. In the version here in *Shaarey Kedushah,* however, it states explicitly that it was sent "to his son from Acco to Barcelona." Also see *Shem HaGedolim,* Nun 7.

48. See Chapter 4, notes 79, 81.

49. *Ibid.* note 6.

50. See introduction of R. Shlomo Alkavitz in *Maggid Mesharim,* p. 18, quoted in *Shnei Luchot HaBrit, Mesechta Shavuot* (288a).

51. *Shaarey Kedushah,* Part Four, p. 16a.

52. *Maggid Mesharim,* p. 4, 5.

53. *Shivechey R. Chaim Vital,* pp. 37, 38.

54. *Shaarey Kedushah,* Part Four, p. 16a.

55. See *Shagigah* 12b. *Cf.* Chapter 2, note 18.
56. *Chayay Olam HaBah,* p. 20b. *Cf. Shaarey Tzedek,* p 64b.
57. *Otzar Chaim,* p. 70b. Also see p. 106b.
58. *Yerushalmi, Shekalim* 6:1 (25b), *Shir HaShirm Rabbah* 5:9, *Zohar* 2:84b, 2:114a, 2:226b, 3:132a, 3:154b, *Tikuney Zohar* 56 (90b).
59. Above, p. 39 ff. Also see *Meditation and the Bible* 2:2, 2:8.
60. *Tanna De Bei Eliahu* 9. See Chapter 6, note 18.
61. Paraphrase of Psalm 84:12.
62. See Chapter 2, notes 6, 7. Also see *Meditation and the Bible,* Part 2, note 118.
63. *Avot* 4:13. See Chapter 6, note 42.
64. Commentary on Deuteronomy 11:22.
65. *Iggeret HaKodesh* 5, quoted in *Kitvey Ramban,* volume 2, p. 333. See note 46. Also see Recanti quoted in that note. The story is in *VaYikra Rabbah* 16:4, *Shir HaShirm Rabbah* 1:10.
66. *Cf. Yoma* 86a, that such sins are normally only expiated by suffering or death.
67. See *Or HaSekhel, Chayay Olam HaBah,* quoted above, pp. 88, 96, *Shaarey Tzedek,* p. 72a, *Sulam HaAliyah* (in *Kitvey Yad BaKabbalah*) p. 227.
68. See above, p. 24.

Chapter 6: The Ari

1. *Avkat Rokhel* 136.
2. *Emek HaMelekh,* Introduction 6 (p. 13a), Meir Benayahu, *Toldot HaAri* (Jerusalem, 1967) p. 217. *Cf. VaYakhel Mosheh,* Introduction (Zolkiev, 1741) p. 3a.
3. See *Shivechey R. Chaim Vital,* p. 25a, where he calls the Radbaz the Ari's master. Also see *Korey HaDorot,* p. 40b.
4. *Shem HaGedolim,* Yud 332.
5. See *Shaar Ruach HaKodesh,* p. 36b, quoted below, page 229.
6. See *Shivechey R. Chaim Vital,* p. 34. On 15 Tammuz and 13 Ab, both before and after the Ramak's death on 23 Tammuz, he dreamed about this commentary. See *Toldot HaAri,* p. 162.
7. *Shivechey HaAri,* p. 9a, *Toldot HaAri, ibid.*
8. See *Shaar HaGilgulim,* p. 125, that this meeting was on the New Moon of the month of Adar, 5331 (1571). See *Shaar HaGilgulim,* p. 148, that this was apparently their first meeting.
9. *Shivechey R. Chaim Vital,* p. 27. See *Toldot HaAri,* p. 204. In *Korey HaDorot,* p. 41a, however, we find that he died in 1573. See Shechter, *Studies in Judaism,* Second Series (Philadelphia, 1945) p. 327, note 163.
10. *Shivechey HaAri,* p. 2a. *Emek HaMelech,* Introduction 2 (10b), *Toldot HaAri,* p. 152.
11. *Shulchan Aruch HaAri* (Jerusalem, 1961), p. 97a. *Cf. Nagid U'Metzavah* (Lublin, 1929) p. 2b. See *Toldot HaAri,* p. 163.
12. *Recanti, Naso,* p. 36d. See Chapter 4, note 2.
13. Commentary to *Yad, Lulav* 8:5. See Chapter 4, note 1.

14. Commentary to *Yad, Bet HaBechirah* 6:14. Paraphrase of Psalm 25:14.

15. See above, page 22.

16. *Zohar* 2:74b. See above, Chapter 4, note 128. One of the things that the Ari would not teach R. Chaim Vital was the mystery of Chiromancy, see *Toldot HaAri*, p. 167. See *ibid*, p. 156, that the Ari was expert in this.

17. *Zohar* 3:188a.

18. See Chapter 4, note 60.

19. Introduction to *Etz Chaim* (Tel Aviv, 1960) p. 18 ff.

20. *Emek HaMelech*, Introduction 3 (10d), *Toldot HaAri*, p. 179.

21. Alluding to Genesis 31:10. These are universes in the upper levels of Adam Kadmon. See *Etz Chaim, Shaar Shevirat HaKelim* 4 (p. 129), *Shaar Akudim* 1 (p. 75).

22. This is a teaching that the creation described in the Bible is only the latest "Sabbatical," and that it was preceded by a number of others. See *Sefer Temunah*, Introduction to *Temunah* 3 (Koretz, 1784), p. 31a ff., *Tshuvot Rashba* 423, *R. Moshe Cordevero, Shiur Komah* 83; Radbaz, *Magen David, Gimel, Dalet; Metzudot David* 298; Isaac of Acco, *Otzar Chaim*, p. 86b, R. Joseph Tzayach, *Tzaror HaChaim*, p. 83b, 85b; *Shaarey Gan Eden, Orach Tzadikim* 1:1 (Cracow, 1881) p. 1b. Also see Bachya, Recanti, Tzioni, on Leviticus 25:8, Ramban on Genesis 2:3, *Sefer HaChinukh* 330, Ibn Ezra on Genesis 1:5, 8:22. For a philosophical discussion, see *Drush Or HaChaim* 3, at the end of *Tiferet Yisrael* on *Mishnayot Nezikin*. The Ari, however, disputed this teaching, and no mention of it is made in the Zohar.

23. *VaYakhel Mosheh*, p. 3a.

24. *Bereshit Rabbah* 3:7.

25. *Pardes Rimonim* 11:1, quoting R. Hai Gaon.

26. *Shaar HaKavanot* (Tel Aviv, 1962), Volume 2, p. 25. See *Pri Etz Chaim, Inyan Shabbat* 4.

27. *Rayeh Mehemna, Zohar* 2:92a. See R. Chaim Vital's note *a.l.* #1, 2.

28. In Hebrew "foot" in *Regel* (רגל), which has a numerical value of 223. This is also the numerical value of the sum of Ab, Sag, Mah and Ben, when an additional unit is added for the whole. It is also the sum of Ab (72) and the expansion of Ehyeh which is 161.

29. See *Bereshit Rabbah* 20.

30. See above, pages 33, 34.

31. *Pesikta Zutrata* on Deuteronomy 30:20 (52a).

32. *Otzar Chaim*, p. 102a.

33. *Shaar HaGilgulim*, p. 158. *Cf. Shivechey R. Chaim Vita*, p. 25.

34. See note 79.

35. See note 78.

36. *Edduyot* 5:7.

37. See below, p. 234.

38. *Shaar HaGilgulim*, p. 140.

39. Introduction, p. 9.

40. *Zohar* 1:168b, 169a.

41. *Zohar* 2:59a.

42. Avot 4:13. See above, Chapter 5, note 63.

43. *Zohar* 2:100b.
44. See above, Chapter 3, note 141.
45. See above, page 129.
46. *Shaar Ruach HaKodesh*, p. 29.
47. The Ari, however, maintained that these two Tetragrammatons are not included in the Thirteen Attributes. See *Etz Chaim, Shaar Arikh Anpin* 9; *Zohar* 2:4b, 3:131b. For other opinions, see Rashi, Ibn Ezra, Ramban, *etc. ad loc.*, *Tosefot, Rosh HaShanah* 17b "*Shalosh*," *Sefer Chasidim* 250, *Makor Chesed ad loc.* 250:3.
48. *Shaar Ruach HaKodesh*, p. 30.
49. *Ibid.* p. 33. See *Shaar HaGilgulim*, p. 131.
50. *Berakhot* 30b.
51. *Cf. Yad, Lulav* 8:15.
52. See *Shabbat* 30b, *Pesachim* 117a. See *Shaarey Kedushah*, Part Four, p. 15b, that music is only played to initiate the meditative process, but then it is stopped.
53. *Pesachim* 66b.
54. See *Shaar HaKavanot*, Volume 1, p. 20a.
55. *Ibid.* p. 76b. These letters change form at the end of a word, see *Megillah* 2b, *Shabbat* 104a, *Bereshit Rabbah* 1:15, *BaMidbar Rabbah* 18:17, *Tanchuma, Korach* 12.
56. *Shaar HaMitzvot, VeEtChanan* (Tel Aviv, 1962) p. 84 ff., *Shulchan Arukh HaAri*, p. 80 ff.
57. *Zohar* 1:113a in *Midrash Ne'elam*. The law is that a synagogue must have windows, see *Berakhot* 34b, Rashi *ad loc.*, "*Chalonot*."
58. See *Zohar* 3:119a, 3:120b, 3:198b, *Zohar Chadash* 18b, 88b, *etc.*
59. *Zohar* 1:83a, 1:122a (in *Midrash Ne'elam*), 1:130a, 1:200a, 2:198b.
60. *Nefilat Apayim* (Falling on the Face) is a short prayer said after the Amidah, when one hides one's face under his arm. Part of this prayer in the Sefardic ritual consists of Psalm 25 (In the Ashkenazic rite, it is the 6th Psalm).
61. *Shaar HaKavanot*, Volume 1, p. 349.
62. *Ibid.* p. 69a.
63. See *Etz Chaim, Shaar RaPaCh Netzutzim* 1 (p. 255), *Mavo Shaarim* 2:2:9, *Shaar HaPesukim, Bereshit*, p. 3. The number 288 is four times 72, and hence is the power of Ab (72) in the four Tetragrammatons. See Chapter 7, note 64.
64. *Shaar Ruach HaKodesh*, p. 38b.
65. The Third Rectification, ibid. p. 41a.
66. See Chapter 2, note 52.
67. *Avodah Zarah* 35b.
68. See *Shaarey Orah*, quoted above, p. 134. The Satan is identified with the Angel of Death. *Bava Batra* 16a.
69. See above, pp. 47, 48.
70. See *Yerushalmi, Sanhedrin* 10:3 (53a), *Tanchuma Re'eh* 13, *Zohar* 1:6b, 1:62b. *Cf. Sh'mot Rabbah* 51:7.
71. *Shaar Ruach HaKodesh*, p. 74.
72. See *Zohar* 1:6a. *Cf.* note 37.
73. *Zohar* 2:95a.

74. *Taanit* 5a.

75. *Shaar Ruach HaKodesh*, p. 110. Yichudim that are designated for specific purposes rather than general enlightenment, have been omitted.

76. *Minachot* 29b, *Bahir* 16, 88, 160, 172.

77. *Tikuney Zohar* 13 (29b).

78. This is the second Yichud mentioned above. See note 35.

79. This is the first Yichud, see note 34. This Yichud is also described in detail in *Benayah ben Yehoyada* (Jerusalem, 1911) Part 2, page 30.

80. See *Sifra DeTzneuta* 2, *Zohar* 2:177b.

81. See *Sefer Yetzirah* 1:3.

82. *Shaar HaKavanot*, Volume 2, p. 246.

83. See above, Chapter 1, note 3.

84. See above, page 185.

85. *Etz Chaim, Shaar AChaP* 4.

86. The reference here is to the various parts of the morning service that correspond to these four Universes. See below, p. 285.

87. See *Reshit Chokhmah, Kedushah* 7 (154c, top).

Chapter 7: The Hasidim

1. *Emek HaMelekh, Shasuey HaMelekh* 55 (Amsterdam, 1653) p. 9d. See Chapter 3, note 109.

2. See Chapter 4, note 137.

3. This is found in *HaTamim*, 1935-1938. They are published in English translation by N. Mindel, as *Lubavitcher Rabbi's Memoirs* (Kehot, New York, 1971). See letters printed in *Gedulat Rabenu Yisrael Baal Shem Tov* (Jerusalem, 1959), p. 95f.

4. *Tshuvot Chakham Zvi* 93, *Tshuvot R. Yaakov Emdin* 2:82. Chakham Zvi was a grandson of Rabbi Ephraim Katz (1616-1678), author of *Shaar Ephraim*, who was in turn married to a grandaughter of R. Eliahu of Chelm. This Rabbi Ephraim also discusses said Golem, see *Shem HaGedolim*, Alef 163. See Chaim N. Dembitzer, *Klilath Yofi* (Cracow, 1888), p. 78b in note, for a discussion as to whether R. Eliahu Baal Shem of Worms is the same as the one from Chelm. According to the Lubavitcher tradition, however, they were both the same individual. According to his *Haskamah* on R. Baruch Genezen's *Gedulat Mordechai* in 5375 (1615), he was still in Worms at the time, and was associated with the Maharal. There was another R. Eliahu Luantz, also known as Eliahu Baal Shem, who did not come to Worms until 1630, at least six years after the first Baal Shem left.

5. See *Haskama* on *Mifaalot Elokim*, dated 5485 (1725), where Rabbi Yoel Haprin of Zamoshtch writes that he is a grandson of Rabbi Yoel Baal Shem.

6. See *Kuzari* 3:53 (64a); *Sheva Netivot HaTorah* (in Jellinek, *Philosohie und Kabbalah)* p. 22. The earliest one to have this title was R. Benjamin ben Zerach (1010-1070), see Eliezer Landshut, *Amud HaAvodah* (Berlin, 1587) p. 72. Another was R. Elchanan Baal Shem, who lived in the Seventeenth Century, see *Klilat Yofi*, p. 78b; *Shem HaGedolim HeChadash, Sefarim, Ayin* 71.

7. See Chapter 4, note 52.

8. *Lubavitcher Rabbi's Memoirs*, Volume 2, p. 150. Here he states that he had been leader of the movement for 7 years, had been R. Joel's disciple for 15 years, and had entered his Yeshiva at the age of 33. He was therefore 55 at the time. From p. 145, we see that this took place around 1710. He was therefore born in 1655. Some identify this Adam with R. David Moshe Abraham (whose initials are Adam) of Troys, author of the *Markava HaMishnah* on the *Mekhilta*. Others identify him with Adam Zerweiker. It is also possible that Adam was used as an anonym to protect his identity.

9. *Tshuvot Mabit* 1:176.

10. We see that the name Adam was in use, see *Birkey Yosef, Yoreh Deah* 265:6 (Livorno, 1774); *Shem HaGedolim, Alef* 34 (first published in Livorno, 1774), *Yosef Ometz* 11 (Livorno, 1798). See *Tshuvah MeAhavah* 1:35, *Pitchey Tshuvah, Yoreh Deah* 265:6. The name Noah is not found in *Nachalat Shivah*, published in 1667, but is found in *Bet Shmuel, Shemot Gittin*, first published in 1689. Among the earliest sages to be called Noah were Noah Mindes of Vilna, born around 1720, and Noah Chaim Zvi Berlin, born around 1730.

11. *Kav HaYashar* 69.

12. *Ibid.* 102. Also see *Yichus Chernoble* 1:7; *Tzion* 5:122-131 (1940), 6:80-84, 89-93 (1941).

13. *Shoshan Yesod Olam*, p. 522. See Chapter 4, note 115.

14. Published at the end of *Ben Porat Yosef* (Koretz, 1781), and in *Keter Shem Tov* (Kehot, New York, 1973) #1.

15. The Baal Shem Tov's spiritual master was Ahiyah the Shilonite see *Toldot Yaakov Yosef, Balak* (Koretz, 1780) p. 156a top, *Keter Shem Tov* 143. Ahiyah is mentioned in 1 Kings 11:29, 14:2, and is said to have been from the generation of the Exodus. He was also said to be the teacher of the prophet Elijah (the one who normally reveals himself to those who are worthy). See *Bava Batra* 121b, Introduction to *Yad; Zohar* 1:4b, 3:309a.

16. According to the Talmud, these are Adam, Seth, Methusalah, Abraham, Jacob, Moses and David. *Sukkah* 52b.

17. Paraphrase of Proverbs 5:16.

18. *Cf.* Judges 18:6, Proverbs 5:21.

19. Paraphrase of Proverbs 4:21.

20. Proverbs 9:9.

21. *Shivechey HaBaal Shem Tov* (Jerusalem, 1969) 1. 43.

22. *Ibid.* pp. 48, 50, 53.

23. *Ibid.* p. 46. See above, p. 38.

24. *Ibid.* p. 58.

25. *Likutim Yekarim* (Jerusalem, 1974) #29.

26. *Ibid.* #38.

27. *Tzavaat HaRivash* (Kehot, New York, 1975) #133.

28. *Likutim Yekarim* #13. See Chapter 4, note 145.

29. Rabbi Menachem Mendel of Vitebsk, *Pri HaAretz, Lech Lecha* (Jerusalem, 1970) p. 3b. Also see *Keter Shem Tov* 2; *Siddur* [Rabbi Schneur Zalman of Liadi] (Kehot, New York, 1971), pp. 147a, 315a. See above, p. 215.

30. *Etz Chaim, Shaar Mochin DeKatnut* 3, p. 314.
31. *Toldot Yaakov Yosef, Tazria,* p. 84b (bottom).
32. *Likutim Yekarim* 74.
33. *Tzafnat Paneach* (Pieterkov, 1884) 2b; *Sefer Baal Shem Tov, Bereshit* 46.
34. *Ketonet Passim* (Lvov, 1866) 11b, *Sefer Baal Shem Tov, Bereshit* 68.
35. *Toldot Yaakov Yosef, Emor,* p. 103b.
36. *Likutim Yekarim* #171, 172.
37. *Ibid.* #17,19, *Tzavaat HaRivash* #67,69.
38. *Toldot Yaakov Yosef, Yitro,* p. 48b. Regarding the Constriction, see *Bereshit Rabbah* 21:5, *Yafah Shaah* on *Etz Chaim* (Tel Aviv, 1960), p. 1.
39. *Yebamot* 105b.
40. Commentary on R. AlFasi, *Berakhot, Rif* 22b. See *Nefesh HaChaim* 2:14 in note; Ramban on Leviticus 18:4.
41. *Tur, Orach Chaim* 98, quoted in *Shulchan Arukh, Orach Chaim* 98:1.
42. *Toldot Yaakov Yosef, Acharey,* p. 88c.
43. *Lekutim Yekarim* #41, *Tzavaat HaRivash* #62.
44. *Lekutim Yekarim* #16, *Tzavaat HaRivash* #66.
45. *Lekutim Yekarim* #21, *Tzavaat HaRivash* #70,71.
46. *Lekutim Yekarim* #224, *Tzavaat HaRivash* #73.
47. *Magid Devarav LeYaakov* (Jerusalem, 1971) #52.
48. *Ibid.* #53.
49. *Likutim Yekarim* 22.
50. *Ibid.* 73.
51. *Berakhot* 6b.
52. *Toldot Yaakov Yosef, Shlach,* p. 134b, *Keter Shem Tov* #138.
53. *Zohar* 2:254a, 2:266b. See *Berakhot* 8a.
54. *Cf. Tikuney Zohar* 18:34a. The word *Shakhav* (שכב) contains the letters *Kaf Bet* (כב), which in Hebrew, is the number 22. This allludes to the 22 letters of the Hebrew Alphabet. See *Tikuney Zohar* 70 (132b), *Etz Chaim, Shaar HaYareach* 3.
55. *Keter Shem Tov* #44.
56. *Likutim Yekarim* 2, *Tzavaat HaRivash* 34.
57. *Shabbat* 104a, *Yoma* 38b. See notes 67, 75.
58. *Tzavaat HaRivash* #36,37; *Likutim Yekarim* #183,168.
59. *Likutim Yekarim* #210, 211, *Tzavaat HaRivash* #104,105.
60. *Likutim Yekarim* #3.
61. *Magid Devarav LeYaakov* #66.
62. *Likutey Yekarim* #63, *Tzavaat HaRivash* #72.
63. *Berakhot* 4:4 (28b).
64. See Chapter 6, note 63.
65. *Toldot Yaakov Yosef, VaYakhel,* p. 67d. *Sefer Baal Shem Tov, Noah* 120.
66. *Lekutim Yekarim* #185, *Keter Shem Tov* #222.
67. See note 57.
68. *Maggid Devarav LeYaakov* #232.
69. *Ketonet Passim,* p. 43b; *Sefer Baal Shem Tov, Noah* 134.
70. *Likutim Yekarim* 6, *Keter Shem Tov* 166. *Cf. Sichot HaRan* 16.
71. *Likutim Yekarim* 32. See Chapter 3, note 80.

72. *Zohar* 3:168a.
73. *Likutim Yekarim* 33.
74. *Ibid.* 55.
75. See note 57.
76. *Likutim Yekarim* 168.
77. *Toldot Yaakov Yosef, VaYetze,* p. 23a.
78. *Ibid. VaEreh,* p. 39a.
79. *Ibid. VaYakhel,* p. 67d.
80. *Likutim Yekarim* #12, *Keter Shem Tov* #195.
81. *Likutim Yekarim* #36.
82. *Ibid.* #48. See above, p. 224.
83. See *Or Torah* (Kehot, New York, 1974), p. 69d.
84. *Cf. Likutim Yekarim* #169, 175.
85. *Likutim Yekarim* #49. See *Keter Shem Tov* #199.
86. *Likutim Yekarim* #50.
87. *Ibid.* #52.
88. *Ibid.* #175. See *Keter Shem Tov* #216.
89. *Keter Shem Tov* #56.
90. *Zohar* 2:82a.
91. *Or Torah,* p. 69d.
92. *Maggid Devarav LeYaakov* #67.
93. The two feet correspond to the Sefirot Netzach and Hod, and are an aspect of faith. See *Zohar* 1:21b, 1:146a, 1:166a.
94. *Maggid Devarav LeYaakov* #188.
95. *Brit Menuchah* (Warsaw, 1884) p. 7a. This was written by R. Abraham of Granada (15th Century). See Numbers 11:24, 33:16, Deuteronomy 9:22. Also see *Degel Machaneh Ephraim, Ekev* (Jozefov, 1883), p. 70a.
96. *Tzafanat Poneach,* p. 33b, *Keter Shem Tov* #121, *Sefer Baal Shem Tov, Noah* 13.
97. *Pardes Rimonim* 23:1. See *Sotah* 21b, *Zohar* 1:156b, 2:221a, 3:290b.
98. *Pardes Rimonim* 3:1.
99. See Chapter 3, note 132.
100. *Maggid Devarav LeYaakov* #96.
101. *Ibid.* 159.
102. *Ibid.* 97.
103. *Imrey Tzadikim (Or HaEmet:* Zitamar, 1901) p. 19c.
104. *Ibid.* p. 23d.
105. *Or Torah,* p. 72a.
106. *Imrey Tzadikim,* p. 18c. *Cf. Bava Metzia* 10a.
107. *Imrey Tzadikim,* loc. cit.
108. *Or Torah, Bereshit,* p. 2d.
109. *Imrey Tzadikim,* p. 28b.
110. *Zohar* 3:53b.
111. See *Shaar HaMitzvot,* Introduction (Tel Aviv, 1962) p. 4; *Toldot Yaakov Yosef,* Introduction, p. 2c. Regarding *ATBaSh,* see p. 225.
112. *Kedushat Levi, Bereshit* (Jerusalem, 1958) p. 1.
113. *Ibid.* p. 5.

114. *Likutey Moharan* 52.
115. *Likutey Moharan Tinyana* 25.
116. *Ibid.* 96.
117. *Sichot HaRan* 47.
118. *Ibid.* 227.
119. *Likutey Moharan Tinyana* 11.
120. *Sichot HaRan* 68.
121. *Ibid.* 274, 275.
122. *Kochavey Or, Anshey Moharan* 23 (Jerusalem, 1933) p. 76.
123. *Likutey Moharan Tinyana* 97.

Index

BIBLICAL QUOTATIONS